Why Do You Need this New Ed...

If you're wondering why you should buy this new ed...
of *Texas Government*, here are 7 good reasons!

1. New **learning objectives** appear at the start of each chapter in the "What Should I Know About . . ." boxes to prime you for the material you are about to read and to help you navigate the chapters more efficiently. These objectives also appear in the body of the chapters and inform the structure of the "What Should I Have Learned?" summary sections.

2. New **"Test Yourself" quizzes** at the end of each chapter provide you with avenues to check your understanding and reinforce each chapter's learning objectives. Each quiz consists of ten questions: one multiple choice question (with five answer choices) for each objective, with the remaining short answer and essay questions focused on critical thinking.

3. All **photo, figure, and table titles appear as questions,** to encourage you to think critically about every visual element.

4. Revised **Analyzing Visuals features** include targeted critical thinking questions that encourage you to progressively engage in deeper understanding and analysis. These features take you beyond answering solely the "what" of the visual and help you to better focus on the "why."

5. Streamlined **Join the Debate boxes** prompt you to develop your own well-thought-out arguments "for" and "against" each position. New to this edition is a debate over the income tax in Texas.

6. **Thinking Nationally** features highlight Texas' differences from and commonalities with other states in the U.S. New to this edition are comparisons of the top conservative states (Chapter 1), a look at poverty among the states (Chapter 1), an examination of tort reform (Chapter 6), regional patterns in executions (Chapter 8), and children and mental health (Chapter 8).

7. New news article excerpts in all of the **Politics Now** boxes help guide you through an in-depth examination of contemporary issues.

TIMELINE: Selected Events in Texas Government and Politics

1836 **Texas Independence**—Following the Battle of San Jacinto, Texans win independence from Mexico, transforming their values and historical experiences into a distinguishable Texan Creed.

1850 **Popular Election of Texas Supreme Court**—A constitutional amendment passes providing for the popular election of Texas Supreme Court justices.

1861 **Constitution**—Texas joins 12 other states in seceding from the United States. The new constitution reflects the principle of state's rights.

1740s **Spanish Colonization**—The Spanish begin to colonize Texas with limited success.

1815–16 **Anglo Settlement**—The first Anglo settlers arrive south of the Red River.

1858 **Incorporation of Cities**—The first statute related to the incorporation of cities is enacted by the Texas Legislature.

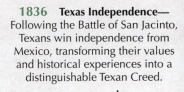

1845 **Constitution**—Texas joins the United States and adopts a state constitution, which is deemed by scholars to be Texas's best constitution. James Pinckney Henderson takes office in 1846 and is the state's first governor.

1869 **Constitution**—Proponents of Reconstruction control the U.S. Congress and force Texas to write a new constitution.

CONSTITUTION

OF THE

STATE OF TEXAS,

ADOPTED BY THE

CONSTITUTIONAL CONVENTION

CONVENED UNDER THE RECONSTRUCTION ACTS OF CONGRESS
PASSED MARCH 2, 1867, AND THE ACTS
SUPPLEMENTARY THERETO;

TO BE SUBMITTED FOR RATIFICATION OR REJECTION
AT AN ELECTION TO TAKE PLACE ON THE
FIRST MONDAY OF JULY, 1869.

AUSTIN, TEXAS:
PRINTED AT THE DAILY REPUBLICAN OFFICE.
1869.

1874 **Democratic Party Dominance**—Democrats dominate Texas politics, and no Republican wins a statewide office until John Tower is elected to the U.S. Senate in 1961. During this era, Texans often referred to themselves as "yellow dog Democrats" meaning they would vote for a yellow dog, if he ran on the Democratic ticket.

1891 **Court of Criminal Appeals**—To manage the increasing workload, the Texas Court of Appeals is limited to hearing only criminal cases. Intermediate courts of civil appeals are created for different geographical regions of the state.

1913 **Home-Rule Charters**—Cities over 5,000 in population are permitted to adopt home-rule charters, enabling them to legislate on any issue that does not conflict with existing state law or the Texas Constitution.

1876 **Constitution**—Democrats call for a constitutional convention in 1875 to rewrite the state's charter; it is overwhelmingly ratified in early 1876.

1904 **Poll Tax**—A poll tax is required to register to vote in Texas.

1924 **First Woman Governor**—Miriam A. Ferguson is the first woman elected governor of Texas.

Texas Politics and GOVERNMENT

ROOTS AND REFORM

Fourth Edition

Gary A. Keith

University of the Incarnate Word

Stefan D. Haag

Austin Community College

with L. Tucker Gibson, Jr. and Clay Robison

Longman

Boston   Columbus   Indianapolis   New York   San Francisco   Upper Saddle River
Amsterdam   Cape Town   Dubai   London   Madrid   Milan   Munich   Paris   Montreal   Toronto
Delhi   Mexico City   São Paulo   Sydney   Hong Kong   Seoul   Singapore   Taipei   Tokyo

Executive Editor: Reid Hester
Editorial Assistant: Elizabeth Alimena
Marketing Manager: Lindsey Prudhomme
Production Manager: Eric Jorgensen
Project Coordination, Text Design, and Electronic Page Makeup:
    Electronic Publishing Services Inc., NYC

Senior Cover Design Manager/Cover Designer: Nancy Danahy
Cover Image: © Bill Heinsohn/Getty Images, Inc.
Photo Researcher: Julie Tesser
Senior Manufacturing Buyer: Roy L. Pickering, Jr.
Printer and Binder: Courier Kendallville
Cover Printer: Lehigh–Phoenix Color Corp.

For permission to use copyrighted material, grateful acknowledgment is made to the copyright holders acknowledged throughout the book, which are hereby made part of this copyright page.

Chapter opening image credits: p. 2, Reproduced from the Collections of the Library of Congress; p. 3, Ron Scott/Alamy; p. 34, The Granger Collection, New York; p. 35, Courtesy of Texas State Library & Archives Commission; p. 62 AP/Wide World Photos; p. 63, Bob Daemmrich Photography; p. 98, Courtesy of Texas State Library & Archives Commission; p. 99, Alamy; p. 138, Courtesy of Texas State Library & Archives Commission; p. 139, Bob Daemmrich Photography; p. 178, Courtesy of L. Tucker Gibson; p. 179, Bob Daemmrich Photography; p. 206, Reproduced from the Collections of the Library of Congress; p. 207, Mark Wilson/Getty Images; p. 234, Courtesy of Texas State Library & Archives Commission; p. 235, Jeremy Woodhouse/Superstock

Library of Congress Cataloging-in-Publication Data

Texas politics and government : roots and reform / Gary A. Keith ... [et al.]. — 4th ed.
    p. cm.
Includes bibliographical references and index.
ISBN 978-0-205-07863-9
1. Texas—Politics and government—1951—Textbooks.   I. Keith, Gary

JK4816.H33 2011
320.4764—dc22

2010054524

1 2 3 4 5 6 7 8 9 10—CRK—14 13 12 11

Longman
is an imprint of

www.pearsonhighered.com

ISBN-13: 978-0-205-07863-9
ISBN-10: 0-205-07863-X

To Jacqueline,
whose work in public health
is so affected by Texas politics, and to Gabe and David,
whose choices in life will similarly be influenced by Texas politics

Gary A. Keith

To my wife, Pat, for her love, patience, and support.

Stefan D. Haag

For Dorothy, the love of my life,
whose tenacity in the face of adversity
has provided inspiration for many.

L. Tucker Gibson, Jr.

For Taylor,
Adrian and my newest Texan, Caroline

Clay Robison

Contents

CHAPTER 5   The Governor and the Executive Branch   138

ROOTS OF the Executive Branch in Texas   140

CHAPTER 6   The Judicial Branch   178

ROOTS OF the Texas Judiciary   181

List of Features

Thinking Nationally

Timeline

John Steinbeck wrote that "*Texas* is the obsession, the proper study and the passionate possession of all Texans." It certainly is one of our passions as authors and teachers.

The politics and government of Texas have not only fashioned much of the quality of civic life in the state, but have also influenced the direction of the nation as a whole. We hope, in our classrooms and in this textbook, to stir in students a healthy intellectual curiosity in all things Texan.

The national presence and profile of Texans during President George W. Bush's administration suggests that Texas has come of age and provides national political and policy leadership to match even Texas bragging rights. Yet, this prominence in national politics should not overshadow the rich past of Texas as a national political contributor, from Sam Houston through Colonel Edward House, Cactus Jack Garner, Jesse Jones, Sam Rayburn, Landslide Lyndon Johnson, Big John Connally, Jim Wright, Lloyd Bentsen, James Baker, and George H. W. Bush.

Though Texas has long been a part of the United States of America, its unique history, vast landscape, diverse population, border-state identity, and other aspects have combined to create a political culture that sets it apart from the rest of the nation. Texans who diverge from each other on characteristics such as ideology, ethnicity, income, and education nevertheless unite under a rallying sense of Texas pride. Texas lore is full of cowboys, oilmen, gutsy frontier women, and colorful political characters. Taken as a whole, Texans have, as the late Governor Ann Richards once remarked, been a little too rowdy for their own good.

We believe that understanding Texas's current socio-economic and political alignment as well as its prominence in national politics requires not only an analysis of what is happening now, but a clear view and comparison with what Texas has been. Thus, our subtitle, *Roots and Reform,* reflects the approach of this book as one that draws on history and contemporary political and governmental dynamics to provide the proper study that Steinbeck suggested.

Highlights of the Text

Throughout the eight chapters of this book students will find numerous examples of the historical roots and significant reforms in Texas politics and government. Institutions that were created when Texas was a rural, agrarian state during the late nineteenth century have survived along with a constitution that was created for a society quite different from that of contemporary Texas.

There have also been numerous changes. We doubt that the framers of the 1876 Texas Constitution would recognize that document as it exists today with its more than 450 amendments, but it would not be totally foreign to them either. The continuity that has kept Texas moored to its roots would be evident to them, as would the changes that have been required to make government more relevant to the twenty-first century.

In the politics of Texas, reform is also compelling. At first glance, party competition seems to have been completely turned upside down over a century of change. Democrats ruled Texas from the 1870s to the 1970s with little opposition; today, Republicans are so dominant that no Democratic statewide officeholders were elected in 2002, 2004, 2006, 2008, or 2010. Yet, when one looks below the party labels to ideology, voting patterns, and voting outcomes, one finds a battle between a populist (and often lower-income) segment of the population and a business-affiliated, conservative segment of the population. This socio-economic cleavage happened between populists and Democrats in the late nineteenth century; it happened within the Democratic

Party during its long period of hegemony; and it persists now in a new two-party configuration.

Each of this book's eight chapters, then, will take the historical roots of the topic covered and use them to illustrate the roots and the reform that Texans have seen over a century and a half. By understanding the time dimension and its influences on current politics, government, and policy, students should be better able to analyze for themselves what is happening in Texas politics now, and as it unfolds in the coming years.

Organization

We first examine the social, economic, and constitutional milieu in Texas, then proceed to the heart of its politics, examining political behavior through interest groups, parties, and voting. Next, we focus on governmental institutions, before concluding with a look at some of the outcomes of Texas politics and government, as evidenced in public policies. Each chapter begins with a vignette exploring a recent event, personality, or group related to the chapter's topic. We then lay the foundation for the reading by looking at the roots and historical development of that topic in Texas.

The first two chapters provide the context for a study of Texas politics and government. **Chapter 1:** Ideas, People, and Economics in Texas Politics discusses the various peoples of Texas (past and present), and the likely trends in population growth and change. It then explores the ideological context, which is essential to the examination of politics in later chapters. A look at the basic economic structure of Texas is next, and the chapter ends with a spotlight on the politics of wealth and poverty. **Chapter 2:** Constitutionalism begins with a brief march through the five constitutions from Texas's independence up to 1876. We lay out a lengthier examination of the politics that led to the 1876 adoption of the current constitution before highlighting its substance, then the dilemmas and problems caused by its statutory nature. Finally, we examine twentieth-century efforts, successful and unsuccessful, to revise the Texas Constitution.

Chapter 3: Voting and Participating: Political Parties, Interest Groups, and Elections combines the *institutions* and *dynamics* of political behavior. No analysis of Texas politics would be complete without a look at the system of one-party dominance for more than a century. We then investigate party organization, party in the electorate, and party in government. Parties' sister organizations, interest groups, are then highlighted, focusing on types of groups in Texas and their political activities. We then focus on the arenas closest to voting Texans: elections and campaigns, including campaign finance, voters' decisions, and voter turnout results.

The next four chapters present Texas's state and governmental institutions. **Chapter 4:** The Legislative Branch describes the roots of the legislature as a series of conclaves engaging the Mexican national government, followed by the Texas Congress and a series of constitutional conventions. The 1876 Constitution then put its stamp on the new Texas legislature, and we examine its structure, powers, pay, and biennial setup. Next, we look at legislative membership, how legislators organize politically, and the law-making and budgeting functions. Finally, we explore how legislators make decisions, including the role of the governor in legislative decision making. **Chapter 5:** The Governor and Executive Branch shows that the Texas governorship is rooted in the Spanish monarchical administration, then the presidency of the Lone Star Republic and the series of expansive constitutions after that. We examine the current constitutional roles of the governor and the slow redevelopment of power that had been stripped away by the original 1876 Constitution. We then describe the governor as policy maker and political leader. Next, we turn to the executive branch that serves alongside the governor, including the plural executive, the modern Texas bureaucracy, and how the legislature attempts to make bureaucracy accountable. **Chapter 6:** The Judicial Branch finds the Texas judiciary rooted in English and Spanish law. We describe the court structure, from local courts to the top appellate courts, and the judges who serve those courts. Next, we examine the debates over reforming the court structure and the judicial selection method. Finally, we outline the judicial process. The last institutional chapter is **Chapter 7:** Local Governments. In nineteenth-century Texas, rural government grew out of the Mexican establishment of districts and the American establishment of counties. For modern times, we look at the structure, authority, and finances of counties, cities, and special districts, then at the politics of local governance.

Once we have explored the context for *Texas Politics and Government,* then looked at the state and local institutions, we conclude the book with a look at what it all means to Texans. **Chapter 8:** Public Policy in Texas finds modern policy rooted in the populist and social welfare policy battles of the late nineteenth and early twentieth century. We then describe the policy process and who the policy actors are, and we put policy outcomes into their political-economy context. The chapter then details modern policy in the areas of state finance, education, criminal justice, health and human services, and the environment.

Features

Tables and figures provide up-to-date data throughout the book. Each chapter also contains a uniform set of features to provide additional depth, context, interest, and opportunities for critical thinking:

- *Roots of* and *Toward Reform* sections highlight the text's emphasis on the importance of the history of Texas politics and government, as well as the dynamic cycle of reassessment and reform that allows Texas to continue to evolve. Every chapter begins with a "Roots of" section that gives a historical overview of the topic at hand, and the chapter ends with a "Toward Reform" section devoted to a particularly contentious aspect of the topic being discussed.

- *What Should I Know About . . . and What Should I Have Learned?* sections now include learning objectives that allow students to preview and review the key topics and concepts explored in each chapter. Every chapter begins with a set of *What Should I Know About . . .* learning objectives tied to the sections within the chapter. These objectives, as well as a bulleted list of section descriptions that follows the opening vignette, preview the key content of the chapter and help to focus student attention on the overall chapter structure. A *What Should I Have Learned?* section at the end of every chapter revisits each of the learning objectives and answers it with a succinct summary paragraph.

- *Thinking Nationally* highlights Texas's differences from and commonalities with other states in the United States. Examples of this feature include a comparison of the U.S. and Texas constitutions (in Chapter 2) and a comparison of budget preparations in Texas and other states (in Chapter 4).

- *Timelines* appear in all chapters and provide students with a clear understanding of the development of key topics in Texas politics. For example, Chapter 3 includes a timeline devoted to the development of local government in Texas.

- *Politics Now* highlights reform through a focus on recent events. News articles about current political personalities or political developments are paired with critical thinking questions to allow students to learn more about Texas politics. For example, Chapter 2's *Politics Now* focuses on the controversy over marriage in Texas as a result of a 2005 constitutional amendment.

- *The Living Constitution* places the chapter topic into its Texas constitutional context by explaining a topical section, its intent, and how it affects Texas today. For example, Chapter 8 highlights a 1917 constitutional amendment dealing with water districts that is at the center of twenty-first century "water wars" in Texas.

- *Analyzing Visuals* is a visual literacy exercise, with graphs, maps, charts, or cartoons that are accompanied by critical thinking questions that ask students to interpret the information provided. (See Analyzing Visuals: A Brief Guide, immediately following this Preface for more information about assessing visual information.)

- *Join the Debate* is a critical thinking exercise that asks students to develop their own well-thought-out arguments "for" and "against" controversial issues. The feature examines topics like the use of red-light cameras at intersections, which is debated in Chapter 3.

- *Key terms* with page references are provided in a list at the end of each chapter, and each term is also defined in the margin on the page where it is used and highlighted. Key terms are also listed in a glossary at the end of the text.

- *In the Library* sections list books that are relevant to key chapter topics.

- *On the Web* sections list Web sites that students can access to find more information on a chapter's main topics. For example, official Web sites of the Texas legislature are listed in Chapter 4.

The Ancillary Package

The ancillary package for *Texas Politics and Government: Roots and Reform* reflects the pedagogical goals of the text: to provide information in a useful context and with colorful examples. We have tried to provide materials that are useful for instructors and helpful to students.

Instructor's Manual/Test Bank: The Instructor's Manual portion offers chapter summaries, outlines, key terms, teaching suggestions, discussion topics, and Web activities that reflect recent news and political events. The Test Bank portion contains questions in multiple-choice, true-false, short-answer, and essay format, which address all levels of Bloom's taxonomy and have been both reviewed and class-tested for accuracy and effectiveness.

MyTest: This flexible, online test-generating software includes all questions found in the printed Test Bank.

Digital Transparency Masters: These PDF slides contain all maps, figures, and tables found in the text. Available on the Instructor Resource Center.

Study Site: Online set of practice tests, Web links, and flashcards organized by major topics and arranged according to this book's table of contents.

PowerPoint Presentation: Slides include a lecture outline of the text, graphics from the book, and quick check questions for immediate feedback on student comprehension. www.pearsonamericangovernment.com

Acknowledgments

We would like to thank Eric Stano at Longman for his constant encouragement and support over the years. Our students at the University of Texas, Austin Community College, the University of the Incarnate Word, and other places where we have taught have helped pique our interest in things Texan, hone our skills, and keep us on our toes.

We would also like to thank Rex Peebles, a colleague with whom we collaborated on an earlier book, and other colleagues who have helped enrich our understanding of politics. We are grateful to Karen O'Connor and Larry Sabato for their support on this and other publishing projects.

Finally, we wish to acknowledge our families— Jacqueline, Gabe, and David, and Patricia, Jeff, and Joel, and their integral roles in our writing as one small but important part of our broader lives.

GARY A. KEITH
STEFAN D. HAAG

Analyzing Visuals

Visual literacy—the ability to analyze, interpret, synthesize, and apply visual information—is essential in today's world. We receive information from the written and spoken word, but knowledge also comes in visual forms. We are used to thinking about reading written texts critically, but we do not always think about "reading" visuals in this way. We should, because images and informational graphics can tell us a lot if we read and consider them carefully. In order to emphasize these skills, the Analyzing Visuals feature in each chapter prompts students to think about the images and informational graphics they will encounter throughout this text, as well as those they see every day in the newspaper, in magazines, on the Web, on television, and in books. Critical thinking questions assist students in learning how to analyze visuals.

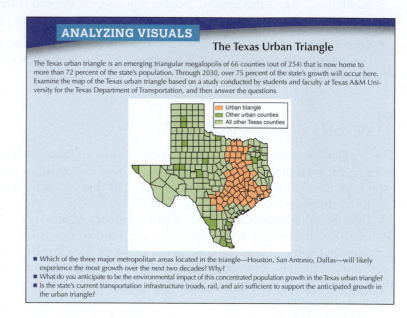

ANALYZING VISUALS

The Texas Urban Triangle

The Texas urban triangle is an emerging triangular megalopolis of 66 counties (out of 254) that is now home to more than 72 percent of the state's population. Through 2030, over 75 percent of the state's growth will occur here. Examine the map of the Texas urban triangle based on a study conducted by students and faculty at Texas A&M University for the Texas Department of Transportation, and then answer the questions.

- Urban triangle
- Other urban counties
- All other Texas counties

■ Which of the three major metropolitan areas located in the triangle—Houston, San Antonio, Dallas—will likely experience the most growth over the next two decades? Why?
■ What do you anticipate to be the environmental impact of this concentrated population growth in the Texas urban triangle?
■ Is the state's current transportation infrastructure (roads, rail, and air) sufficient to support the anticipated growth in the urban triangle?

Tables

Tables consist of textual information and/or numerical data arranged in tabular form, in columns and rows. Tables are frequently used when exact information is required and when orderly arrangement is necessary to locate and, in many cases, to compare the information. All tables in this edition include questions that encourage critical thinking.

Students are encouraged to ask the following kinds of analytical questions about the tables:

Table 4.12 *Which constitutional requirements limit who can run for office?*	Senate	House
Residency	5 years in Texas, 1 year in district	2 years in Texas, 1 year in district
Minimum age	26 years	21 years
Term of office	4 years	2 years
Citizenship	United States	United States
Voting status	Qualified (registered) voter	Qualified (registered) voter
Salary	$600 per month	$600 per month
Conflict of interest	Must disclose any personal interest in a bill; may not hold any other state office or contract	Must disclose any personal interest in a bill; may not hold any other state office or contract

Source: Texas Constitution, Article 3.

- What is the purpose of the table? What information does it show?
- What information is provided in the column headings (provided in the top row)? How are the rows labeled?
- Is there a time period indicated, such as January to June 2010? Or, are the data as of a specific date, such as June 30, 2010?
- If the table shows numerical data, what do these data represent? In what units? Dollars a special interest lobby provides to a political party? Estimated life expectancy in years?
- What is the source of the information presented in the table?

Charts and Graphs

Charts and graphs depict numerical data in visual forms. Examples that students will encounter throughout this text are line graphs, pie charts, and bar graphs. Line graphs show a progression, usually over time (as in how membership in the Texas Senate has changed over time). Pie charts (such as ones showing Texas city revenue demonstrate how a whole (total Texas city revenue) is divided into its parts (different sources of revenue). Bar graphs compare values across categories, showing how proportions are related to each other (as in the number of amendments added to the Texas Constitution since 1877). Bar graphs can present data either horizontally or vertically. All charts and graphs in this edition are based on questions that encourage critical thinking.

Students will learn to ask the following kinds of questions about visual information:

- What is the purpose of the chart or graph? What information does it provide? Or, what is being measured?
- Is there a time period shown, such as January to June 2009? Or, are the data as of a specific date, such as June 30, 2009? Are the data shown at multiple intervals over a fixed period, or at one particular point in time?
- What do the units represent? Dollars a candidate spends on a campaign? Number of voters versus number of nonvoters in Texas? If there are two or more sets of figures, what are the relationships among them?
- What is the source? Is it government information? Private polling information? A newspaper? A private organization? A corporation? An individual?
- Is the type of chart or graph appropriate for the information that is provided? For example, a line graph assumes a smooth progression from one data point to the next. Is that assumption valid for the data shown?
- Is there distortion in the visual representation of the information? Are the intervals equal? Does the area shown distort the actual amount or the proportion?

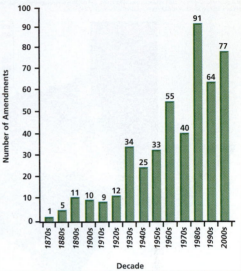

Figure 2.1 *How many amendments were added to the Texas Constitution from 1877 to 2009?*

Source: Secretary of State, Elections Division; Texas Legislative Library, Constitutional Amendments, www.lrl.state.tx.us.

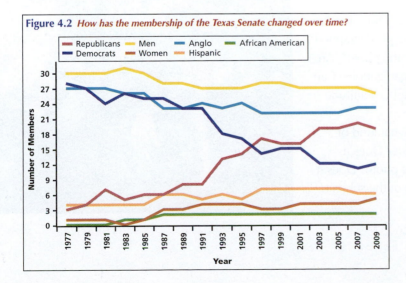

Figure 4.2 *How has the membership of the Texas Senate changed over time?*

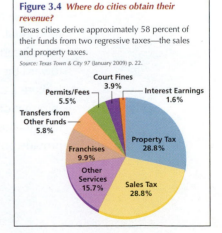

Figure 3.4 *Where do cities obtain their revenue?*

Texas cities derive approximately 58 percent of their funds from two regressive taxes—the sales and property taxes.

Source: Texas Town & City 97 (January 2009) p. 22.

Figure 7.4 *Which party controlled most Texas counties in the 2000s?*

The map reflects the strength of the Texas Republican and Democratic parties based on votes for Republican and Democratic candidates in selected general election contests during the 2000s.

Sources: Based on county election results from the 2000 presidential election, 2002 gubernatorial election, 2004 presidential election, 2006 gubernatorial election, 2006 lieutenant governor election, and the 2006 attorney general election. Texas Secretary of State Web site, Historical Election Results, www.sos.state.tx.us/elections/historical/70-92.shtml.

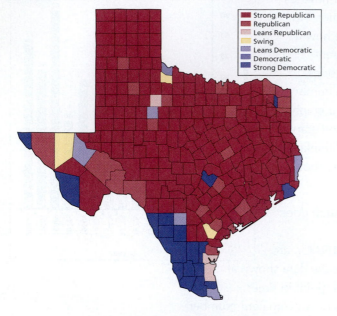

■	Strong Republican
■	Republican
■	Leans Republican
■	Swing
■	Leans Democratic
■	Democratic
■	Strong Democratic

Maps

Maps—of the United States, of particular regions, or of the world—are frequently used in political analysis to illustrate demographic, social, economic, and political issues and trends. All maps in this edition include questions to encourage critical thinking.

Students learn to consider the following issues when analyzing maps:

- Is there a title that identifies the purpose or subject of the map?
- What does the map key/legend show? What are the factors that the map is analyzing?
- What is the region being shown?
- What source is given for the map?
- Maps usually depict a specific point in time. What is the point in time being shown on the map?

News Photographs

Photos can have a dramatic—and often immediate—impact on politics and government. Visual images usually evoke a stronger emotional response from people than do written descriptions. For this reason, individuals and organizations have learned to use photographs as a means to document events, make arguments, offer evidence, and even in some cases to manipulate the viewer into having a particular response.

Students are encouraged to consider the following about photographs:

- When was the photograph taken?
- What is the subject of the photograph?
- Why was the photo taken? What appears to be the purpose of the photograph?
- Is it spontaneous or posed? Did the subject know he or she was being photographed?
- Who was responsible for the photo? (An individual, agency, or organization?) Can you discern the photographer's attitude toward the subject?
- Is there a caption? If so, what kind of information does it provide? Does it identify the subject of the photo? Does it provide an interpretation of the subject?

Political Cartoons

Some of the most interesting commentary on American politics takes place in the form of political cartoons. The cartoonist's goal is to comment on and/or criticize political figures, policies, or events. The cartoonist uses several techniques to accomplish this goal, including exaggeration, irony, and juxtaposition. For example, the cartoonist may point out how the results of governmental policies are the opposite of their intended effects (irony). In other cartoons, two people, ideas, or events that don't belong together may be joined to make a point (juxtaposition). Knowledge of current events is helpful in interpreting political cartoons.

Students learn to appreciate the nuances of political humor and satire by asking the following kinds of questions:

- What labels appear on objects or people in the cartoon? Cartoonists will often label some of the elements. For example, a building with columns might be labeled the "Texas Legislature."
- What does the caption or title contribute to the meaning or impact of the cartoon?
- Can any of the people shown be identified? Governors, well-known members of the Legislature, and state leaders are often shown with specific characteristics that help to identify them.
- Can the event being depicted be identified? Historical events, such as Texas Independence, or contemporary events, such as the 2010 statewide elections, are often the subject matter for cartoons.
- What are the elements of the cartoon? Objects often represent ideas or events. For example, a donkey is often used to depict the Democratic Party.
- How are the characters interacting? What do the speech bubbles contribute to the cartoon?
- What is the overall message of the cartoon? Can you determine what the cartoonist's position is on the subject?

Texas Politics and GOVERNMENT

ROOTS AND REFORM

Fourth Edition

1

Ideas, People, and Economics in Texas Politics

Texas—the Lone Star State—is often perceived by outsiders to have a unique political culture and style of politics, characterized by a sense of individualism and a highly conservative political philosophy. Although more than 80 percent of the population resides in urban areas and the economy is highly diverse, the images of wide-open spaces, large herds of cattle, cowboys, and wildcatters searching for oil and gas persist. Most Texans understand that the widely publicized motto, "Don't Mess with Texas," was part of a statewide environmental effort, but another meaning might be attributed to the phrase—leave Texas alone. It didn't help recently when the governor of Texas made public remarks that some interpreted to suggest that Texas could secede from the United States.

Texans have experienced dramatic changes over the past decades that require a revision in our understanding of who Texans are and the political context or environment in which they now live.

Texas is a populous state with more than 25 million people. The U.S. Census of 1840 counted 200,000 Texans. For the past five decades, the state's rate of population growth has been much larger than that of the nation.[1] Population growth in the latter years of the twentieth century was built, in part, on immigration from other states. More recently, foreign-born immigrants have had a disproportionate impact on the state's population growth. Current projections place the state's population in 2040 at 35 million.[2]

Anglos, non-Hispanic whites, were the dominant population from the period of Texas independence to the early part of the twenty-first century, but the combined populations of

For most of its history, the Texas economy was driven by agriculture and petroleum. At left, oil workers add a length of pipe to a drill stream in 1939. At right, dock workers unload pipes at a port in present day Houston, Texas. While oil is still important, over the past four decades, extensive changes have occurred in the basic structure of the economy, including the dramatic development of high-tech industries and a major role in the worldwide economy.

Hispanics, African Americans, and Asian Americans now exceed the Anglo population. Current population estimates anticipate that Hispanics will comprise 50 percent of the estimated 35 million Texans by 2040.[3]

Less than five percent of Texans lived in urban areas in 1850, but now more than eighty percent of the population lives in urban areas, with a large part concentrated in the Texas urban triangle, which connects the urban areas of Houston, San Antonio and the Dallas-Fort Worth Metroplex.

The state's economy now exceeds $1 trillion a year, larger than most countries in the world. Texas has the third largest state economy, following California and New York. Across the thirteen economic regions of the state, the story is one of economic diversification, high-tech industries, and globalization.

What Should I Know About . . .

After reading this chapter, you should be able to:

★ **1.1** Trace the roots of Texas government and the impact of the state's cultural diversity on its politics, p. 4.

★ **1.2** Identify the core political values Texans hold, and distinguish between four distinct ideologies, p. 13.

★ **1.3** Outline the transformation of the Texas economy from its dependence on agriculture and petroleum to a highly diverse, global economy, p. 24.

★ **1.4** Analyze how disparities in wealth, income, and poverty among races and classes influence politics in Texas., p. 26.

★ **1.5** Assess the potential for welfare reforms within the context of the state's political culture, p. 29.

Demographics, economics, and the political culture of Texas are at the heart of politics. Governments across the state act in response to the demands and expectations of their citizens. Understanding the historical roots of the state's political system and the widespread changes that are occurring is central to a critical analysis of Texas government and politics.

In this chapter, we will describe the historical, demographic, social, ideological, and economic context of Texas politics and government. By understanding this context, we gain an understanding of the institutions and politics Texas shares with other states as well as those that are unique to Texas.

- First, we will examine *the roots of Texas politics and government,* focusing on the ethnic and racial groups that settled and now live in Texas.

- Second, we will analyze *the ideological context* for Texas politics and government, noting how a set of ideas—shared with other Americans—has been modified by Texas's unique experiences.

- Third, we will examine the transformation of *the economy of Texas* from one dependent on agriculture and petroleum to the trading and industrial center that is now the eleventh largest economy in the world.

- Fourth, we will describe the disparities in *income, wealth, and poverty in Texas.*

- Finally, we will examine *political culture and welfare reform* describing prospects for reforms that could potentially improve conditions for those with limited economic resources and enhance the quality of life for all Texans.

ROOTS OF Texas Politics and Government

★ **1.1** . . . **Trace the roots of Texas government and the impact of the state's cultural diversity on its politics.**

The political culture of Texas first emerged among the early settlers who inhabited an area of 267,339 square miles. In part, the state's geography shaped the core values of the new political system. Texas is larger than most nations and contains every major landform: mountains, plains, plateaus, and hills. West of the Pecos River, in far West Texas, are the Chisos and Davis Mountains, a part of the Rocky Mountain chain. Plains constitute the major landform in Texas, covering much of West Texas, North Texas, the Gulf Coast, and Northwestern Texas. The Edwards Plateau, in west central Texas, is the major plateau, or tableland, in Texas. Hills are found in many parts of Texas, but they are especially prominent in the German Hill Country, located northwest of San Antonio. The variety of landforms and the geographical size of Texas have an effect on its inhabitants, including their settlement patterns, voting behavior, economic activities, partisan proclivities, and their political ideas.

Taming a land of such great size and variety is not accomplished easily, but many different peoples have tried. With more than 25 million residents in 2010, Texas is the second largest state in population and in territory.[4] Texas's population is almost as diverse as its geography. Whereas the United States in 2008 was 56.6 percent Anglo,

Does anybody live out here? The image of wide-open spaces and sparsely settled land persists for many, but the lion's share of the state's population lives in the hundred counties designated the Central Texas triangle.

Photo courtesy: Peter Arnold, Inc./Alamy

20.5 percent Hispanic, 15.3 percent African American, and 3.9 percent Asian American, Texas in the same year was 47.2 percent Anglo, 36.5 percent Hispanic, 11.2 percent African American, and 5.1 percent Asian American and others.[5] The Institute of Texan Cultures identifies twenty-seven ethnic groups in contemporary Texas. From the beginning, Texas's population was diverse. The first inhabitants, of course, were the American Indians. (To learn more about how the population of Texas compares with those of other large states, see Table 1.1.)

American Indians

There are few American Indian tribes in present-day Texas. However, from prehistoric times, American Indians representing four different cultural traditions established permanent residence in Texas, and members of many more tribes and nations, some of whom are still present in Texas, were brief inhabitants.

In the coastal areas of the state and extending into all of South Texas, the Coahuiltecan and Karankawan tribes maintained an imperiled existence in a harsh

Table 1.1 *How does the population of Texas compare to those of other large states?*

	Total Population 2009	Anglo Population 2008	Hispanic Population 2008	African American Population 2008	Asian American Population 2008	Median Age* 2008	Persons Under 18 2008	Persons 65+ 2008
General Population Characteristics								
Texas	24,782,302	47.2%	36.5%	11.2%	3.4%	33.2	27.6%	10.1%
California	36,961,664	42.0%	36.6%	5.9%	12.2%	34.9	25.5%	11.2%
New York	19,541,453	59.7%	16.7%	14.7%	6.9%	38.0	22.6%	13.4%
Florida	18,537,969	60.1%	21.0%	14.8%	2.2%	40.3	21.8%	17.4%

*Median age (ages of half of the population above and half below).

Source: U.S. Census Bureau, *American Community Survey, 2008 and 2009,* factfinder.census.gov/home/saff/main.html?_lang=.

environment by hunting and gathering. In Central Texas, scattered bands of American Indians, known contemporarily as the Tonkawa, established themselves during the 1500s. By the eighteenth century, they had become a buffalo-hunting, tepee-using, horse-riding Plains people. To the north of the Tonkawa were the ancestors of the Lipan Apache. Other Plains tribes associated with Texas in those early days were the Kiowa Apache, the Kiowa, and especially the Comanche.[6] The Jumano, related to the Puebloan culture of the American Southwest, were present from historical times, especially in the Rio Grande Valley from El Paso to the confluence of the Rio Grande and Mexican Rio Conchos. Spanish Fort on the Red River was the headquarters for a group of semi-sedentary tribes, known today as the Wichita, who extended to Waco in Central Texas. The Wichita had much in common with the Caddo, but after their adoption of horses in the eighteenth century, their culture became more Plains-like. In eastern and northeastern Texas, tribes of the Caddo who had joined together in confederacies possessed a complex culture built around intensive farming and agriculture.

The American Indian legacy in Texas is substantial. The Caddo established economic and cultural patterns—involving farming, trading, and trotline fishing—on which subsequent inhabitants of Texas expanded. The Caddo also greeted early Spanish explorers as *Tayshas,* meaning "friends." The term was subsequently Hispanicized to *Tejas,* and then Anglicized to *Texas.* Similarly, the most feared and respected American Indians in Texas, the Comanche, displayed many of the characteristics of individualism that Anglo Texans on the frontier most admired.[7] Also, their resistance to Anglo expansion forced the farmers and ranchers to become horsemen and to adapt to the challenges of existence on the frontier.

By the late 1800s, few American Indians remained in Texas, a result of epidemics of diseases such as cholera and smallpox, military campaigns, and their forced removal to reservations in other states. American Indians constitute a small percentage of Texas's population, and their political influence reflects their small numbers. Currently, there are only three American Indian tribes on reservations in Texas: the Alabama-Coushatta in Polk County (in East Texas), the Kickapoo near Eagle Pass (in South Texas on the Rio Grande River), and the Tigua near El Paso (in far West Texas). The oldest, the Alabama-Coushatta reservation, was established in 1854 as compensation for the tribe's neutrality during the war for Texas independence in 1836.

The Tigua first became embroiled in Texas politics when they opened their Speaking Rock Casino in 1993. In 1987, Congress recognized the Tigua, and in exchange, the tribe agreed to prohibit gambling in all forms and to obey Texas laws. Nevertheless, the tribe filed a lawsuit, which they lost, attempting to force the state to negotiate a casino compact with the tribe under the 1988 Indian Gaming Regulatory Act. In 1999, Texas Attorney General John Cornyn sought an injunction to halt gambling on tribal property. In 2001, a federal district court granted a permanent injunction against the tribe's casino and ordered it to close by November 30, 2001. The Tigua appealed this ruling and were allowed to keep the casino open during their appeals. In February 2002, the casino was forced to close.

Other tribes in Texas have tried to establish gambling operations. In 1999, the Alabama-Coushatta tribe voted to bring gambling to its Texas reservation and opened a casino in November 2001. In July 2002, a federal district court ordered it to close. Currently, the only tribal gaming facility is the Kickapoo Lucky Eagle Casino in Eagle Pass. In 2007, the tribe received permission from the U.S. Interior Department to offer Class III games (slots, roulette, and black jack), but the U.S. Court of Appeals reversed the department's decision. Today, the casino offers limited gambling, including poker and bingo.

The desire for additional revenues to fund public education in Texas fueled efforts by Texas American Indians to pressure the legislature to authorize video slot machines on their reservations. However, conservative religious groups opposed any additional gambling in Texas and garnered the support of a majority of legislators.

Is gambling the solution? The Kickapoo tribe has staked its economic development on a limited gambling casino located on its reservation outside of Eagle Pass.

Photo courtesy: J. Lara/San Antonio Express-News/ZUMA Press

Hispanic Americans

Spaniards explored Texas in the sixteenth century, but they did not establish permanent settlements until the early eighteenth century. An early colony in Nacogdoches was followed by a *presidio*, San Antonio de Bexar, and a mission, San Antonio de Valero, along the San Antonio River. A colony in La Bahia (Goliad) followed. The Spaniards did not colonize the land along the Rio Grande until the 1740s and 1750s, although these became some of their most successful settlements.

The mainstays of Spanish colonization included four institutions: (1) the mission, which performed civilian as well as religious functions; (2) the *presidio*, which provided frontier defense; (3) the *rancho*, which sustained civilian life; and, (4) towns or civilian settlements. By the end of the eighteenth century, only about 5,000 *pobladores* (settlers) inhabited Texas.[8] Nonetheless, their legacy far exceeds what their numbers suggest. They created a culture that valued "egalitarianism, a sense of duty, and a respect for physical prowess and gallantry in the face of adversity."[9] They also provided cultural norms for ranchers, sheep herders, and goat raisers. In addition, Spanish legal traditions, such as those pertaining to women's property rights, endured, as did customs protecting debtors.[10]

Mexico declared independence from Spain in 1821, but Mexican colonization of Texas was no more successful than the Spanish attempts had been. In 1836, when Texas became an independent republic, no more than 7,000 or 8,000 Spaniards, Christianized American Indians, and *mestizos* (people of mixed European and American Indian ancestry) resided in Texas. In 1850, the U.S. Census recorded a Hispanic population of only 14,000—less than 7 percent of Texas's population. As late as 1887, the state census counted only 83,000 Hispanics, only 4 percent of the Texas population. Concentrated in the border counties along the Rio Grande, Hispanics were outnumbered even by German Americans. However, between 1890 and 1910, a major influx of Mexicans occurred, resulting in a doubling of the Hispanic population of 1887. Between 1910 and the 1980s, the Hispanic population in Texas grew tenfold, caused largely by an explosive birthrate in Mexico and the steady industrialization of Texas.

How many elected public officials in Texas are Hispanic? Julian Castro, shown here, was elected mayor of San Antonio in 2009. In 2009, there were 2,435 Hispanic elected public officials in Texas.

Photo courtesy: Bob Daemmrich Photography, Inc.

During the late 1940s, Hispanics displaced African Americans as the largest ethnic minority in Texas.[11]

Now, Hispanics exercise considerable political clout in Texas. By 2009, there were 2,435 Hispanic elected public officials in Texas, more than in any other state. And, six Hispanics—Texas Supreme Court Justices Raul A. Gonzalez, Alberto R. Gonzales, and David M. Medina; Attorney General Dan Morales; and Texas Railroad Commissioners Tony Garza and Victor Carrillo—had been elected to statewide office.[12]

In 2010, a large majority of Hispanic elected officials were Democrats. The Republican Party has made a concerted effort to attract Hispanic voters in recent elections, appealing to Hispanics' desires for educational advancement, personal responsibility, and economic opportunity.[13] But when Republican Railroad Commissioner Victor Carrillo was unseated by an unknown challenger in his party's primary in 2010, he blamed his loss on his Hispanic surname. Carrillo had outspent his challenger by twelve to one and had enjoyed the support of other Republican leaders.

African Americans

African Americans have inhabited Texas since Spanish rule but probably made up no more than 12 percent of the population in Texas prior to 1836. This was due to the Mexican government's opposition to slavery. Most early settlers in Texas came from the southern mountain states, where slavery was less common. In the late 1830s, however, an influx of African Americans accompanied Anglo planters from coastal southern states. With slavery legalized in the Republic of Texas, the number of African Americans increased rapidly, composing 20 percent of the population by 1840. The growth of the African American population in Texas was effectively halted by the Civil War. Between 1865 and 1880, only 6 percent of immigrants were African American, and the percentage of African Americans has continued to decline since 1865, the year in which nearly one-third of Texas's population was African American.[14]

The bulk of the settlement by African Americans in Texas occurred between 1836 and 1865. The states that contributed the largest number of slaves were Alabama, Virginia, Georgia, and Mississippi, and the area of greatest settlement for African Americans lay east of a line connecting Texarkana and San Antonio. This was also the area dominated by Anglos from the lower South. By 1860, thirteen Texas counties had African American majorities. All of these counties were located along the major rivers of eastern and southeastern Texas, especially the lower Brazos, Colorado, and Trinity Rivers. After emancipation, freed African Americans remained in that area; consequently, in 1887, twelve counties had African American majorities. However, with the decline of the sharecropper system, African Americans abandoned the rural areas of East Texas for the urban centers that were closest to the old plantation districts—Houston and Dallas. In 1930, only four counties had African American majorities, and by 1980, there were none.[15]

How many African Americans have been able to win statewide offices? Texas Supreme Court Chief Justice Wallace B. Jefferson, seen here delivering the biennial State of the Judiciary Address before the Texas Legislature, is one of four African Americans to win statewide office.

Photo courtesy: Bob Daemmrich Photography, Inc.

African Americans in Texas held 466 elected offices in 2002.[16] Texas ranked ninth among the states in the number of African American elected officials. Among the elected officials in Texas, two African Americans were U.S. Representatives, two were state senators, fourteen were representatives, twenty were county officials, 282 were municipal officials, forty-four were judicial or law enforcement officials, and ninety-five were elected to school boards and other elected education positions. Four African Americans have been elected to statewide office in Texas. They are Railroad Commissioner Michael Williams, Texas Supreme Court Chief Justice Wallace Jefferson, and Texas Supreme Court Justice Dale Wainwright, all Republicans; and former Texas Court of Criminal Appeals Judge Morris Overstreet, a Democrat.

Another prominent African American politician in Texas is former Dallas Mayor Ron Kirk. In November 2001, Kirk resigned as mayor and later won the Democratic Party's nomination for U.S. senator, but lost the general election. In 2009, President Barack Obama appointed Kirk to the post of United States Trade Representative. Three African Americans have been appointed speaker pro tempore of the Texas House.

Asian Americans

The first permanent resident Asian Americans in Texas were probably Chinese immigrants who arrived in Houston in 1869 to clear land for the Houston and Texas Central Railway. Chinese laborers also worked for the Southern Pacific Railroad and the Texas and Pacific line during the 1870s and 1880s. In the early 1900s, a distinguished Japanese businessman, Seito Saibara, was invited to the United States to help develop the rice industry on the Gulf Coast. In 1903, Harris County officials invited him to start a colony in Webster, just south of Houston. Saibara bought 304 acres and began bringing families from Japan. Several Japanese colonies were subsequently

Where do you find the Asian American population? Small numbers of Asian Americans live throughout the state, but the significant concentration of these populations is in the larger cities, particularly Houston.

Anglos
Non-Hispanic whites.

established in the Rio Grande Valley and in Orange County. During the 1970s, thousands of Vietnamese immigrants came to Texas when the South Vietnamese government neared collapse and ultimately fell to North Vietnam.

In 2008, there were 939,000 Asian Americans in Texas, primarily of Vietnamese, Chinese, Indian, Filipino, Korean, and Japanese ethnicity. The larger cities in Texas contain Asian neighborhoods. In Houston, which has the largest Asian American population, there are two China-towns: an historic district near the George R. Brown Convention Center and a newer area on Bellaire Boulevard. In fact, a number of small malls, many along Bellaire, have signs in Chinese, Japanese, Vietnamese, and other Asian languages.

Tom Lee of San Antonio, who served in the 1960s, is believed to be the first Asian American to serve in the Texas House. Martha Wong, longtime community activist, served on the Houston city council from 1993 until 1999 and won election to the Texas House in 2002 and in 2004. She was the first Asian American woman elected to the Texas Legislature. In 2004, Hubert Vo was elected to the Texas House, narrowly defeating veteran Representative Talmadge Heflin. Asian Americans have been elected to city councils, state and local courts, and boards of education.[17] In recent election cycles, there is evidence of increased numbers of Asian Americans running for office, supported in part by groups such as the Asian-American Democrats of Texas and the Indian American Coalition of Texas.

Anglos

As the term is used in Texas, **Anglos** are non-Hispanic whites. During the early period of Anglo settlement in Texas, 1815 to 1836, the Anglo immigrants to Texas were predominantly upper Southerners from Tennessee, Kentucky, Arkansas, and North Carolina. By 1820, these people had firmly established themselves in Northeast Texas. During the 1820s, the *empresario* program of the Mexican government, which granted land to contractors who promised to bring settlers, drew additional upper Southerners to the Austin, DeWitt, and Robertson colonies in South Central Texas. Missouri, Kentucky, Tennessee, and Arkansas provided most of these settlers.

In the southeastern border area of Texas, known as the Atascosita District, Anglos began drifting in after 1819. These settlers were lower Southerners, mostly poor whites from Louisiana, Mississippi, and Alabama.

North of the Big Thicket, between the Trinity and Sabine Rivers, a few small Anglo settlements developed. Most of these settlers were upper Southerners, although many slave-owning planters were attracted by the fertile Redlands area. Thus, by 1836, more than 60 percent of Anglos in Texas were from the upper South, about 25 percent were from the lower South, and about 10 percent were New Englanders.[18]

From Texas's independence to the Civil War, Anglo immigration increased, drawing more heavily from the lower South. The legalization of slavery in the Texas Republic resulted in the first major wave of lower Southerners, primarily from Alabama, Georgia, Mississippi, and Louisiana. According to the 1850 Census, lower Southerners had become almost as numerous as the upper Southerners. The two groups, however, occupied different areas of Texas. Most of eastern and southeastern Texas was successfully settled by lower southern planters, and the continuing waves of upper Southerners were directed to the western interior of Texas.

In the post–Civil War period, upper and lower southern immigration continued in roughly equal proportions. The western expansion to the New Mexico border by 1880 was primarily an achievement of upper Southerners, who settled most of West Texas, and lower Midwesterners (from Illinois, Kansas, and Iowa), who dominated the upper Panhandle.

Anglos have dominated politics and government in Texas since its independence from Mexico in 1836. Since statehood, Anglos have provided all of Texas's governors and lieutenant governors, almost all of its statewide elected officials, an overwhelming majority of its legislators, and most of the members of its administrative boards and commissions. However, the changing composition of Texas's population presages a likely challenge to the Anglo dominance in politics and government.

The Contemporary Population of Texas

The patterns of settlement established by Texas's first residents are still evident today, providing a measure of continuity. But new patterns are emerging as Texas becomes more heavily populated, more urbanized, and more diverse ethnically.

The state's population today exceeds 25 million. Over the past five decades, the state's population has increased at a substantially higher rate than the nation's population, and since 2000, the Texas population has increased by more than 4 million and has, as a result, picked up an additional handful of congressional seats. Texas continues to be the second largest state, exceeded only by California.

Population growth is explained by both immigration and natural increases based on birthrates. During the 1970s, approximately 59 percent of the population growth was due to in-migration (immigration minus emigration) from other states or countries. Although in-migration has slowed down, rising birthrates, particularly among the minority populations, have taken on more significance in explaining the increase in the state's population.

Approximately 61 percent of Texas residents were born in the state. More than 22 percent were born in other states, and approximately 16 percent were born in another country. More than 70 percent of approximately 4 million foreign-born residents are from Latin American countries.[19]

During the decade of 1940 to 1950, Texas became an urban state, and the process of urbanization has continued. Despite the rural image and wide-open spaces frequently associated with Texas, approximately 88 percent of the population now lives in urban areas. Houston, San Antonio, and Dallas are among the ten most populous cities in the United States. The fastest growing areas are within the Texas urban triangle in the center of the state and along the Mexican border from Brownsville to Laredo.[20]

The dramatic increases in the state's population are matched by changes in its ethnic and racial composition. In 1950, Anglos comprised 74 percent of the state's 7.7 million residents, and African Americans and Hispanics accounted for approximately 13 percent each. Fifty years later, the population had grown to approximately 21 million. The Anglos' share was 53 percent, Hispanics, 32 percent, and African Americans, approximately 12 percent. Additionally, the Asian American communities exceeded 3 percent of the population.[21] By 2008, the Anglo proportion of the population had dropped to 47 percent, while the Hispanic population was almost 37 percent. Based on current estimates, the composition of the state's population will continue to change with Hispanics eventually becoming the majority population. (To learn more about Texas's changing populations, see Analyzing Visuals: Texas Population Projections.)

ANALYZING VISUALS

Texas's Population Projections

Examine the chart depicting population projections for Texas for the next thirty years, and then answer the questions.

Year	Total	Anglo	Black	Hispanic	Other
2015	26,156,723	11,694,520	2,913,062	10,436,546	1,112,595
2020	28,005,740	11,796,448	3,052,417	11,882,980	1,273,895
2025	29,897,410	11,830,578	3,170,964	13,448,459	1,447,409
2030	31,830,575	11,789,274	3,268,623	15,140,100	1,632,578
2035	33,789,697	11,682,022	3,345,687	16,934,464	1,827,524
2040	35,761,165	11,525,089	3,403,163	18,804,311	2,028,602

Source: Texas State Data Center, "Projections of the Population of Texas and Counties by Age, Sex and Race/Ethnicity for 2000–2040," February 2009, txsdc.utsa.edu/tp epp/2008 projections/2008_txpopprj_txtotnum.php.

■ Are the Anglo and African American populations projected to decrease in terms of absolute numbers?
■ Why is the Hispanic percentage of the population increasing in relationship to the Anglo and African American populations?
■ What changes in public policy and partisan control of the state's government are likely to accompany these population changes?

As Hispanics become the principal ethnic group, politics and government will definitely change, but political scientists disagree on the effect of the changes. First, most political analysts agree that Hispanics will enjoy greater political clout in Texas. Hispanics are more likely to be Democrats than Republicans (in Texas, Democrats outnumbered Republicans by a two-to-one margin in party identification among Hispanic voters).[22] However, many Hispanics, who were formally or informally excluded from the political process prior to the application of the Voting Rights Act to Texas in 1975, are likely to claim no partisan affiliation or an attachment to some other party.[23]

Nationally, Hispanics voted overwhelmingly for Democrat Barack Obama over Republican John McCain in the 2008 presidential race—by a margin of 67 percent to 31 percent, according to exit polls analyzed by the Pew Hispanic Center.[24] In a subsequent national survey, Hispanics listed the economy (57 percent), education (51 percent), health care (45 percent), and national security (43 percent) as the most important issues facing the Obama administration.[25] Historically, Hispanics have been more likely than Anglos to mention social issues as areas of concern. In education, Hispanics want more schools, smaller classes, and greater cultural sensitivity. They are also concerned about crime, drugs, assistance for the elderly, and responding to prejudice and discrimination.[26]

The most important economic issue for Hispanics is jobs. Although self-identified conservatives, Hispanics are willing to pay more taxes for an expanded government role in combating crime, preventing drug abuse, providing public education, increasing health care and child care, and protecting the environment. This is especially true for Hispanic Texans.[27] Furthermore, government is viewed positively by Hispanics as a problem solver in society.[28]

The positive view of government, however, may be suffering because of the prolonged controversy over immigration, research by the Pew Hispanic Center indicates.

According to the survey, "Just over half of all Hispanic adults in the U.S. worry that they, a family member or a close friend could be deported." Nearly two-thirds said Congress' failure to enact an immigration reform bill had made life more difficult for all Hispanics.[29]

Given the policy preferences of Hispanics and presuming an increase in their political influence, several policy changes can be anticipated. The tax structure in Texas, which takes 12.2 percent of the income of poorest Texans (incomes less than $18,000 annually) and only 3.0 percent of the income of the richest Texans (incomes greater than $463,000 annually), will likely be revised to become less regressive. But the battle for tax changes will be long and arduous.[30] State spending for elementary and secondary education will probably increase, given the increasing school-age population and the need for a better-educated workforce. Spending on health care will increase as the population ages, with increased demand for long-term care. In 2009, more than one in four Texans (26.9 percent) were without health insurance, the highest uninsured rate in the nation.[31] Although thousands of children in Texas are covered by Medicaid and the Children's Health Insurance Program (CHIP), some 20 percent of Texas's children were uninsured in 2009. (To learn more about health insurance, see Politics Now: Sad Statistics.) In subsequent chapters, we return frequently to the topic of Texas's people; however, we now shift our focus to the ideological context for Texas politics and government.

The Ideological Context

⭐ **1.2 . . . Identify the core political values Texans hold, and distinguish between four distinct ideologies.**

The ideological context for Texas politics and government centers on a Texan Creed. The Texan Creed incorporates many of the same ideas that were influential for other Americans: individualism, liberty, constitutionalism, democracy, and equality. The features that distinguish the Texan Creed from the ideas held by other Americans arise from the unique historical experiences of Texas and Texans, especially between the 1820s and 1880s. Texas has changed substantially since the late 1800s, but the repetition of the prior historical experiences, whether mythical or not, keeps the creed alive and perpetuates it in each new generation. Consequently, we first explore how these experiences have shaped the five ideas of the Texan Creed.

The Texan Creed

The **Texan Creed** consists of a set of ideas that identify Texans and provide the basis for their politics and government. For a majority of Texans, there is a consensus on the importance of these ideas. Contemporary Texas is more heterogeneous than nineteenth-century Texas, but the ideas that were established during that century are still important today. Among the five ideas, individualism holds a special place for most Texans.

INDIVIDUALISM For most Americans, **individualism,** which is the belief that each person should act in accordance with his or her own conscience, is the product of seventeenth-century Protestantism. Historian T. R. Fehrenbach cites individualism as the reason that early Anglo settlers came to Texas in the first place:

> The early Texans descended from clans and families, heavily Scotch Irish, who deserted the panoply of Europe, despising its hierarchies and social organism . . . and who plunged into the wilderness. These folk sought land and opportunity, surely— but they were also consciously fleeing something: a vision of the world in which community and state transcended the individual family and its personal good.[32]

Texan Creed

A set of ideas—primarily individualism and liberty—that shape Texas politics and government.

individualism

The belief that each person should act in accordance with his or her own conscience.

Sad Statistics

February 13, 2010
San Antonio Express-News
www.expressnews.com

By Melissa Fletcher Stoeltje, Staff

Almost a quarter of the children in Bexar County lived in poverty and lacked health insurance in 2008, according to a new study on poverty in Texas.

And while the numbers dropped slightly compared with a similar study the year before, this still means roughly one in four children struggled with the byproducts of poverty: poor school performance, health woes, hunger and circumscribed futures. . . .

The Center for Public Policy Priorities, a nonprofit dedicated to improving the economic and social conditions of low- and moderate-income Texans, put forth the report, called the *State of Texas Children 2009-10: Texas KIDS COUNT Annual Data Book.*

It found that in Bexar County, 102,413 children, or 23.1 percent, lived below the poverty level. The federal poverty line for a family of three in 2008 was an annual income of $17,600 or less.

Compared with their peers, children living in poverty are more likely to drop out of school, have worse health in adolescence and adulthood, and work at lower-paying jobs.

The outlook is likewise bleak when it comes to poor children and their health care coverage. For the 10th consecutive year, Texas has the highest rate of uninsured children in the nation, with 20 percent of Texas children uninsured, nearly twice the national average.

When it comes to food insecurity, Texas has the second-highest rate of childhood hunger in the nation, with 1.4 million Texas households unsure where their next meal will come from.

Sad Statistics

- Children in Texas living in poverty: 23 percent
- Children in the U.S. living in poverty: 18 percent
- Bexar County children in poverty: 23.1 percent
- Uninsured children in Texas: 20 percent
- Uninsured children in Bexar County: 24.5 percent
- Bexar County children on food stamps: 136,920 in February 2010
- Food stamp applications not processed on time in Texas: 38 percent

Critical Thinking Questions

1. Do most Texans recognize the extent of poverty within the state?
2. In addition to the problems mentioned in this article, what are some of the other difficulties these children routinely face?
3. What are the consequences of these poor conditions for the future economic development of the state?

Coming to Texas in the late eighteenth century, these people created a society dedicated to individualism. According to the ideal, the individual is responsible for the benefits that she or he receives in life and in the hereafter. In reality, the feeling for the soil that these Texans developed created the society. For Texans, land possesses both a symbolic and a practical meaning. During the nineteenth century, Texans created a social environment in which every person, whether dirt farmer or rancher, could be a landowner, independent and supreme over his or her "country." The landowners' ethos remains in contemporary Texas, a legacy of early Texas individualism. For most Texans, the landowner remains the ideal and is accorded the highest social status.[33]

The individualism created in Texans' attachment to the land was nurtured by the frontier experience. For most Americans, the frontier era was short lived, lasting usually no more than a decade. Civilization advanced rapidly. For Texans, however, the **frontier era**—the period when Texas was a border between American civilization and an area inhabited by a hostile indigenous population—lasted four decades (1830s to 1870s).

frontier era
The period when Texas was a border between American civilization and an area inhabited by a hostile, indigenous population.

It involved three distinct challenges: a battle with Mexico for cultural and political dominance, a more dangerous conflict for survival with an American Indian population, and a struggle to conquer a difficult land. The frontier era had an enormous impact on Texans.

For Texans, the most dangerous frontier was the western, American Indian frontier. By 1834, Texan colonists had placed themselves within range of the Comanche. Previous wars between American Indians and Anglos followed a common pattern: Anglo encroachment engendered American Indian retaliation, which incited a military response that subdued the American Indians. The Plains Indians, such as the Comanche, were not stationary, agricultural peoples. They were nomads who followed the bison herds over the seemingly boundless prairie. They avoided contact with Anglo settlers, except for raids on established settlements. Thus, the conflict involved an Anglo farming population and powerful, warlike American Indians who held a decided advantage in military tactics, weapons, and mobility. The Comanche were never numerous, but they were defending their territory from intruders, and their raids exacted a terrible toll. As historian T. R. Fehrenbach notes, "Between 1836 and 1860, 200 men, women, and children were killed each year by Indians on the Texas border; between 1860 and 1875 at least 100 died or were carried off annually. The trek through Central Texas cost seventeen white lives per mile."[34]

In order to survive on the frontier, Anglo farmers and ranchers had to adapt. They became true horsemen, they learned to survive in American Indian country, and they adapted their agriculture to raising stock. The most important adaptation, however, involved frontier defense—the creation of the **Texas Rangers,** a mounted force of armed volunteers that provided order on the frontier. Companies of Texas Rangers date from Austin's colony, having been formed as early as 1823. However, only after Texas independence was their presence significant. Characterized as an early state police, the rangers were in reality unique. The state authorized the rangers as a mounted militia, a paramilitary organization that the state assisted when it could—usually not often. The rangers were composed of farmers and ranchers threatened by the native population; they were young, adventuresome, courageous volunteers. Though the rangers were less numerous than their enemies, they quickly found that the best defense was to attack, dominate, and subdue. Though moral and ethical questions surround their tactics, few have questioned their success in seeking out their enemies' weakness and then attacking it without mercy. These characteristics and the use of Samuel Colt's revolving pistol, which gave each ranger the firepower of six, enabled the rangers to subdue their enemies.[35] However, as Fehrenbach admits,

Texas Rangers
A mounted force of armed volunteers that provided order on the frontier.

> The Rangers never halted all the lawlessness and violence, of course, and the Army, not they, waged all the final campaigns against the Indians. . . . But Texans applauded their efforts. . . . For Rangers, born of the frontier, embodied many of the bedrock values of the frontier. They were brutal to enemies, loyal to friends, courteous to women, kind to old ladies; they never gave up, claiming that no power on earth could stop the man in the right who kept "a-coming." These were male values, warrior values.[36]

The final contribution to individualism came from the cowboy, who experienced the closing of the frontier and its way of life. Similar to the ranger in many of his values, the cowhand adopted a semi-feudal notion of loyalty to his boss and brand, taken from the Mexican cattle-ranching culture. To herd half-wild cattle over thousands of miles required physical courage, but not recklessness. However, no respectable cowboy backed away from a fight that was forced upon him.[37] In all its manifestations, individualism has produced in Texans "a hard pragmatism and absence of ideology, a worship of action and accomplishment, a disdain for weakness and incompetence, and a thread of belligerence—and finally, a natural mythology stemming from the Alamo."[38] (The Alamo is discussed in the next section on liberty.)

TIMELINE: The Changing Milieu of Texas Government and Politics

1700s   American Indians in the Pre-modern Era— Approximately twenty-three American Indian tribes live in Texas.

1740s   Spanish Colonization— The Spanish begin to colonize Texas with limited success.

1815–16   Beginning of Anglo Settlement— The first Anglo settlers arrive south of the Red River.

1836   Texas Independence— Following the Battle of San Jacinto, Texans win independence from Mexico, transforming their values and historical experiences into a distinguishable Texan Creed.

liberty
The belief that government should not infringe upon a person's individual rights.

LIBERTY   Closely related to individualism and nearly as important to the Texan Creed is the idea of liberty. For most Americans, liberty is a product of the eighteenth century's Age of Enlightenment, with its emphasis on natural rights, the social contract, and a limited role for government. Complementing individualism, **liberty** is the belief that government should not infringe upon a person's individual rights. For Texans, a passion for liberty has additional sources: it was the reason for Texas's revolt against Mexico and the battle for the Alamo.

The decision by Texans to declare their independence from Mexico in 1836 had many causes, but the most important ones involved Mexico's attempts to exert greater control over Texas and Texans. Perhaps the cultural differences between the Anglo settlers and their Mexican governors were such that conflict was inevitable. However, Stephen F. Austin's leadership had enabled the settlers to avoid involvement in domestic Mexican factional disputes for many years. Minor problems—religious requirements imposed on the settlers and Mexican opposition to slavery—offered potential areas of greater conflict, but a more serious concern involved the lack of an adequate local government through which the settlers could exercise a voice in the administration of their own affairs and the maintenance of order.[39] This grievance and Mexican suspicions of Anglo motives led the Mexicans to ban further immigration in 1830 and, two years later, to enforce the collection of tariff duties. In response to these Mexican actions, the colonists dispatched Stephen F. Austin to request separate statehood for Texas and other reforms. Until 1835, Texans considered themselves loyal Mexican citizens and were attempting to uphold the principles of the liberal, federal Mexican Constitution of 1824. Only when the futility of such a position became evident were the "Texians," as they called themselves, willing to revolt against Mexico itself.[40]

1940s **Urban Texas—** Texas becomes an urban state developing extensive metropolitan areas.

1993 **NAFTA—**The United States, Canada, and Mexico enter into the North American Free Trade Agreement, transforming Texas into a center of international trade.

2000s **Eleventh Largest World Economy—** Economic growth and job creation exceed that of the nation.

1970s **Economic Diversification—**Texas begins to diversify its economy, which up until now has relied primarily on petroleum and agriculture.

2010 **Ever-Increasing and Diverse Population—**With a diverse population now exceeding 25 million, Texas, the second largest state, is likely to acquire additional seats in the U.S. House of Representatives.

In October 1835, Mexican President Antonio Lopez de Santa Anna replaced the federal Constitution of 1824 with the *Siete Leyes* (the "Seven Laws"), which established a centralized government under the president's control. The *Siete Leyes* signaled the end of republicanism in Mexico, converted the states into departments under the central government, and replaced the elected governors with appointed ones. At the same time, Mexican troops took up positions in Texas. When Mexican troops attempted to take a cannon in Gonzales, a skirmish ensued, and Texians prepared for war. A summons to arms in 1835 appealed to the Texians: "Fellow citizens, Your cause is a good one, none can be better; it is republicanism in opposition to despotism; in a word it is liberty in opposition to slavery. You will be fighting for your wives and children, your homes and firesides, for your country, for liberty."[41] With the adoption of this declaration, Texas established the right to revolution and laid the foundation for its subsequent government.

More than any historic event, the loss of the **Alamo** exemplifies Texans' passion for liberty. The Alamo, a former Spanish mission in the heart of San Antonio, once separated Mexican forces from Anglo settlements. In February and March of 1836, Lieutenant Colonel William Barret Travis and his band of about 180 volunteers fought to their deaths there against a Mexican army of more than 5,000. The Alamo defenders lost the battle, but historian Joe Frantz contends that they "set the stage for ultimate Texas unification and victory" and created a legacy that inspires and defines Texans more than a century and a half later.[42] Over the years, fact and legend have intertwined so that the real story of the Alamo is impossible to discover. However, the true story is unimportant, for the power of the Alamo as a symbol of Texan independence and liberty transcends any measure of the truth. To a significant degree, the importance of the Alamo is embodied in the statements

Alamo
A San Antonio mission that was defended by Texans during their war for independence.

17

Does Texas have its own mythology? The Texan Creed is based, in part, on the events that occurred at the Alamo and San Jacinto, commemorated below, when Texans defeated the troops of Santa Anna on April 21, 1836.

and the alleged actions of its heroes: David Crockett, William Barret Travis, and Jim Bowie.

Upon his arrival in Texas in 1836, David Crockett was administered the oath of allegiance by Judge John Forbes, who was forced to pause during his reading. Crockett had "noticed that he was required to uphold 'any future government' that might be established. That could mean a dictatorship. He refused to sign until the wording was changed to 'any future *republican* government.'"[43] Similarly, when he reached the Alamo, Crockett, noted for his verbal excesses, announced that "all the honor that I desire is that of defending as a high private, in common with my fellow citizens, the liberties of our common country."[44] For Crockett and others of his generation, the defining historical event was the American Revolution. To these men, the similarities between the American Revolution and the revolt by Texans were overpowering.

William B. Travis, the youthful commander of the Alamo, probably best exemplifies the ideal of individual liberty and freedom. In his appeal for assistance, which was addressed "To The People of Texas & All Americans in the World," Travis pledged never to surrender or retreat and called on Americans everywhere "in the name of liberty, of patriotism & everything dear to the American character, to come to our aid."[45] In a letter to a friend, Travis explained his stand at the Alamo: "He felt the spirit of the times—the conviction that liberty, freedom and independence were in themselves worth fighting for; the belief that a man should be willing to make any sacrifice to hold these prizes."[46]

Whether Travis really drew a line in the dirt is disputed. Nevertheless, his speech in which he gave his men three choices—surrender, escape, or fight to the end—is a cornerstone of the Alamo legacy. Travis urged his men to fight with him, but he left the choice to each individual. Aware that no reinforcements were coming, all but one man crossed the line, choosing to fight and die with Travis. Jim Bowie, confined to a cot by typhoid-pneumonia, allegedly said, "Boys, I am not able to go to you, but I wish some of you would be so kind as to remove my cot over there."[47]

The symbolic power of the Alamo reaches all Anglo Texans, regardless of political ideology. To a conservative, the Alamo symbolizes rugged individualism on the frontier and the need to defend liberty. A liberal sees in the Alamo the struggle for a sense of community, justice, and civil liberties.[48] Both visions offer insight into Texas and its politics. For ***Tejanos*** (native Texans of Mexican descent), the Alamo is an ambiguous symbol. Although Texas independence was the result of an alliance between Anglos and *Tejanos,* who played a crucial role, the ambivalence that *Tejanos* feel "stems from . . . the long use of the Alamo as an everyday symbol of conquest over Mexicans, as a vindication for the repressive treatment of Mexicans."[49]

Tejanos
Native Texans of Mexican descent.

CONSTITUTIONALISM AND DEMOCRACY   Texans grant nearly equal status to the ideas of **constitutionalism** and democracy. Perhaps Texans give a slight edge to constitutionalism because of its greater harmony with the dominant values of individualism and liberty. Following a tradition established in the United States, Texas has, for each of its governments, adopted a formal, written constitution, which clearly and distinctly limits the authority of government. (To learn more about one limit on government's authority, see The Living Constitution: Article 1, Section 3A, Texas Equal Rights Amendment.) In fact, from their first constitution in 1836, Texans created what historian T. R. Fehrenbach considers a "state that did not and could not plan society—they saw this as an immoral intrusion upon personal liberty—and in fact had almost no control over society in general."[50] Further support for the connection

constitutionalism
Limits placed on government through a written document.

The Living Constitution

Equality under the law shall not be denied or abridged because of sex, race, color, creed, or national origin. This amendment is self operative.

—TEXAS EQUAL RIGHTS AMENDMENT, ARTICLE 1, SECTION 3A

In 1957, the Texas Federation of Business and Professional Women launched a campaign to convince the Texas Legislature to put a Texas Equal Rights Amendment (ERA) on the ballot. The legislature finally approved the necessary resolution in 1971, and the amendment was ratified by Texas voters in 1972. In 1973, women legislators took advantage of the amendment to win passage of laws prohibiting sex-based discrimination in processing loan and credit applications and preventing husbands from abandoning and selling homesteads without their wives' consent. In 1974, Texas Attorney General John Hill, citing the amendment, struck down laws restricting the hours that women could work.

In the first case involving the amendment, the Texas Supreme Court established a three-pronged test for cases alleging a violation of the Texas ERA. First, a court had to decide whether equality under the law had been denied. If it had, the ERA's language required the court to determine "whether equality was denied because of a person's membership in a protected class of sex, race, color, creed, or national origin." If the court concluded that equality was denied because of membership in a protected class, the challenged action violated the ERA unless (and this is the third prong) it was narrowly tailored to serve a compelling governmental interest.[a]

In 1993, a suit was filed in an Austin district court on behalf of all low-income women in Texas. The suit challenged the Texas Medical Assistance Program (TMAP), which provides public funds for abortions for Medicaid recipients only when the pregnancy is the result of rape or incest or endangers the life of the mother. The plaintiffs argued that a number of health problems may be caused or aggravated by pregnancy and that, as a result, women were being denied medically necessary treatments. Men, they noted, had all

medically necessary conditions treated under Medicaid. The Texas Supreme Court agreed in December 2002 that women on Medicaid were being treated differently than men but ruled the disparity didn't violate the ERA. The unequal treatment was not because of the women's sex but because the Texas Legislature would cover only those Medicaid treatments for which the state would be reimbursed by the federal government, the court said. Congress had refused to reimburse states for abortions since the passage of the Hyde Amendment in 1976.

In 1998, John Geddes Lawrence and Tyron Garner were arrested, convicted, and fined $200 in Houston for sodomy. On appeal to the 14th Texas Court of Appeals, they argued that since the law prohibited sexual acts only between individuals of the same sex, it violated the Equal Rights Amendment. The appellate court disagreed and upheld the anti-sodomy law. Subsequently, the law was overturned by the U.S. Supreme Court as a violation of the U.S. Constitution's Fourteenth Amendment.[b]

CRITICAL THINKING QUESTIONS

1. Based on your understanding of the Hyde Amendment, could Texas fund abortion procedures with state funds?
2. Do you concur with the reasoning of the Texas Supreme Court that the Texas Medical Assistance Program did not violate the Texas Equal Rights Amendment? Why or why not?
3. Has the U.S. Supreme Court's decision in the case involving Lawrence and Garner basically eliminated any authority of Texas to restrict consensual sex between persons of the same gender? Explain your answer.

[a]*In re McLean*, 725 S.W.2d Tex. (1987).
[b]*Lawrence v. Texas*, 539 U.S. 558 (2003).

between constitutionalism and liberty is seen in the inclusion, in all of Texas's constitutions, of an extensive Bill of Rights (we will examine the constitutions of Texas and their provisions in detail in **chapter 2**). Texans' desire for democracy was reflected in their commitment to creating Jeffersonian democracy—that is, a male, slave-owning democracy of property holders.

equality
The belief that all individuals should be treated similarly, regardless of socioeconomic status.

EQUALITY   The idea of **equality**—the belief that all individuals should be treated similarly, regardless of socioeconomic status—that developed in Texas during the nineteenth century was a product of the social system. Although there were substantial differences in social and economic statuses of Anglo males, no rigid social or political hierarchy existed. The commitment to social and political equality reflected a society based on land ownership, and land was a plentiful commodity. However, the equality accorded Anglo males did not extend to other members of the society. For non-Anglos, the inequality was palpable and perverse. Historian Fehrenbach describes slavery for African American Texans as "a system of the entrepreneurial exploitation of labor for profit, based on a law and society that was explicitly racist, in that the servitude of black people was justified by their racial inequality with whites."[51] The end of slavery was followed by the legal segregation of African Americans. Though no longer supported by law, there are still, in many areas of contemporary Texas, two societies—one Anglo and one African American, separate and unequal. The Anglo response to Hispanics has been similar, and Mexican Americans have been subjected to segregation and discrimination as well.

American Creed
A set of ideas that provide a national identity, limit government, and structure politics in America.

The Texan Creed is similar to the American Creed. According to political scientist Samuel Huntington, the **American Creed** consists of five ideas—individualism, equality, liberty, constitutionalism, and democracy—that provide Americans with a national identity, limit government authority, and are the foundation for American politics.[52] Like the American Creed, the Texan Creed provides the ideas that are the foundation for politics and government. Though similar to the American Creed, the Texan Creed has been shaped by historical events to place more emphasis on individualism and liberty than does the American Creed. If the Texan Creed is to endure, it must be transmitted from generation to generation, and Texans make a concerted effort to ensure its transmission.

As people acquire additional knowledge about politics and government, there is a growing need to organize that information and make it meaningful. For those who are most involved and active in politics, it means the development of a political ideology. A political ideology is a group's or individual's coherent set of values and beliefs about the government's purpose and scope. People who adhere to a particular ideology are called ideologues.

Political Ideologies in Texas

Politics involves conflicts over different ideas about the proper scope and purpose of government. If everyone agreed about what government should do and to what extent it should do it, there would be no need for politics. The Texan Creed allows different conceptions of government's role. Some people may want the government to regulate individual behavior so that greater liberty is enjoyed by all; others may claim that the individual's right should be supreme and absolute. For example, for some Texans, the law that required motorcyclists to wear protective helmets infringed unnecessarily on individualism in the interest of the general welfare. Similarly, some people may want government to promote equal rights and protections for all immigrants, regardless of their legal status, whereas others may want government to lower the number of immigrants allowed into the United States.

A person's ideas of the scope of government (how much government should do) and the purpose of government (what goals are legitimate for government) determine

Figure 1.1 *What are the four ideologies?*

The axes represent people's attitudes concerning the use of government to achieve certain goals. The horizontal axis represents a person's willingness to use governmental power to limit personal freedoms to maintain order. The vertical axis represents a person's willingness to use governmental power to promote equality. Each ideology reflects a choice between conflicting values. For example, liberals oppose the use of governmental power to limit personal freedoms to maintain order, but support the use of governmental power to promote equality over protecting personal freedoms. On the other hand, conservatives support the use of governmental power to maintain order over protecting personal freedoms and support the protection of personal freedom over the use of governmental power to promote equality. Libertarians support the protection of personal freedom over the use of governmental power either to promote equality or to maintain order. Populists support the use of governmental power to maintain order and to promote equality over the protection of personal freedom.

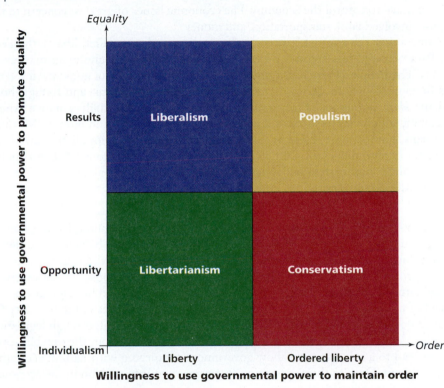

the person's political ideology: libertarian, populist, conservative, or liberal.[53] (To learn more about this connection, see Figure 1.1.)

LIBERTARIANS   Libertarianism is "a highly individualistic extension of classical liberalism. . . . Libertarians emphasize very strongly the autonomy of the individual and the minimal role required of government."[54] Compared to conservatives, who view government as a necessary evil, libertarians see government as an evil, limiting the ability of individuals to make choices and achieve their own destinies. In Texas, Libertarian Party candidates have been on the ballot for statewide and local offices since 1980. In most contests, however, the candidates received only 3 to 5 percent of the vote. The party has never elected a member to state office, and most voters, even if they share the libertarian ideology, consider the Libertarian Party either too extreme or unable to win against a major party candidate. However, this lack of support for the Libertarian Party's candidates is not a valid measure of the support for the ideology.

populists
People who support the promotion of equality and of traditional values and behaviors.

POPULISTS   In contrast to libertarians, **populists** favor government intervention both to promote equality and to establish or maintain an ordered liberty. Populists support the greatest scope of government action. Populism swept the nation in the 1880s and 1890s, becoming one of the largest social movements in American history. Texas has a strong populist tradition. Started in Comanche County by Thomas Gaines in 1886 as a protest against its Democratic Party's leaders, the People's Party led the political struggle for the ideas promoted by the Farmers' Alliance. The fundamental value championed by the People's Party was the equality of humankind. The view was incorporated in the Farmers' Alliance slogan: "Equal rights to all, special privileges to none." Despite the supposed equality of humans, the People's Party noted that certain economic inequalities existed in America, which placed a burden on all working people and most especially on the agricultural classes. These inequities had to be eliminated, and this could only be accomplished with the assistance of the government's power. Thus, the People's Party sought government intervention to regulate or, if necessary, to control the economy. The economic issues of greatest concern to the populists involved land, transportation, and money.[55]

Concerning the conflict between individualism and an ordered liberty, the People's Party showed less tolerance for diversity and individual choice in matters of morality. The People's Party had a strong Protestant religious flavor and drew few converts in counties where African Americans, Mexican Americans, and foreign-born residents were numerous. The populist movement was essentially a native Anglo movement, which was unsuccessful with foreign-born Texans and ignored Mexican Americans. For example, Germans, who were courted by the populists, viewed the movement as anti-alien, anti-Catholic, anti-liberal, and prohibitionist.[56] The Populist Party no longer nominates candidates for public office, but populism persists to this day as an ideology in Texas.

CONSERVATIVES   Conservatives believe that government should not promote equality, but they support government regulation of individual behavior in order to ensure an ordered liberty. The contradiction that conservatives exhibit in terms of the scope of government action can be explained by American conservatism's view of human nature. According to this view, humans are selfish, flawed by original sin, and in need of moral guidance. Thus, American conservatism believes in the necessity for moral principles to guide human behavior and allows government, through legislation and other devices, to apply those principles. Similarly, doubts about the capabilities of humans lead to a reluctance to allow government tampering with natural economic and social laws. Despite their opposition to government intervention in the economy, contemporary conservatives recognize the value of some forms of economic promotion and regulation. This concession to government involvement in the capitalist economy by contemporary conservatives has forced some traditional conservatives to abandon conservatism in favor of libertarianism.

In contemporary Texas, self-identified conservatives are prominent in both of the major political parties and both state and local government, as well as the population generally.[57] Economic issues have provided the basis for Texas conservatism. Conservatives view government programs to provide public services as unnecessary and anti-capitalist. However, some of Texas's most intense confrontations historically have involved the use of government authority to protect traditional values—for example, the prohibition of alcohol in the early 1900s and restrictions on abortions in the 2000s. Increasingly, in Texas as well as in other states, conservatives are joined by libertarians in battles that involve government's regulation of the economy.

LIBERALS   Liberalism favors a government that uses its authority to promote equality but that leaves an individual free to make moral or personal decisions. Modern liberalism in Texas is traceable to the effects of industrialization and the economic and

Where do they fit ideologically? A tea party rally in San Antonio in 2009 brought together a diverse group of individuals with a number of anti-government complaints. Pundits continue to assess the political and ideological basis of their positions.

Photo courtesy: Bob Daemmrich Photography, Inc.

social dislocations associated with it. The events that define modern American liberalism are the Great Depression, which promoted the use of government authority to limit the economic effects of dramatic swings in the business cycle, and the civil rights movement, which promoted the use of government authority to ensure equality for all elements of society. While favoring government's promotion of economic, political, and social equality, modern liberals oppose government infringement on each individual's freedom to make personal choices on moral issues, such as the decision by a woman to terminate a pregnancy. In Texas, liberals have always constituted a minority of the population.

We revisit the ideologies frequently in subsequent chapters. For now, understanding the ideologies in Texas is important for two reasons. *First, most issues in Texas politics are expressed in terms of a preference either for individualism or for an ordered liberty or in terms of a preference either for equality or for individualism.* Almost every political issue in Texas politics can be viewed as a conflict over ideas in the Texan Creed. For example, the conflict over affirmative action programs involves the ideas of individualism and equality. As Figure 1.1 illustrates, the choices are usually between individualism and equality or

THINKING NATIONALLY

Conservatism and Party Support

The Gallup Poll completed a national study in 2010 in which respondents self-identified on a conservative continuum. The ten most conservative states were Alabama, Mississippi, Louisiana, Idaho, Oklahoma, Utah, North Dakota, South Carolina, South Dakota, and Arkansas, with 44 to 49 percent of the population identifying themselves as politically conservative. Yet, only five of these states were ranked as the most Republican states in 2008. Texas, which ranked in the top ten Republican states, reported a conservative population of 43.5 percent.

- What geographic patterns do you discern in the states with the highest percentage of conservatives?

- What demographic characteristics, if any, do these states have in common?

- Are there any cultural commonalities among these conservative states? What might these be?

between individualism and social order. Furthermore, although only a small fraction of Texans are ideologues, they are the ones who frame the political debates over issues. They are the most sophisticated and active people politically. Understanding the bases for their views helps you understand political discussions and the positions of the participants and, if you are so inclined, allows you to join in.

Second, most people in Texas have ideological tendencies. Most Texans are not ideologues, but they do hold consistent attitudes in a general policy area, such as social policy or economic policy. Most political debates play to these tendencies because political activists realize that this is how most people organize their political information.

As political scientist V. O. Key Jr. noted more than fifty years ago, Texas politics is about economics, and Texas "voters divide along class lines in accord with their class interests."[58] We will turn next to an examination of the evolving Texas economy.

The Economy of Texas

★ **1.3** . . . **Outline the transformation of the Texas economy from its dependence on agriculture and petroleum to a highly diverse, global economy.**

Until quite recently, the Texas economy was land-based and colonial in structure. Texas produced, processed, and shipped its agricultural and mineral products to outside markets. Thus, the Texas economy was dependent on external demand and the prices paid for its cotton, cattle, or petroleum.

Cotton

The first real economy in Texas was created by southern planters and resembled the early southern seaboard of the United States. In the 1830s, the economy was based on large slave plantations. The money crop, cotton, was barged down Texas rivers to the Gulf of Mexico because reefs prevented the development of ports at the mouths of Texas rivers. The cotton was then shipped to Europe or the United States, mostly through New Orleans. Later, Galveston was developed as a port, and it was the commercial center of Texas from the 1840s to the 1880s. During Texas's experience as a republic, and during its early statehood, cotton was the economic heart. Consequently, the region flourished during the cotton boom that preceded the Civil War. Although the plantation system didn't survive the Civil War, cotton production did. In 2009, Texas produced 5 million bales of cotton, 40 percent of the total cotton production in the United States.[59]

Cattle

The cattle kingdom, inherited from the Mexicans, spread across the entire American West and captured the fancy of Texas and the world in the late nineteenth century. Initially, the cattle business involved rounding up stray cattle and driving them to the Kansas railheads. The demand for beef created a link between the western frontier and the industrial marketplace. Like King Cotton, the cattle kingdom drew people and money from afar and involved agricultural products shipped to distant markets. For example, the largest ranch in Texas, the XIT, involved a Chicago syndicate, which was given 3 million acres in return for constructing the state capitol in 1881. Covering parts of nine counties in the Panhandle, the XIT ranch, which operated until the early 1900s, featured more than 1,500 miles of fence.[60] Despite the decline in cattle production resulting from an extended drought that finally broke in late 2009, Texas continued to rank first among the states in cattle production with 13.3 million head.[61]

Petroleum

For much of the twentieth century, petroleum was the basis for the Texas economy. From the first major oil discovery in 1901 at Spindletop, near Beaumont, by mining engineer Captain A. F. Lucas, Texas and the production of crude oil have been synonymous. Between 1900 and 1901, Texas oil production increased fourfold. In 1902, Spindletop alone produced 17 million barrels, 94 percent of the state's production. In 1923, the success of Santa Rita No. 1 ushered in the West Texas oil industry. The largest Texas oil field, the East Texas field, was discovered by C. M. "Dad" Joiner in 1930. However, the discovery of the East Texas field created a surplus of petroleum in a depressed economy. After World War II, the U.S. market sought cheaper oil in the Middle East. However, the oil embargo by the Organization of Petroleum Exporting Countries (OPEC) in 1973, a year after Texas reached its peak in oil production, caused an economic boom during the 1970s as prices were driven upward. This boom was followed by the bust of the 1980s when, in 1986, the price for West Texas crude fell below ten dollars a barrel. In 1981, the petroleum industry contributed 27 percent of the state's gross state product (GSP). Eighteen years later, in 1999, the industry contributed only 7.5 percent to the GSP, due to the lower price for crude oil and America's greater dependence on foreign oil.[62] But when oil prices approached $150 a barrel prior to the global recession that began in 2008, this figure jumped to 15 percent of the state's economy for a short period of time.[63]

The Contemporary Economy

The transformation of the Texas economy from one dependent primarily upon agriculture and petroleum to a highly diverse, technology-based economy that is global in scope has been dramatic. Economic diversification has been tied to high-tech industries, including companies that produce semiconductors, microprocessors, computer hardware, software, telecommunications devices, fiber optics, aerospace guidance systems and medical instruments. The high-tech sector also includes biotechnology industries that produce new medicines, vaccines, and genetic engineering of plants and animals. The state has undergone a series of recessions since the 1970s, with the most recent in 2009, but it is the third largest state economy with a gross state product in 2009 of $1.25 trillion.

Texas has thirteen distinct economic regions, and there are marked differences in their economic characteristics. The heavily populated regions of Texas, such as the Metroplex area of Dallas–Fort Worth, are the most diverse. Some continue to be heavily dependent on agriculture, whereas others have strong manufacturing, financial, or commercial bases. Even the economic regions of Texas that were most dependent on oil and natural gas—the Gulf Coast, West Texas, and portions of South Texas—have substantially altered their economies. This diversity allows the state to withstand economic setbacks in one or more industries or economic regions.[64] Moreover, some regions may be undergoing rapid economic growth, while others are stagnant. Currently, the greatest population and economic growth is occurring in a core area anchored by Houston, Dallas–Fort Worth, and San Antonio, often referred to as the Central Texas triangle or the Texas urban triangle. Today, the Texas economy more closely resembles the diversity of the national economy.

With few exceptions, the Texas economy outpaced the overall national economy each year from 1990 through 2008. For most years throughout this period, Texas led the nation in job growth. Some sectors of the economy—agriculture and mineral extraction—witnessed a decline in the number of jobs, but job growth occurred in most sectors of the economy. Job growth in construction jobs increased, bolstered by low interest rates and increasing demand for residential and nonresidential construction. Manufacturing jobs increased dramatically, as did jobs in government and the service sectors.

The globalization of the state's economy is demonstrated by its exports to countries throughout the world. In 1999, Texas exported some $83 billion in merchandise to other countries. By 2008, total exports were $192 billion, with approximately one-third of its exports going to Mexico. The North American Free Trade Agreement (NAFTA) among the United States, Mexico, and Canada created a trading zone of more than 450 million people with combined gross national products of more than $17 trillion.[65]

But the recession that broke across the nation in the summer of 2008 had arrived in Texas by late winter of 2009.[66] The worldwide crisis in financial and credit markets was linked to subprime lending, accounting scandals, overextended credit to consumers, dramatic declines in manufacturing and trade, and a loss of confidence on the part of the consumer. With massive federal intervention, a concerted effort was made to stop the slide. As the economy restructures in an attempt to recover, local governments across Texas have begun to feel a recessionary impact on their budgets.

Several lessons can be drawn from the state's recent economic history. The health of the state's economy for much of the twentieth century was directly tied to the price of oil. Even during national recessions, high oil prices served to insulate Texas. In effect, the Texas economy grew or contracted in relationship to the price of oil.

Initiatives to diversify the state's economy, which began some fifty years ago, have transformed the economy's basic structure. With economic diversification paralleling the structure of the national economy, Texas is in a much stronger position to minimize the impact of economic downturns.

It also is critical to recognize the relationship of the Texas economy to the Mexican economy. In earlier periods, economic declines in Mexico were felt primarily in the counties along the Mexican border. But NAFTA and the *maquiladora* program (a program whereby parts are imported into Mexico to be assembled or manufactured and then the finished product is exported back to the United States or another country) have linked most areas of the state to the Mexican economy.

High-tech industries continue to be the engines of economic growth and expansion in Texas. The question remains as to whether the state's future workforce will be sufficiently educated to handle the demands of skilled, high-tech jobs. Texas is still struggling with an inadequately and inequitably funded education system, and increasing numbers of students in the public schools do not have the English language skills necessary to earn a high school diploma, let alone a college degree. (To learn more about bilingual education, see Join the Debate: Should Texas Provide for Bilingual Education?)

Income, Wealth, and Poverty in Texas

⭐ **1.4** . . . Analyze how disparities in wealth, income, and poverty among races and classes influence politics in Texas.

There are wide disparities in the distribution of income and wealth across the state. In 2008, the median household income in Texas was $50,043, and the median family income was $58,765, both below national income levels (To learn more about the

Join the DEBATE | Should Texas Provide for Bilingual Education?

Immigration from non-English speaking countries, primarily Mexico, has generated a lengthy debate over the best approach to educating children with English language deficiencies. More than one-third of Texans older than five speak languages other than English at home. Many are bilingual, but more than 3 million Texans report that they do not speak English well, a situation that challenges many Texas public school teachers. English deficiencies are most pronounced among the Hispanic and Asian populations.

Hispanic legislators won enactment of the Texas Bilingual Education Act in 1973, which required all Texas public schools that enrolled 20 or more students of limited English proficiency in a given grade level to provide bilingual education for these children. An estimated 800,000 Texas school children had a limited proficiency in English in 2009, a figure that reflects the English language deficiency of the general population. A large proportion of these children perform academically below grade level, leading to high dropout rates and reduced levels of educational attainment. Under these circumstances, should Texas provide increased funding for bilingual education?

To develop an ARGUMENT FOR bilingual education, think about how:

- **Bilingual education is essential for the success of children of immigrants.** If children enter classes in which they cannot understand English, how can they be expected to master the concepts or materials? If children don't master the basic materials, won't they inevitably fall behind?
- **Bilingual children will grow up to play an important role in Texas's economy.** How can bilingual children contribute to Texas's economic success? For Texas to remain a leading center for international trade and high-tech development, what skills do Texas schoolchildren need to acquire to become a valuable component of its workforce?
- **Literacy transfers across languages.** How will teaching students in their primary language lead to literacy and understanding in English as well?

To develop an ARGUMENT AGAINST bilingual education, think about how:

- **Bilingual education is expensive.** What additional costs do school districts have to expend in order to provide for a bilingual education? Are specialized teachers needed to provide bilingual education? Do regular classroom teachers need to be trained?
- **Bilingual education separates students by language.** How does bilingual education segregate and isolate children from the majority of students? In what ways does it lead to feelings of low self-esteem, contributing to an attitude of failure?
- **Bilingual education allows limited English proficiency students to resist assimilation.** If students find comfort in classes in which their native languages are used, won't they avoid learning English and delay adopting the values and expectations of the broader society? How will this create social tension and economic challenges?

What is the best method for teaching students who have limited English proficiency? Texas students in a dual language class are taught English and Spanish, which is an effective method of teaching non-English-speaking students English while English-speaking students are taught Spanish.

Photo courtesy: Bob Daemmrich Photography, Inc.

Table 1.2 *How do U.S. and Texas incomes compare?*

| | U.S. | Texas | | | | |
	All Persons	All Persons	Anglos	Hispanics	African Americans	Asian Americans
Median Income						
Household	$52,029	$50,043	$61,471	$36,855	$36,598	$66,347
Families	63,366	58,765	77,356	39,382	44,893	77,802
Per Capita						
Income	27,589	25,096	34,611	14,646	18,307	29,416
Percent of All Persons Below						
Poverty Level	13.2%	15.8%	8.3%	24.0%	22.9%	10.7%

Source: U.S Census Bureau, *2008 American Community Survey.*

distribution of income among Texans, see Table 1.2). Approximately 25 percent of Texas households reported incomes of less than $25,000 per year. By contrast, 20 percent of Texas households reported incomes in excess of $100,000. Income disparities are evident among the different regions of the state. The median household income for Collin County, north of Dallas, was $81,875 in 2008. The median household income for Hidalgo County on the border with Mexico was $30,513. Thirty-seven counties reported household incomes of less than $33,000, or two-thirds of the state figure, in 2008. Sixteen were in West Texas and had populations of less than 3,000 people. Sixteen heavily Hispanic border and South Texas counties with a total population of 450,000 also reported household incomes in 2008 below $33,000. This group included sparsely populated counties as well as the cities of Brownsville, Edinburg, and McAllen.[67]

Although many Texans are suffering economically, others make large salaries and have significant assets, including those on the *Forbes Magazine* annual list of the 400 richest Americans. Forty-one Texans made the list in 2009, with a reported net worth ranging from $950 million to $19.3 billion.[68] Their combined wealth was estimated to be over $120 billion. The vast majority of Texans, however, have incomes or assets that are nowhere near those of the super wealthy.

On all measures of income, Hispanics and African Americans fall significantly below the Anglo population. According to an *American Community Survey,* 33.2 percent of Hispanic households and 35 percent of African American households in Texas reported incomes less than $25,000, but only 18 percent of Anglo households and a similar portion of the Asian American population reported incomes below that level. By contrast, 41 percent of Anglo households, but only 18.6 percent of Hispanic and 19.5 percent of African American households, reported incomes of more than $75,000.[69]

Some of the nation's poorest counties are in Texas. These are border counties (Dimmit, Hidalgo, Maverick, Starr, Willacy, Zapata, and Zavala) with

THINKING NATIONALLY

Poverty Among the States

The National Center for Children in Poverty, using 2008 census data, estimated that 23 percent of Texas's children lived in families below the poverty level (for example, $21,200 for a family of four). Other states that had significant poverty levels included Mississippi (28%), Kentucky (23%), Louisiana (23%), Arizona, Arkansas, New Mexico, and West Virginia (all with 22%).

States with the lowest poverty levels for children included New Hampshire (7%), Alaska (10%), and Connecticut, Maryland, and Utah (all with 11%).

- What differences in the political cultures of states might explain the differences in the poverty levels of children?

- What differences in state government programs and spending for welfare services might explain these differences in poverty levels?

- Are there social or demographic factors that provide some explanation for these differences in poverty levels? What might these be?

large Hispanic populations and unemployment rates that are twice the state average. The per capita income (total state income divided by the population) for Texas was $25,096 in 2008. For the Anglo population, it was significantly higher, $34,611, but for African Americans, the figure was $18,307, and for Hispanics, $14,646.

Poor people do not usually participate actively and routinely in politics and government in Texas or in the other states. The wealthy tend to be more aware of what they could gain or lose through policy changes, and they more actively protect their interests. They have more resources, time, and social connections. As we note in subsequent chapters, the economic leaders in Texas engage in many political activities. In the past, wealthy Texans influenced state politics either by recruiting and funding candidates for public office or by seeking public office themselves.

TOWARD REFORM: Political Culture and Welfare Reform

⭐ **1.5** . . . Assess the potential for welfare reforms within the context of the state's political culture.

Political culture affects the adoption and implementation of political reforms. Political scientist Daniel Elazar developed a typology of political culture in the United States that identified three political cultures.[70] He termed the three cultures moralistic, individualistic, and traditionalistic. According to this typology, Texas's political culture is a mixture between the individualistic and traditionalistic political subcultures, reflecting a governing preference for individual responsibility and maintaining traditional social values. Furthermore, states with traditionalistic and individualistic political subcultures feature lower levels of political participation, less professional bureaucracies, and less competitive political parties.

This philosophy contrasts sharply with states, such as Massachusetts, dominated by the moralistic subculture. The moralistic subculture considers government a positive instrument with a responsibility to enhance the social and economic well-being of its citizens.

The effect of political culture can be seen in how Texas adopted and implemented welfare reform during the 1990s and early 2000s. In 1996, Congress adopted the Personal Responsibility and Work Opportunity Reconciliation Act (PRWOR), which replaced the Aid to Families with Dependent Children (AFDC) entitlement program with the Temporary Assistance for Needy Families (TANF) block grant program. The welfare system was transformed from a cash assistance program to a workforce training program. Although federal guidelines accompanied TANF, each state developed and implemented its own program.

In comparison to other states, Texas ranks close to the bottom on many public policies and budgetary issues that benefit the poorer and less well-educated segments of the population. Here are a few examples of Texas's rankings:

- 45th in percentage (76 percent) of children aged 19 to 35 months who were immunized (2006)
- 46th in the quality of its health care program (2008)
- 47th in state revenues per capita ($4,850 in fiscal year 2007)

- 48th in the percentage of children above the poverty level (71% in 2006–2007).
- 49th in mental health expenditures ($34.57 per capita, 2006)
- 50th in the percentage of its population with health care insurance (74.8 percent in 2008)[71]

A study that compared several states, representing different political subcultures, indicated that states with moralistic political subcultures performed better than states with traditionalistic or individualistic political subcultures in adopting and implementing welfare reform. Texas, for example, performed poorly in developing a coherent policy, in providing the necessary funds for the reforms, and in implementing the reforms.[72] In so doing, Texas was following its own tradition. From mental services to Medicaid expenditures to public school finance, the state has a history of improving social programs only after being required to do so by court order.

What Should I Have LEARNED?

Now that you have read this chapter, you should be able to:

⭐ **1.1 Trace the roots of Texas government and the impact of the state's cultural diversity on its politics, p. 4.**

The expansive land mass was sparsely populated when Texas declared its independence from Mexico in 1836, but it is now home to more than 25 million. American Indians and Hispanics preceded the Anglo population, but from the creation of the state through the twentieth century, Anglos dominated the state's politics and government. American Indians, now a very small part of the state's population, gave Texas its name. The early Hispanics contributed to the state's legal system and organization of local government. Slavery was prohibited under Mexican law, but soon after statehood, African Americans were brought into the state and played a prominent role in the development of the state's agricultural economy. Race and ethnicity have shaped the state's political culture and politics and continue to be dominant themes in politics and public policy. The mosaic of the state's population became more complex in the last part of the twentieth century with new arrivals from Asia. Texans are now highly urbanized and participants in the global economy and are undergoing population changes of an enormous magnitude.

⭐ **1.2 Identify the core political values Texans hold, and distinguish between four distinct ideologies, p. 13.**

Texans share the core values held by most other Americans. Anglos were proponents of individualism, liberty, equality, constitutionalism, and democracy, and

these values were prominent in the way in which Texans shaped their institutions and gave form to their politics. Early Texans started as residents of Mexico, moved through a period of independent nationhood, and then became citizens of the United States. These events helped shape a set of views or attitudes identified as the Texan Creed, distinguished by its heavy emphasis on individualism, liberty, and views of limited government. Although there are variations on these values with sharp differences of opinion over public policy, there are common core values, such as property rights and freedom, that provide some basis for comity and cooperation.

⭐ **1.3 Outline the transformation of the Texas economy from its dependence on agriculture and petroleum to a highly diverse, global economy, p. 24.**

The gross state product now exceeds $1.2 trillion, and the state's economy is the eleventh largest economy in the world. Not only has the state moved to mirror the general diversity of the nation's economy, it is internally diversified with thirteen distinct economic regions. The state is a major player in the global economy with numerous sectors of the state's economy being major sources of the nation's exports.

⭐ **1.4 Analyze how disparities in wealth, income, and poverty among races and classes influence politics in Texas, p. 26.**

Although some Texans are very wealthy, and a large number of Texans live comfortably, there are a large number of Texans who are very poor, living in substandard conditions with limited access to health care. Low-income and less-educated Texans are to be found disproportionately among Hispanic and African American populations. These economic and social factors translate into politics, giving Anglos greater influence in the policy process. Even as minority populations now become the majority, they continue to have less influence on policy than the Anglo population and remain underrepresented in government positions.

⭐ **1.5 Assess the potential for welfare reforms within the context of the state's political culture, p. 29.**

Despite the state's huge and vibrant economy, expenditures for social services and the needs of the poor are low in comparison to many of the other highly industrialized states. On many per capita measures such as health care, mental health care, and education, Texas allocates much less than other states. The culture of individualism and self-help comes into direct conflict with social policies. Moreover, the state's highly regressive tax system places a much heavier burden on the poor than the wealthy. Reforms in many areas are likely to occur only after litigation in the courts.

Test Yourself: Ideas, People, and Economics in Texas Politics

⭐ **1.1 Trace the roots of Texas government and the impact of the state's cultural diversity on its politics, p. 4.**

Anglos constituted a majority of the state's population until
A. the period immediately after World War II.
B. the first decade of the twenty-first century.
C. the extensive immigration from other states in the 1970s.
D. the increased immigration from other countries in the 1990s.
E. the late 1980s.

⭐ **1.2 Identify the core political values Texans hold, and distinguish between four distinct ideologies, p. 13.**

Which of the following is NOT a significant component of the Texan Creed?
A. Individualism and personal responsibility
B. Limited government and freedom from government infringement on the individual
C. A commitment to constitutionalism
D. A strong commitment to the principle of the common good and communitarianism
E. Commitment to political equality

⭐ **1.3 Outline the transformation of the Texas economy from its dependence on agriculture and petroleum to a highly diverse, global economy, p. 24.**

Which of the following statements does NOT describe the current economy of Texas?
A. It is highly diversified with far less dependence on petroleum and agriculture.
B. There are thirteen distinct economic regions in the state.

C. It usually lags behind the national economy.
D. It is a major player in the global economy.
E. It is dominated by the Central Texas triangle.

⭐ **1.4 Analyze how disparities in wealth, income, and poverty among races and classes influence politics in Texas, p. 26.**

Which group reported the lowest per capita and household incomes in 2008?
A. Anglos
B. Hispanics
C. African Americans
D. Asian Americans
E. Persons of two or more races

⭐ **1.5 Assess the potential for welfare reforms within the context of the state's political culture, p. 29.**

Seemingly, the most significant deterrent to welfare reform in Texas is
A. the general population's ignorance of the problems of the poor.
B. the limited number of groups advocating the needs or interests of the poor.
C. a conservative political culture based, in part, on individualism.
D. general disdain or contempt for the poor.
E. the lack of financial resources.

Essay Questions

1. What demands will the projected population increases in Texas place on the infrastructures of the state and local governments?
2. Is the Texan Creed simply a set of myths or stories about the state's history, or can it be identified in contemporary beliefs and attitudes of Texans toward their governments and public policy? Explain your answer.

3. With the changing demographics of the state, will Texas have an adequate workforce to sustain the economic growth experienced in the past? What can the state government do to meet this challenge?

4. How do you account for the wide disparities in income and wealth in Texas?

5. Why are Texans so reluctant to fund many social and welfare programs?

Key Terms

Alamo, p. 17
American Creed, p. 20
Anglos, p. 10
constitutionalism, p. 18

equality, p. 20
frontier era, p. 14
individualism, p. 13
liberty, p. 16

populists, p. 22
Tejanos, p. 18
Texan Creed, p. 13
Texas Rangers, p. 15

To Learn More on Ideas, People, and Economics in Texas Politics

In the Library

Anderson, Gary Clayton. *The Conquest of Texas: Ethnic Cleansing in the Promised Land, 1820–1875.* Norman: University of Oklahoma Press, 2005.

Barr, Alwyn. *Black Texans: A History of African Americans in Texas, 1528–1995,* 2nd ed. Norman: University of Oklahoma Press, 1996.

Brands, H. W. *Lone Star Nation.* New York: Doubleday, 2004.

Campbell, Randolph B. *Gone to Texas: A History of the Lone Star State.* New York: Oxford University Press, 2003.

Davis, William C. *Lone Star Rising: The Revolutionary Birth of the Texas Republic.* New York: Free Press, 2004.

Elazar, Daniel J. *American Federalism: A View from the States.* New York: Thomas Y. Crowell, 1966.

Fehrenbach, T. R. *Lone Star: A History of Texas and the Texans,* updated ed. Cambridge, MA: Da Capo, 2000.

———. *Seven Keys to Texas,* rev. ed. El Paso: Texas Western Press, 1986.

Himmel, Kelly. *Conquest of the Karankawas and the Tonkawas, 1821–1859.* College Station: Texas A&M University Press, 1999.

La Vere, David. *The Texas Indians.* College Station: Texas A&M University Press, 2004.

Maddox, William S., and Stuart A. Lilie. *Beyond Liberal and Conservative: Reassessing the Political Spectrum.* Washington, DC: Cato Institute, 1984.

Murdock, Steve H., Md., Steve White, Md., Nazrul Hoque, Beverly Pecotte, Xuihong You, and Jennifer Balkan. *The New Texas Challenge: Population Change and the Future of Texas.* College Station: Texas A&M University Press, 2003.

Newcomb, W. W., Jr. *The Indians of Texas: From Prehistoric to Modern Times.* Austin: University of Texas Press, 1961.

O'Connor, Robert F., ed., *Texas Myths.* College Station: Texas A&M University Press, 1986.

Tijerina, Andres. *Tejanos and Texas Under the Mexican Flag, 1821–1836.* College Station: Texas A&M University Press, 1994.

On the Web

To learn more about Texas's cultural history and people, go to the Institute of Texan Cultures Web site at **www.texancultures.utsa.edu.**

To learn more about Texas population estimates and projections, go to the Texas State Data Center Web site at **www.txsdc.utsa.edu.**

To learn more about a variety of Texas topics in an encyclopedic format, go to the Handbook of Texas Online at **www.tshaonline.org.**

To learn more about economic development in Texas and the Texas economy, go to the Texas governor's Business Research Web site at **governor.state.tx.us/ecodev/business_research.**

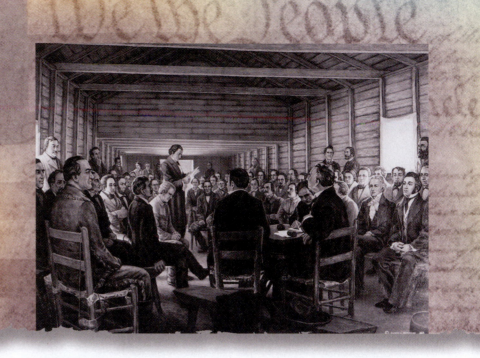

2 Constitutionalism

The current Texas Constitution has provided the framework for Texas government since 1876. To make the document applicable to solving contemporary problems, it has been amended 467 times since its adoption. With each amendment, the Texas Constitution has become longer, more detailed, and more confusing.

Between 1971 and 1975, the Texas Legislature struggled to produce a new constitution that would meet the needs of Texans and provide an acceptable substitute for the current constitution. Their attempts failed miserably. For members of the legislature who had served as the Constitutional Convention of 1974, there were few political benefits in advocating constitutional reform, especially when they calculated the political costs of failure. Consequently, constitutional revision, except for the constant

parade of amendments, was abandoned for nearly a quarter of a century.

In 1999, House Appropriations Committee Chair Rob Junell, a Democrat from San Angelo, thought that the legislature might be ready for a major revision to the 1876 Texas Constitution. Representative Junell and Senator Bill Ratliff, a Republican from Mount Pleasant, proposed a new constitution that would have reduced the 376 sections and approximately 90,000 words to 150 sections and 19,000 words. Despite a public opinion poll that showed 49 percent of the population thought constitutional revision was a "very important" or "somewhat important" issue, the proposed new constitution never left committee. Ratliff told the *Austin American-Statesman,* "Any document that you have to amend twenty times every other year is broke. It's sort of a Texas tragedy, actually, that we

Did the circumstances make a difference? The men who met in the small settlement of Washington-on-the-Brazos (shown in the artist's rendition to the left) hastily declared their independence on March 2, 1836; wrote the Constitution of the Republic, which was adopted on March 16, 1836; and made a swift exit with news of the advancing Mexican armies. At right, after three years of preparation and deliberations, the proposed Constitution of 1974 failed by three votes in the final hectic session of the Constitutional Convention, when the gallery was filled with interested onlookers, including many representatives of labor and other interest groups.

can't seem to come to grips with the fact that we need a new, basic document going into the next century and the next millennium."[1] Proponents of a new Texas Constitution continue to wait for that realization, and they are likely to be waiting a long time.

Constitutional issues are important to academics and many special interest groups, particularly those that benefit from special provisions in the current constitution. But major constitutional revision won't happen without a strong demand from the general public, and most constitutional provisions are of little interest to the vast majority of everyday Texans, even those who vote regularly. As long as most voters have little interest in streamlining and modernizing the Constitution, few state leaders are going to take on that politically difficult task.

What Should I Know About . . .
After reading this chapter, you should be able to:

★ **2.1** Trace the roots of the political values and institutions in the Texas Constitution by summarizing the characteristics of Texas's previous constitutions, p. 36.

★ **2.2** Analyze the current constitution as a product of the political and social forces in 1876, p. 41.

★ **2.3** Compare and contrast the benefits and shortcomings of each method of constitutional revision, p. 51.

★ **2.4** Assess the obstacles and prospects for a major revision of the Texas Constitution, p. 57.

Texas has drafted six constitutions since it declared its independence from Mexico in 1836. Each constitution has been written to deal with changing political conditions in Texas. In 1836, Texas became an independent republic. In 1845, Texas joined the United States as the twenty-eighth state, which required a new constitution. Texas seceded from the United States in 1861 to join the Confederate States of America during the American Civil War. To reenter the union required two constitutions: one in 1866 and one in 1869. After Reconstruction, Texas adopted its current constitution in 1876. Since then, attempts to modernize the Texas Constitution have resulted in political struggles.

In order to understand the Texas Constitution and its evolution in the face of a variety of reform efforts, we will examine the following topics:

- First, we will examine *the roots of the Texas Constitution,* including the legacy of Texas's first five constitutions, which established the foundation for the current constitution.

- Second, we will discuss *the current Texas Constitution,* examining the convention that framed it, its provisions, and its impact on the structure of Texas government.

- Third, we will assess *constitutional revision* in Texas, considering both piecemeal reform through constitutional amendments and comprehensive reform efforts through the drafting of a new constitution.

- Finally, we will analyze *the obstacles and prospects for a major revision* of the Texas Constitution.

ROOTS OF the Texas Constitution

2.1 . . . **Trace the roots of the political values and institutions in the Texas Constitution by summarizing the characteristics of Texas's previous constitutions.**

Like most other states, Texas has had several written constitutions. Constitutions serve several purposes. First, and possibly foremost, constitutions establish the structures and powers of government. Constitutions also provide a method of constitutional change, allowing them to be adapted to changing social, economic, and political conditions. Finally, constitutions specify the civil liberties of individuals by placing limits on the government's ability to restrict an individual's basic rights. We consider each Texas constitution in turn.

The 1836 Texas Constitution

Prior to its independence, Texas was governed as a part of Mexico under the Mexican Constitution of 1824, which established a federal republic and provided that each state should write its own constitution. Combined as a single state, Texas and Coahuila established a constitution in 1827. Because of escalating tensions between Mexicans and Texans (see **chapter 1**), Texas declared its independence in 1836, established the Republic of Texas, and adopted the Constitution of 1836.

The 1836 Texas Constitution contained a declaration of rights that consisted of seventeen articles. It also created a bicameral Congress, consisting of a Senate and House of Representatives, whose members were popularly elected and exercised powers similar to those of the U.S. Congress. The executive branch included a president and vice president, whose powers resembled the powers of the U.S. president and vice president. The judiciary consisted of courts at four levels: justice, county, district, and supreme courts. The fifty-nine delegates who assembled at Washington-on-the-Brazos to draft the document borrowed heavily from the U.S. Constitution and contemporary state constitutions and were guided by their political experiences. They produced a document quickly because of the imminent threat of attack by the Mexican cavalry.[2]

The 1836 Texas Constitution included a preamble; the incorporation of a separation of powers combined with checks and balances; recognition of slavery; a definition of citizenship that excluded Africans, the descendents of Africans, and Indians; a bill of rights; adult male suffrage; and an amending process. However, the amending process proved so complex that although several amendments were proposed during the constitution's existence, none were adopted.

Several provisions reflected state constitutions with which the delegates were familiar. For example, clergy were prohibited from holding public office, imprisonment for debt was abolished, and terms of office were short, ranging from one year for representatives to four years for some judges.

Spanish-Mexican law also found its way into the constitution. Community property rights were established, homesteads were protected and exempted from taxation, and Texas courts were not separated into distinct courts of law and equity. However, the delegates' preference for English common law prevailed when deciding all criminal cases.[3]

The 1845 Texas Constitution

When Texas ceased to be an independent republic and joined the United States, a new constitution was necessary. In June 1845, President Anson Jones called a meeting of the Texas Congress to discuss offers by the United States to annex the Republic of Texas as a state. At the same time, he called a convention to assemble in July, which approved the offer of annexation with the Texas Congress and drew up a constitution, which the voters ratified in October 1845. The U.S. Congress accepted the 1845 Texas Constitution on December 29, 1845, and Texas became the twenty-eighth state to join the United States. The actual transfer of power occurred in February 1846.

From the beginning, was it the intention of most Texans to become part of the United States?
Anson Jones, the last president of the Republic of Texas, is portrayed lowering the Texas flag in February of 1846.

Photo courtesy: Texas State Library and Archives Commission

TIMELINE: Texas's Constitutions

1836 1836 Constitution—Texas declares independence from Mexico and drafts a constitution for the Republic of Texas.

1861 1861 Constitution—Texas joins 12 other states in seceding from the United States. A new constitution is written reflecting the principle of state's rights.

1869 1869 Constitution—Proponents of Reconstruction now control the U.S. Congress and force Texas to write a new constitution.

1845 1845 Constitution—Texas joins the United States and adopts a state constitution, which is deemed Texas's "best constitution."

1866 1866 Constitution—Texas rejoins the Union and writes a new constitution in compliance with Reconstruction policies.

CONSTITUTION
OF THE
STATE OF TEXAS,
ADOPTED BY THE
CONSTITUTIONAL CONVENTION

AUSTIN, TEXAS;
1866.

Often cited as among the best of all state constitutions of its time, the 1845 Texas Constitution was noted for its straightforward, simple form. It created a bicameral legislature consisting of a Senate and House of Representatives that met biennially (once every two years). The governor served a two-year term and was limited to serving no more than four years in any six-year period. The attorney general and secretary of state were appointed by the governor and confirmed by the Senate; the comptroller and treasurer were elected by the legislature biennially in a joint session of the legislature. The governor could convene the legislature, was commander in chief of the state militia, granted pardons and reprieves, and could veto legislation, which could be overridden by a two-thirds vote of both chambers. The judiciary included a supreme court, district courts, and additional courts created by the legislature. The supreme court consisted of three judges, appointed by the governor for six-year terms. The constitution created district courts, whose judges were also appointed by the governor. A district attorney was elected for each district by a joint session of the legislature for a two-year term.

The longest article was entitled General Provisions, which primarily limited the legislature's powers. For example, bank corporations were prohibited; the state debt was limited to $100,000; homesteads and community property of husband and wife were protected. The constitution also created a public school system and what were called Permanent and Available School Funds, and it continued the general land office to oversee Texas's public lands.

Amendments required proposal by a two-thirds vote of both chambers, and ratification both by a majority of voters in an election and by a two-thirds vote of the next legislature. Only one amendment survived these requirements. Adopted in 1850, it provided for the election of state officials who were originally appointed by the governor or the legislature.

1972 **Constitutional Convention Authorized—** Texas voters overwhelmingly approve a constitutional amendment creating a constitutional convention to begin work on a new state charter in 1974.

2010 **Constitution of 1876 Endures—**Despite efforts of two leading legislators in 1999, Texas government continues to function under the Constitution of 1876, now with 467 amendments and more than 90,000 words in length.

1876 **1876 Constitution—** Democrats regain control of Texas government in 1874, call for a constitutional convention in 1875, and rewrite the state's charter more to their liking. The new document is overwhelmingly ratified in early 1876.

1974 **Constitutional Convention Unsuccessful—**The constitutional convention, composed of state legislators, fails to get the required votes of the delegates for submission of a new constitution to voters.

The 1861 Texas Constitution

When Texas seceded from the United States in February 1861 at the beginning of the Civil War, the convention that had proposed secession reconvened to direct the transition of Texas into the Confederacy and replace the 1845 Constitution. Changes necessitated by secession were made as well as a defense of slavery and states' rights. A provision in the 1845 Constitution that provided for the emancipation of slaves was deleted. However, many changes that some secessionist leaders had advocated were not incorporated, such as legalizing the resumption of the African slave trade, taking an extreme position on states' rights, and making major changes to existing laws.[4]

The 1866 Texas Constitution

When Texas reentered the Union after the Civil War, federal Reconstruction required certain changes in the state's charter, such as the abolition of slavery. In addition, the Constitutional Convention of 1866 proposed a series of amendments, which were narrowly adopted in June 1866. In the executive branch, the governor's term was increased to four years, but the governor was prohibited from serving more than eight years in any twelve-year period. The governor was given a line-item veto over appropriations, and the governor's salary was increased from $3,000 to $4,000 annually. The attorney general, comptroller, and treasurer were to be elected to four-year terms. The legislators' salaries were increased significantly, although the structure and powers of the legislature changed only slightly. Only white men could serve as legislators. The state supreme court was increased to five judges, who were elected for ten-year terms.

Did his commitment to the union cost him the governorship? Governor Sam Houston, who played a pivotal role throughout the formative period of Texas history, opposed the state's secession from the United States and was replaced on March 16, 1861, by Governor Ed Clark.

Photo courtesy: Courtesy of L. Tucker Gibson

Also elected were district judges, but their terms were shorter. The jurisdiction of each court was specified in detail.

An additional method of constitutional revision was adopted, which allowed the legislature by a three-fourths vote of each chamber and approval of the governor to call a convention to propose changes. Provisions of the constitution also called for internal improvements in the state and a system of public education, segregated by race and directed by a superintendent of public instruction. State land was set aside to support public education, to create and support a university, and for charitable institutions.[5]

The 1869 Texas Constitution

When the U.S. Congress ended Reconstruction in 1867, additional requirements were placed on Texas's readmission to the Union. Texas was required to have another constitutional convention, with delegates elected by all male citizens over the age of twenty-one, regardless of race, color, or previous condition of servitude. In what was called congressional Reconstruction, Congress required that the convention write a new state constitution that would provide for universal adult male suffrage. When the constitution had been written and the state had ratified the Fourteenth Amendment to the U.S. Constitution, Congress would consider the case for Texas's readmission to the union. The vote on holding the convention and electing delegates produced a lopsided victory for a convention, primarily due to an overwhelmingly favorable African American vote. A majority of registered voters, however, did not vote.

When the ninety delegates met in June 1868, they represented four different voting blocs, differentiated by geography, party, and issues. The convention's principal task—writing a new constitution—was overshadowed by other issues as each bloc pushed its own agenda. By August, the convention had exhausted its funding without even starting its consideration of a new constitution. A special tax allowed the convention to reconvene, but the delegates still failed to consider the convention's principal task until the last month of the convention. In February 1869, the convention broke up in confusion. Forty-five of the ninety delegates signed a partially assembled constitution. Military officers gathered the materials together after the convention and, in July 1869, voters approved the convention's proposals as the 1869 Constitution.[6]

The constitution met the requirements of congressional Reconstruction. In addition, it extended the term of senators to six years, increased the governor's salary, and allowed the governor to appoint the attorney general and secretary of state. The number of state supreme court justices and the length of their terms were reduced. All judicial offices were appointive. Overall, the constitution created a strong and expensive state government with annual legislative sessions, a system of centralized public education, higher salaries for public officials, and a lack of controls on state and local taxing powers.[7]

With the transition from military rule to civilian government under the Constitution of 1869, Republicans won control of the Texas House and Senate, but their control was short lived. When rank-and-file Democrats regained control of the legislature in 1873 and won the governorship in 1874, the constitution was bound to change once again.

Was acceptance of the 1869 Constitution too heavy a price to pay for readmission to the Union? The 1869 Constitution was a response to the demands of congressional Reconstructionists who required the state to expand its suffrage to newly released slaves and adopt the Fourteenth Amendment as a precondition for readmittance to the Union.

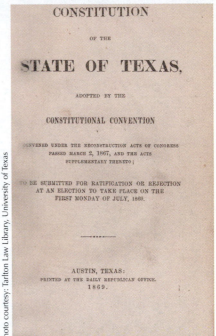

Photo courtesy: Tarlton Law Library, University of Texas

The Current Texas Constitution

⭐ **2.2** . . . Analyze the current constitution as a product of the political and social forces in 1876.

The adoption of a new constitution for Texas was shaped by the effects of Reconstruction. Although Texas Democrats agreed that the constitution needed to be changed, there were differences concerning the method and scope of the change. Governor Richard Coke and the legislature's Democratic leadership favored a constitution written by a legislative committee rather than by a constitutional convention. They believed that only a document drafted by a legislative committee would ensure a short, liberal constitution and allow a more activist government. A majority of House members, however, considered anything but a convention "anti-democratic." Through a series of parliamentary maneuvers, a joint legislative committee was formed to produce a constitution. The result was a constitution that shared many similarities with its predecessors. However, the joint committee's proposed constitution failed when the Texas House rejected it. Public pressure resulted in Governor Coke's calling for a special legislative session to assemble a constitutional convention in 1875.[8]

According to newspaper accounts of the Constitutional Convention of 1875, the delegates were not a distinguished group. However, a reappraisal, based on interviews with the delegates, reveals a group both more experienced and better trained than earlier accounts had indicated. Of the ninety elected delegates, seventy-six were Democrats and fourteen were Republicans. Six African Americans, all Republicans, were originally elected as delegates, but one resigned after the first day and was replaced by a white man. Of the ninety delegates, thirty-eight identified themselves as members of the Patrons of Husbandry, or Grange, an organization of farmers created in response to the economic panic of 1873. Seventy-two delegates were immigrants from other southern states, principally Tennessee, Kentucky, and Alabama. Seven delegates were European immigrants. Only four were native Texans.

Among the delegates claiming a single occupation, there were thirty-three lawyers, twenty-eight farmers, three merchants, three physicians, two editors, two teachers, two mechanics, one minister, and one postmaster. The other fifteen delegates pursued two or more occupations. These were usually farmers, lawyers, or physicians who also claimed at least one other occupation.

Who were the delegates to the 1875 Constitutional Convention? Ninety delegates, including six recently emancipated African Americans, were elected to the Constitutional Convention of 1875.

Photo courtesy: Texas State Library and Archives Commission

Averaging forty-five years of age, the delegates had a wealth of political experience. Eleven had been members of a previous Texas constitutional convention—most commonly the 1861 Convention. At least thirty had served at least one term in the Texas Legislature, and several had served in other states' legislatures, the U.S. Congress, and the Congress of the Confederate States of America. Five delegates had been judges, and four had executive and administrative experience. As political scientist Joe E. Ericson concluded, "The Convention of 1875 was composed, therefore, of a much abler group of men on the basis of their previous experience and training than is generally conceded. Their background and training compare favorably with that of the delegates to any previous constitutional convention held in Texas. If their product is inferior, then the cause must lie elsewhere."[9]

Reasons for the 1876 Constitution

What accounts for the 1876 Constitution, a constitution that is quite different from previous Texas constitutions and the U.S. Constitution? Three factors explain the adoption of an organic, restrictive Texas Constitution. First, the 1876 Constitution was, to some extent, a reaction to Reconstruction. Certainly the adoption of the 1869 Constitution angered many Texans. To many, the 1869 Constitution was an illegitimate constitution that Texas had been forced to accept by the Reconstructionist government.

Second, the 1869 Constitution had led to Governor E. J. Davis's regime. During that administration, power had been centralized in the state government. The Enabling Act allowed Governor Davis to appoint district attorneys, district clerks, sheriffs, mayors, aldermen, and other local officials. In all, Davis appointed more than 8,000 officials. The legislature granted the governor extraordinary powers to maintain public order. For example, the governor controlled a state police that could operate anywhere in the state. Additionally, the Militia Bill allowed the governor to declare martial law in any Texas county, suspend the laws, and assess punishments for violators.

The legislature had also adopted expensive programs that increased taxes dramatically. Universal, compulsory education for all children under the direction of a state superintendent of education was a progressive but expensive policy. In addition, the legislature had provided bond subsidies to railroads. After only two years, state and county property tax rates in Texas had increased from fifteen cents on $100 property valuation to $2.18 on $100 property valuation. In addition, there were occupation taxes, city taxes, poll taxes, and taxes to retire the railroad bonds. Wanting to avoid similar governments in the future, the convention delegates of 1875 attempted to hobble government.

The third factor affecting the 1876 Constitution was a movement that swept through the United States in the 1870s, calling for a politics of substantive issues and restrictive constitutionalism.[10] Using the ideological labels explained in **chapter 1**, the movement had both populist and libertarian elements. As a result of this movement, many states, both southern and northern, revised their constitutions.

At the 1875 Constitutional Convention, this movement took the form of "retrenchment and reform." For the members of the Grange and their allies, who were anti-Coke Democratic delegates, the 1869 Constitution had violated important Texas ideals, including a belief that government should be limited in its purpose. Historian Patrick Williams, studying the convention journals, notes: "There were distinct patterns to their [the delegates'] votes, especially when it came to government promotion of economic growth and social welfare."[11]

The division among Democrats at the convention was more complex than support or opposition to government activism; it also involved the *way* that government should be active, and it resulted in four distinct groupings. One group supported rapid commercial and agricultural growth and believed that the government's principal role was to nurture private enterprise, but that otherwise government's role should be limited. A second group also supported rapid economic growth and believed that government's role should include assistance to private enterprise, but they further believed that government should invest in Texas's human resources, such as schools. A third group wanted government's role to be almost exclusively the promotion of those activities that private enterprise would not or could not accomplish, such as education and frontier defense. A fourth group favored less government generally, whether the purpose of government was economic assistance to private enterprise or to the state's social welfare.[12]

The provisions of the 1876 Constitution, therefore, are not only a reaction to Reconstruction and the Davis regime but also the product of a national movement and a complex mix of motives among the convention delegates.

Why was Edmund J. Davis detested by so many Texans? A Union general and later governor of Texas (1870–1874), Davis was perceived by many Texans to be repressive in his policies and actions.

Photo courtesy: Texas State Library and Archives Commission

Provisions of the 1876 Constitution

The current Texas Constitution has seventeen numbered articles. (To learn more about the articles, see Table 2.1.) Article 13, Spanish and Mexican Land Titles, was deleted by amendment in 1969.[13] Many of the provisions of the constitution are

Table 2.1 *What are the articles of the Texas Constitution?*

Preamble

Article	1	Bill of Rights
Article	2	The Powers of Government
Article	3	Legislative Department
Article	4	Executive Department
Article	5	Judicial Department
Article	6	Suffrage
Article	7	Education
Article	8	Taxation and Revenue
Article	9	Counties
Article	10	Railroads
Article	11	Municipal Corporations
Article	12	Private Corporations
Article	13	Spanish and Mexican Land Titles (repealed August 5, 1969)
Article	14	Public Lands and Land Office
Article	15	Impeachment
Article	16	General Provisions
Article	17	Mode of Amending the Constitution of This State

liberal constitution

Constitution that incorporates the basic structure of government and allows the legislature to provide the details through statutes.

statutory constitution

Constitution that incorporates detailed provisions in order to limit the powers of government.

nearly identical to the way they were written when ratified in 1876, but others have been amended extensively. Like the U.S. Constitution, the Texas Constitution incorporates many principles of American constitutional theory. However, because the U.S. Constitution is a **liberal constitution**—a constitution that incorporates the basic structure of government and allows the legislature to provide the details through statutes—and the Texas Constitution is a **statutory constitution**—a constitution that incorporates detailed provisions in order to limit the powers of government—the two are quite different.

Article 1 of the Texas Constitution contains the Texas Bill of Rights. Many of its provisions are similar to the U.S. Constitution's Bill of Rights, but the Texas Bill of Rights is longer and in some respects more extensive. Because of the framers' experience during the Davis administration, the Texas Bill of Rights contains provisions stating that the "writ of *habeas corpus* is a writ of right, and shall never be suspended" and that the Bill of Rights "is excepted from the general powers of government, and shall forever remain inviolate."[14] Amendments incorporating equal rights for women, ensuring rights for victims of violent crimes, and defining marriage as only the union of one man and one woman were added later.

Article 2 of the Texas Constitution establishes a separation of powers among the legislative, executive, and judicial branches in Texas government and prohibits an individual from holding positions in more than one branch simultaneously.

Article 3 establishes the legislative branch, specifying its structure and powers. The 1876 Constitution continued the bicameral legislature, comprising a Senate with thirty-one members and a House of Representatives that can never exceed 150 members. House members' terms continued to be two years, but senators' terms were reduced to four years. To limit the legislature's power, the constitution created regular legislative sessions that are biennial, meeting in odd-numbered years, and attempted to limit the length of the regular legislative session. Originally, legislators received their full pay—a per diem of five dollars a day—only for the first sixty days of a regular session. Their pay was then cut by 60 percent for the remaining days of the session—a powerful incentive for short sessions. The framers of the constitution reasoned that if the legislature is not in session, it cannot pass laws, thereby limiting the government's authority.

Article 3's provisions also include legislative procedures, such as a requirement that a bill's title clearly indicate its content. Other provisions place limits and requirements on the legislature, such as specifying, in great detail, the purposes for which the legislature can levy taxes. Another provision of Article 3 specifies that the legislature is prohibited from passing special or local legislation for certain purposes, such as creating offices and assigning duties for counties, cities, and other local governments.

Article 4 establishes the executive branch. The governor's term was reduced to two years (it was reinstated to four years in 1974), and the governor's salary was reduced. To ensure the independence of other executive officers from the governor's control, the major executive officers—lieutenant governor, attorney general, comptroller, treasurer, and land commissioner—were elected independently. The addition of numerous elected and appointed boards and commissions in Texas by constitutional amendment and legislation has further diminished the governor's control over the executive branch. A seeming anomaly to the reduction of the governor's powers was the retention of the governor's line-item veto. However, the framers probably viewed the line-item veto as another check on the legislature's spending powers.[15]

In Article 5, the constitution created a judicial system that included a supreme court (the highest state court for civil matters), a court of appeals (the highest state court for criminal matters), district courts, county courts, commissioners courts, and justice of the peace courts. The judicial branch was also subject to popular control. Judges for each of the courts are currently selected in partisan elections. Article 5 also specifies in detail the qualifications of judges, the jurisdiction of the courts, and even the operation of the courts.

Article 7, the education article, created a public school system that differed dramatically from the system that the Davis administration had created. (To learn more about the education article in the Texas Constitution, see The Living Constitution: Article 7, Section 1.) The superintendent of public instruction's position and compulsory school attendance were eliminated, schools were segregated by race, and the constitution made no provision for local school taxes. The constitution funded public education through a poll tax, general funds, and interest earned on the principal in the Permanent School Fund.

Constitutional provisions relating to local governments are found in several articles. In fact, Article 9, which is entitled "Counties," provides no information about the structure of county government and its officials. That information is contained in Article 5, the Judicial Article. In all, four articles must be consulted to find all of the constitutional provisions relating to counties.

In several articles, the 1876 Constitution limits the legislature's discretion in enacting fiscal policies—taxing and spending. First, it mandates a balanced budget. Except for war or insurrection, debt is prohibited unless voters approve the necessary constitutional amendments. Seventy-four provisions in the original 1876 Constitution dealt with taxation, spending state money, and the use of private property.[16]

As an additional check on government spending, the constitution contains provisions for dedicated funds, which require that certain tax monies be deposited in particular funds. The money in a dedicated fund may be used only for specified purposes. For example, 75 percent of the state portion of the gasoline tax is deposited into the Highway Trust Fund, which may be spent only to build and maintain roads and bridges in Texas. The other 25 percent is deposited into the Permanent School Fund, which generates money for the public schools. The balanced-budget and dedicated-fund provisions of the Texas Constitution serve to limit the discretion of the legislature. Funding schemes may also lead to resistance from entities within the state.

Article 17 establishes the process for amending the Texas Constitution. Amendments are proposed by a joint resolution, which must receive a two-thirds majority vote of the Texas House of Representatives and the Texas Senate. After the two-thirds vote by each chamber, the secretary of state prepares a statement that describes the proposed amendment. The statement must be approved by the attorney general and published twice in Texas newspapers that print official state notices. Ratification of a proposed amendment requires a simple majority of those

A Comparison of the U.S. and Texas Constitutions

The table compares the U.S. and Texas Constitutions. Review the table, and then answer the questions.

	U.S. Constitution	Texas Constitution
General principles	Popular sovereignty; limited government; representative government; social contract theory; separation of powers	Popular sovereignty; limited government; representative government; social contract theory; separation of powers
Context of adoption	Reaction to weakness of Articles of Confederation—strengthened national powers significantly	Post-Reconstruction—designed to limit powers of state government
Style	General principles stated in broad terms	Detailed provisions
Length	7,000 words	90,000-plus words
Date of implementation	1789	1876
Amendments	27	467
Amendment process	Difficult	Relatively easy
Adaptation to change	Moderately easy through interpretation	Difficult; often requires constitutional amendments
Bill of Rights	Amendments to the Constitution—adopted in 1791	Article 1 of the Constitution of 1876
Structure of government	Separation of powers, with a unified executive based on provisions of Articles I, II, III	Separation of powers with a plural executive defined by Article 2
Legislature	Bicameral	Bicameral
Judiciary	Creation of one Supreme Court and other courts to be created by the Congress	Detailed provisions creating two appellate courts and other state courts
Distribution of powers	Federal	Unitary
Public policy	Little reference to policy	Detailed policy provisions

■ In what ways are the U.S. and Texas Constitutions similar?

■ What are the most significant differences between the U.S. Constitution and the Texas Constitution?

■ What are the differences between a statutory constitution and a liberal constitution?

The Living Constitution

A general diffusion of knowledge being essential to the preservation of the liberties and rights of the people, it shall be the duty of the legislature of the state to establish and make suitable provision for the support and maintenance of an efficient system of free public schools.

—ARTICLE 7, SECTION 1

At the Constitutional Convention of 1875, no issue was more vigorously debated than public education. Article 7, section 1, reflected the majority's opinion that "an elaborate and expensive system [of public education] like the one devised by the hated Republicans" should be prevented.[a]

Public education in Texas is financed by a combination of state and local revenues, a system that has produced wide disparities in education spending among the state's school districts. The legislature's intermittent efforts to resolve the problem have produced only limited success. Recognizing that the problem was likely to worsen, the state legislature began to provide hundreds of millions of dollars in "equalization" funds to property-poor districts, but the gap between the wealthy and poor school districts widened. In 1984, a lawsuit was initiated by proponents of equalization in a state district court. The district court ruled in *Edgewood* v. *Kirby* that the state's funding law violated the Constitution of Texas. In 1989, the Texas Supreme Court agreed and ordered the legislature to replace the existing law by May 1, 1990.[b]

There is no language in the constitution that requires an equal dollar amount be spent on every child in every school district, but Article 1, section 3, expresses the principle that all citizens have equal rights. The district court's ruling tied this provision to Article 7, section 1, which called for "the support and maintenance of an efficient system of free public schools." In effect, the funding system used by the state was inefficient, relied too heavily on local property taxes, and produced significant disparities in per capita expenditures for education across the state.

After several attempts, the legislature finally came up with a plan in 1993—often referred to by its opponents as "Robin Hood"—that required wealthy districts to share their property tax revenues with poorer districts. The Texas Supreme Court upheld the law in a 5–4 decision in 1995, and the state legislature continued to increase its funding for education.[c]

A challenge to the 1993 funding mechanism by wealthy districts resulted in a district court decision in 2004 that held a statewide property tax was prohibited under Article 8, section 1, of the constitution. Upon appeal, the Texas Supreme Court in 2005 ruled the statewide reliance on property taxes for school funding was unconstitutional, and ordered the state to correct the problem by June 1, 2006.[d]

A special session of the legislature was called in the spring of 2006. A new funding law was enacted, which cut school property tax rates by as much as one-third. The budget surplus was used to cover lost revenues, a new, broad-based business tax was enacted, and the cigarette tax was increased by $1 per pack. However, the funding issues are not resolved, and with a projected $18 billion shortfall in 2011, the legislature will have to revisit the problem.

CRITICAL THINKING QUESTIONS

1. Should school districts that have a wealthy property tax base be required to share their funds with property-poor districts?
2. Why has the Texas Legislature been reluctant over the years to enact a major overhaul of school funding?
3. Is a state income tax the only viable solution for funding public education in Texas?

[a]George D. Braden, *The Constitution of the State of Texas: An Annotated and Comparative Analysis*, vol. 2 (Austin: Texas Advisory Commission on Intergovernmental Relations, 1977), 506.

[b]*Edgewood Independent School District v. Kirby*, 777 S.W.2d 394 Tex. (1989); *Edgewood Independent School District et al. v. William Kirby et al.*, 777 S.W.2d 391 Tex. S.Ct. (1989).

[c]*Edgewood v. Meno*, 893 S.W.2d 450 Tex. (1995).

[d]*Neeley v. West Orange–Cove Consolidated ISD*, 176 S.W.3d 746 (2005).

who actually cast ballots in an election. The ratification of constitutional amendments may occur in a general election, which is conducted in even-numbered years in November, or in special elections, which are conducted at other times. The legislature determines when the election to ratify a constitutional amendment will be held.

In the 1980s, the legislature established a pattern of conducting constitutional amendment elections primarily in odd-numbered years in November. At this time, only constitutional amendments and local issues are on the ballot, which results in lower voter turnout and in a lower adoption rate for amendments. (To learn more about constitutional amendment elections, see Analyzing Visuals: Constitutional Amendments and Voter Turnout.)

Having a statutory constitution that requires constitutional amendments to make major and even minor changes in government also means that the constitution has been amended many times. Through 2009, the Texas Constitution had been amended 467 times. In contrast, the U.S. Constitution has survived since 1789 with only twenty-seven amendments. Because the first ten amendments to the U.S. Constitution, the Bill of Rights, were necessary to achieve ratification and because the Twenty-First Amendment repeals the Eighteenth Amendment, there have been only fifteen actual changes to the U.S. Constitution since its ratification.

ANALYZING VISUALS

Constitutional Amendments and Voter Turnout

Constitutional amendments are submitted to Texas voters in three different types of elections—presidential, gubernatorial, or special. This table shows the percentage of the voting age population who took part in each election, the number of amendments voted on, and how many of those amendments were adopted. Review the table and then answer the questions.

Decade	Type of Election	Voter Turnout[a]	Considered Amendments	Adopted Amendments	% Adopted
1970s	General: Presidential	45.52	15	12	80.0
	General: Gubernatorial	25.47	16	12	75.0
	Special	5.42	26	16	61.5
1980s	General: Presidential	45.81	20	16	80.0
	General: Gubernatorial	29.44	10	10	100.0
	Special	10.23	77	65	84.4
1990s	General: Presidential	45.31	0	0	0.0
	General: Gubernatorial	30.41	1	1	100.0
	Special	9.47	91	63	69.2
2000s	General: Presidential	45.20	0	0	0.0
	General: Gubernatorial	29.35	1	1	100.0
	Special	8.00	78	76	97.0

[a]Voter turnout indicates the percentage of voting-age people who voted. For the 1970s, special election turnout figures are only for the 1977 and 1979 special elections (no figures were available for 1971, 1973, or 1975).

- In which decade were the most amendments considered? In which decade were the most amendments adopted?
- What relationship, if any, exists between voter turnout and the percentage of amendments adopted? What about the relationship between the number of considered amendments and the percentage of amendments adopted?
- If you were a member of the Texas Legislature anticipating considerable opposition to your proposed constitutional amendment, at which type of election would you schedule your amendment for vote?

Source: Secretary of State, Election Results, Turnout and Voter Registration Figures (1970–present); Texas Legislative Council, "Amendments to the Texas Constitution Since 1876," www.tlc.state.tx.us.

Criticisms of the 1876 Constitution

With so many amendments, one might think that Texans would have been able to make a nineteenth-century constitution applicable to the twenty-first century. In many respects, however, the constitutional amendments have not fundamentally changed the basic structure of Texas government, and for many Texans, the 1876 constitution does not provide an adequate foundation for governing in the twenty-first century.

TOO LONG AND DISORGANIZED   With the addition of so many amendments, Texas has earned the distinction of having one of the longest constitutions in the United States. (To learn more about the constitutions of some other large states and to compare them with the Texas Constitution, see Table 2.2.) Only Alabama's constitution contains more words. The amendments have also exacerbated the disorganization that plagued the 1876 Constitution originally. In the most heavily amended articles, the numbering of sections is almost impossible to follow because of missing letters and duplication. For example, until a 1999 amendment corrected the errors, there was no Article 3, section 48c, but as if to compensate, there were two 48e's, each dealing with a separate topic. Both 48e's were added by the 70th Legislature in 1987. A similar problem existed in section 52.

AMENDMENTS POORLY WRITTEN   Some constitutional amendments have been so poorly written that they produced consequences never intended by their sponsors and advocates. In 1933, Texans approved a progressive amendment that gave counties home rule authority (the right of local governments to govern themselves). But, thanks to contradictory interpretations and restrictive procedures, no county established home rule government before the amendment was repealed in 1969. In 2001, Texans adopted a constitutional amendment that supposedly permitted most local governments to exempt travel trailers from local property taxes. The purpose was to encourage "winter Texans" from other states to continue making South Texas their winter homes. Upon its implementation, however, it was discovered that the wording of the amendment actually placed a tax on the very trailers that were to be exempt. Finally, in 2005, Texas became the eighteenth state to add a ban on same-sex marriage to its constitution when voters overwhelmingly approved Proposition 2. While the language appeared straightforward, it became an issue in the 2010 race for attorney general when Barbara Ann Radnofsky, the Democratic candidate, challenged the amendment's language. (To learn more about this controversy, see Politics Now: Texas Marriages in Legal Limbo due to 2005 Error, Democrat Says.)

LIMITED EXECUTIVE POWER   Some of the most serious concerns relate to the three branches of Texas government. The plural executive has been criticized because it limits the executive power of the governor to implement public policy. By dividing

Table 2.2 *How does the Texas Constitution compare to those of other large states?*

	Number of Constitutions Since Statehood and (Last Adoption Date)	Number of Words in Constitution (2009)	Number of Amendments (2009)
Texas	5(1876)	90,000	submitted 614, ratified 467
California	2(1879)	54,645	submitted 870, ratified 518
New York	4(1894)	51,700	submitted 293, ratified 218
Florida	6(1968)	51,456	submitted 148, ratified 115

Source: Council of State Governments, *The Book of the States 2009* (Lexington, KY: Council of State Governments, 2009).

POLITICS NOW

| WORLD | NATION | LOCAL | **POLITICS** | OPINION | HEALTH & SCIENCE | ARTS | SPORTS | LEISURE |

Texas Marriages in Legal Limbo due to 2005 Error, Democrat Says

By David Montgomery

November 18, 2009
Fort Worth Star-Telegram
www.star-telegram.com

Texans: Are you really married?

Maybe not.

Barbara Ann Radnofsky, a Houston lawyer and Democratic candidate for attorney general, says that a 22-word clause in a 2005 constitutional amendment designed to ban gay marriages erroneously endangers the legal status of all marriages in the state.

The amendment, approved by the legislature and overwhelmingly ratified by voters, declares that "marriage in this state shall consist only of the union of one man and one woman." But the troublemaking phrase, as Radnofsky sees it, is Subsection B, which declares:

"This state or a political subdivision of this state may not create or recognize any legal status identical or similar to marriage."

Architects of the amendment included the clause to ban same-sex civil unions and domestic partnerships. But Radnofsky, who was a member of the powerhouse Vinson & Elkins law firm in Houston for 27 years until retiring in 2006, says the wording of Subsection B effectively "eliminates marriage in Texas," including common-law marriages.

She calls it a "massive mistake" and blames the current attorney general, Republican Greg Abbott, for allowing the language to become part of the Texas Constitution. Radnofsky called on Abbott to acknowledge the wording as an error and consider an apology. She also said that another constitutional amendment may be necessary to reverse the problem.

"You do not have to have a fancy law degree to read this and understand what it plainly says," said Radnofsky. . . .

Abbott spokesman Jerry Strickland said the attorney general stands behind the 4-year-old amendment. "The Texas Constitution and the marriage statute are entirely constitutional," Strickland said without commenting further on Radnofsky's statements. "We will continue to defend both in court."

A conservative leader whose organization helped draft the amendment dismissed Radnofsky's position, saying it was similar to scare tactics opponents unsuccessfully used against the proposal in 2005. "It s a silly argument," said Kelly Shackelford, president of the Liberty Legal Institute in Plano. Any lawsuit based on the wording of Subsection B, he said, would have "about one chance in a trillion" of being successful. Shackelford said the clause was designed to be broad enough to prevent the creation of domestic partnerships, civil unions or other arrangements that would give same-sex couples many of the benefits of marriage.

Radnofsky acknowledged that the clause is not likely to result in an overnight dismantling of marriages in Texas. But she said the wording opens the door to legal claims involving spousal rights, insurance claims, inheritance and a host other marriage-related issues. "This breeds unneeded arguments, lawsuits and expense which could have been avoided by good lawyering," Radnofsky said. "Yes, I believe the clear language of B bans all marriages, and this is indeed a huge mistake.". . .

Critical Thinking Questions

1. On the basis of your reading of the constitutional proposition, do you find it confusing or ambiguous?
2. How is it that different lawyers can reach different conclusions as to what the amendment means?
3. Do you anticipate future litigation over this constitutional amendment?

the executive authority among several officials, who are elected statewide to four-year terms (just as the governor is), the constitution makes these officials co-equals of the governor. Though the constitution declares that the governor is the state's chief executive, it also denies the governor the powers necessary to perform that role. The governor's executive authority is further diminished by the numerous appointed boards and commissions that make up a substantial portion of the executive branch of Texas government.

Political scientist and Texas Constitution expert Janice May has stated: "Texas has probably the most disintegrated and fragmented administrative organization in the country."[17] Despite efforts in the early 1990s to transfer more control to the governor, the executive branch remains badly fragmented. Consequently, Texas governors are in a much weaker position to influence public policy than are most of their counterparts in the rest of the United States (see **chapter 5**).

PART-TIME LEGISLATURE   In the legislative branch, the most important criticisms relate to the constitutional provisions that make the legislature a part-time, citizen legislature. Among these provisions are the requirement for 140-day biennial sessions and the low, constitutionally mandated salary for legislators. Meeting every two years for such a short time makes governing a large urban state difficult. Particularly burdensome is the need to prepare a budget for a two-year period, anticipating economic conditions, so that revenues will cover appropriations and the next legislature will not face a large deficit. A legislator's salary of $7,200 per year, which has not changed since 1975, plus a per diem for expenses, affects who can afford to serve financially and who can afford the time away from their primary occupation to attend regular and special sessions. This helps explain the high percentage of lawyers and businesspeople in the Texas Legislature, as well as the influence of lobbyists.

PARTISAN ELECTION OF JUDGES   The structure of the Texas judiciary and the method of selecting judges are also frequently criticized. The court system in Texas consists of a bewildering number of courts, divided into several levels, many with overlapping jurisdictions. The Texas Constitution creates most of these courts. Capping the court system are two supreme courts: the Texas Supreme Court, which is the highest state court for civil cases, and the Texas Court of Criminal Appeals, which is the highest state court for criminal cases. Each court has nine members, elected on a partisan ballot, as are almost all members of Texas courts. Many political scientists, attorneys, and even Texas judges have questioned whether partisan election is the best way to select judges (see **chapter 6**).

RESTRICTIONS ON LOCAL GOVERNMENT   The 1876 Constitution places severe restrictions on local governments. First, the structure of county government is established in the constitution, which means that the smallest and the largest counties in Texas have a commissioners court, a county judge, and a number of independently elected officials to run the various county departments. The structure may be effective in rural Texas counties, but urban counties, where more than 80 percent of Texans currently reside, find the structure inefficient. Any change in the structure of a county's government, such as the elimination of an outdated county office (county surveyor), requires a constitutional amendment, which must be approved by a majority of the voters statewide.[18] Also, counties are limited in their ability to raise revenue and provide needed services. The restrictions placed on county and city government in Texas have resulted in the creation of thousands of special districts across Texas (see **chapter 7**).

With all the criticisms of the 1876 Constitution, legislators and citizens have often called for wholesale revisions to the document. In the next section we compare and contrast the methods of constitutional revision.

Constitutional Revision

⭐ **2.3** . . . Compare and contrast the benefits and shortcomings of each method of constitutional revision.

Constitutional revision in Texas can occur through two methods. First, the constitution can be revised through amendments intended to add new provisions, remove obsolete portions, clarify ambiguous sections, or consolidate sections that pertain to a single topic. This is usually referred to as **piecemeal revision.** The second method, known as **comprehensive revision,** involves the adoption of an entirely new constitution, such as what the 1974 Constitutional Convention tried to do.

piecemeal revision
Constitutional revision through constitutional amendments that add or delete items.

comprehensive revision
Constitutional revision through the adoption of a new constitution.

Piecemeal Revision Efforts

As we noted earlier, the Texas Constitution has been amended frequently, and the addition of amendments occurred almost immediately after its adoption. The first amendment was proposed in 1877. Since then, amendments have been considered by every legislature, but the addition of amendments accelerated in the 1930s, 1960s, and in every decade since the 1980s. (To learn more about the pace at which constitutional amendments have been adopted, see Figure 2.1.)

Ironically, many piecemeal changes in the Texas Constitution have resulted from attempts to produce comprehensive reform. For example, the League of Women Voters became interested in constitutional revision in 1949 and, in 1957, was successful in getting the legislature to direct the Legislative Council to study each section of the constitution and make recommendations. The legislature also created a Citizens Advisory Committee to follow the council's work, do its own research, and report to the legislature. In its report, the Legislative Council found that the 1876 Constitution, "despite its age and alleged deficiencies, is still overall a sound document and generally reflects the governmental philosophy of the people of Texas for their government."[19] The Citizens Advisory Committee disagreed with the assessment of the Legislative Council and sought a constitutional commission to study the need for constitutional revision and the elimination of "deadwood" and repetitive sections, a logical arrangement of contents, and clarification of ambiguous provisions of the constitution.

Similarly, between 1966 and 1969, Governor John Connally led an effort to revise the Texas Constitution. Although Connally's efforts to call a constitutional convention failed, the legislature created a Texas Constitutional Revision Commission to study the constitution and make recommendations to the legislature in 1969. The commission provided momentum for the earlier Citizens Advisory Committee's proposal to eliminate the deadwood provisions of the Texas Constitution through a single amendment. The amendment, which removed fifty-two provisions—including Article 13 on Spanish Land Titles—and reduced the constitution's length by 10 percent, was passed by the legislature and adopted by the voters in August 1969.[20]

In the 1990s, Representative Anna Mowery led an attempt to revise the constitution by removing sections that were duplicative, archaic, obsolete, previously executed, or ineffective. In 1997, she introduced a constitutional amendment that changed the wording in several articles. Then, in 1999, Mowery introduced a proposal amending sixty-four

Figure 2.1 *How many amendments were added to the Texas Constitution from 1877 to 2009?*

Source: Secretary of State, Elections Division; Texas Legislative Library, Constitutional Amendments, www.lrl.state.tx.us.

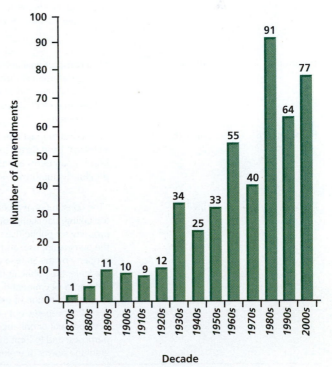

provisions and repealing seventeen provisions; most of the proposed revisions focused on the legislative article, and none of the proposed changes significantly altered the powers of government, the rights of individuals, or the structure of Texas state and local government.[21] Voters approved of Mowery's amendment in November 1999. In 2001, another amendment by Mowery won legislative approval and was ratified by voters. This amendment eliminated duplication and clarified provisions of the constitution.

The language of proposed amendments follows a prescribed legal style, written to summarize the content of the enabling legislative resolution. There is no detailed description of the effect of amendments or the "pro-con" debates surrounding their passage by the legislature, and there have been occasions when amendments have been written to obscure their very purpose. Often, without reading the explanations of proposed constitutional amendments provided by the Texas Legislative Council or other organizations, the ballot language is incomprehensible. (To learn more about the ballot language from the 2009 Constitutional Amendment Election, see Table 2.3.)

Table 2.3 *How do voters make sense of the ballot language?*

Selected Propositions from the November 3, 2009, Constitutional Amendment Election

Proposition Number	House Joint Resolution Number	Ballot Language Explaining the Amendment	Explanation
Proposition 1	HJR 32	"The constitutional amendment authorizing the financing, including through tax increment financing, of the acquisition by municipalities and counties of buffer areas or open spaces adjacent to a military installation for the prevention of encroachment or for the construction of roadways, utilities, or other infrastructure to protect or promote the mission of the military installation."	As the city of San Antonio has expanded to the north, it has encroached on Camp Bullis, a 28,000 acre military base. Urban development threatens the use of this base, and this amendment authorizes counties or cities to issue bonds to purchase buffer zones around military installations.
Proposition 2	HJR 36	"The constitutional amendment authorizing the legislature to provide for the ad valorem taxation of a residence homestead solely on the basis of the property's value as a residence homestead."	The appraisal of property is always difficult, especially when a home is in proximity to commercial development. To guard against a large increase in the appraisal of a home, this amendment limits an appraisal to the residential value of the home, not its potential commercial use.
Proposition 5	HJR 36	"The constitutional amendment authorizing the legislature to authorize a single board of equalization for two or more adjoining appraisal entities that elect to provide for consolidated equalizations."	Each county is required to maintain an appraisal district, but there are political subdivisions that are situated in two or more counties and subject to more than one appraisal district. This amendment provides for consolidation of appraisal functions.
Proposition 6	HJR 116	"The constitutional amendment authorizing the Veterans' Land Board to issue general obligation bonds in amounts equal to or less than amounts previously authorized."	Under existing provisions, the Veterans' Land Board is limited in the amount it can borrow to assist veterans in their purchase of homes. This amendment provides additional bonding authority by the board.
Proposition 11	HJR 14	"The constitutional amendment to prohibit the taking, damaging, or destroying of private property for public use unless the action is for the ownership, use, and enjoyment of the property by the State, *a* political subdivision of the State, the public at large, or entities granted the power of eminent domain under law or for the elimination of urban blight on a particular parcel of property, but not for certain economic development or enhancement of tax revenue purposes, and to limit the legislature's authority to grant the power of eminent domain to an entity."	Under eminent domain, governments can take (if they pay for it) private property for certain "public uses," such as highways. An expansive interpretation of this power has resulted in some governments taking property for the primary purpose of economic development or enhancement of tax revenues. This amendment attempts to clarify restrictions on use of eminent domain for economic development.

Many Texans believe that only a thorough rewriting of the Texas Constitution will make it more uniformly applicable to modern Texas. Professor Dick Smith's observations, made nearly forty years ago, seem especially prophetic today: "Even if, in due time, many non-substantive changes are made, through the overworked amending process, it will still be an inadequate, outdated fundamental law for the state."[22]

Comprehensive Revision Efforts

The legislature's first attempt to call a constitutional convention for a comprehensive revision occurred in 1877. It was the first in a long series of such attempts. In 1917, the legislature passed a resolution calling for a constitutional convention without referring the question to the voters. Governor James Ferguson refused to issue a proclamation calling for the election of delegates, and the effort failed. In 1919, the legislature tried again, but this time they submitted the call for a convention to the voters. In November 1919, the proposal was soundly defeated by a nearly three-to-one margin.

Despite the defeat, the proposals for constitutional reform continued. Between 1919 and 1949, the legislature regularly considered proposals for a constitutional convention. Four House Concurrent Resolutions, three Senate Concurrent Resolutions, eight Joint House Resolutions, and four Senate Joint Resolutions were introduced. None of the resolutions calling for a constitutional convention or creating a revision commission was approved by the legislature. In 1949, Governor Beauford Jester invited a group of citizens to the capitol for a conference. The group formed a Citizens Committee on the Constitution, which asked the legislature to form a Commission on the Texas Constitution to thoroughly study the constitution and to suggest how to proceed if a revision was deemed necessary. The resolution to create the commission received an unfavorable committee report and was never considered by the House.[23]

For over fifty years, numerous advocates proposed major constitutional revisions, including governors, state legislators, and citizen reform groups. Rarely, however, was there a public outcry for broad constitutional reforms, and without it, legislators failed to see any urgency to support change. Many citizens held the view that if the constitution wasn't broke, why fix it? It takes a concerted effort to orchestrate a constitutional convention, and legislators perceived little electoral advantage in leading a revision effort, especially when there were groups that would try to defeat any calls for a constitutional convention.

When the legislature failed to consider the constitution produced by the 1967–1968 Constitutional Revision Commission and voters ratified the 1969 amendment to eliminate the deadwood in the 1876 Constitution, most political observers expected constitutional revision to wane in importance. However, the 62nd Legislature, meeting in 1971, created the first constitutional convention in Texas in nearly a century.

THE 1974 CONSTITUTIONAL CONVENTION In 1971, a group of recently elected representatives led the efforts to revise the constitution. They were intensely committed to constitutional reforms, and they won the backing of the legislative leadership. They proposed a constitutional amendment that called for the Texas Legislature of 1973 to sit as a constitutional convention in 1974 and required the legislature to establish a **Constitutional Revision Commission**—a group established to research and draft a constitution for a constitutional convention. The voters overwhelmingly approved the amendment in November 1972 (61 percent to 39 percent). Although the Texas electorate had previously rejected calls for a constitutional convention, success was achieved through sustained leadership, the widely discussed recommendations of the revision commission, the media's coverage, and the timing of the election—the 1972 presidential election had higher voter turnout than a special or gubernatorial election.

Constitutional Revision Commission
Group established to research and draft a constitution for a constitutional convention.

According to the amendment, legislators, meeting as a constitutional convention, were authorized to submit either a new constitution or revisions to the old constitution for voter approval. They also were allowed to present alternative sections or articles of either the old or the new constitution. The only substantive limitation on the legislature involved Article 1—the Bill of Rights—which could not be changed. There was also a time limit on the convention. The convention would automatically end on May 31, 1974, unless the convention voted to adjourn earlier or to extend the session for not more than sixty days after the May deadline.

In 1973, the legislature quickly adopted a resolution establishing the Constitutional Revision Commission.[24] A six-member committee composed of the governor, lieutenant governor, Speaker of the House, attorney general, chief justice of the Texas Supreme Court, and presiding judge of the Texas Court of Criminal Appeals appointed the thirty-seven members of the commission, who could not be public officials. The governor chaired the committee, and the votes of four members were required for an appointment. The committee also selected the commission's chair— Robert W. Calvert, a former chief justice of the Texas Supreme Court—and vice chair—Beryl Buckley Milburn, a prominent Republican civic leader. The commission's membership was finalized in March 1973, and the commission began meeting immediately. From April through June, the commission held nineteen public hearings across the state, meeting with citizens and local advisory committees. On November 1, 1973, the commission submitted a draft constitution to the members of the legislature.

The convention started with great expectations. The 181 members of the 1973 legislature (150 state representatives and 31 state senators) met as a constitutional convention on January 8, 1974. The amendment authorizing the process had been passed by the voters by a substantial margin. The Constitutional Revision Commission had prepared a draft constitution from which the convention could begin its work. The convention only had to make whatever modifications it desired to the commission's draft and submit it to the voters for ratification.

Most political observers expected a revised constitution to be presented to Texas voters at the 1974 general election. However, the convention adjourned on July 30, 1974, without producing a new constitution. The final vote fell three short of the two-thirds

Would they have served if they had known what the outcome of the constitutional convention would be? The Constitutional Revision Commission, shown here and chaired by Robert Calvert and co-chaired by Beryl Milburn, worked long, arduous hours to draft a constitution prior to the convention in 1974.

Photo courtesy: Texas State Library and Archives Commission

vote necessary to submit a revised constitution to the voters. How can the failure of the constitutional revision effort be explained? According to political scientist Janice May, a member of the Constitutional Revision Commission, there are several reasons:

First, the legislature was the constitutional convention. Legislatures propose constitutions or constitutional revisions frequently, but they normally do this as a legislature. The Texas constitutional convention experience was unique in that the members of the Texas Legislature met in a separate session, as a unicameral body. In some respects, this was helpful because the legislators were not concerned with other issues and could devote their attention to the constitutional issues. However, being legislators, the convention delegates thought of constitutional revision as "politics as usual." The delegates were influenced by reelection considerations, institutional and personal rivalries between the chambers, pressure from lobbyists, and partisan and ideological differences. The general practice among the states had been to have delegates to a constitutional convention elected by the people. If the convention had been made up of citizen delegates whose political careers might have ended with the adjournment of the convention, the final result might have been different.

The second reason for failure involved the decision rules used in the convention, especially the two-thirds rule. The convention delegates were divided into several substantive and procedural committees. (To learn more about the committees at the convention, see Table 2.4.) The substantive committees were responsible for conducting hearings, taking testimony, and drafting the articles or sections of the new constitution. Once the committee reported out a section, the section was then debated and voted on by the entire convention. For a particular article to be approved by the convention, a simple majority vote was required. However, the final document, made up of all previously approved sections and articles, required a two-thirds majority vote for submission to the voters. This was a rare rule in the history of constitutional conventions.

The third reason for failure, and the single most important policy issue, was the right-to-work provision. A right-to-work provision states that membership or nonmembership in a union cannot be a condition of employment. The Taft-Hartley Act of 1947 allowed states to establish right-to-work laws, and the Texas Legislature passed one in that year. Labor union leaders considered the Taft-Hartley Act a "slave labor" law. Delegates supported by business interests came to the 1974 Constitutional Convention determined to place a right-to-work provision in the Texas Constitution, which would have made it more difficult to repeal. But labor unions refused to support any constitutional revision that contained a right-to-work provision. The issue dragged long-standing partisan, faction, and labor–management battles into the convention.

The fourth reason for the convention's failure was a lack of exceptional political leadership. As president of the convention, Speaker Price Daniel Jr. probably bears most of the responsibility for the lack of leadership. As some delegates noted, Daniel lost the convention with his committee appointments, which included many freshmen legislators and not enough experienced lawmakers. Furthermore, Daniel did not attempt

Table 2.4 *What were the committees of the 1974 Constitutional Convention?*

Substantive Committees	Procedural Committees
Finance	Rules
Local Government	Administration
Education	Submission and Transition
Legislature	Style and Drafting
Judiciary	Public Information
General Provisions	
Executive	
Rights and Suffrage	

Why did he call them cockroaches? Price Daniel Jr., president of the 1974 Constitutional Convention, applied the term "cockroaches" to a group of legislators who were clearly opposed to the proposed constitution and worked continually to block its final passage by the convention.

cockroach

A member of a constitutional convention who opposes any changes in the current constitution.

revisionist

A member of a constitutional convention who will not accept less than a total revision of the current constitution.

to compromise on the right-to-work issue early in the convention by bringing the two sides together for discussions. Having announced before the convention that he would not seek another term as House Speaker in 1975, Daniel was a lame duck, which reduced his ability to influence members of the convention. Of course, other politicians, such as Governor Dolph Briscoe, could have provided leadership, but Briscoe decided to take a neutral public stand on constitutional revision during the convention.

The final reason involves cockroaches and revisionists. In the jargon of constitutional revision, a **cockroach** is a member of a constitutional convention who opposes any changes in the current constitution. About twenty members of the constitutional convention were cockroaches. In addition, several members were **revisionists,** members who would not accept less than a total revision of the current constitution. Essentially, revisionists did not believe the proposed revision went far enough toward giving Texas a good constitution. Together, these two groups were large enough to prevent the adoption of a final resolution.[25]

THE 1975 CONSTITUTIONAL AMENDMENTS   In 1975, the legislature rewrote the constitution that the 1974 Convention had failed to adopt as eight amendments, each dealing with a particular portion of the constitution, and presented them to the voters. The right-to-work provision and certain other controversial proposals were not included. Voter approval of all eight amendments would have given Texas a new constitution. The amendments would have shortened the constitution considerably and provided for annual legislative sessions, veto sessions, a unified judiciary, a single court of last resort, and a flexible structure for county government.

But, on November 4, 1975, Texas voters rejected all eight amendments by large margins. Only two of Texas's 254 counties passed all eight amendments. Several explanations account for the amendments' defeat. First, the constitutional revision efforts of 1974 and 1975 were preceded by the Sharpstown scandal in Texas (in which a number of state officials were involved in alleged stock fraud and bribery) and the Watergate scandal, which forced President Richard M. Nixon's resignation, at the national level. Both scandals damaged the public's trust in government. Second, many Texans feared that the new constitution would make the government too powerful. Third, although Lieutenant Governor Bill Hobby and House Speaker Bill Clayton threw their support behind the new constitution, Governor Dolph Briscoe announced his opposition to the document less than a month before the election. Finally, several groups, representing interests that benefited from provisions of the present constitution, actively campaigned against at least some of the amendments. In the end, voters were not convinced that the proposed amendments justified replacing the existing constitution.

THE 1999 CONSTITUTIONAL REVISION EFFORT   The proposed constitution introduced in 1999 by Representative Rob Junell and Senator Bill Ratliff, two of the legislature's more powerful members, recommended major substantive changes in the structure and operation of Texas government. In the legislative branch, the proposal increased House and Senate members' terms to four and six years respectively, placed term limits on House and Senate members, and created veto sessions, an opportunity for the legislature to call itself into session to override gubernatorial vetoes.

Under the proposal, the governor would have become a true chief executive, heading a Cabinet of nine appointed department heads. Cabinet members would have been confirmed by the Senate and served at the governor's pleasure. Although the lieutenant governor, comptroller of public accounts, and attorney general would have remained independently elected executive officers, the executive branch would have been consolidated and placed under much greater gubernatorial control.

The judiciary would have been simplified into fewer courts. A merit system—incorporating nominating commissions, gubernatorial appointments, and nonpartisan retention elections—would have replaced partisan elections in selecting judges for district courts, courts of appeals, and a single supreme court. The supreme court would have included fourteen justices, divided into seven-member civil and criminal divisions, and would have replaced the two current highest courts.

Other important changes included a definition of an efficient system of public education and an authorization of a statewide property tax to fund public education. Also, individual counties would have been empowered to change their organizational structure. A salary commission would have recommended legislative, executive, and judicial pay and per diems, and the legislature would have set the salaries through legislation. Finally, an addition would have allowed the legislature to call a constitutional convention, subject to voter approval.

The legislature never considered the proposed 1999 Constitution. In the House, Speaker Pete Laney assigned the proposal to a Select Committee on Constitutional Revision, which held several hearings but did not approve the proposed constitutional amendment. Instead, the committee reported favorably on Representative Mowery's proposal for nonsubstantive changes, described earlier in the chapter. The Texas Constitution remained substantially unchanged.

THINKING NATIONALLY

Citizen-Initiated Changes

Texans have many opportunities to approve or disapprove of constitutional amendments submitted to them by the Texas Legislature, but the Texas Constitution does not provide for the initiative or referendum. The initiative, now available in some form to voters of twenty-four states, is a legal process whereby voters can place a proposed law or constitutional amendment on the ballot through a petition process. The referendum, also used in twenty-four states, permits voters by petition to vote on the repeal of a law. These constitutional processes were part of the reforms advanced during the Progressive era to give citizens a direct voice in government.

Across the nation, thousands of local governments use these instruments of direct citizen participation. Issues have included tax provisions, bilingual education, term limits, and redistricting. Voters have considered a tax on marijuana and discounts on insurance (California), a limit on state and local debt (Colorado), medical marijuana (Florida), increased funding for public education (Oklahoma), a periodic call for a constitutional convention (Montana), and the list goes on.

- What are the benefits of citizen-initiated changes to public policies?
- Within the context of Texas's history of voting in elections for constitutional amendments, do you anticipate increased voter interest in initiative propositions?
- If Texas legislators knew that most of the laws they enacted could be challenged through the referendum, would this likely change their decisions on legislation?

TOWARD REFORM: Obstacles and Prospects for a Major Revision

⭐ 2.4 . . . **Assess the obstacles and prospects for a major revision of the Texas Constitution.**

Elected officials, the press, reform groups such as the League of Women Voters, and constitutional experts can point out the many flaws of the Texas Constitution, but attempts at wholesale revision have not been successful. The periodic efforts of reform advocates have failed, and there appears to be no collective political will on the part of the legislature or the plural executive to lead the charge in constitutional reform. Numerous piecemeal changes have been made, but they have not addressed the fundamental criticisms of the charter. (To learn more about a related issue, see Join the Debate: Should Texas Adopt the Initiative Process?)

Join the DEBATE | Should Texas Adopt the Initiative Process?

The initiative was part of a package of reforms advanced by Progressives beginning in the late nineteenth century to curtail corruption in state government by reducing the influence of political parties and interest groups. Initiative procedures, which vary greatly among the states, allow citizens to propose constitutional amendments or legislation for a vote of citizens statewide. If the state legislature refuses to act in response to public demands, needs, or opinions, citizens can enact laws or amendments in spite of the legislature's inaction. The initiative process also provides citizens an opportunity to reverse or modify an action of the legislature.

The constitutions of twenty-four states permit the proposal of legislation or constitutional amendments through a statewide initiative petition. Among these states, the process varies greatly. In some states, citizens can propose laws or constitutional amendments directly, without going through the legislature. In other states, the process is indirect and the proposed legislation or constitutional amendments must first be submitted to the state legislature during a regular session.

The Texas Constitution does not allow for the initiative process. It is not that Texans have been oblivious to the initiative. There was support for the initiative process around 1900, but it never took off. Governor Bill Clements (1979–1983, 1987–1991) was a staunch advocate of the initiative and referendum processes, and for a period, Texas Republicans supported them, but they were taken off the table by Governor George W. Bush through a plank in the party's 1994 platform.

Would the interests of Texans be better served if the state adopted a constitutional amendment for the initiative? Would citizens take the time to become informed when initiatives were submitted for approval? Would the initiative process increase or decrease the influence of special interest groups?

To develop an ARGUMENT FOR adding the initiative to the Texas Constitution, think about how:

- **Citizens cannot impact the policy process in a direct manner.** How does the process by which decisions are currently made in the legislature reduce the influence of the general public? In what ways would the threat of an initiative effort force public officials to be more responsive to the general population?
- **Interest groups play a major role in the formulation and implementation of public policy in Texas.** In what ways can the general population use the initiative process to limit the power or influence of interests groups? Would interest groups have to be more transparent in how they go about their lobbying activities?
- **Texans pay limited attention to the actions of their elected officials.** How do the current structures and processes discourage more general participation? If citizens knew they could directly influence public policy or the actions of their elected officials, how would they be more disposed to participate? In what ways would the initiative provide access for segments of the population who have been excluded historically?

To develop an ARGUMENT AGAINST adding the initiative to the Texas Constitution, think about how:

- **Not many Texas voters participate in the special elections where constitutional amendments are submitted.** If interest and turnout are historically low in these special elections, would turnout likely change with initiative elections?
- **Voters are already ill informed about politics and public policy.** Will voters really take the time to learn about the propositions to be voted on? Without having been involved in the deliberations regarding statewide proposals, will voters have a frame of reference to judge the merits of a proposition?
- **Provisions in the current constitution often reflect narrow interests.** In what ways would the initiative process increase the influence that interest groups have on issues submitted to voters? How does the initiative reduce the power of the legislature and move the deliberations about policy into an often hostile public arena?

Obstacles to a Major Revision

Why has substantial reform been so difficult to achieve? First, Texans have a long history of suspicion of government, and this tradition continues. Most people fear governmental abuses and excesses more than they worry about government's inability to respond quickly and efficiently to the needs of its citizens. In the vernacular of the ordinary citizen, "If it ain't broke, don't fix it." And it is not clear that the ordinary citizen believes the constitution is broken. Moreover, if something needs fixing, it can be done by tinkering through constitutional amendments.

Second, many groups and interests have learned how to use the amendment process to advance their priorities. Others benefit from the existing constitution, and they have demonstrated a collective resolve to minimize change.

Finally, most Texans, as demonstrated by their low participation in special constitutional elections, give little thought to changing the constitution because they are ill prepared to deal with the complexities of the document. Some years ago the *Austin American-Statesman* lamented "amendment fatigue" on the part of Texas voters but saw little possibility that the needed reforms would occur.[26]

Prospects for a Major Revision

Public officials who are advocates of reform recognize that there are limited political benefits to be derived from spending a great deal of their time and energy on constitutional reforms. Legislators know their constituents want them to work on issues that directly impact their districts. A legislator's reelection is not likely to build support on the basis of constitutional revision.

Enormous problems must be overcome if citizens are to be educated and motivated to press for constitutional revision, and the importance of constitutional revision is not likely to occur until there is widespread discontent with existing institutions. Voters will have to perceive a need for change, and this will likely occur only when voters come to believe that their elected officials are so constrained by institutional arrangements that extensive changes are the only solution. It will take a sustained, statewide effort by reform advocates to mobilize the political resources and develop a successful strategy to produce an overhaul of a state constitution, and it will require skillful political leadership to steer reforms through the intense field of political landmines.

What Should I Have LEARNED?

Now that you have read this chapter, you should be able to:

⭐ **2.1 Trace the roots of the political values and institutions in the Texas Constitution by summarizing the characteristics of Texas's previous constitutions, p. 36.**

Texas adopted five successive constitutions, prior to its current constitution. These constitutions reflected Texas's changing status from a state of Mexico to an independent nation (1836), to a member of the United States (1845), to a state in the Confederacy (1861), and to a state readmitted into the Union (1866 and 1869). Each of these documents, especially the 1869 Constitution, provided the roots (or precedents) for the current Texas Constitution. Language or general principles of earlier constitutions can be found in the constitution that now serves the state.

⭐ **2.2 Analyze the current constitution as a product of the political and social forces in 1876, p. 41.**

The provisions of the 1876 Texas Constitution are a product of three forces: the perceived defects of the Constitution of 1869, the widespread anger and hostility toward the administration of Governor E. J. Davis (1870–1874), and a movement in many states, including Texas, toward substantive and restrictive constitutions. The 1876 Constitution fragments and limits authority and responsibilities (e.g., the plural executive, the appellate courts of last resort, and local governments). Significant limits are also placed on the state legislature. The constitution includes excessive details, poorly written provisions, and provisions that are legislative in nature.

⭐ **2.3 Compare and contrast the benefits and shortcomings of each method of constitutional revision, p. 51.**

The state's constitution can be changed by constitutional amendments, a process that has been used some 467 times, or a constitutional convention. Piecemeal tinkering with the document is far easier than change through a constitutional convention. Voters are far less likely to oppose amendments than a complex document that might have one or more objectionable provisions. The piecemeal approach has produced a long and confusing document with excessive detail, confusing and sometimes conflicting provisions, and government structures limited in their abilities to address issues facing Texas. A constitutional convention can be authorized to look at all of the structures of state and local government and adjust them to meet current conditions. Thought can be given to the manner in which the institutions relate to each other. Yet, constitutional revision through a convention is a daunting task given the political landmines that exist.

⭐ **2.4 Assess the obstacles and prospects for a major revision of the Texas Constitution, p. 57.**

Since the failed Constitutional Convention of 1974, there have been proposals for a rewrite of the Texas Constitution, but there has been little interest in the Texas Legislature or elsewhere to take on the task. Without widespread voter dissatisfaction with the present document or the willingness of one or more political leaders, there are few prospects on the horizon for a new state constitution.

Test Yourself: Constitutionalism

⭐ **2.1 Trace the roots of the political values and institutions in the Texas Constitution by summarizing the characteristics of Texas's previous constitutions, p. 36.**

Which of Texas's state constitutions is viewed as its "best" based on its simplicity and inclusion of general constitutional principals?
   A. The Constitution of 1845, when Texas was admitted to the Union as a state
   B. The Constitution of 1861, when Texas joined the Confederate States of America
   C. The Constitution of 1866, adopted under Reconstruction
   D. The Constitution of 1869, adopted in compliance with congressional Reconstruction policies
   E. The Constitution of 1876, adopted at the end of Reconstruction

⭐ **2.2 Analyze the current constitution as a product of the political and social forces in 1876, p. 41.**

All but one of these principles of government organization was included in the Texas Constitution of 1876. The exception is:
   A. a plural executive with the election of the governor, lieutenant governor, attorney general, treasurer, and land commissioner.
   B. a legislature limited to biennial sessions unless called by the governor.
   C. a state court system in which judges are elected.
   D. an amendment process limited to constitutional amendments to be approved by voters.
   E. a restrictive Bill of Rights.

⭐ **2.3 Compare and contrast the benefits and shortcomings of each method of constitutional revision, p. 51.**

The Constitutional Convention of 1974 failed for all but one of the following reasons.
   A. It was comprised of Texas legislators who were thinking about reelection and subject to pressures from lobbyists.
   B. A supermajority of two-thirds of the delegates was required for final passage.
   C. Differences over the "right-to-work" issue were irreconcilable.
   D. The Constitutional Revision Committee had prepared a radical draft of a constitution prior to the convention.
   E. A group of obstructionist delegates were opposed to a new constitution no matter what form it took.

⭐ **2.4 Assess the obstacles and prospects for a major revision of the Texas Constitution, p. 57.**

A major overhaul of the Texas Constitution is most likely to occur when
   A. the U.S. Supreme Court declares a number of its current provisions to be in violation of the U.S. Constitution.
   B. the Texas Legislature determines that it no longer can budget for two years as required by the current constitution.
   C. the Texas Supreme Court declares that the provisions for public education are unconstitutional.
   D. interest groups agree that a new constitution is needed.
   E. the general public recognizes a need for a new constitution.

Essay Questions
   1. What evidence can you find of the influence of earlier Texas constitutions on the Constitution of 1876?
   2. Who should serve as members of a constitutional convention, and how should they be selected?
   3. How is it possible to insulate members of a constitutional convention from excessive political pressure or influence?
   4. Should citizens be able to propose constitutional amendments through the initiative process?
   5. What are the major problems with trying to improve or revise the Texas Constitution through the amendment process?
   6. What are the more significant changes that should be made to the Texas Constitution?

Key Terms

cockroach, p. 56
comprehensive revision, p. 51
Constitutional Revision
    Commission, p. 53

liberal constitution, p. 44
piecemeal revision, p. 51

revisionist, p. 56
statutory constitution, p. 44

To Learn More on Constitutionalism

In the Library

Angell, Robert H. *A Compilation and Analysis of the 1998 Texas Constitution and the Original 1876 Text*. Lewiston, NY: Mellen, 1998.

Bruff, Harold H. "Separation of Powers Under the Texas Constitution." *Texas Law Review* 68 (June 1990): 1337–67.

Braden, George D. *Citizens' Guide to the Texas Constitution*. Austin: Texas Advisory Commission on Intergovernmental Relations and Institute of Urban Studies, University of Houston, 1972.

Cornyn, John. "The Roots of the Texas Constitution: Settlement to Statehood." *Texas Tech Law Review* 26 (1995): 1089–218.

Harrington, James C. "Free Speech, Press, and Assembly Liberties Under the Texas Bill of Rights." *Texas Law Review* 68 (June 1990): 1435–67.

May, Janice C. *The Texas Constitutional Revision Experience in the 1970s*. Austin, TX: Sterling Swift, 1975.

———. *The Texas State Constitution: A Reference Guide*. Westport, CT: Greenwood, 1996.

McKay, Seth S. *Debates in the Texas Constitutional Convention of 1875*. Austin: University of Texas Press, 1930.

———. *Seven Decades of the Texas Constitution of 1876*. Lubbock: Texas Tech College, 1943.

Mauer, John Walker. "State Constitutions in a Time of Crisis: The Case of the Texas Constitution of 1876." *Texas Law Review* 68 (June 1990): 1615–47.

Parker, Allan E. "Public Free Schools: A Constitutional Right to Educational Choice in Texas." *Southwestern Law Journal* 45 (Fall 1991): 825–976.

Tarr, G. Alan. *Understanding State Constitutions*. Princeton, NJ: Princeton University Press, 1998.

Watts, Mikal, and Brad Rockwall, "The Original Intent of the Education Article of the Texas Constitution," *St. Mary's Law Journal* 21 (1990): 771–820.

Williams, Patrick G. *Beyond Redemption: Texas Democrats After Reconstruction*. College Station: Texas A&M University Press, 2007.

Wolff, Nelson. *Challenge of Change*. San Antonio, TX: Naylor, 1975.

On the Web

To learn more about the 1845 Texas Constitution, often cited as the "best" Texas Constitution, go to the Tarlton Law Library at **www.tarlton.law.utexas.edu/constitutions/text/1845index .html.**

To learn more about the 1869 Constitution, go to the Tarlton Law Library at **www.tarlton.law.utexas.edu/constitutions/text /1869index.html.**

To learn more about the amendments to the Texas Constitution, go to the Legislative Reference Library at **www.lrl.state.tx .us/legis/constAmends/lrlhome.cfm.**

To learn more about voter turnout in constitutional elections, go to the Texas Secretary of State at **www.sos.state.tx.us/elections /historical/70-92.shtml.**

3

Voting and Participating: Political Parties, Interest Groups, and Elections

For several years after the Republican Party had become the dominant political party in Texas, political pundits predicted a showdown between two of the state's most popular Republicans, Governor Rick Perry and U.S. Senator Kay Bailey Hutchison, for the governor's office. It finally happened in 2010, when Perry, to the surprise of some political observers—and perhaps to Hutchison— announced that he would seek a third term. Many observers expected Hutchison to be a formidable opponent. She was considered the more moderate of the two and had been handily winning statewide elections in Texas for 20 years.

But Hutchison's campaign was marked by indecision. Initially, she hesitated over whether

to resign from the Senate in mid-term to campaign full time for governor, then she kept putting off her resignation date, and finally, a few months before the primary, she announced that she wouldn't resign after all but would remain in the Senate while she campaigned for governor. Perry, meanwhile, mounted a very aggressive campaign against Hutchison. Tapping into the anti-government tea party movement during the midst of a recession, he campaigned against President Barack Obama, who wasn't popular in Texas, and blamed the federal government for much of the state's and nation's problems, all the while painting Hutchison as a Washington insider. Perry's campaign was extremely effective with the conservative voters who

Prior to the adoption of the party primary, party conventions nominated candidates for elected offices. The primary promotes self-recruitment for office and the candidate-centered campaign. Although the political parties have only a marginal role in candidate selection, the party convention brings party activists together to discuss policy positions, address and resolve rules and procedures, and select delegates to the national presidential conventions. At left, U.S. Senator Lyndon B. Johnson is surrounded by backers at the Texas Democratic State Convention in 1956. At right, Governor Rick Perry and his wife Anita accept congratulations at the Texas Republican Convention.

dominate the GOP electorate. He defeated both Hutchison and a third candidate, ultra-conservative Debra Medina, with 51 percent of the vote in the March 2010 Republican primary.

The victory set off speculation, both in Texas and nationally, that Perry was trying to position himself for a campaign for the 2012 Republican presidential nomination. He denied any interest in the White House but, nevertheless, courted national conservative Republican groups and national media interviews. In the 2010 election, Governor Rick Perry defeated Democratic nominee Bill White, 55 percent to 42 percent, to win his third full term as governor.

What Should I Know About . . .

After reading this chapter, you should be able to:

★ **3.1** Trace the gradual evolution of political parties, interest groups, elections, and campaigns in Texas, p. 64.

★ **3.2** Differentiate among the three components of political parties in Texas, and identify their functions in the state's party system, p. 65.

★ **3.3** Categorize the types of interest groups in Texas and the methods they use to influence elections and public policy in Texas, p. 77.

★ **3.4** Identify the types of election systems held in Texas, and analyze the role of strategies in political campaigns, p. 82.

★ **3.5** Evaluate how recent reforms have impacted political parties, interest groups, elections, and campaigns, p. 93.

Election campaigns, such as the 2010 gubernatorial race, illustrate the role played by political parties and interest groups in campaigns and elections. Governor Rick Perry galvanized the support of the tea party movement to win his party's nomination. By winning the Republican primary, Perry weeded out other candidates and launched a strong campaign for the 2010 general election. Interest groups and political parties represent the interests of their members and promote the adoption of certain government policies, but the activities of interest groups focus on *influencing* government, while the activities of political parties focus on *controlling* government. Interest groups mobilize their members to support candidates and make campaign contributions to political candidates and office holders through individuals and political action committees. The parties nominate the candidates, help finance their campaigns, and try to get them elected. Elections provide the mechanism by which parties gain control of government, and campaigns create a link among the political parties, their candidates, interest groups, and the public.

In this chapter, we will examine political parties, interest groups, elections, and campaigns in Texas and consider them from several vantage points.

- First, we will consider *the roots of political parties, interest groups, elections, and campaigns in Texas,* noting how reforms in these institutions and processes influenced their development in Texas history.

- Second, we will examine *political parties in Texas,* describing the party organization, the party in the electorate, and the party in government and analyzing the functions of these components.

- Third, we will explore *interest groups in Texas,* describing the types of interest groups and the activities that groups employ to influence public policy.

- Fourth, we will examine *elections and political campaigns in Texas,* exploring types of elections; voting behavior; the role of money, media, and marketing (the three Ms), voter turnout; and vote choice.

- Finally, we will assess *recent proposed changes in elections and campaigns,* examining reforms in election and campaign procedures.

ROOTS OF Political Parties, Interest Groups, Elections, and Campaigns in Texas

⭐ 3.1 . . . Trace the gradual evolution of political parties, interest groups, elections, and campaigns in Texas.

Political parties and interest groups developed slowly in Texas. As noted in **chapter 1,** early Anglo settlers in Texas were from the upper and lower South, and many brought their Democratic Party attachments with them. But, until the late 1840s, personality was the dominant force in electoral politics. In 1848, the Democratic Party emerged as a formal organization that actively participated in elections. Until the end of the

Civil War in 1865, personalities still strongly influenced party politics in Texas, providing the basis for factions within the dominant Democratic Party. In 1867, in response to congressional Reconstruction, the Republican Party of Texas formed and took control of Texas politics and government from 1868 to 1874 (see **chapter 2**), when Democrats reasserted their dominance. After Reconstruction, the Democratic Party, though challenged occasionally by the Greenback Party and People's Party, controlled Texas government, making Texas a one-party state.

The era of one-party Democratic dominance (1874–1986) was filled with feuds between contending factions within the party. Issues such as the free coinage of silver and Prohibition caused splits in the Democratic Party during the late nineteenth and early twentieth centuries. In the 1930s, the Great Depression and President Franklin D. Roosevelt's New Deal created a split over economic policy that resulted in the development of liberal and conservative factions, which would battle for control of the party until the end of the one-party era.

Like political parties in Texas, interest groups developed slowly. The most influential interest groups in the nineteenth century represented agrarian interests, and the influence of the Grange, though not monolithic, was evident in the Constitutional Convention of 1875. Groups representing oil and gas interests supplanted agrarian groups during the early twentieth century. After World War II, as the Texas economy and society became more complex and diverse, interest groups proliferated, representing a broader array of interests based on ethnic, social, and cultural divisions in the state. However, economic interests, especially those representing businesses, maintained their preeminence.

Campaigns and elections, which originally were centered on personal loyalties to candidates, became partisan or factional contests. Until the early 1960s, the most important elections were the Democratic primaries, which featured candidates of the contending factions. Democratic candidates always won the general elections, and voter turnout suffered because of the lack of competition. Voter turnout was also hampered by legal impediments to voting, some of which persisted until the 1970s.

Political Parties in Texas

⭐ **3.2** . . . Differentiate among the three components of political parties in Texas, and identify their functions in the state's party system.

Political parties in Texas perform the same functions as the national parties. The parties perform these functions through their three components: party organization, party in the electorate, and party in government. The concept of the three-part political party is frequently linked to the work of renowned scholar V. O. Key, Jr., whose approach permits us to differentiate among the parties' core structures and functions.[1]

Party Organization

The party organization consists of the structures that constitute the party organization and the party activists who occupy positions in the party structure. The party organization includes both a formal organization, established by state law, and a functional organization, which describes how a party actually operates. Party activists, such as precinct and county chairs, usually perform their work in obscurity, unknown and unheralded.

FORMAL ORGANIZATION   Texas state law, as in most states, establishes the formal organization for political parties. There is both a temporary and a permanent party organization for each political party. The **temporary party organization** consists

temporary party organization
Party organization that exists for a limited time and includes several levels of conventions.

TIMELINE: The Texas Political System—From Democratic to Republican Dominance

1874 **Democratic Party Dominance in Texas Politics**—No Republican would win a statewide office until John Tower in 1961.

1904 **Poll Tax**—A poll tax is required to register to vote.

1903 **Terrell Election Law**—This law is enacted to provide for the nomination of candidates by a primary rather than a convention.

1923 **White Primary**—The Texas Legislature adopts the "white primary," which disenfranchises blacks in primary elections.

---

precinct convention
Precinct party meeting to select delegates and adopt resolutions.

How does the Democratic precinct convention fit into the "Texas Two-Step?" Texans do not register by political party, and a registered voter can vote in either primary, thus entitling the voter to participate in the precinct convention held after the polls close. Precinct conventions are held in facilities close to where people voted. Some conventions have only a handful of participants whereas others draw large numbers of party voters, as occurred in 2008.

of conventions at the precinct, the county or state senatorial district, and the state levels. Held every two years, party conventions are attended by party activists and last only a short period of time, ranging from a few hours to a few days. The conventions meet to select delegates to subsequent party conventions, choose party leaders, and establish party policies. They provide an opportunity for interested party members to select the party's leaders and influence its policies.

Every two years, the first party convention occurs at the voting-precinct level. Election precincts are voting districts that usually contain fewer than 3,000 registered voters. On the date of the primary election (currently the first Tuesday of March in even-numbered years) after the polls have closed, the parties hold their **precinct conventions.** The political parties conduct primary elections to select their nominees for elected public office—governor, state senator, state representative, and county judge, for example. A stamp, indicating which party's primary election the person voted in, is placed on the voter's registration card by the primary election official, and any person with such a stamp may participate in the party's precinct convention. Participation is open, but only about 1 percent of the voters in the party's primary election actually attend the precinct conventions. Even in presidential election years, when the precinct conventions in the Democratic Party have an effect on

1944 *Smith v. Allwright*—U.S. Supreme Court declares the white primary a violation of the U.S. Constitution's Fifteenth Amendment.

1975 **Voting Rights Act Is Extended to Cover Texas**—It prohibits "vote dilution" in political districts and requires pre-clearance by the Department of Justice of changes in redistricting plans and other election procedures.

2002 **Republican Party Dominance in Texas Politics**—Republicans are elected to all statewide offices and control both houses of the Texas Legislature.

1966 *Harper v. Virginia*—U.S. Supreme Court declares the poll tax unconstitutional in state elections.

1980s **Evidence of Republican Resurgence**—The number of Republican statewide elected officials, state legislators, and local officials increases.

the selection of delegates to the party's national convention and the choice of the party's presidential nominee, attendance rarely exceeds 10 percent of the eligible participants.

The 2008 presidential primaries in Texas, however, had record turnouts, sparked mainly by the tight race between Barack Obama and Hillary Clinton for the Democratic nomination. More than 2.8 million Texans (a record) voted in the Democratic primary that year, and about 1 million of them (also a record) returned after the polls closed for their precinct conventions. The primaries and the conventions were dubbed the "Texas Two Step" that gave Obama a slight edge over Clinton in Texas delegates to the Democratic National Convention. Clinton won the primary vote, but Obama, whose campaign was well-organized, had stronger support in the precinct conventions. Although the 2008 Republican presidential nomination was all but settled in favor of John McCain before the Texas primary, almost 1.4 million Texans cast ballots in the Republican primary that year for a record, total primary turnout of more than 4.2 million.

The precinct convention's principal task is to select delegates to the party's **county convention** or, in those counties that are in more than one state senatorial district (which included fifteen counties in 2008) to the **state senatorial district convention.**[2] In both the Democratic and the Republican Parties, each precinct in the county or senatorial district is allocated delegates based on the number of votes cast in the precinct for the party's gubernatorial nominee in the most recent gubernatorial election. The allocation system is designed to reward those precincts that provided the greatest electoral support for the party's gubernatorial nominee by giving them a larger voice in selecting party officials and setting party policy. After delegates to the county or senatorial district convention have been chosen, the precinct convention debates and then either adopts or rejects resolutions; the resolutions that are adopted are forwarded to the county or senatorial district convention. Through this process, the party begins to build a party platform by discussing the concerns of party members on issues of public policy.

county convention
County party meeting to select delegates and adopt resolutions.

state senatorial district convention
Party meeting held when a county is a part of more than one senatorial district.

On the third Saturday after the primary election, each party holds its county and senatorial district conventions. The delegates and alternates who were selected in the precinct conventions attend the county and senatorial district conventions. The principal purpose of the county or senatorial district conventions is to select delegates to the party's state convention.

In June, the delegates assemble for the party's **state convention.** The state convention certifies the results of the party's primary (which nominates the party's candidates for public office), drafts and adopts the party's platform, and selects the party's state executive committee, including the state party chair and vice chair. In presidential election years, the state convention also selects the party's slate of presidential electors, nominates the state's members for the party's national committee, and selects the state's delegates to the party's national convention.

The **permanent party organization** consists of the party chairpersons and committees, which purportedly work throughout the year performing party-building and electoral functions. Because of their principal activities, the parties' permanent organizations are tied to electoral districts. Each electoral unit, from the smallest (the precinct) to the largest (the state), is represented in the permanent organization. The political party appears hierarchical in structure, with power concentrated at the top, but party organizations are more accurately described as stratarchies—organizations with power distributed in layers or strata.[3] Consequently, each level of party organization is relatively independent of the other levels and concentrates on electoral activities within its level or strata.

Each precinct in Texas has a **precinct chairperson** who represents the party in that electoral district. The chairperson is elected for a two-year term in the party's primary election. The chairperson is responsible for informing members of the party's activities and issue positions, getting party members to the polls on election days, and serving on the party's county executive committee.

Each county in Texas has a **county chairperson** and a **county executive committee.** The county chairperson is elected in the party's primary for a two-year term. The county executive committee, consisting of the county's precinct chairpersons, assists the county chairperson. At the county level, the party's duties, which are usually performed by the county chairperson, include conducting the party's primary elections, arranging for the county convention, raising funds for the county organization, campaigning for party candidates, and promoting precinct organization efforts.

Formally, the supreme unit of the party's permanent organization is the **state executive committee,** composed of a chairperson and a vice chairperson (state law requires that the chairperson and vice chairperson not be of the same gender) and one man and one woman from each of the state's thirty-one senatorial districts. The representatives from the senatorial districts are elected at the state convention, based on nominations by the individual state senatorial districts, for two-year terms. Consequently, the selection is really made by the delegates from each of the state's senatorial districts. In addition, the Texas Democratic Party allocates committee membership to state party officials and several constituent groups—such as women, Asian Americans, African Americans, *Tejanos,* and young Democrats—which increases the size of the committee to ninety-two

state convention

Party meeting held to adopt the party's platform, elect the party's executive committee and state chairperson, and, in a presidential election year, elect delegates to the national convention and choose presidential electors.

permanent party organization

Party organization that operates throughout the year, performing the party's functions.

precinct chairperson

Party leader in a voting precinct.

county chairperson

Party leader in a county.

county executive committee

Precinct chairpersons in a county who assist the county chairpersons.

state executive committee

Sixty-two-member party committee that makes decisions for the party between state conventions.

Are all county parties well organized? The two parties strive to develop a permanent presence at the local level with a party headquarters, such as the Bexar County Democratic headquarters shown here. Maintaining an office and staffing it with volunteers or a paid staff is costly, and most partisan contributors opt to contribute to a candidate or campaign committee rather than to the party organization.

Photo courtesy: Courtesy of L. Tucker Gibson

Figure 3.1 *Are Texas party organizations highly centralized or decentralized?*

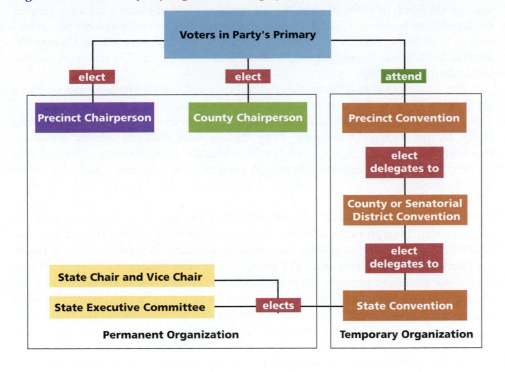

members. The **state party chairperson** and vice chairperson are chosen by the entire convention, but their selection may be influenced by the party's gubernatorial nominee. The state executive committee's duties include certifying the party's candidates for the general election, conducting the state convention, and promoting the party's candidates and issue positions. (To learn more about the formal party organization, see Figure 3.1.)

The formal organizational chart of any organization may not provide the real story of how well the organization functions and where decisions are made. For political parties, although the state chairperson formally heads the party and is elected by the state convention, functional leadership may rest with the governor, who can be instrumental in selecting his or her party's state chairperson and shaping party policy. The formal organization provides a skeleton for the party organization, but its performance is determined by the effectiveness of the people who occupy those positions and who use those positions to further the party's political goals and promote party unity.

DEMOCRATIC PARTY UNITY   Since 1976, control of the Democratic Party organization in Texas has been in ideological liberals' hands. Their control has affected the number of liberals among Democratic candidates for statewide office, their electoral success, and the party's platform. During the 1950s and 1960s, the only liberal Democrat elected to statewide office in Texas was U.S. Senator Ralph Yarborough. However, in 1982, four liberal Democrats—Jim Mattox, Jim Hightower, Garry Mauro, and Ann Richards—were elected to statewide executive offices. All won reelection in 1986, and Ann Richards was elected governor in 1990. In recent elections, however, liberal Democrats have not fared as well. In 1990, Republican Rick Perry, a former conservative Democratic state representative who switched parties, defeated Jim Hightower for agriculture commissioner. Mattox, who unsuccessfully sought the Democratic gubernatorial nomination in 1990, was replaced as attorney general by

state party chairperson
Party leader for the state.

moderate Democrat Dan Morales. In 1994, Ann Richards lost the governorship to George W. Bush. In 1998, Mattox lost his comeback bid to become attorney general to Republican Supreme Court Justice John Cornyn. Mauro, who barely won reelection as land commissioner in 1994, lost his bid to become governor to George W. Bush in 1998. Thus, Republicans replaced the liberal class of 1982 in statewide elective offices during the 1990s.

The success of liberal Democrats in the 1980s and early 1990s also had an effect on the Republican Party, as conservative Democrats, having lost control of the Democratic Party, increasingly abandoned the Democratic Party for the Republican Party. By the 1990s, Democratic Party leaders were overwhelmingly liberal or moderate ideologically. A recent study of Democratic Party activists indicated that 60 percent were self-described liberals, 25 percent were moderates, and 15 percent were conservatives.[4]

REPUBLICAN PARTY UNITY The Republican Party has always been conservative ideologically. Though more cohesive ideologically than the Democratic Party, the Republican Party in Texas also has its intraparty conflicts. Republican Party activists are overwhelmingly conservative (91 percent), with few moderates (7 percent) and even fewer liberals (2 percent).[5] Republican conflicts typically are over goals and policies. Republican pragmatists or economic conservatives emphasize the party's role in elections and governing and its economic policies. More libertarian in political ideology, the pragmatists seek to expand the party's membership, reaching out to people who have not traditionally been members of the Republican coalition, and to pursue policies that advance the economic well-being of its members. Republican ideologues or social conservatives emphasize the party's representation function, stressing the party's conservative political ideology over winning elections and controlling the government. The ideologues are more interested in promoting conservative social policies than electing Republican candidates to office.

The clash between the factions has been evident in every Republican state convention since 1994, when a coalition of religious conservatives and anti-abortion activists dominated the party's state convention and elected their candidate state party chair. The Christian Coalition, a group that favors what they identify as traditional social values, extended its control by electing the party vice chair, Susan Weddington, and a majority of the state executive committee.[6] In 1996, the issue that divided the convention was abortion. Despite the urgings of former governor Bill Clements to focus on the issues that united Republicans in the past, the social conservatives, who made up more than 80 percent of the delegates, attempted unsuccessfully to exclude Senator Kay Bailey Hutchison from the party's national convention delegation because her pro-life credentials were not staunch enough for them.[7]

In 1997, when Susan Weddington was elected state chair, she pledged to unify the party's factions. She reached out to the party's moderates and economic conservatives, many of whom supported abortion rights. However, the election of David Barton, a social conservative like Weddington, as state vice chair raised concerns among some moderate Republicans. Nevertheless, Weddington declared a new leadership and focus for the state party.[8] In 1998, social conservatives initiated a platform provision denying party funding and support to any candidates who refused to endorse a ban on the late-term abortion procedure that social conservatives term partial-birth abortion. The social conservatives, whose candidates had been unsuccessful in the Republican primary earlier in the year, defied the pleas of Governor George W. Bush and other statewide elected officials not to restrict the party's growth in this manner.[9] In 2002, the social conservatives pushed the Republican platform even further, calling for the deportation of immigrants who do not carry the required ID, stricter requirements for voter registration, and the termination of bilingual education programs in Texas.[10] In 2006, state convention delegates adopted a platform that declared "the United States is a Christian nation" and the Ten Commandments "the basis of our basic freedoms and the cornerstone of our Western tradition."[11]

PARTY EFFECTIVENESS: WHAT'S AT STAKE?   Assessing party organizational effectiveness requires us to examine different factors, depending on the level of party organization. Consequently, we consider each level of party organization—statewide, county, and precinct—in turn.

At the state level, party effectiveness is related to the complexity of the party's organization and the capacity of the party's organization to perform its party-building functions. Indicators of organizational complexity include an accessible party head-quarters, a complex division of labor, a substantial party budget, and a professional leadership. In Texas, both parties maintain fairly complex organizations. A state party's ability to perform its party-building duties is calculated in two areas: (1) institutional support activities such as fund-raising, electoral mobilization programs, public opinion polling, issue leadership, and publication of a newsletter; and, (2) candidate-centered activities such as contributions to candidates, recruitment of candidates, selection of convention delegates, and pre-primary endorsements. A comparison of the contemporary Democratic and Republican Parties in Texas reveals that an advantage in both measures of party building is enjoyed by the Republican Party.

At the county and precinct levels, the party organization's primary task is campaigning for the party's candidates and getting voters to the polls. County and precinct chairpersons are most influential in determining the party's effectiveness at this level.[12] Studies of party activities at these levels reveal that Republican Party activists are more likely to involve their members in party and political activities.

How does the examination of the parties' functional organizations help us understand party politics in Texas? The lack of unity in both parties detracts from their effectiveness as organizations and from their ability to represent a majority of Texans. To become the majority party in Texas, Republicans must effectively deal with the differences between the ideologues and the pragmatists by becoming less interested in ideological purity and more interested in representing and governing. Although a majority of Texans consider themselves conservative politically, they are not as conservative as the Republican ideologues. The challenge for Democrats is to ensure that as conservative Democrats are drawn to the Republican Party, the Democratic Party does not become too liberal to represent a majority of Texans on most issues. (To learn more about how party systems in Texas compare to those in other large states, see Table 3.1.)

Table 3.1 *How does the Texas party system compare to the party systems of other large states?*

	Interparty Competition (2002–2008)*	Divided Government (2010)⁺	Party Identification of the Electorate (2009)		Ideological Orientation of Residents (2009)		
			Republican	Democrat	Conservative	Moderate	Liberal
Texas	0.290	No	41.6	40.3	43.5	36.0	16.7
California	0.593	No	31.5	51.2	33.1	37.5	25.4
New York	0.397	Yes	30.5	53.9	31.6	37.7	26.3
Florida	0.187	No	38.5	46.2	39.3	37.0	19.3

*The Ranney index of party competition is a measure of party control of the legislature and the executive. An index of .0500 indicates that control of government is evenly split between the parties. An index of 1.0000 indicates complete Democratic Party control; an index of 0.000 indicates complete Republican control. Authors compiled Ranney Index.
⁺Divided government occurs when one party does not control both houses of the legislature and the governorship.
Sources: Gallup Poll, "Party ID: Despite Republican Gains, Most States Remain Blue," *State of the States*, February 1, 2009, www.gallup.com/poll/125450/Party-Affiliation-Despite-GOP-Gains-States-Remain-Blue.aspx?CSTS=tagrss#1; Jeffrey M. Jones, "Ideology: Three Deep South States Are the Most Conservative," Gallup Poll, February 3, 2010, www.gallup.com/poll/125480/ideology-three-deep-south-states-conservative.aspx.

Party in the Electorate

The most important function for the party organization is winning elections, which means mobilizing interest in the party's goals and candidates among the voters—the electorate. The party in the electorate consists of those people who identify with a political party and consider themselves members. In slightly more than half of the states—not including Texas—voters register as members of a particular political party or as independents.

Because Texans don't register by political party, opinion polls are used to determine the party identifications of Texans.[13] Party identification is a psychological attachment that is formed early in life but can be altered by events, issues, and political personalities. Partisan attachments are considered important in determining a party's chances for electoral victory and, consequently, its ability to control government.

DISTRIBUTION OF PARTY ATTACHMENTS   In 1952, when survey research began measuring party identification in Texas, only 6 percent of Texans identified themselves as Republicans, and 66 percent identified themselves as Democrats. Since 1952, however, the percentage of Democrats has declined and the percentage of Republicans has increased. In 1991, the percentages of Republicans and Democrats were identical. In public opinion surveys conducted since 1999, there have been more Republicans than Democrats in Texas. In 2010, 39 percent of Texans identified with the Republican Party, and 38 percent identified with the Democratic Party. (To learn more about the Republican rise and Democratic decline, see Figure 3.2.)

The changes in party affiliation among Texans involve more than just a decrease in Democrats and an increase in Republicans. The percentage of independents—individuals who identify with neither major political party—has also increased in Texas. Independents constituted a larger percentage of the population (39 percent) than either the Democratic or Republican Party. Thus, whereas 72 percent of the

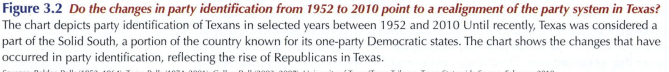

Figure 3.2 *Do the changes in party identification from 1952 to 2010 point to a realignment of the party system in Texas?*
The chart depicts party identification of Texans in selected years between 1952 and 2010 Until recently, Texas was considered a part of the Solid South, a portion of the country known for its one-party Democratic states. The chart shows the changes that have occurred in party identification, reflecting the rise of Republicans in Texas.
Sources: Belden Polls (1952, 1964); Texas Polls (1974–2001); Gallup Poll (2003–2007); University of Texas/*Texas Tribune, Texas Statewide Survey,* February 2010.

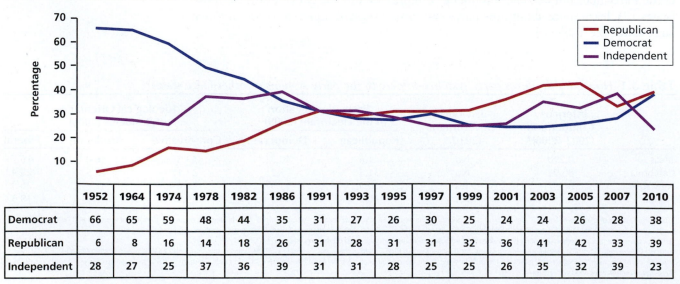

	1952	1964	1974	1978	1982	1986	1991	1993	1995	1997	1999	2001	2003	2005	2007	2010
Democrat	66	65	59	48	44	35	31	27	26	30	25	24	24	26	28	38
Republican	6	8	16	14	18	26	31	28	31	31	32	36	41	42	33	39
Independent	28	27	25	37	36	39	31	31	28	25	25	26	35	32	39	23

population in Texas identified with one of the major political parties in 1952, only 64 percent did in 2009. Consequently, people with attachments to the Democratic or the Republican Party constitute a smaller percentage of the electorate now than in 1952. This is not a good sign for supporters of strong political parties or for the view that strong parties are essential to democracy.

PARTY REALIGNMENT IN TEXAS   Realignments, triggered by critical elections, produce profound changes in the distribution of partisan attachments. According to some political scientists, Texas has experienced an attenuated realignment (or secular realignment). They offer the following evidence:

- Young voters were more likely to identify with the Republican Party than the Democratic Party during the 1980s and 1990s. Among party identifiers, young people—age eighteen to twenty-nine—were much more likely to identify with the Republican Party than were older people. Consequently, generational replacement favored the Republicans. However, surveys conducted in 2007 indicate that nearly half of those age eighteen to twenty-nine are independents. The same percentage of young people (28 percent) identify with the Republican or Democratic Party.

- Some Democrats switched to the Republican Party. These conversions were most likely among conservative Democrats of an upper-level socioeconomic status who were bringing their party identification into line with their ideology and status.

- New residents of Texas were more likely to identify with the Republican Party than were native Texans or long-term residents. Between 1970 and 2000, when Texas experienced an influx of immigrants, most of the new residents brought an identification with the Republican Party, which they kept.

- Party identification, especially among Republicans, is important in determining vote choices in elections. Between 80 and 90 percent of Republicans voted for Republican candidates in recent elections. Also, in the two largest counties of Texas, a majority of voters cast straight-ticket ballots, voting for all candidates of one party.

- Republican candidates won more counties (especially the most populous counties) than Democrats in recent presidential, gubernatorial, and other statewide elections. Indeed, a map of voting trends in the 1970s is dramatically different from a map of voting trends from the 2000s.[14] (To learn more about vote choices in the 1970s and 2000s, see Figures 3.3 and 3.4.)

In 2008, Republican candidates won every statewide election, continuing their hold on all twenty-nine statewide elected offices. Republicans also retained control of the Texas Senate, which they have controlled since 1997, and the Texas House, which they have controlled since 2003. Generally speaking, Republican candidates are more successful in large electoral districts. For example, 80 percent of the court of appeals judges were Republicans in 2005, but only 37 percent of the county judges and 36 percent of the county commissioners were Republicans. Nevertheless, the total number of Republican elected officials had increased to approximately 2,400 by 2008.[15] As political scientists Gregory Thielemann and Euel Elliott contend, "The transformation from hard-core 'yellow dog' Democratic Party dominance to Republican supremacy has been thorough and complete."[16]

Another possible interpretation of the surveys on party identification in Texas is that Texans are not realigning but dealigning. In a dealignment, party affiliations weaken, and the importance of party affiliation to the population's political attitudes and behavior also weakens. The dealignment interpretation concludes that although

Figure 3.3 *Which party controlled most Texas counties in the 1970s?*
The map reflects the strength of the Texas Republican and Democratic Parties based on votes for Republican and Democratic candidates in selected general election contests during the 1970s.

Sources: Based on county election results from the 1972 presidential election, 1974 gubernatorial election, 1976 presidential election, 1978 gubernatorial election, 1978 lieutenant governor election, and the 1978 attorney general election. Mike Kingston, Sam Attlee, and Mary G. Crawford, *The Texas Almanac's Political History of Texas* (Austin: Eakins, 1992); *Texas Almanac, 1980–1981* (Dallas: A. H. Belo, 1979).

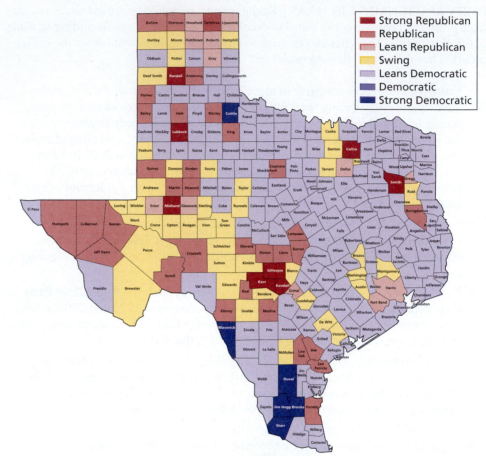

there are more Republican identifiers and fewer Democratic identifiers, the most important fact is the growth in independent identifiers, who do not identify with any political party. According to this interpretation, Texas is not becoming a Republican state; it is becoming a no-party state. The large percentage of independents is cited as evidence that party identification is less important, and elections are not about parties but about candidates. However, given the Republican Party's advantage in most elections, this interpretation is more difficult to support.

CONTEMPORARY PARTY COALITIONS   As a result of the changes in party identification among Texans, the party coalitions have become more like their national counterparts. Increasingly, people in the upper income categories identify with the Republican Party; people in the lower income categories identify with the Democratic Party. In addition, the Democratic Party is the party of liberals and populists, African Americans and Hispanics, and women; the Republican Party is the party of conservatives and libertarians, Anglos, males, the Christian Right, and now members of the tea party movement.

Figure 3.4 *Which party controlled most Texas counties in the 2000s?*

The map reflects the strength of the Texas Republican and Democratic parties based on votes for Republican and Democratic candidates in selected general election contests during the 2000s.

Sources: Based on county election results from the 2000 presidential election, 2002 gubernatorial election, 2004 presidential election, 2006 gubernatorial election, 2006 lieutenant governor election, and the 2006 attorney general election. Texas Secretary of State Web site, Historical Election Results, www.sos.state.tx.us/elections/historical/70-92.shtml.

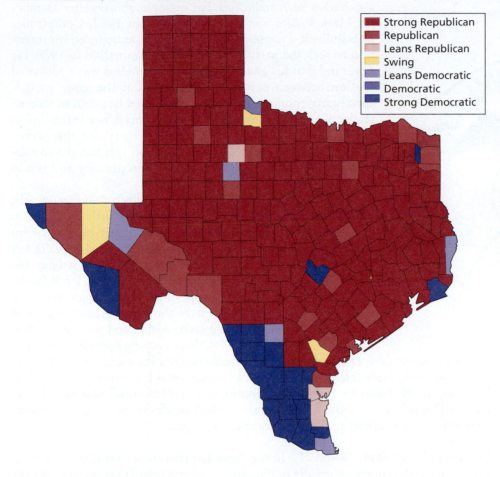

Legend:
- Strong Republican
- Republican
- Leans Republican
- Swing
- Leans Democratic
- Democratic
- Strong Democratic

Party in Government

The party in government is a political party's mechanism for establishing coopera-tion among the separate branches of government. In theory, all public officials who are appointed or elected under the same party label work together to establish and implement public policies that represent the party's positions on issues. How strong is the party in government in Texas, and how well does it perform this unifying function?

IN THE EXECUTIVE BRANCH   For members of the executive branch in Texas, the Texas Constitution establishes several impediments to cooperation. Foremost is the independent election of the most important executive officers in Texas. Even the governor and lieutenant governor do not run as a team on the ballot (see **chapter 5**). Consequently, the relationship between the governor and lieutenant governor, even when they are members of the same political party, may be strained. Also, because

Are there any "yellow dogs" left? During the era of Democratic dominance of state politics, Texans often referred to themselves as "yellow dog Democrats." This was understood to mean, "I'd vote for a yellow dog if he ran on the Democratic ticket." There are still a few yellow dog Democrats left in Texas, but the political landscape has changed over the past three decades, resulting in a dying breed.

Photo courtesy: Courtesy of L. Tucker Gibson

the Texas attorney general's office has often been used as a stepping stone by politicians who aspire to be governor, the relationship between those two officials may not be the most cordial, even when they are members of the same political party. Other statewide elected officials in the executive branch may also harbor such ambitions. For example, shortly after Democrat Mark White was elected governor in 1982, Comptroller Bob Bullock, a member of White's party, announced his intention to seek the party's gubernatorial nomination in 1986. He never did, but his announcement nevertheless was a source of tension between two office holders from the same party.[17] Intra-party conflict surfaced in 2006 when Republican Comptroller Carol Keeton Strayhorn announced her intention to challenge Republican Governor Rick Perry for the party's gubernatorial nomination. She backed off this threat and subsequently decided to skip the Republican primary and run in the general election as an independent.

Because the executive officers are elected independently, candidates of the same political party have little incentive to campaign together or even to coordinate their campaigns for public office. Typically, each office-seeker establishes his or her own campaign organization. This practice further reduces the likelihood of cooperation after the election. In 1982, faced for the first time with Republican opposition in all major executive races, the Democratic candidates showed a greater degree of cooperation than normal and even coordinated portions of their campaigns. In 1990 and 1994, despite strong opposition in many executive contests, the Democrats failed to coordinate their campaigns. In 1998, John Sharp and Paul Hobby, Democratic candidates for lieutenant governor and comptroller, respectively, failed to endorse the Democratic gubernatorial nominee, Garry Mauro. Republican candidates for statewide executive offices have usually demonstrated a similar tendency to run independent campaigns.

IN THE LEGISLATIVE BRANCH   In the Texas Legislature, as noted in **chapter 4**, partisan considerations are usually minimized. Until recently, Texas was one of only five states that did not hold inclusive party caucuses, elect party leaders, or create party committees. Party caucuses and committees are formed to provide information to party members on policy issues and to formulate the party's position on issues. Party leaders are selected to provide leadership for a party's caucus and committees. In 1981, a group of Democratic members of the Texas House of Representatives formed a Democratic caucus. By 1987, the caucus included all Democrats, including the Speaker of the House and all Democrats on his team, a practice that has continued in subsequent sessions. By 1989, the Speaker's team and the caucus began to work together, reducing the tension that had characterized the earlier years.[18] From 1993 to 2003, while Pete Laney was House Speaker, the Democratic caucus was not very active. In 2003, when Republicans gained control of the House and elected a Republican Speaker, the caucus became more active. Similarly, since 1999, Senate Democrats, faced with a Republican governor and lieutenant governor, decided to give the caucus a more prominent role. Caucus chairs called frequent meetings, discussed policy and strategy, and held press conferences to publicize the Democrats' position on issues before the legislature.

Prior to 1989, the Republicans avoided party organization in the House, preferring to work with the Speaker and conservative Democrats through the Texas Conservative Coalition. However, in 1989, the Republicans organized a caucus, "formed a policy committee to screen suggested legislation before it went to the full caucus for endorsement, and maintained a political arm called the Republican Campaign Legislative Committee."[19] Also, Governor Bill Clements, who had opposed a Republican organization in the House in 1979, endorsed it during his second term (1987–1991). As their numbers passed the one-third threshold, Republicans began to feel their independence from the Speaker and conservative Democrats. Breaking the one-third threshold allowed the Republicans to prevent an override of a governor's veto, prevent a constitutional amendment from passing, keep a law from becoming effective immediately, and prevent a suspension of the rules. More importantly, it allowed the Republicans to create a working majority if they could maintain party unity and attract the votes of only one-fourth of the Democrats.

During recent legislatures, the House Republican caucus has met, but it does not have much influence. Despite predictions to the contrary, the Texas Legislature continues to operate with strong institutional leaders, eschewing the opportunity to build strong party organizations.[20]

IN THE JUDICIAL BRANCH   In Texas, all judges, except municipal court judges, are elected on a partisan ballot. Consequently, a reluctance to politicize the judiciary, which is evident in some states, is less pronounced in Texas. However, candidates for legislative and executive positions rarely team with members of their party seeking judgeships in a coordinated campaign. Thus, the elections are usually conducted independently.

The influence of party is often dominant in the appointment of judges when a vacancy occurs through a judge's death, resignation, retirement, or removal. Because a large percentage of judges are initially appointed to their positions by the governor, he or she has many opportunities to reward party members with judicial appointments. A comparison of judicial appointments by Governor Bill Clements during his last term (1987–1991) and Governor Ann Richards during her term (1991–1995) indicates that each appointed an overwhelming majority of judges who shared the governor's party affiliation.[21] More recently, when Governor Rick Perry was given the opportunity to fill vacancies on the Texas Supreme Court, he chose Republicans.

Appointments of judges by governors could also be viewed as an attempt to fill the courts with judges who share the governor's political ideology. This assumes that judges, in interpreting the law, can exercise some discretion and that Republican judges and Democratic judges differ in how they interpret the law and decide cases. Evidence in certain kinds of cases indicates that this assumption is correct. In civil suits, Democratic judges are more likely to take the plaintiff's side. Republican judges, on the other hand, are more likely to support the defendant when businesses are being sued. For example, during the 2005–2006 term, the Texas Supreme Court, on which Republicans held all of the seats, decided for business interests in 82 percent of its cases. In 1985, when Democrats controlled the Supreme Court, defendants won only 28 percent of the cases.[22]

Interest Groups in Texas

⭐ **3.3** . . . **Categorize the types of interest groups in Texas and the methods they use to influence elections and public policy in Texas.**

Recall that when people form groups, they must decide whether to act as a political party or as an interest group. We now turn from parties to interest groups, considering first the types of interest groups and then their political activities.

Types of Interest Groups

Usually, political scientists classify interest groups according to the type of interest that the group represents. We have adopted a classification that focuses on the policy goals of the group: business groups and trade associations, professional associations, labor groups, racial and ethnic groups, and public-interest groups.

BUSINESS GROUPS AND TRADE ASSOCIATIONS   Interest groups representing businesses in Texas are diverse, but business groups and trade associations generally agree that their primary goal is to maintain a favorable climate for businesses in Texas. More specifically, these groups attempt to ensure that business taxes remain low, that labor union influence is restricted, and that favorable business regulations exist. Some business interest groups (e.g., Texas Association of Business and Texas Taxpayers and Research Association) represent business interests generally. Others, known as trade associations, represent specific industries and their interests. Among the more influential trade associations are the Texas Automobile Dealers Association, the Texas Bankers Association, the Mid-Continent Oil and Gas Association, and the Texas Chemical Council. To increase their influence, many corporations (AT&T, for example) also hire their own lobbyists.

PROFESSIONAL ASSOCIATIONS   Some of the most influential interest groups in Texas represent professional associations, such as trial lawyers, physicians, teachers, and realtors. The Texas Trial Lawyers Association (TTLA) represents the interests of lawyers who make their living representing people in personal-injury lawsuits or product-liability suits. The Texas Medical Association (TMA) represents physicians, and the Texas State Teachers Association (TSTA), the Texas Federation of Teachers (TFT), the Association of Texas Professional Educators (ATPE), and the Texas Classroom Teachers Association (TCTA) compete to represent public-school teachers. The Texas Association of Realtors (TAR) works for realtors in Texas. All of these groups attempt to influence regulations and public policies that affect their professions.

LABOR GROUPS   Although labor groups have never been strong in Texas, their influence is greatest in the industrialized areas, such as Houston, Dallas, Fort Worth, and especially in the Golden Triangle area of Beaumont, Port Arthur, and Orange. Labor unions attempt to establish rights for their members to collective bargaining, occupational safety, and increased wages. The membership of the American Federation of Labor–Congress of Industrial Organizations (AFL-CIO) has declined since the 1980s. Within the AFL-CIO, the more influential unions are the American Federation of Teachers (AFT), the American Federation of State, County, and Municipal Employees (AFSCME), and the Communication Workers of America (CWA).

RACIAL AND ETHNIC GROUPS   Racial and ethnic groups promote political, economic, and social equality for their members, freedom from discrimination, and representation in public offices. Because they are the largest ethnic minorities in Texas, Hispanics and African Americans have the greatest number of groups representing their interests. The oldest and largest Hispanic group, the League of United Latin American Citizens (LULAC), is involved in efforts to change the method of selecting judges in Texas, and the Mexican American Legal Defense and Educational Fund (MALDEF) was instrumental in the lawsuit that led to greater equality in funding for public education in Texas. The National Association for the Advancement of Colored People (NAACP) supported the challenge to the Democratic Party's white primary, fought to end segregation in public education, and continues to fight for increased economic and social opportunities for African Americans.

PUBLIC-INTEREST GROUPS Public-interest groups advocate public policies intended to benefit the public interest. Among the more active groups in Texas are the Baptist Christian Life Commission, Clean Water Action, the Sierra Club, Public Citizen, Texans for Public Justice, Texas Alliance for Human Needs, Texas Citizen Action, the AARP, NOW, and Americans Disabled for Attendant Programs Today (ADAPT). These groups seek public policies that protect consumers, the environment, the poor, the elderly, the young, the disabled, and women, and some promote stronger ethical standards in government.

Political Activities of Interest Groups

Interest groups usually engage in three distinct, but related, types of political activities: lobbying, electioneering, and litigation. In this section, we identify and explain each of these activities.

LOBBYING When most people think of interest-group activities, lobbying is probably the first thing that comes to mind. Indeed, lobbying may be the universal activity of interest groups. Most groups practice direct and indirect lobbying.

Attempting to influence public officials through direct contacts defines direct lobbying. Because public officials reside in all three branches of government (legislative, executive, and judiciary) and at all levels of government (national, state, and local), we would expect lobbyists (the people who lobby) to attempt to influence all of them. Indeed, lobbyists are evident wherever public policy and political decisions are made.

In 1987, there were approximately 800 lobbyists in Texas. In 2009, there were 1,690 lobbyists registered with the Texas Ethics Commission, and they were paid somewhere between $167 million and $344 million for their services to approximately 2,900 clients.[23] Many had more than one client. Texas laws requiring lobbyist registration and placing restrictions on lobbying activity have been passed in several legislative sessions since the 1950s. In some respects, the laws are broad and encompassing. Lobbying is defined as efforts to influence the legislative and the executive branches, and the law applies even when the legislature is not in session. Furthermore, individuals who register as lobbyists must indicate their employers, provide information about their expenditures, and indicate the bills or regulations about which they are concerned. Individuals who engage in direct communications with members of the legislature or executive branch of government to influence legislation or administrative action must register as lobbyists if they receive more than $1,000 in any calendar quarter as pay for lobbying, or they spend more than $500 in any calendar quarter for transportation and lodging, food and beverages, gifts, awards, entertainment, or attendance at a political fundraiser or charity event to influence legislation or administrative action.[24] In 1991, the legislature limited the annual amount that a lobbyist could spend on a public official to $500. Pleasure trips and honoraria paid for by lobbyists were also prohibited. In 2001, the legislature established new conflict-of-interest rules for registered lobbyists.

In the late 1980s, two trends characterized lobbyists in Texas. First, there was an increase in the number of contract lobbyists ("hired guns")

Does Austin have its version of K Street? K Street, located in Washington, D.C., is home to some of the most influential lobbyists in the nation's Capital, and for many critics of lobbying, it represents all that is wrong with interest group politics. There are not nearly as many lobbyists in Austin as in Washington, nor are the headquarters of interest groups and lobbyists as concentrated. But more than thirty associations and offices of lobbyists are located in these three buildings, just a few blocks from the Texas Capitol.

Photo courtesy: Courtesy of L. Tucker Gibson

who work for more than one client. Many of these contract lobbyists were former members of the legislative or executive branches. In the 1990s, that trend continued, as more former legislators and bureaucrats took positions representing interest groups. By 2005, seventy ex-legislators were lobbyists in Texas, the state with the most ex-legislators turned lobbyists.[25] The second trend involved greater ethnic and gender diversity among lobbyists. By 1999, the number of women, Hispanics, and African Americans had increased significantly.[26] This trend reflects the changing ethnic and gender composition of government, as well as the tendency for interest groups to assemble a team of lobbyists who are individually assigned to specific legislators or bureaucrats, based on a number of shared characteristics.

According to lobbyists, their principal job involves access to public officials and presenting information about their issues. To present information to legislators or administrators though, lobbyists first need to gain access to public officials. Access comes from the lobbyist's reputation and from the interest group's contributions to the legislator's campaign (a technique that we discuss more fully in the next section of this chapter). Consequently, many lobbyists are former public officials who have established personal relationships with the people to whom they now want access. Furthermore, their previous experience in public office increases their credibility with current legislators and bureaucrats. As lobbyist and former Democratic legislator Bill Messer states, "The real job is to articulate a position and to state a constituency. If you don't have a constituency, then you don't have any influence."[27]

The days when lobbyists could rely on wining and dining public officials in Texas have passed. Currently, lobbyists must rely on their information and integrity. As the late Bill Clayton, former Democratic Texas House Speaker and lobbyist, stated, "Integrity is the one thing that counts more than anything. If you lie to one of the members, you won't ever get a job again."[28] Despite the personal friendships that many lobbyists have cultivated with legislators and administrators, lobbyists have to make their case on its merits. Currently, with increased personal and committee staffs, legislators are less dependent on lobbyists for information than they were twenty years ago; however, lobbyists still provide information that is useful to legislators because it is processed, interpreted, and packaged.

The information provided by lobbyists can be substantive (usually technical) or political. Substantive information provides details about the content of the legislation. Political information indicates how the legislation will affect the legislator's constituents and supporters. Furthermore, lobbyists can provide experts to testify at legislative hearings. Probably the most persuasive information provided by lobbyists involves what other states have done concerning a particular issue and the effects of those measures. For example, if the legislature is considering welfare reform, lobbyists can provide information on what other states have done and the effects of those efforts. Although the lobbyists represent particular interests, the case for or against a bill must be made in terms of good social policy, not the benefits to the particular interest.[29]

From legislative session to session, the interests that lobbyists represent vary according to the legislative agenda, but some interests are always present. Most prevalent are business interests. In 2009, the Texas businesses that employed the greatest number of lobbyists were energy and natural resource companies, which established 1,228 contracts worth as much as $62 million. In second place among businesses were health industry clients with 986 contracts worth up to $41.8 million, and third place belonged to the miscellaneous businesses, which included alcohol and gambling interests and which spent up to $37.6 million on 830 contracts.[30]

The individuals targeted by lobbyists vary. Some lobbyists pursue a "top-down" strategy, concentrating their efforts on the leadership. Because the Texas Speaker of the House and president of the Senate (lieutenant governor) have considerable powers, lobbying the leadership can be productive. However, most lobbyists focus their efforts on the committees with jurisdiction over legislation that affects the interests of the group. Committee chairs receive more attention than committee members, but lobbyists cannot ignore committee members entirely because committee members' votes can be crucial to their success or failure. As their numbers have increased, legislative staff members are also among the lobbyists' targets, particularly those staffers who are considered influential with the legislator. Finally, on the House and Senate floors, lobbyists concentrate their efforts on legislators who are undecided, rather than those who have committed to vote for or against a given measure.[31]

Lobbyists do not confine their activities to the legislature. Interactions between lobbyists and administrators of state agencies and departments are frequent in Texas. A 1982 study of executive agencies in Texas indicated that interest-group-initiated contacts with agencies occurred frequently or very frequently and that half of the contacts were administration-initiated. These contacts usually involve an exchange of information or an attempt to influence policies. For example, an environmental group, such as the Sierra Club, might contact the Texas Commission on Environmental Quality (TCEQ) to relay information about water and air pollution in Texas or to lobby the commission for stronger environmental regulations. Administrative agencies contact interest groups to ascertain the effects of their programs on group members and to solicit input on proposed regulations. Interest groups, on the other hand, contact agencies to obtain information about their programs and to influence the agencies' rules and regulations.

THINKING NATIONALLY

Legislators Who Become Lobbyists

Twenty-five states, including California, New York, and Florida, but not Texas, require a waiting period that ranges from six months to two years before former legislators are allowed to register as lobbyists. This "cooling-off period" is intended to reduce the likelihood that former legislators' political connections will be used to promote their clients' interests. Among the states, Texas has the largest number of former legislators who are lobbyists. In 2009, the Center for Public Integrity identified 63 former legislators working the corridors of the Capitol during the legislative session.

■ What advantages do ex-legislators bring to the practice of lobbying?

■ Should Texas require a waiting period for former legislators who want to register as lobbyists? Why or why not?

■ Does a waiting period violate an individual's right to earn a living, or should a different set of rules apply to former legislators? Explain your answer.

In addition to direct lobbying, interest groups also engage in a form of lobbying called indirect or "grassroots" lobbying. There are actually two forms of indirect lobbying. In the first form, interest groups attempt to activate their members, urging them to contact their representatives or executive officials to influence public policy. For example, the Texas Automobile Dealers Association (TADA) could encourage its members to write or email their representatives about pending legislation and could even provide a sample letter. The second, increasingly common form attempts to change the climate of public opinion, largely through television advertising. Political activists have termed some of these lobbying efforts "Astroturf," because although they look like grassroots political efforts, they are actually manufactured by interest groups. Despite their artificial quality, they offer a semblance of popular support for a position. In 2003, Astroturf interest groups led the efforts to limit tort liability for doctors, hospitals, and insurance companies.

ELECTIONEERING   Electioneering has become a major political activity of interest groups since the mid-1970s. Interest groups maintain that their involvement in political campaigns is to ensure access to public officials. As one lobbyist notes, the price of access is a $1,000 contribution to a senator's campaign and a $250 contribution to a representative's campaign.[32]

Like most states, Texas has experienced a great deal of activity by political action committees (PACs), which are groups formed to solicit funds and then to use those funds to help elect or defeat candidates for public office. In 2008, there were 1,209 general-purpose PACs as well as PACs in other categories registered with the Texas Ethics Commission. By 2010, the total of all PACS exceeded 1,700.[33] The general-purpose PACS reported spending approximately $120 million during the 2007–2008 election cycle, an increase of 21 percent over the previous cycle. Of the

Figure 3.5 *What are the Texas PAC lobbying expenditures by sector?*

Sources: Texans for Public Justice, "Texas PACs: 2008 Election Cycle Spending," April 2009 info.tpj.org/reports/txpac08/pacs2008.pdf.

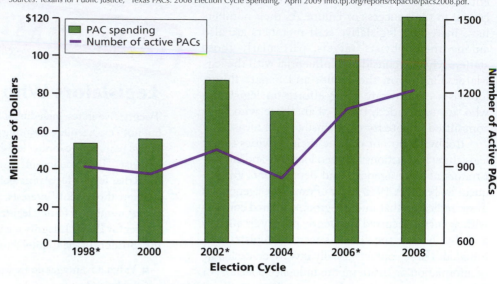

*Gubernatorial election year.

$120 million spent on the 2008 election, business PACs spent $62.7 million (55 percent), ideological and single-issue PACs contributed $50 million (42 percent), and labor PACs contributed $6.3 million (5 percent).[34] (To learn more about PACs in Texas, see Figure 3. 5.)

PACs and individuals do not give money willy-nilly. The general purpose of campaign contributions is to help elect individuals who are sympathetic or receptive to a group's or individual's interests or policy positions. Contributions are generally allocated where they will do the most to further a group's interest. Campaign money flows to legislators, particularly incumbents and committee chairs, whose committees have jurisdiction over policy that affects a group. Although there are some groups that are more inclined to support one party over the other, such as the Texas Trial Lawyers Association, interest groups want winners and access to the decision making process. Candidates of the party in power generally receive the lion's share of PAC funds.

LITIGATION   Practiced extensively by civil rights and environmental groups in the 1960s and 1970s, litigation recently has become a more common weapon in the arsenal of interest-group activities. Much of the increased use of litigation can be attributed to the new judicial federalism, which has made state courts more likely to entertain such lawsuits (see **chapter 6**). The purpose of litigation is to effect or prevent changes in public policy. Litigation can also be used as a delaying tactic to slow change.[35] However, because litigation is expensive, the groups that are most likely to pursue litigation are those who are prosperous enough to afford the expense, and who have been unsuccessful in lobbying and campaigning and therefore pursue the legal route as a last resort.

Elections and Political Campaigns in Texas

⭐ **3.4** . . . **Identify the types of election systems held in Texas, and analyze the role of strategies in political campaigns.**

This section discusses the various types of elections that are conducted in Texas—primary elections, special elections, general elections, and local elections—and examines political campaigns and voting behavior.

Types of Elections

In Texas, elections are frequent, and the ballot tends to be longer than in other states. The legislature has established regular dates for general and special elections, but elections can occur at other times as well.

PRIMARY ELECTIONS   By Texas law, any party whose candidate for governor receives more than 20 percent of the vote must hold a primary election to nominate candidates. Parties whose gubernatorial candidates receive less than 20 percent of the vote can nominate their candidates in primary elections or in party conventions. In Texas, the Democratic Party has held primary elections every two years since 1906. The Republican Party held primaries only five times between 1906 and 1962. Since 1962, the Republican Party has held primaries every two years.

Primaries were established in Texas in 1905 with the passage of the Terrell Election Law, which required a combination of the primary election and a state convention to determine the party's nominees. In 1907, the law was amended to establish a direct primary election, with a plurality vote necessary to secure the nomination. In 1918, the legislature adopted a majority vote requirement to win the primary and established a second, or runoff, primary between the first- and second-place vote-getters if no candidate received a majority of the vote in the first primary.[36] For example, in the 1990 Democratic primary, Jim Mattox, Ann Richards, and Mark White sought the nomination for governor. Because none of the three candidates received a majority of the vote in the primary, the top two vote-getters in the first primary—Ann Richards and Jim Mattox—participated in the second primary.

Although primary elections in Texas are supposedly closed elections, voters can still choose to participate in the opposition party's primary election, making them operate more like open primaries. For example, in the 1994 Democratic gubernatorial primary, incumbent Governor Ann Richards was challenged by Gary Espinosa, a political unknown who received 22 percent of the primary vote. Republicans contended that Espinosa's vote indicated that more than one-fifth of Richards's party members did not support her. However, a county-by-county analysis indicated that a large percentage of Espinosa's vote came from Republicans who "raided" the Democratic primary, attempting to discredit the popularity of the incumbent governor.[37]

Participation in primary elections is usually low in Texas, especially in runoff primaries. However, between 1906 and 1962, a larger percentage of Texas voters participated in the Democratic primaries than participated in the general elections. Participation in the Democratic primaries was high because they often included contests reflecting the ideological split in the party, making the results more important than the general elections, which were almost always won by the Democratic candidates. In 1962, for the first time in Texas history, the number of voters in the general election in a nonpresidential election year exceeded the number of voters in the Democratic primary election. Since then, as participation in the general election has increased, participation in the Republican primary has increased while participation in the Democratic primary has decreased. This change reflects the rise of the Republican Party in Texas and the resulting increase in the importance of the general election.[38] In 2008, the record turnout of 2.8 million voters in the Democratic primary in Texas represented only 16.2 percent of the voting-age population. The almost 1.4 million voters who participated in the Republican primary in Texas that year represented only 7.7 percent of the voting-age population.

Because primary elections are party elections, each party is responsible for administering its own primary election, which includes preparing the ballots, conducting the elections, tabulating and certifying the results, and financing the election. Candidates for statewide office file for positions on the ballot with the state party chair; candidates for county or precinct office file with the county party chair; candidates for district office (e.g., court of appeals, state senator) file with each county party chair in the district.

special election
Election held at a time other than general or primary elections.

SPECIAL ELECTIONS   **Special elections** are held in Texas to fill vacancies in state legislative and U.S. congressional offices, to approve local bond proposals, and if the legislature chooses, to approve amendments to the Texas Constitution (see **chapter 2**). Executive and judicial vacancies are filled by gubernatorial appointment. The dates for special elections are set by the legislature for amendments to the Texas Constitution, by the governor to fill legislative and congressional vacancies, and by the local government to approve bond proposals. The parties do not hold primaries to nominate candidates for special elections; thus, access to the ballot for legislative or congressional vacancies is through filing fees or signatures on petitions. Consequently, the number of candidates in special elections tends to be large. For example, the May 1993 special election for U.S. senator drew twenty-four candidates. Candidates who seek an office in special elections are identified by political party on the ballot, and they must receive a majority of the votes cast to win the office. If no candidate receives a majority of the vote, a runoff election between the top two vote-getters is held one month after the first election.

Participation in special elections is usually extremely low but varies, depending on the issues involved in elections to approve constitutional amendments or the competitiveness among candidates in elections to fill vacancies. Bond-approval elections draw even fewer voters.

GENERAL ELECTIONS   General elections are interparty contests to determine which candidates will hold public office. In Texas, as in most states, the general election is held on the first Tuesday after the first Monday in November of even-numbered years. Since 1974, when Texas adopted a four-year gubernatorial term, the governor and other statewide elected executive officials who also serve four-year terms are elected in nonpresidential years. Other elected officials in Texas, because of the tenure of their offices, may be chosen in presidential or nonpresidential years. In elections for state, district, and county offices, the person who receives the most votes—a plurality— wins the election.

General elections are administered and funded by the state. The secretary of state, the state's chief election official, is responsible for certifying state and district candidates, ensuring that the county clerks certify local candidates and that the county commissioners court appoints the necessary officials to administer the election, and report and maintain the election results.

local election
Election conducted by local governments to elect officials.

LOCAL ELECTIONS   **Local elections** are conducted to elect city councils, mayors, school-board members, and special district boards. Races for city councils, local school boards, and special district governing boards are nonpartisan. Some cities require a majority vote to win, necessitating a runoff election if no candidate receives a majority in the first election. Some local elections generate high voter interest and turnout, but most do not. Recent legislation now permits local governments to cancel an election if no offices are contested, and canceled elections have occurred in numerous communities across the state.

Political Campaigns in Texas

As noted earlier, there are ample (some say too many) opportunities to vote in Texas. How do Texans find out about the candidates, their party affiliations, and their positions on issues of public policy in all of these elections? Political campaigns are supposed to perform that function.

Ideally, election campaigns should offer the electorate an opportunity to compare the candidates and their views on the major issues of public policy. Then, armed with this knowledge, voters should choose among the competing political views and, thereby, determine public policy. Unfortunately, contemporary political campaigns do not meet this standard. As political scientist W. Lance Bennett has noted, contemporary political campaigns are about the three M's—money, media, and marketing.[39] We will consider the influence of these factors in Texas campaigns before analyzing voters' decisions in recent gubernatorial campaigns.

MONEY: THE MOTHER'S MILK OF POLITICS   Everyone knows that contemporary political campaigns are expensive. In the 2006 gubernatorial campaign in Texas, incumbent Governor Rick Perry raised more than $21 million and spent $29.3 million to win reelection.[40] In 2008, candidates who won election to the Texas House raised an average of $337,000 in campaign contributions to the losers' average of $150,000. Incumbent House candidates raised an average of $325,000 while challengers raised an average of $142,000. In 2008, candidates who won Texas Senate contests raised an average of $1,047,000 while losers raised an average of $533,000. Incumbent Texas senators raised an average of $949,000 to their challengers' average of $341,000.[41] Money does not guarantee electoral success, but winning candidates generally outspend their opponents. Why are election campaigns so expensive in Texas, and how do the candidates raise the money necessary to be competitive?

The geographic size of Texas makes money important in electoral campaigns. As journalist Kaye Northcott noted, "Money doesn't just talk in Texas elections: it does tap dances and sings the state anthem in three-part harmony."[42] In 1982, Peyton McKnight, a conservative Democratic state senator, spent $1.5 million of his own fortune attempting to win the Democratic nomination for governor. On the filing deadline for the primary election, a media consultant informed McKnight that another $1 million was necessary to raise his name recognition to a winnable percentage. Rather than ante up, McKnight folded. McKnight was replaced by Buddy Temple, son of Arthur Temple Jr., an East Texas timber magnate. The key to name recognition, as Temple learned in an earlier statewide race for a seat on the Texas Railroad Commission, is television advertising. After spending nearly ten months traveling the state, meeting people and giving speeches, Temple had raised his name recognition from 5 to 12 percent. When his television advertising campaign started, two days yielded an increase from 12 to 24 percent. As Temple noted, "That made a believer out of me. If you don't have the money to make a good showing on television, you don't have a chance in Texas."[43]

Some 110,000 campaign contributions were made in 2008. The lion's share of the contributions fell in the range of $101 to $1,000. However, the 33,000 contributions under $100 accounted for only three percent of the money raised, while "candidates owed 22 percent of their war chests ($21 million) to 702 whopper checks that were each worth $10,000 or more."[44] Moreover, "legislative candidates raised 82 percent of their money ($78 million) from mailing addresses outside the districts that they sought to represent."[45] In addition to contributions from the "fat cats" or large contributors, contributions from groups, through their PACs, have become more important, especially to incumbents in state legislative contests. In 2008, PACs contributed 51 percent of the $24.6 million raised by candidates for the Texas Senate, and individuals contributed 49 percent. PACs contributed 56 percent of the $70 million raised by Texas House candidates, and individuals contributed 44 percent.

Not only is political money important in Texas, but there are also few restrictions placed on its use in political campaigns. In Texas, campaign finance regulation has usually come as a response to blatant, both legal and illegal, excesses by campaign contributors. One significant reform was passed in 1973 in the wake of the Sharpstown scandal (see **chapter 4**). However, even the scandal did not produce strong legislation. The law merely required candidates to designate a campaign treasurer and to report contributions and expenditures. There were numerous loopholes in the legislation, such as the requirement that only "opposed" candidates must report contributions and expenditures.[46] After poultry producer Lonnie "Bo" Pilgrim passed out checks for $10,000 to Texas state senators during debate on workers' compensation legislation in 1989, the legislature, at the urging of Governor Ann Richards, attempted to strengthen the regulation of campaign finance in 1991. The legislature created the Ethics Commission, which now receives the contribution and expenditure reports for candidates for state office, and it did close some of the loopholes in the previous law. In 1999, the legislature adopted a law requiring candidates for statewide offices, the state legislature, and many district offices to file their contribution and expenditure reports electronically. However, there are still no limits on contributions by individuals or PACs to legislative and executive candidates in Texas. Contribution limits have been imposed on judges and judicial candidates, and the periods during which they can raise campaign money are restricted.

MEDIA: LINKING THE CANDIDATES AND THE VOTERS

Although politicians once believed that campaigning should be conducted personally and should involve face-to-face contacts with the voters at campaign rallies, technology has made personal contacts less effective. Campaign communications are now conducted through the media. This is especially true for statewide political campaigns, but it is also becoming more common in district and local campaigns as well. In a state the size of Texas, candidates can effectively reach potential voters through the state's nineteen media markets. As political consultant Mark McKinnon noted, "It's impossible to effectively communicate with voters in Texas any other way but television. TV is the next best thing to being there. TV allows the candidate to be in everybody's living room, up close and personal."[47] And, increasingly, campaigns make use of Web sites and blogs. (To learn more about developing name recognition and exposure to voters, see Politics Now: Texas Democrat Is Striving to Make His Name Known).

As more people have become detached from their partisan affiliations, party leaders have lost the skills necessary to organize campaigns capable of electing candidates to public office. Thus, candidates have turned to political consultants, specialists in the modern campaign technology, to plan and organize their campaigns.[48] The specialized knowledge possessed by campaign consultants has led to the third component of contemporary campaigns—marketing.

MARKETING: SELLING THE CANDIDATE

The transition from party-centered to candidate-centered campaigns was facilitated by political consultants. At first, political consultants offered candidates only their technical expertise, probably gained from experience in commercial marketing or advertising. However, as candidates' dependence on media and the techniques of commercial advertising increased, political consultants in Texas expanded their influence in the campaign, as well as the specialization of their services to candidates. Despite the proliferation of consultants and their specialization, the most important consultants operate in the area of opinion polling and media services.

Candidates use several techniques to assess the public's concerns and desires, but public opinion polls have become the most commonly used technique. The earliest and most comprehensive opinion survey is the benchmark poll to assess the public's general mood, how readily people recognize the candidate's name, and the public's perception of the candidate's strengths and weaknesses, as well as the strengths and weaknesses of the candidate's likely opponent or opponents. The results of the benchmark poll are used to design the campaign's main themes and to establish the candidate's image. As the campaign progresses, tracking polls are used to determine the effectiveness of the campaign's theme and advertising, to detect shifts in voters' preferences among various segments of the population, and to evaluate changing images of the candidates. Focus groups or small discussion groups of voters are used by pollsters to provide qualitative information about campaign hot-button issues, candidates' performances in televised debates, and campaign ads.

The most important campaign consultants provide media services to their candidates. These media consultants furnish a number of campaign services, such as the creation of the media messages and the coordination of

How do candidates make themselves known to voters? Texas is such a vast state that the only real way for candidates to make themselves known to voters is through the media. However, candidates must still take opportunities to meet with voters face-to-face on the campaign trail. Here, 2010 Democratic gubernatorial candidate Bill White greets voters in Huntsville, Texas, at the Walker County Democratic Headquarters. White lost the 2010 election to incumbent Rick Perry.

Photo courtesy: Bob Daemmrich Photography, Inc.

POLITICS NOW

| WORLD | NATION | LOCAL | **POLITICS** | OPINION | HEALTH & SCIENCE | ARTS | SPORTS | LEISURE |

Texas Democrat Is Striving to Make His Name Known

By James C. McKinley Jr.

May 1, 2010
New York Times
www.nytimes.com

Midland, Tex.—On the same day *Newsweek* magazine anointed Gov. Rick Perry on its cover as a conservative icon, his Democratic opponent, Bill White, was slogging through small-scale campaign stops in a Republican stronghold, needling the governor, saying he paid more attention to his career than to bread-and-butter issues like schools.

"We need a governor more interested in the state's future than his political future," Mr. White said to about 100 curious oil company lawyers and executives at the Petroleum Club.

But after the stump speech, a local lawyer piped up with the question on everyone's mind. How was Mr. White going to beat a well-known and well-financed Republican incumbent like Mr. Perry in a state where a Democrat has not won in 20 years?

"I'm going to get more votes than he does." . . . "So what's my strategy?"

By all accounts, Mr. White has his work cut out for him . . . trying to make his name better known and to define himself as a pro-business, fiscal conservative palatable to Republicans and independents.

The match-up between Mr. Perry and Mr. White this fall promises not only to test the depth of the conservative backlash against President Obama, but also to shed light on just how Republican the state has become. . . .

Conventional wisdom holds that this is a bad year to run as a Democrat in a state like Texas. Since the mid-1990s, Republican candidates have started off with a 10-point advantage. . . . What's more, most political scientists and strategists say the pendulum is swinging back against the Democrats after Mr. Obama's victory in 2008.

The backlash among staunch conservatives, who are angry about the bailout of banks and deficit spending to create jobs, has given rightwing politicians [an advantage]. . . . Indeed, Mr. Perry has actively courted disaffected voters angry with Washington, appearing with Sarah Palin and Glenn Beck and building Mr. Perry's national profile.

Yet . . . Mr. White has credentials as a fiscal conservative, having cut property tax rates in Houston, where he was a three-term mayor. And in Houston, he proved that he can win over Republicans and independents. It is also difficult for an opponent to pigeonhole Mr. White on social issues—he favors abortion rights but opposes gun control and supports the death penalty.

And there is a feeling among some moderate Republicans and independents that Mr. Perry has moved too far to the right . . . by expressing sympathy for secessionists last year [and supporting] . . . religious conservatives on the state school board.

Mr. White . . . hits those notes often on the campaign trail . . . [while charging that] the governor did nothing to [combat] . . . high school [drop out rates] or [skyrocketing] tuition at state universities. . . .

Critical Thinking Questions

1. Given the recent record of Republican dominance of statewide races, why would Bill White run for governor in 2010?
2. What appears to be the core strategy used by White?
3. What appears to be the core strategy used by Perry?

those messages with the campaign theme. The importance of media messages, particularly negative ads, was demonstrated in the 2002 gubernatorial campaign between Rick Perry and Tony Sanchez, when Perry commercials accused Sanchez's Tesoro Savings and Loan of laundering money for drug cartels and contributing to the death of a Drug Enforcement Agency (DEA) agent.[49]

The ultimate goal in a political campaign is winning, which requires that eligible voters who support the candidate participate in the election and vote for the candidate. Thus, our attention in the next section shifts to the factors that influence the voters' decisions.

The Voters' Decisions

In an election, the potential voter faces two decisions. The first decision is whether to participate. The second decision, which applies only if the person has chosen to participate, involves which candidates to support. In Texas, fewer than half of the age-eligible voters (people eighteen years of age and older) participate in presidential elections, and fewer than one-third participate in gubernatorial elections. Why is voter turnout—the percentage of voting-age people who vote—so low in Texas, ranking last among the fifty states in 2008?

VOTER TURNOUT   Like most decisions concerning political participation, the decision to vote is the result of a calculation that weighs the costs of voting against the benefits of voting. People vote when they believe that voting will yield benefits.

Voting is generally perceived as requiring little effort, but it does involve costs. For example, a voter must find out when the election is held and where the polling place is located, take the time to travel to the polling place, and most importantly, meet the legal requirements to vote. Until the mid-1960s, a number of legal restrictions in Texas, including a poll tax and a white-only Democratic primary, made voting costly, especially for particular groups or categories of Texans. The legal restrictions fell most heavily on the poor, the uninformed, Hispanics, and African Americans.

In contemporary Texas, the legal requirements for voting are minimal. The nominal requirements include U.S. citizenship, being eighteen years of age or older, residency in the state, and registration. The only people who are prohibited from voting are the "mentally incompetent" (as declared by a court of law) and convicted felons who have not completed their sentence, including any term of incarceration, parole, supervision, or probation. Thus, the only real legal barrier to voting is registration, which in Texas is relatively easy. A person who wants to vote must register at least thirty days prior to the election. After registering, a person is permanently registered and will receive a new registration certificate every two years unless he or she moves during that period, which necessitates completing a new registration form. However, forms are readily available and are printed in both Spanish and English on postage-free postcards.

In 1991, the Texas Legislature adopted a motor-voter registration system, which allows a person who is obtaining a driver's license or a Department of Public Safety (DPS) identification card the opportunity to register to vote at the same time. Also, registration forms were made even more accessible by placing them in public buildings. The effect of the motor-voter registration system has been to increase significantly the percentage of the population that is registered to vote—from 65 percent before motor-voter in the 1980s to a high of 85 percent in 2000. Since then, registration has fluctuated between 75 and 80 percent.

Why was there so much opposition to a poll tax of $1.50? The poll tax, effective in 1904, was a requirement for voting in Texas until it was eliminated by a constitutional amendment. To register, the voter would pay a tax of $1.50 to $1.75—a hefty sum in 1904—at the courthouse, a tactic designed to prevent the poor and minorities from voting.

Photo courtesy: Courtesy of L. Tucker Gibson

The Texas Legislature reduced the cost of voting with the adoption of early voting in 1987. Presently, early voting extends over a two-week period, commencing seventeen days before the election and continuing through the fourth day prior to the election. In most urban counties, there are numerous permanent and mobile early voting sites, such as supermarkets, schools, and churches. The effect of early voting on turnout has been negligible. Early voting has had an impact on the political parties' get-out-the-vote efforts, moving the start of activities to an earlier date and requiring an adjustment in organization and volunteer-recruitment schedules.[50] In the 2006 gubernatorial election, 39 percent of the votes were cast during the early voting period. A comparison of early voters and Election Day voters indicated that early voters are more partisan, older, more conservative, more likely to be male, and require less mobilization than Election Day voters. Candidates can allocate their resources to turn out their core supporters early and then concentrate their campaign efforts on those voters who require stronger issue and candidate appeals to obtain their votes on Election Day.[51]

To increase the ease of actually casting a vote, Texas has been introducing electronic voting systems. But, questions have been raised about electronic voting. (To learn more about voting systems, see Join the Debate: Are Electronic Voting Systems Better than Paper Ballots?) Nevertheless, although the costs of voting have been reduced significantly in Texas over the past thirty years, a large percentage of Texans still fail to vote. To complete an explanation of voter turnout, we need to consider the benefits of voting.

The most obvious benefit of voting involves election outcomes—the party and candidates who win the offices contested in the election. Although the results of elections have significant effects on people's lives, an individual does not have to vote in an election to receive the benefits. The benefits, in terms of the election outcomes, are collective. That means the potential benefit of election results are available to nonvoters as well as to voters. Consequently, the value of a person's vote is not equal to the benefits derived from a given election outcome but to the probability that his or her individual vote will decide a given election. Therefore, the value of voting in most elections is quite small, and it raises questions about why anyone would bother to vote, since there are some costs involved. Apparently, the answer lies in the fact that people derive benefits from voting that are not dependent on deciding the outcome of an election.

In other words, there are selective benefits associated with voting. According to political scientist Ruy Teixeira, the selective benefits are basically expressive, which means that the person must find his or her vote meaningful.[52] For some people, voting expresses a general commitment to a political party, a social category (ethnicity, gender, or social class), or society in general. These benefits are largely symbolic because they are not directly connected to which candidate wins the election. For instance, an individual may find meaning in his or her commitment to the working class and may use the vote to express that commitment. For other people, voting expresses a concern about the election's effect on who holds public office and public policy. These benefits are instrumental because they express a desire to achieve certain results through the election of a particular candidate or political party. An individual who votes because he or she strongly supports the policy goals of a certain candidate would be an example.

A connection to politics—which is achieved through an identification with a political party, through an involvement in public affairs, and through a sense that government is responsive to people's demands—makes voting meaningful and influences the decision to vote. Many Texans lack a strong connection to politics for several reasons. First, as noted earlier, party identification is weak in Texas. The growing strength of the Republican Party in Texas and the resulting increase in electoral competition have probably increased some people's connection to politics, but there are still many Texans who do not identify with a political party. Second, feelings that the government is responsive to popular demands are low in Texas. Finally, involvement in public affairs—indicated by campaign interest, reading campaign news stories, watching campaign television, and following government and public affairs—is low in Texas.

Voter turnout in gubernatorial elections in nonpresidential years over the past century has exhibited several trends. After reaching its zenith in the 1890s, when more than 75 percent of the eligible voters voted, voter turnout in Texas fell precipitously

THINKING NATIONALLY

Same-Day Voter Registration

Ten states—Idaho, Iowa, Maine, Minnesota, Montana, New Hampshire, North Carolina, Washington D.C., Wisconsin, and Wyoming—used same-day or Election Day voter registration in 2008. In other words, an eligible citizen can register and cast a ballot on the day of the election. Some form of convenience voting is used by many other states, including extended early voting and no-excuse absentee voting. South Dakota does not require voters to register.

In states with same-day voter registration, voter turnout averaged 71 percent of the voting-eligible population (VEP) in the 2008 presidential election; the national average was 62 percent of the VEP. On the other hand, eight states that required pre-election registration reported turnout rates between 68 and 70 percent. In Texas, the VEP turnout was approximately 55 percent.

- Should Texas adopt same-day voter registration?
- What benefits, in addition to higher turnout rates, might result from same-day voter registration?
- What problems might same-day voter registration create?

Join the DEBATE | Are Electronic Voting Systems Better than Paper Ballots?

Like other states, Texas began eliminating punch-card voting systems and lever machines to comply with the Help America Vote Act (HAVA) of 2002. Texas also decided there should be at least one direct-recording electronic (DRE) voting system at each polling place to accommodate disabled voters. However, some experts have raised questions about the security of electronic voting.

In the 2008 election, Texas's counties employed three election systems for voting. A total of 176 counties used direct recording electronic systems as their primary method of voting. Optical scanning of ballots was used in 61 counties, and paper ballots were used in 73 counties. All counties were required under the Americans with Disabilities Act (ADA) to provide voting devices for those with disabilities.

As more governments across the nation adopt electronic voting, problems and security issues have surfaced. Isolated examples of hardware and software problems have been reported in every election cycle. The potential for "hacking" elections systems also remains. Without a paper trail of each person's vote, election counts cannot be verified or validated. Electronic voting is not going away, but are electronic voting systems better than paper ballots?

To develop an ARGUMENT FOR electronic voting systems, think about how:

- **Texans elect many officials—from the governor to the precinct constable.** How can an electronic voting system reduce confusion over the ballot format or "style" and guide the voter from office to office? In what ways does electronic voting eliminate problems with mechanical voting machines, punch cards, or optical-scan ballots?
- **The length of the ballot often leads to voter mistakes.** How will electronic voting systems prevent over-voting (voting for more than one candidate for an office) and warn voters of under-voting (not voting for a candidate for an office)?
- **Accurate and rapid tabulation of votes is essential to the legitimacy of elections.** In what ways is the computer much more accurate than paper ballots in terms of the tabulation of votes? How does using computers increase the legitimacy of elections?

To develop an ARGUMENT AGAINST electronic voting systems, think about how:

- **Electronic voting systems do not provide an avenue for verifying votes.** If the outcome of an election is in question, how is a recount conducted to verify votes without a corresponding paper trail? In what ways will electronic voting lead to an increased number of disputed elections?
- **Electronic voting is not secure.** With so many different governments across the state responsible for administering elections, how will the security of electronic voting be maintained? In what ways is it possible and even likely that sophisticated hackers will penetrate the security of election systems and distort the actual vote?
- **Computers are prone to hardware, software, and virus problems.** Are there backup systems available to deal with such problems when voting occurs in a 12-hour period of time? What happens when an entire system goes down?

Photo courtesy: Courtesy of L. Tucker Gibson

How has HAVA increased voting opportunities?
Electronic voting machines are mandated for the disabled. Electronic voting is now prevalent in heavily populated Texas counties.

for the next decade, finally stabilizing at approximately 24 percent of the eligible voters by 1910. In the 1920s, voter turnout dipped again, falling into the low teens and remaining there for the next two decades. During the 1950s and 1960s, voter turnout rose to a twentieth-century high of nearly 35 percent in 1970, before falling into the low 20 percent range during the 1970s. Voter turnout increased during the 1980s, but it never exceeded 30 percent until the 1990s. (To learn more about voter turnout, see Analyzing Visuals: Voter Turnout in Texas.)

Several factors, involving both the effort required to vote and the benefits of voting, have contributed to the variation in Texas voter turnout. The initial decline after the 1890s is partly due to the establishment of the poll tax in 1904; however, voter turnout had already declined to approximately 40 percent by the general election in 1902. In 1904, a presidential election year, voter turnout continued its decline to approximately 35 percent. Thus, the increased costs of voting are probably less important than a reduction in benefits in explaining the decline. After 1896, the Populist Party was no longer a threat to Democratic Party dominance. As Texas returned to a one-party Democratic state, general elections became less competitive, and voter turnout declined.

ANALYZING VISUALS

Voter Turnout in Texas

The figure shows voter turnout in Texas for gubernatorial, presidential, and legislative elections from 1958 through 2010. Review the chart, and then answer the questions.

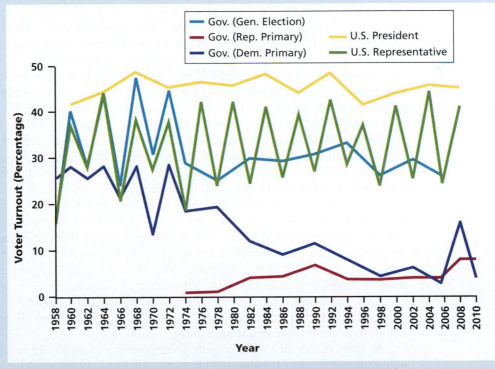

Sources: For 1958–1968, Clifton McCleskey, Allan K. Butcher, Daniel E. Farlow, and J. Pat Stephens, *The Government and Politics of Texas,* 7th ed. (Boston: Little, Brown, 1982), 41; for 1970–2004, Secretary of State, "Turnout and Voter Registration, 1970–current," www.sos.state.tx.us; authors' calculation.

■ In which election was voter turnout the highest? The lowest?
■ What do you think explains the differences in voter turnout for different types of elections? What might explain the changes in voter turnout in gubernatorial general elections since 1972?
■ Why do you think voter turnout showed no significant spikes when Texans were running for president?

The changing composition of the electorate also affected voter turnout. The decline in the percentage of voter turnout during the 1920s and the 1970s is associated with the enfranchisement of women and young people, respectively. With the ratification of the Nineteenth Amendment, extending suffrage to women, the percentage of voter turnout decreased as the number of eligible voters nearly doubled. Similarly, when the minimum voting age was reduced from twenty-one to eighteen in 1972, a large number of former nonvoters were enfranchised, and voter turnout, as a percentage of eligible voters, declined. However, when groups who have been disenfranchised have their right to vote restored, as when legal restrictions on voting are removed, voter turnout increases, as it did during the 1950s and 1960s, after the white primary and the poll tax were eliminated.

Undoubtedly, making voting easier increases voter turnout, but high rates of turnout cannot be achieved solely by minimizing the effort required to vote; people must be motivated by the benefits of voting. During the 1890s, political campaigns in Texas were party-centered. Party workers and their supporters marched strong partisans to the polls. The parties were supported by a partisan press, and they distributed campaign literature to a politically active citizenry. Partisan politics occupied a central role in people's lives, both as a social activity and as a statement of personal identity. Obviously, one cannot recreate the society or the politics of the late nineteenth century, but efforts can be made to connect people with politics by providing the institutional means for people to find meaning in political participation. On the other hand, because of attempts to reduce the effort required to vote in Texas, the percentage of Texans who are registered to vote has increased. However, early voting procedures have not increased turnout, as only 45.5 percent of the age-eligible Texans voted in the 2008 presidential election, and only 26.4 percent voted in the 2006 gubernatorial election.

THE VOTE CHOICE: PARTIES, ISSUES, AND CANDIDATES   During the entire nineteenth and first part of the twentieth century, the vote choice was party-oriented. Most voters practiced straight-ticket voting, voting for the same party's candidates for all national, state, and local offices. Currently, the vote choice is more office-oriented and person-oriented, meaning that the basis for the vote choice varies by political office and is more dependent on issues and candidates. Thus, more voters engage in split-ticket voting, voting for some candidates from one party and some from another.

Most explanations of the vote choice focused on three psychological factors: party identification, issues, and candidate characteristics. Party identification was seen as providing stability in the voter's choice, and assessments of candidate characteristics were considered primarily responsible for the variation in the voter's choice. Issues were considered less important. Based on an analysis of voters' choices in presidential elections, the authors of *The American Voter* implied that vote choices in other elections were motivated by the same factors. However, recent changes in electoral behavior indicate that partisanship is no longer able to structure the vote because of declining partisanship in the electorate and declining strength of partisanship among those members of the electorate who are partisan.[53] Because of the electorate's greater volatility, predicting and explaining the vote choice have become more difficult. Nonetheless, a comparison of the 1986 and 2002 gubernatorial elections in Texas helps clarify the relative importance of the factors.

In 1986, an incumbent Democratic Texas governor, Mark White, was seeking a second term over former Governor Bill Clements, a Republican whom White had unseated four years earlier. Clements won the Republican primary handily, while White won the Democratic primary with only 53 percent of the vote over five unknown and poorly financed candidates. In the general election, which Clements won, party identification favored White, the Democrat. But White won only 82 percent of the votes of Democratic Party identifiers, while Clements won 92 percent of the Republican vote. Also, among those demographic categories that traditionally support Democratic candidates (low- and moderate-income voters, African Americans, and Hispanics), voter turnout was lower, and support was less enthusiastic than it had been in the gubernatorial election of 1982.[54] Finally, among reasons given for their vote, 20 percent of White's voters and a mere 4 percent of Clements's voters noted party loyalty.

For a large number of voters in 1986, the most important factors were the candidates themselves. The largest percentage of Clements's voters (38 percent) indicated that they voted for Clements as a vote against White. Almost a fifth (19 percent) of White's voters indicated that they were voting against Clements.[55] As one study demonstrated, voters weigh candidates on several characteristics, including personal qualities, integrity, reliability, charisma, and competence.[56] Of these dimensions, competence is usually the most important and was the basis for the vote against White. Of course, the judgments of the candidates' competence included some content issues. Voters seemed less confident in White's ability to deal with the fiscal situation, which included an estimated $5.3 billion revenue deficit for the next biennium, especially because he had presided over large tax and fee increases during his tenure. Also, the education reforms that White had championed, especially the "no pass, no play" restrictions for students and a one-time competency test for public-school teachers, hurt White in many areas of the state, especially in rural West Texas and the Texas Panhandle. Teachers were angry over the competency test, even though White had delivered on a pay raise he had promised them during his 1982 campaign. More than anything else, the 1986 election demonstrated that although party labels were still important to at least a portion of the electorate, "the better candidate with the better issues and the better campaign can win in most areas regardless of party label."[57]

In 2002, Rick Perry was seeking election as governor after succeeding George W. Bush, who resigned as governor to become U.S. president. Perry was unopposed in the Republican gubernatorial primary. In the Democratic primary, Tony Sanchez, a wealthy Laredo businessman, defeated former Texas Attorney General Dan Morales. It was the first head-to-head race between two Hispanics for a gubernatorial nomination in Texas, and it was a highly contentious race.

In 2002, the Republican Party held an advantage among Texans in party identification, and the advantage was even greater among voters. Among their respective party identifiers, both nominees did well in the general election, but many more Democrats than Republicans defected to the opposition candidate.

Perry and Sanchez voters differed on the issues that were most important to them. Perry voters were more likely to be concerned about taxes, while Sanchez voters were more concerned about the state of the economy, education, and health care. According to Fox News Election Day polls, voters were equally divided on the factor that most determined their vote choice for governor (47 percent cited positions on the issues, and 47 percent cited personal character and experience). Only 23 percent identified political party as the basis for their vote choice. Whatever voters' reasons, Perry won.[58]

TOWARD REFORM: Recent Proposed Changes in Elections and Campaigns

⭐ **3.5** . . . **Evaluate how recent reforms have impacted political parties, interest groups, elections, and campaigns.**

In 2007, the 80th legislature considered several reforms in campaign and election procedures. One of the more significant, though unsuccessful, proposals would have moved the primary election date from the first Tuesday in March to the first Tuesday in February. In 2008, the front-loading of presidential primaries and caucuses

The Living Constitution

(a) The following classes of persons shall not be allowed to vote in this State:

    (1) persons under 18 years of age;

    (2) persons who have been determined mentally incompetent by a court, subject to such exceptions as the Legislature may make; and

    (3) persons convicted of any felony, subject to such exceptions as the Legislature may make.

(b) The legislature shall enact laws to exclude from the right of suffrage persons who have been convicted of bribery, perjury, forgery, or other high crimes.

—ARTICLE 6, SECTION 1

The Texas Constitution establishes the exclusions from the right to vote in Article 6, section 1. Of the various disqualifications, the provisions relating to convicted criminals have the greatest impact. The prohibitions on voting by criminals have appeared in every Texas Constitution. In 1836, the Constitution of the Republic disqualified persons "convicted of bribery, perjury, or other high crimes and misdemeanors." The 1845 Constitution changed the language slightly to prohibit voting by persons "convicted of bribery, perjury, forgery, or other high crimes." The same language appeared in the Texas Constitutions of 1861, 1866, and 1869. The Constitution of 1869 also disqualified all felons. Although the convention delegates in 1875 debated which crimes should result in disqualification, they retained the felony disqualification. However, they did allow the legislature to make exceptions.[a]

The legislature originally allowed no exceptions, and convicted felons were barred from voting for life. However, in 1983, the legislature allowed convicted felons to vote five years after completing their sentences. Later, the waiting period was reduced to two years. In 1997, the legislature adopted the current provision, which excludes from the disqualification anyone who has not been convicted of a felony, or if convicted, has completed any sentence resulting from the conviction, which includes any incarceration, probation, parole, or supervision. Also, a person is not disqualified if he or she has been pardoned or "otherwise released from the resulting disability to vote." Consequently, without a pardon, convicted felons must complete the sentence imposed by the court before they are eligible to vote.[b]

In Texas, the number of convicted felons who are disenfranchised approaches 500,000 adults. According to political scientist Michael McDonald of George Mason University, there were 172,116 prisoners, 431,967 probationers, and 101,916 parolees in Texas in 2008. Of those, McDonald estimates that 490,016 are ineligible felons, the largest number in any state in the United States.[c]

CRITICAL THINKING QUESTIONS

1. What arguments can you offer for restoring a convicted felon's right to vote after a set period of time?
2. Does this issue of restoring a felon's right to vote have any implications for either of the two political parties' electoral base?
3. Does this ineligible population of felons reduce the political influence of any key segments of the state's population? Explain your answer.

[a]George D. Braden, *The Constitution of Texas: An Annotated and Comparative Analysis*, vol. 2 (Austin: Texas Legislative Council, 1977), 483.
[b]Juan Castillo, "Did Your Time? Groups Want You to Vote," *Austin American-Statesman* (April 26, 2004): A1.
[c]Michael McDonald, 2008 General Election Turnout Rates, United States Elections Project, George Mason University, elections.gmu.edu-Turnout_2008G.html.

increased, resulting in more than twenty states scheduling their delegate selection contests on February 5, 2008 (the earliest date allowed by party rules). With so many states holding contests on that date, most political observers thought that the nomination contests would be over before Texas's primary election in March.[59] However, when Hillary Clinton and Barack Obama emerged from the February round of primaries and caucuses with nearly identical delegate counts, the Texas Democratic primary, held on its unchanged date in March, gained added significance.

Additional proposed election changes included legislation to notify former prisoners when their voting rights were restored and a bill to require voters to produce a form of photo identification at the polls. The notification of former prisoners was vetoed by Governor Perry, who stated that he found it "unseemly that the state would make a greater effort to register former inmates to vote than we would any other group of citizens in this state."[60] (To learn more about the issue of convicted felons and voting, see The Living Constitution: Article 6, Section 1.)

The voter photo identification proposal, a major priority of Republicans who insisted it was necessary to guard against voter fraud, was one of the most divisive partisan issues of the session. Democrats opposed it because they believed it was designed to discourage elderly and minority voters, who likely would support Democratic candidates, from going to the polls. In 2009, the Republican Senate majority voted to bypass the two-thirds rule to pass a similar bill, but Democrats used delaying, parliamentary tactics to kill the measure in the House that session (see **chapter 4**).

Successful reforms involved general-purpose PACs and corporate contributions. One reform requires general-purpose PACs that accept large contributions or make sizeable expenditures shortly before an election to report them before the election occurs, a requirement that already pertained to candidates for public office. Previously, PACs did not report these contributions until mid-January, long after the election was over. This measure promotes greater transparency and accountability in campaign contributions and expenditures. Also, the ban on corporate campaign contributions to political candidates was amended to ensure that the ban applied to corporations organized under the Texas For-Profit Corporation Law and Texas Nonprofit Corporation Law.

What Should I Have LEARNED?

Now that you have read this chapter, you should be able to:

⭐ **3.1 Trace the gradual evolution of political parties, interest groups, elections, and campaigns in Texas, p. 64.**

Any semblance of a two-party system was aborted by the Civil War and Reconstruction. One-party politics dominated by the Democrats followed Reconstruction until the mid-1980s. In the state's early history, there were aggregations of interests centering around a few sectors of the economy, but the contemporary complex, diversified interest group system is a product of the middle part of the twentieth century. Continued changes in the state's election system have expanded the electorate, increased the variety of elections, and produced changes in voting behavior and party identification.

⭐ **3.2 Differentiate among the three components of political parties in Texas, and identify their functions in the state's party system, p. 65.**

The party organizations in Texas include a formal organization and a functional organization. At all levels,

the Republican Party's organization is stronger than the Democratic Party's organization. Since 1952, the party in the electorate has become more Republican, less Democratic, and more independent in its party attachments. Partisan changes in the 1980s and 1990s made the parties in Texas more like their national counterparts. Although some political scientists maintain that Texas has experienced a partisan realignment, others claim that Texans have dealigned. The party in government in Texas is very weak.

⭐ **3.3 Categorize the types of interest groups in Texas and the methods they use to influence elections and public policy in Texas, p. 77.**

Interest groups—representing business groups and trade associations, professional associations, labor groups, racial and ethnic groups, and public-interest groups—engage in a variety of political activities, such as direct and indirect lobbying, electioneering, and litigation. The most powerful groups represent business and professional interests.

★ 3.4 Identify the types of election systems held in Texas, and analyze the role of strategies in political campaigns, p. 82.

Primary elections, general elections, special elections, and local elections are conducted to nominate candidates, select public officials, fill vacancies in elected offices, and vote on constitutional amendments and local bond issues. Contemporary political campaigns in Texas are candidate-centered affairs, dominated by the three M's—money, media, and marketing. Voting decisions include a decision to vote, which requires registration, and a choice among candidates, which requires some information about the candidates. Although the costs of voting have been reduced significantly over the past twenty-five years, voter turnout remains low in Texas. Vote choices are less predictable in contemporary Texas than in the past.

★ 3.5 Evaluate how recent reforms have impacted political parties, interest groups, elections, and campaigns, p. 93.

The 80th Legislature attempted unsuccessfully to move the Texas primary elections to early February. The failure to move the primary, which most political pundits criticized, actually benefited Texas Democrats in 2008. Another proposed change, which also failed in both the 80th and 81st legislatures, would have required voters to produce a form of photo identification before casting ballots. One reform that passed requires PACs to more quickly report large contributions that were made close to an election date.

Test Yourself: Voting and Participating: Political Parties, Interest Groups, and Elections

★ 3.1 Trace the gradual evolution of political parties, interest groups, elections, and campaigns in Texas, p. 64.

From the end of Reconstruction to the mid-1980s, the state's political system is best characterized as
  A. a multiparty system.
  B. a two-party system.
  C. a no-party system.
  D. a Republican-dominated system.
  E. a Democratic-dominated system.

★ 3.2 Differentiate among the three components of political parties in Texas, and identify their functions in the state's party system, p. 65.

Realignment, or a profound change in partisan attachments, occurred
  A. rapidly, in a critical election.
  B. when the Voting Rights Act was extended to Texas in 1975.
  C. as a result of the sharp divisions over the New Deal.
  D. slowly or over time in what is called secular realignment.
  E. when Rick Perry was elected governor.

★ 3.3 Categorize the types of interest groups in Texas and the methods they use to influence elections and public policy in Texas, p. 77.

When an interest group attempts to influence the policy process by mobilizing or activating its membership, it is engaged in
  A. stealth lobbying.
  B. surreptitious lobbying.
  C. indirect lobbying.
  D. direct lobbying.
  E. defensive lobbying.

★ 3.4 Identify the types of election systems held in Texas, and analyze the role of strategies in political campaigns, p. 82.

The elections that generate the highest level of voter turnout in Texas are
  A. hotly contested local elections.
  B. hotly contested primary elections.
  C. presidential elections.
  D. controversial constitutional amendment elections.
  E. gubernatorial elections.

★ 3.5 Evaluate how recent reforms have impacted political parties, interest groups, elections, and campaigns, p. 93.

Democrats opposed the voter photo identification proposal introduced in the 80th and 81st legislatures because
  A. it violated the civil rights of voters.
  B. it was costly and time consuming in its administration.
  C. it imposed an excessive hardship on voters.
  D. it would discourage elderly and minority voters.
  E. it would exclude former felons from voting.

Essay Questions

1. What explanations can you give for the partisan realignment that occurred in Texas during the last part of the twentieth century?
2. How do you account for the low rates of participation in most Texas elections?
3. Interest groups and political parties often engage in similar activities—candidate recruitment, electioneering, and campaign fund-raising—but there are significant differences in their functions. What are these differences?
4. How do you account for the ever-increasing costs of political campaigns in Texas?
5. What are some of the factors that shape a voter's decision about a specific candidate?

Key Terms

county chairperson, p. 68
county convention, p. 67
county executive committee, p. 68
local election, p. 84
permanent party organization, p. 68

precinct chairperson, p. 68
precinct convention, p. 66
special election, p. 84
state convention, p. 68
state executive committee, p. 68

state party chairperson, p. 69
state senatorial district convention,
 p. 67
temporary party organization,
 p. 65

To Learn More on Voting and Participating: Political Parties, Interest Groups, and Elections

In the Library

Berry, Jeffrey M., and Clyde Wilcox. *The Interest Group Society*, 4th ed. New York, NY: Pearson Longman, 2007.

Black, Earl, and Merle Black. *The Rise of Southern Republicans*. Cambridge, MA: Harvard University Press, 2002.

Bridges, Kenneth. *Twilight of the Texas Democrats: The 1978 Governor's Race*. College Station: Texas A&M University Press, 2008.

Davidson, Chandler. *Race and Class in Texas Politics*. Princeton, NJ: Princeton University Press, 1990.

Davidson, Chandler, and Bernard Grofman, eds. *Quiet Revolution in the South: The Impact of the Voting Rights Act, 1965–1990*. Princeton, NJ: Princeton University Press, 1994.

Goodwyn, Lawrence. *Texas Oil, American Dreams: A Study of the Texas Independent Producers and Royalty Owners Association*. Austin: Texas State Historical Association, 1996.

Grantham, Dewey W. *The Life and Death of the Solid South: A Political History*. Lexington, KY: University Press of Kentucky, 1988.

Green, George Norris. *The Establishment in Texas Politics: The Primitive Years, 1938–1957*. Westport, CT: Greenwood, 1979.

Hadley, Charles D., and Lewis Bowman, eds. *Southern State Party Organizations and Activists*. Westport, CT: Praeger, 1995.

Hardin, Stephen and Angus McBride. *The Alamo 1836: Santa Anna's Texas Campaign*. Oxford: Osprey Publishing, 2002.

Hobby, William P. *The Power of the Texas Governor*. Austin: University of Texas Press, 2009.

Martin, Roscoe. *The People's Party in Texas: A Study in Third-Party Politics*. Austin: University of Texas Press, 1970.

Murray, Richard, and Sam Attlesey. "Texas: Republicans Gallop Ahead," in Alexander P. Lamis, ed., *Southern Politics in the 1990s*, 305–42. Baton Rouge: Louisiana State University Press, 1999.

Olien, Roger M. *From Token to Triumph: The Texas Republicans Since 1920*. Dallas, TX: SMU Press, 1982.

Texans for Public Justice. *Texas PACs: 2008 Spending Cycle*. Austin: Texans for Public Justice, 2009.

On the Web

To learn more about the Texas Democratic Party, go to **www.txdemocrats.org**.

To learn more about the Republican Party of Texas, go to **www.texasgop.org**.

To learn more about voter registration, turnout, and election results in the state of Texas, go to the Web site of the Secretary of State, Election Division at **www.sos.state.tx.us/elections/**.

To learn more about the influence of money in Texas politics, go to the Web site of Texans for Public Justice at **www.tpj.org**.

4 The Legislative Branch

The Republican takeover of the Texas House of Representatives in 2003 was a watershed event in Texas politics. It marked the first GOP majority of that body since the 1870s and ensured the election of veteran lawmaker Tom Craddick of Midland as the first Republican House Speaker since Reconstruction.

Craddick quickly imposed an autocratic style of leadership over the House and—with the help of Republican Governor Rick Perry and a Republican majority in the state Senate—advanced a conservative GOP agenda. Republican leaders closed a $10 billion revenue shortfall that year by imposing deep cuts in health care and other public services and, in a bitter partisan fight, redrew congressional district lines to give Republicans a majority of the Texas delegation elected to the U.S. House of Representatives.

But Craddick's heavy-handed tactics soon began to erode his support, even among

Republicans. In subsequent elections, Democrats reclaimed several House seats from Republicans who had been loyal to Craddick. It was believed that Craddick had pressured some of the unseated GOP lawmakers to vote against the interests of their own districts on such critical issues as public education. Craddick survived a leadership challenge from a fellow Republican in 2007 but was unseated by Republican Joe Straus of San Antonio in 2009 after Democrats had narrowed the Republican majority in the 150-member House to 76–74 in the 2008 elections.

Straus had served in the House for only two terms and had never been a committee chair but emerged as the choice of eleven anti-Craddick Republicans shortly before the 2009 session convened. His election as Speaker resulted when 64 Democrats also endorsed his selection. Straus, who had a more relaxed leadership style than Craddick, was criticized by some Republicans for securing pivotal

The Texas Capitol, second only in size to the U.S. Capitol, was completed in 1888. Texas paid for its construction in land—some 3 million acres in the Panhandle. Its style is Renaissance Revival, and the exterior is constructed with "sunset red" granite. Austin's population in 1890 was less than 15,000. Today, the Capitol complex meets the needs of a large, highly urbanized state. Underground office space and committee meeting rooms were completed in 1993, legislative support services have been moved to nearby office buildings, and the Supreme Court and Court of Criminal Appeals have been moved to their own building.

support from Democrats and failing to secure House passage of a key Republican priority—a bill to require voters to provide photo identification before casting ballots. But, he received mostly positive assessments at the end of the session and claimed to have enough support to be reelected Speaker in 2011. After Republicans made huge gains in the 2010 election—boosting the GOP to a two-thirds House majority—some conservative Republicans began waging a campaign for a new, more conservative speaker, one without Democratic ties.

The contentious circumstances surrounding Straus's selection as Speaker also reflect the changes in the structure of the state's party system as well as broader changes in the political environment in which the Texas Legislature functions. Over the past several decades, the legislature has moved from a "citizen" legislature characterized by part-time service, low pay, limited staff, and high rates of turnover to a "professional-citizen" legislature with increased staff, lower turnover, and more demands on the time of legislators.

What Should I Know About . . .

After reading this chapter, you should be able to:

★ **4.1** Trace the historical development of Texas's legislative branch, p. 101.

★ **4.2** Identify the provisions of the state constitution that apply to the Texas state legislative branch, p. 102.

★ **4.3** Characterize the membership of the two houses of the Texas state legislature, p. 106.

★ **4.4** Outline the structure of the Texas Legislature, p. 114.

★ **4.5** Summarize the process through which the Texas Legislature enacts laws and establishes the state budget, p. 122.

★ **4.6** Describe the factors that influence how legislators make decisions, p. 129.

★ **4.7** Assess the governor's role in the legislative process, p. 132.

★ **4.8** Evaluate proposals to reform the legislature, p. 133.

Т he leadership turnover and other recent legislative experiences have reflected some of the enormous social, political, and economic changes that have occurred in Texas during the past generation. Forty years ago, the rural-dominated legislature operated within the context of one-party Democratic control and an interest group system dominated by oil, finance, and agriculture. Today, Texas is the country's second most populous state, the third largest state economy, ethnically and racially diverse, more than 80 percent urban, and now dominated by the Republican Party. Despite these major demographic and political changes, however, lawmakers still have to operate under outdated constitutional restrictions that were written for a rural state in a bygone era.

The Texas Legislature continues to serve the same functions: to represent the people in government; to legislate, budget, and tax; to perform constituent casework; to oversee the bureaucracy; to consider constitutional amendments; to confirm the governor's appointees; to redistrict; and to impeach and remove from office corrupt officials.

There is much to learn about the Texas Legislature's structure, procedures, and members. But, were we to study the legislature alone, we would not fully understand its place in the political system. We must also look at external forces that influence its actions—such as elections, lobbyists, governors, and the media.

- First, we will examine *the roots of the legislative branch*.

- Second, we will look at provisions of *the state constitution* that define and limit *the legislative branch of government*.

- Third, we will focus on *who the members of the legislature are*.

- Fourth, we will explore *how the Texas Legislature is organized*.

- Fifth, we will study *how the legislature makes laws and budgets*.

- Sixth, we will examine *how legislators make decisions*.

- Seventh, we will look at *the governor's role in the legislative process*, indicating how the governor wields influence with legislators.

- Finally, we will look at some proposals put forward to *reform the legislature*.

How was he able to pull it off? In a surprising turn of events, Joe Straus (R–San Antonio) successfully challenged Tom Craddick for Speaker at the beginning of the 2009 legislative session. His election was atypical in that the majority of his support came from Democratic members of the House rather than the members of his own party.

Photo courtesy: Texas House of Representatives

ROOTS OF the Legislative Branch

⭐ **4.1** . . . **Trace the historical development of Texas's legislative branch.**

The predecessors to the Texas Legislature were Mexican legislatures, a series of elected conventions, and the Congress of the Republic of Texas. Mexico won its war of independence from Spain in 1821, and by 1824 it adopted a constitution that provided for a federal republic. The provinces of Tejas and Coahuila were joined together. The State of Coahuila y Tejas drafted a constitution in 1827 and organized a legislature. Originally, Tejas got only one deputy in the state legislature. As the population of Tejas grew, its representation in the state legislature grew to three.[1] Texans grew disenchanted with their representation and with Mexican policies, and they met in conventions in 1832, 1833, and 1835 that called for separate statehood and a separate state legislature. Another convention assembled in 1836 and, with civil war erupting, declared Texas's independence.[2]

The first Congress of the Republic of Texas convened in 1836 and consisted of thirty representatives and fourteen senators. Members of the Senate served three-year terms, but members of the House were elected for one-year terms, so each Congress lasted one year. The Republic of Texas had nine congresses.[3] When Texas joined the United States in 1846, the Congress of the Republic dissolved and the 1st Legislature of the State of Texas convened. A legislature sat for a two-year period. The numbering of the legislative sessions was not changed when new constitutions were later adopted. Thus, the first legislature to meet under the current constitution (in 1876) was the 15th Legislature.

The population of Texas has been diverse from its origins, but over its 177-year history, its institutions have been dominated by Anglos. The state's constitutional conventions as well as the various legislative bodies have had few Hispanics or African Americans. A number of Tejanos were not only members of the government under the Constitution of Coahuila y Tejas (1827) but also participated in the opposition movement to the Mexican government, which attempted to extend its direct control over Tejas. Some Tejanos were leaders in the 1836 conventions, most notably Lorenzo de Zavala, who then served as interim vice president of the Republic of Texas.[4] Other Hispanics associated with the political establishment during this period of the Republic included Jose Antonio Navarro and Juan Seguin. For a number of reasons, relationships between Hispanics and Anglos were often hostile. There was even an effort at the Constitutional Convention of 1845 to strip Hispanics of the right to vote.[5]

For a period of time after the Civil War, African Americans were an integral part of the Texas political process. During Reconstruction, African Americans were elected to the Constitutional Convention of 1868 and to the Texas Legislature from 1869 to 1874, then in reduced numbers up to the 1890s. The end of Reconstruction brought about the end of representation for African Americans when white supremacists regained power. The Constitutional Convention of 1875 included a small number of African American delegates, and a few African Americans won election to the legislature into the 1890s; 1895 was the last year that an African American served in the legislature until 1967, after passage of the federal Voting Rights Act of 1965.[6] The nine African American representatives and two African American senators in the 1871–1872 legislature were not surpassed in number until 1977.

TIMELINE: The Evolution of the Texas Legislature

1827 **Constitution of Coahuila y Tejas Creates Unicameral Congress**—Members, elected for a term of two years, are required to be residents of Mexico for at least eight years, owners of property, and at least twenty-five years of age.

1866 **Failed First Effort to Rejoin Union**—Texas makes efforts to rejoin the Union but rejects the Fourteenth Amendment and refuses to consider the Thirteenth Amendment. The U.S. Congress rejects the new constitution.

1845 **Creation of a Bicameral Legislature**—The state constitution of 1845 provides for a Senate (19 to 35 members) and a House (45 to 90 members). House members must be at least 21, while senators must be at least 30 years old.

1861 **Secessionist Legislature**—The new constitution requires all public officials to take an oath of loyalty to the Confederacy and no longer requires U.S. citizenship for Texas legislators.

The State Constitution and the Legislative Branch of Government

⭐ **4.2** . . . Identify the provisions of the state constitution that apply to the Texas state legislative branch.

bicameral Texas legislature
The legislature has two bodies, a House of Representatives and a Senate.

The Texas Legislature, like all state legislatures except that of Nebraska, is bicameral—it has two chambers. The **bicameral Texas legislature** consists of a Senate of thirty-one members, ranking fortieth in size among the states, and a House of Representatives of 150 members, ranking eighth.[7] The 1876 Constitution set the size of the Senate but allowed the House to grow to a maximum of 150, which it reached in 1921. (To learn more about representation in the Senate, see The Living Constitution: Article 3, Section 25.)

Both the House and Senate must pass a bill for it to become law. Nonetheless, there are a few differences in the duties of the two chambers. The House has the responsibility of initiating action to raise state revenue. The Senate has the responsibility of confirming the governor's appointees to many state offices. Article 15 of the Texas Constitution allows the House to impeach public officials and the Senate to try and, if convicted, remove impeached officials from office.[8] It does not specify any breach of standards of conduct or any other reasons that must be given for the impeachment. Impeachment requires a majority vote in the House, and conviction requires a two-thirds vote in the Senate. This process was invoked only once, when Governor James "Pa" Ferguson was removed from office in 1917.

Article 3 of the Texas Constitution includes numerous rules governing the legislative process, including setting out a designated regular order of business

1876 **Restrictions on the Legislature-** The reaction to Reconstruction produces a new constitution approved by voters in 1876. The governor is given the power to set the agenda for a special session, and extensive restrictions are placed on the legislature's powers. The Capitol building is completed in 1888.

2011 **Redistricting after the 2010 Census**—The legislature receives the population data from the 2010 U.S. Census, and changing population and partisan characteristics of Texans are reflected in the new districts.

1869 **Reconstruction Legislature**—Passed under congressional Reconstruction, the Constitution of 1869 draws from many of the legislative provisions of earlier constitutions. With the provisional legislature's adoption of the Thirteenth, Fourteenth, and Fifteenth amendments, Texas satisfies the requirements for readmission to the Union. Republicans hold a majority of seats, and African Americans serve in this session.

1965–2003 **Reapportionment Comes to the Texas Legislature**—The Texas Legislature redistricts its seats in both houses. With the extension of the federal Voting Rights Act to Texas in 1975, minority representation must now be considered.

for a legislative calendar. It provides broad rules, but it also contains more specific restrictions that are so specific the legislature often overrides them. For instance, the part of the regular order of business limiting the legislature to some types of action early in the session and others later in the session is routinely suspended at the beginning of each session. Occasionally tension over the House Speaker's election roils a session, as it did in 1981, 1983, and 2007, when the House was unable to get the four-fifths vote required to suspend the constitutional rule.[9]

Constitutional Provisions Affecting Legislators

The Texas Constitution sets out the length of legislators' terms of office, requirements that a person must meet to serve as a legislator, provisions for legislators' pay, and provisions limiting what a legislator may do in office. (To learn more about these constitutional provisions, see Table 4.1.)

LENGTH OF TERMS Representatives are elected for two-year and senators for four-year terms, with no limit on the number of terms they may serve. Senate elections are staggered: fifteen seats are up for election; then, two years later, the other sixteen are up for election. In the first election after redistricting, all senators must run because new district boundaries are drawn. Senators then draw lots to see who serves a two-year term and who gets a four-year term, so that membership terms return to a staggered system.

Table 4.1 *Which constitutional requirements limit who can run for office?*

	Senate	House
Residency	5 years in Texas, 1 year in district	2 years in Texas, 1 year in district
Minimum age	26 years	21 years
Term of office	4 years	2 years
Citizenship	United States	United States
Voting status	Qualified (registered) voter	Qualified (registered) voter
Salary	$600 per month	$600 per month
Conflict of interest	Must disclose any personal interest in a bill; may not hold any other state office or contract	Must disclose any personal interest in a bill; may not hold any other state office or contract

Source: Texas Constitution, Article 3.

TEMPORARY ACTING LEGISLATORS   In 2003, the constitution was amended (Article 16, section 72) to provide that a representative or senator who goes into active military service may appoint a temporary replacement legislator (subject to majority approval by the appropriate chamber) for the period of his or her active military duty, up to the remainder of the term. The replacement legislator must meet the same constitutional requirements as other legislators; in addition, the replacement must be of the same political party as the elected legislator. Under this new provision, Representative Rick Noriega (D–Houston) appointed his wife, Melissa, as his replacement when he was deployed to Afghanistan in 2005; Representative Carl Isett (R–Lubbock) appointed his wife, Cheri, as his replacement when he was deployed to Kuwait in 2006; and, Representative Frank Corte (R–San Antonio) appointed his wife, Valerie, as his replacement when he was deployed to Iraq in 2006.

per diem

Legislators' per day allowance covering room and board expenses while on state business.

COMPENSATION   Table 4.2 shows that Texas legislators are among the lowest paid in the nation. Legislative salaries are established in the constitution at $600 per month for each month of the term of office (or $7,200 per year). Legislators also get a **per diem,** a per day allowance to cover room and board expenses when they are in session. Nationwide, state legislative annual salaries in 2010 ranged from the top levels of $95,291 in California, $79,650 in Michigan, and $79,500 in New York, to the lowest level of $100 in New Hampshire (with no per diem).[10]

Table 4.2 *How does the Texas Legislature compare to those of other large states?*

	Regular Sessions	Special Sessions	Number of House Members	Number of Senate Members	Annual Salaries (2010)	Women as Percentage of the Legislature (2010)
Texas	140 calendar days, biennial	30-day limit, called only by governor	150 (8th)	31 (40th)	$ 7,200 (39th)[a]	23.8 (25th)
California	no limit on length	no limit, called only by governor	80 (35th)	40 (18th)	95,291 (1st)	27.5 (17th)
New York	no limit on length	no limit, called by governor or 2/3 of legislators	150 (8th)	62 (2nd)	79,500 (3rd)	24.1 (24th)
Florida	60 calendar days (extended by 3/5 vote)	20-day limit (extended by 3/5 vote), called by governor, legislative leaders, or legislators	120 (16th)	40 (18th)	29,697 (19th)	23.8 (25th)

[a]Ranking could be lower; eight states pay by the number of days or weeks in session. If their sessions go long, their pay could exceed Texas pay.

Sources: Council of State Governments, *The Book of the States 2009,* vol. 39, 76–94; Center for American Women and Politics, www.cawp.rutgers.edu.

The Living Constitution

The State shall be divided into Senatorial Districts of contiguous territory according to the number of qualified electors as nearly as may be, and each district shall be entitled to elect one Senator; and no single county shall be entitled to more than one Senator.

—ARTICLE 3, SECTION 25

The basis for representation in the Texas Senate has changed over time. The Texas Constitution of the Republic (1836) based representation in the Senate on "free population (free negroes and Indians excepted)" and entitled each district to only one senator. The 1845 Texas Constitution based representation on the "number of qualified electors." No change in the provision occurred until the 1876 Texas Constitution, which retained the "number of qualified electors" as the basis for representation but also limited a county, regardless of its population, to one senator.[a]

During the 1960s, the U.S. Supreme Court and lower federal courts issued several opinions that affected Texas. In *Reynolds* v. *Sims* (1964), the U.S. Supreme Court decided that the equal protection clause of the Fourteenth Amendment to the U.S. Constitution requires that both chambers of a bicameral legislature be apportioned solely on the basis of population. In *Kilgarlin* v. *Martin* (1966), a U.S. federal district court, applying the standards set in *Reynolds* v. *Sims*, declared the 1961 Texas Senate redistricting unconstitutional because it limited a single county to one senator, regardless of the county's population. However, basing representation in the Senate on "qualified voters" rather than the "total population" was not affected by the ruling. As Justice William J. Brennan noted, writing for the majority in *Burns* v. *Richardson* (1966), "We start with the proposition that the Equal Protection Clause does not require the States to use total population figures derived from the federal census as the standard by which this substantial population equivalency is to be measured." Continuing, Justice Brennan stated, "Neither in *Reynolds* v. *Sims* nor in any other decision has this Court suggested that the States are required to include aliens, transients, short-term or temporary residents, or persons denied the vote for conviction of crime, in the apportionment base by which their legislators are distributed and against which compliance with the Equal Protection Clause is to be measured."[b] Despite the fact that Texas was not required to use the total population as the basis for representation in the Senate, the legislature employed that figure during redistricting in the 1960s and 1970s, primarily because it was more readily available.

The issue was settled in 1981 when Comptroller Bob Bullock asked Attorney General Mark White whether the legislature was required by the Texas Constitution to use "qualified electors" for redistricting. Attorney General White responded, "The section 25 requirement that the state be divided into senatorial districts on the basis of qualified electors is unconstitutional on its face as inconsistent with the federal constitutional standard."[c] White cited *Kilgarlin* v. *Martin* (1966) as the basis for his assertion. Unless challenged in court and overturned, the attorney general's opinion stands. In 2002, the Texas Constitution was changed to read: "The state shall be divided into Senatorial Districts of contiguous territory, and each district shall be entitled to elect one Senator."[d]

CRITICAL THINKING QUESTIONS

1. In the total population of Texas, which now exceeds 24 million people, who would be "unqualified" to vote?
2. The U.S. Senate is based not on population but geographical units: each state is allocated two senators. Why shouldn't the Texas Senate be apportioned on the basis of geography?
3. If the basis for representation in the Texas Senate were "qualified voters" or geographical areas such as a county or combination of counties rather than the "total population," which groups would benefit? Why?

[a] George D. Braden, *The Constitution of the State of Texas: An Annotated and Comparative Analysis*, vol. 1 (Austin: Texas Legislative Council, 1977), 147.
[b] *Burns* v. *Richardson*, 384 U.S. 73 (1966).
[c] Mark White, Attorney General Opinion, Opinion No. MW-320, May 30, 1981, www.oag.state.tx.us.
[d] Texas Constitution, Article 3, section 25, amended November 6, 2001, www.capitol.state.tx.us.

Texas legislators' pay was last raised, by constitutional amendment, in 1974. In 1991, voters amended the constitution to allow the new Ethics Commission to propose a higher salary, subject to approval by the voters. The commission may also propose higher salaries for the House Speaker and the lieutenant governor. The commission has taken no action under this new authority. The 1991 amendment allows the Ethics Commission to set the per diem rate at an amount no higher than the maximum federal tax deduction for business expenses. The commission adopted the rate of $139 per day for the 2009 legislative session.

Sessions of the Legislature

biennial legislature
A legislative body that meets in regular session only once in a two-year period.

Texas has a **biennial legislature:** it meets regularly once every two years. Biennial state legislatures were common in the nineteenth and into the twentieth century, out of the belief that "citizen" legislators could tend to the affairs of the state in a short period of time, then return to their jobs and families. Today, forty-four states have annual sessions, and Texas is the only large, urban state that uses biennial sessions.[11]

regular session
The biennial 140-day session of the Texas Legislature, beginning in January of odd-numbered years.

special (called) session
A legislative session of up to thirty days, called by the governor, during an interim between regular sessions.

The constitution calls the biennial session of the legislature a **regular session** with a 140-day limit. **Special (called) sessions** of the legislature lasting up to thirty days each can be called only by the governor. Despite its pedigree as a biennial, part-time body, the Texas Legislature has met so often in special sessions in recent decades, and has upgraded its professional structure so much, that the National Conference of State Legislatures now considers Texas a "hybrid" legislature, with legislators spending more than two-thirds of their time on legislative business.[12] They continue, however, to receive minimal pay.

Who Are the Members of the Legislature?

★ 4.3 . . . **Characterize the membership of the two houses of the Texas state legislature.**

Members of the Texas Legislature *represent* the public in government. Differences over the nature of representation, how to achieve representation, and equality of representation are core issues in democratic theory and practice.

Variables Affecting Members' Elections

Two election variables are significant in determining who the members of the legislature are. First, members run from districts, so we examine how the lines for those districts are drawn. Second, members may run for reelection to an unlimited number of terms, so we examine the stability or turnover in legislative membership.

REDISTRICTING   Legislators are chosen in single-member districts, where each legislator represents a separate, distinct election district. Because districts become unequal in population size over time, the U.S. and Texas Constitutions require that the district lines be redrawn every decade to assure citizens equal representation regardless of where they live. The legislature usually redistricts—both itself and

Texas's U.S. House seats—in the year after the U.S. Census. Early in the twentieth century, when the rural-dominated Texas Legislature was called on to redistrict itself, it faced a dwindling rural population and a burgeoning urban population. When it came time to redistrict, rural legislators simply could not or would not do it, since redistricting meant giving up seats (and incumbent legislators) to urban areas. The result was malapportionment of legislative districts, and those disparities worsened throughout the decades, becoming so extreme that the legislature was forced to act.

In 1947, the legislature proposed a constitutional amendment to establish a Legislative Redistricting Board, with the power to act if the legislature ever again failed to pass a redistricting bill after the U.S. Census. Voters approved the amendment in 1948, and it had its intended effect. In 1951, the legislature approved the redistricting bills rather than let the board take action. Yet, the redistricting still did not effect equal representation. It was the U.S. Supreme Court that finally ended the "rotten boroughs" by making courts watchdogs over legislative redistricting to assure equalization.[13] Consequently, the Texas Legislature was compelled to redistrict in 1965 under the new standards and has adhered more closely to equal representation in recent decades.

The ultimate goal of redistricting is to create districts with equal-sized populations. From 2000 to 2010, the population of Texas, as measured by the Census, rose from about 21 million to approximately 25 million people. On the basis of 31 Senate districts and 150 House districts, the ideal size of these districts increased by over 100,000 persons and 25,000 persons, respectively.[14]

Reaching that goal of equality is a process laden with political intrigue and hidden traps. Political parties, incumbents running for reelection, courts, the U.S. Department of Justice, and racial and ethnic groups are the primary players in redistricting politics, and their goals are often at odds. Legislators often gerrymander districts, drawing the lines to enhance or diminish the power of one party or of one racial or ethnic group.

The U.S. Voting Rights Act of 1965 declares that states with a history of electoral discrimination against minority groups—including Texas—must preclear redistricting plans with the U.S. Department of Justice or the U.S. District Court of the District of Columbia.[15] Also, the U.S. Supreme Court has ruled that redistricting raises constitutional questions of equal representation, so courts (federal and state) have jurisdiction to review redistricting plans. The U.S. Supreme Court is divided over the issue of racial gerrymandering and has given mixed signals about it.

In the 1991 redistricting, Democrats had a majority in both chambers, and Democrat Ann Richards had just been elected governor. Republicans, Mexican Americans, and African Americans all proposed redistricting maps that would be to their greatest advantage. Anglo Democratic incumbents wanted to protect their seats but knew that if they protected themselves too strongly, the courts could reject their plan and write their own plan. That is exactly what happened.

The new districts drawn by the courts for 1993 resulted in an increase for Republicans in the Texas Senate and for minorities in both chambers. In 1993, the new Senate redrew lines in a way that would benefit minorities but would not benefit Republicans so much. A federal district court upheld this new plan. In 1994, Republicans still gained an additional seat. In 1995, a group of Republican voters sued the state to overturn the House plan. The House negotiated with the plaintiffs and redrew some districts in metropolitan areas, and the U.S. Department of Justice and a federal court panel approved the new plan. The 1990s redistricting skirmishes led to increased Republican representation, including Republican majority Senates in 1997, 1999, and 2001.

In 2001, the Democratic-controlled House, Republican-controlled Senate, and Republican Governor Rick Perry did not reach an accommodation on redistricting during the regular session, so the Legislative Redistricting Board (with four Republicans and one Democrat) approved Senate and House plans (by 3–2 votes) that distinctly favored Republicans. Several groups sued, and the U.S. Department of Justice objected to one part of the House plan. A three-judge federal panel in Tyler approved the board's Senate plan, then approved its House plan with modifications requested by the Department of Justice.

The 2001 legislature also failed to redistrict congressional lines, leaving that task to the courts. A state district court in Austin established a congressional redistricting plan, but the Texas Supreme Court threw it out. Then the federal judges in Tyler drew their own plan, using as criteria historic district locations, compactness and contiguity of the districts (following city and county boundaries where possible), and protection of incumbents.[16] The panel concluded that additional minority districts were not required by federal law, so it would not impose them, and in 2002 the U.S. Supreme Court approved the plan.

During the regular session of the 78th Legislature in 2003, the Republican-controlled legislature tried to redistrict Texas's congressional districts to give Republicans a majority of the U.S. House delegation from Texas. Their plans were thwarted when more than 50 Democratic members of the Texas House fled to Oklahoma to break a quorum and halt work on the plan. Governor Rick Perry called the state legislature back into special session that summer to redraw the congressional districts. After Lieutenant Governor David Dewhurst announced that he would not observe the traditional two-thirds rule that would have blocked consideration of the bill in the state Senate, eleven Democratic senators flew to Albuquerque, N.M., for more than a month to shut down the state Senate. Finally, Senator John Whitmire (D–Houston) broke with his fellow Democrats and returned to Austin, restoring a Senate quorum. The remaining Democratic senators also returned to Austin, and the Republican-dominated legislature passed a new congressional redistricting plan that gave Republicans a 20–12 majority in the Texas delegation in the U.S. House. That ended the careers of several Democratic representatives from Texas.

In 2004, the U.S. Supreme Court upheld Pennsylvania redistricting plans (*Vieth* v. *Jubelirer*) but suggested that partisan issues in redistricting could be so extreme as to render plans unconstitutional. When the Texas congressional redistricting plan got to the Supreme Court, instead of deciding it, the Court sent the case back to the lower court with the instruction to reconsider it in light of *Vieth*. The lower court upheld it again, and on a new appeal to the Supreme Court in 2006, the Court (with two new members) approved most of the plan but required the redrawing of some district lines in south Texas, where Hispanic voting had been illegally diluted. (To learn more about redistricting, see Join the Debate: Should Redistricting Be Conducted by a Nonpartisan Commission?)

REELECTION RATES AND TURNOVER OF MEMBERSHIP　In the early years of the Texas Legislature, more than four-fifths of the legislators served a single term and did not seek reelection.[17] Now, most incumbents seek reelection, and most are successful. Around the nation, the average

Where did the "Killer Ds" go? The simple answer is, Oklahoma. As the Republicans attempted to redistrict congressional seats for the second time in two years to provide additional winnable seats, more than 50 Democrats took their leave of the House and fled to Oklahoma to break the necessary quorum required for action on the redistricting bill.

Photo courtesy: AP/Wide World Photos

Join the DEBATE | Should Redistricting Be Conducted by a Nonpartisan Commission?

After the round of redistricting triggered by the 2000 U.S. Census, Pennsylvania, Texas, Georgia, and Colorado all experienced high-profile court cases challenging the results of their redistricting plans. While disagreement over redistricting is as old as the nation, the intense partisan clashes, some approaching the silly or absurd, since the election of 2000 have elevated the issue of the consequences—and legitimacy—of redistricting plans drawn by partisan bodies for partisan purposes.

The Center for Voting and Democracy has long pushed nonpartisan redistricting proposals, believing that redistricting in the hands of partisan office holders creates noncompetitive districts that take away real choices from voters. There is evidence that legislative races have become less competitive. In California's 2008 elections, for instance, not one congressional seat and only three of 100 state legislative seats changed parties. In Texas, redistricting in 2001 helped Republicans in 2002 win majority control of both the House and Senate for the first time in 130 years. New congressional districts had been created in the 2001 legislature, but with their new majorities, the Republican legislature pushed through another congressional redistricting plan in 2003 with the stated intent of increasing Republican representation in the U.S. House. The U.S. Supreme Court, in 2006, approved most of the plan with the exception of some districts where Hispanic voting had been illegally diluted.

The campaign for nonpartisan redistricting in Texas has been led by Senator Jeffrey Wentworth (R–San Antonio). Since 1993, he has introduced legislation calling for congressional redistricting by an independent bipartisan commission whose members are appointed by the state legislature. In some instances, he has been able to move his proposal through the state Senate, only to have it die in the House.

Should the legislators who have the most to gain by redistricting themselves safe seats be in charge of the process? Does the creation of so many safe or noncompetitive seats result in lower voter interest and participation in elections? Has the creation of safe seats increased ideological divisions in the state's political system in general and the legislature in particular?

To develop an ARGUMENT FOR using a nonpartisan commission to conduct redistricting, think about how:

- **A nonpartisan commission would confer legitimacy on the redistricting process.** How would a nonpartisan commission make the redistricting process fairer? In what ways would using a nonpartisan commission allow for competition between the political parties?
- **The Texas Legislature has a long history of highly partisan redistricting fights.** How does redistricting result in knocking off competent legislators who have helped develop significant state policies? In what ways does the legislative redistricting process often protect weak, ineffective, or obstructionist legislators?
- **A nonpartisan commission would consider factors other than partisan affiliation in designing legislative districts.** Should districts divide communities or natural boundaries to simply "pack" or "crack" partisan voters? What other factors besides partisan affiliation are significant in determining districts? How would a nonpartisan commission encourage transparency and more citizen participation?

To develop an ARGUMENT AGAINST using a nonpartisan commission to conduct redistricting, think about how:

- **It is impossible to create a truly independent or nonpartisan redistricting body.** Will parties and office holders who have much at stake really give up power to a nonpartisan redistricting body? How might legislators create the trappings and public perceptions of independence and nonpartisanship but covertly control the process?
- **The current redistricting process eliminates the need for a nonpartisan commission.** How does the public's access to geographic information systems (GIS) and data on voting patterns, registration, and demographics make the process more transparent and reduce some of the political deception of the past? By what means may individuals or groups participate in the redistricting process that were not available to them in the past?
- **The redistricting process should be political.** Why do advocates of reform think that redistricting should be depoliticized? What are the benefits for citizens of a political redistricting process?

How long does reform take? Senator Jeff Wentworth has been a long-suffering advocate of nonpartisan congressional redistricting. In every session of the Texas Senate since 1993, he has introduced a proposal for reform, but his efforts have met with opposition.

Photo courtesy: Bob Daemmrich Photography, Inc.

term limits
Restrictions that exist in some states about how long an individual may serve in state or local elected office.

turnover in state legislative races in 2006 was 23 percent in the House and 17 percent in the Senate.[18] The turnover rates for the Texas House were 18 percent in 2006, 15 percent in 2008, and 23 percent in 2010; the turnover rates for the Texas Senate were 6 percent in 2004, 16 percent in 2006, 6 percent in 2008, and 6 percent in 2010. Turnover rates typically decline in the election before redistricting because parties push their incumbents to run again (knowing that incumbents usually win) as a strategy to maximize their strength for redistricting. The election after redistricting is often the most volatile; incumbents must run in reconfigured districts, with new voters, and the districts may be drawn in ways to alter party balance in the district.

Today, many legislators make a career of politics. In 2007, the average tenure of incumbents was 13.6 years in the Texas Senate (combining Senate and House experience where present) and 8 years in the House.[19] Across the United States, frustration, born out of a sense that the system of representation and election is biased in favor of incumbents staying in office, fueled a 1990s political movement for **term limits**. Fifteen states now limit the number of terms that legislators may serve. However, Texas does not have the systems of initiative and referendum—the methods used to force term limits in most states—and it is unlikely that Texas legislators will approve limits for themselves.[20]

Personal and Political Characteristics of Members

An examination of member characteristics such as party affiliation, ideology, occupation, race, ethnicity, gender, and age can reveal who represents Texans in the legislature and can show whether there are distinctive patterns to that representation. (To learn more about characteristics of the legislative membership over the past thirty years, see Figures 4.1 and 4.2.)

OCCUPATION, EDUCATION, AND RELIGION   Across the nation in the nineteenth and early twentieth centuries, nearly half of state legislators were farmers and about half were lawyers, businesspeople, and other professionals. The majority of legislators were probably middle class. In state legislatures today, the number of business owners, farmers, and attorneys is declining, and the number of teachers, preachers, public organizers, and former legislative aides being elected to legislatures is increasing. In 2007, 42 percent of Texas senators and 59 percent of representatives were businesspeople, while 32 percent of senators and 33 percent of representatives were attorneys.[21] One possible explanation for continued dominance of lawyers and businesspeople is the low level of pay and part-time nature of the Texas Legislature—which ensures that most legislators must have flexible schedules and must be able to take time off from work without losing their jobs and income. The increasing number of Republicans in both chambers also reduced the percentage of attorneys and increased the percentage of professionals and businesspersons.

In 2007, every senator and all but seven House members had attended some college, and a majority of legislators had graduate degrees. Understandably, more Texas legislators have law degrees than any other type of graduate degree, with master's degrees second.

Figure 4.1 *How has the membership of the Texas House of Representatives changed over time?*

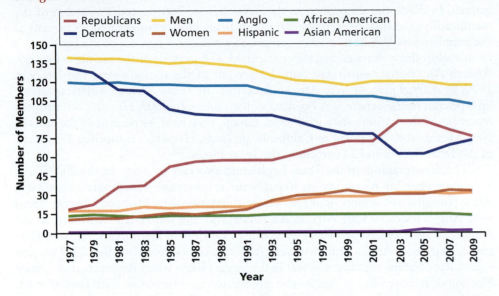

With the diversification of the legislature since the 1970s has come a broadening of the representation of religious denominations. While Baptists traditionally had the highest number of members in the legislature, by the 1990s Roman Catholics were the largest group, followed by Baptists, Methodists, and Episcopalians.

GENDER, RACE, ETHNICITY, AND AGE   Historically, most state legislators across the nation have been Anglo males. The recent trend in legislatures is an increase in minorities and women. By 2009, 24.2 percent of state legislators were women.[22] There is still a tremendous difference among the states, ranging from New Hampshire,

Figure 4.2 *How has the membership of the Texas Senate changed over time?*

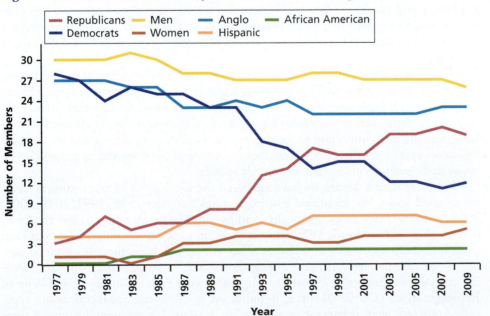

where 37.3 percent of legislators were women, to South Carolina, where 10 percent were women. Southern and border states tend to have the lowest representation of women. In 2009, the six women in the Texas Senate constituted 19 percent of the membership; the thirty-seven women in the Texas House constituted 25 percent of the membership. Whereas women comprised a meager 7 percent of the legislature's membership thirty years earlier, they comprised 23.8 percent of the members in 2009. African Americans constituted only 2.2 percent of the nation's state legislators in 1970; by 2009, 9 percent were African American. In Texas, African Americans made up 6 percent of the Senate and 9 percent of the House. In 2009, Hispanics constituted 3 percent of the nation's state legislators, though they held 44 percent of the seats in New Mexico and 23 percent in California. In Texas, Hispanics comprised 19 percent of the Texas Senate and 21 percent of the Texas House.[23]

The demographics of the Texas Legislature also vary by party. In the 2009 Texas House membership of seventy-six Republicans, seventy-five were Anglo and one was Asian American; of seventy-four Democrats, thirty-two were Hispanics, twenty-seven were Anglo, fourteen were African American, and one was Asian American. In the Senate, all nineteen Republicans were Anglo. Of Senate Democrats, six were Hispanic, four were Anglo, and two were African American. After the 2009 session ended, Republicans regained one seat in the Texas House when Representative Chuck Hopson of Jacksonville, an Anglo who represented a conservative East Texas district, switched from the Democratic to the Republican Party. That gave Republicans a 77–73 lead in the House.

Most Texas legislators are in their forties or fifties in terms of age. House members tend to be young to middle aged, while senators tend to be middle aged to older—though there certainly are exceptions. In 2009, two-thirds of the members of the Texas Legislature were over the age of fifty. The average age of the senators was 56, with an age range of 38 to 68. Ages of the members of the House ranged from one representative under thirty to four who were seventy or older.[24]

PARTY AND IDEOLOGY   Historically, Democrats have won far more seats in the Texas Legislature than have Republicans. Republicans won a legislative majority only in 1870, but as Reconstruction ended, Republicans became a small minority and remained so over the next hundred years. By 1971, there were only 10 Republicans in the House and two in the Senate. Then, in the last two decades of the twentieth century, Texas, along with many of the other states in the "Solid South," underwent a process of realignment; Republicans won control of the Senate in 1996 and the House in 2002.

The four kinds of ideology described in **chapter 1**: liberal, populist, libertarian, and conservative, can be useful in analyzing legislative voting patterns in Texas. Different groups rank legislators' votes on ideological dimensions, though they are usually two-dimensional, rather than four-dimensional. The groups simply choose votes on issues that are most important to them, given their policy perspectives, and see whether legislators agree with them. Of course, these results tend to be skewed, as groups choose issues that clearly divide legislators on their agenda.[25]

For more than a decade, we have measured the ideology of House members based on selected votes. We identified (for legislatures between 1995, 1999, 2001, 2003, 2005, and 2007) five votes on equality and five on liberty measures to test the four-part ideological framework. While the distribution varies some each session, and each session also has its own dynamics that affect voting behavior, there is a general pattern—and that pattern was borne out again in 2007.[26] (To learn about the 2007 voting analysis, see Analyzing Visuals: Ideological Voting Patterns in the Texas House of Representatives.) Of the 80 voting Republicans in 2007 (the Speaker does not typically vote), 68 were conservative, 4 were libertarian, 5 were populist, and 3 were

ANALYZING VISUALS

Ideological Voting Patterns in the Texas House of Representatives

Roll call analysis is used by students of legislatures to identify and measure the impact of ideology on legislators' decisions. Many votes cast by Texas legislators are unanimous or near-unanimous, shaped by factors other than ideology. Legislators divide ideologically when core values are perceived to be directly related to policy choices. Examine the distribution of legislators on the ideology quadrant, and then answer the questions.

	Liberal (33 Democrats, 3 Republicans)		**Populist** (33 Democrats, 5 Republicans)		
	8	8	14	7	2
3	2	6 and 1	5	3 and 1	
	3	3 and 2	2 and 1	2	1
		2	2 and 6	3	7
		1	11	10	10
		1	10	6	5
	Libertarian (4 Republicans)		**Conservative** (68 Republicans, 2 Democrats)		

- Which ideologies are most common among the members of the Texas House of Representatives? Which are least common?
- What is the ideological difference between members of the Democratic Party and members of the Republican Party in the House?
- Is the difference what you expected based on your understanding of Democrats and Republicans?

Source and Methodology: An ideological voting pattern was identified from five roll-call votes in the 2007 sessions selected on equality/opportunity and five roll-call votes selected on liberty/order. *House Journal* record votes 136, 384, 1022, 1035, and 1438 were used to measure legislators' placement on the liberty/order axis, while record votes 267, 284, 375, 1582, and 1976 were used to measure legislators' placement on the equality/opportunity axis. For instance, on record vote 1976, an aye vote was a vote against the bill to give colleges more flexibility in deciding whom to admit, rather than requiring them to admit the top 10 percent from a high school graduating class; it was categorized as a vote for "equality" and against "opportunity." On record vote 1035, an aye vote was a vote to allow police greater powers to obtain private communications (pen registers); it was categorized as a vote for "order" and against "liberty." Each legislator was then placed on the thirty-six-point grid based on the thirty-six possible combinations of scores, from 0–0 to 5–5.

liberal. Of the 68 voting Democrats (one member was ill most of the session), 33 were liberal, 33 were populist, and 2 were conservative.

The data for all the sessions studied reveal a distinct difference between legislative Democrats and legislative Republicans. The center of the House Democratic Party is liberal, with some populist elements, while the center of the House Republican Party is solidly conservative and libertarian (in 1995, 1999, and 2005, it had stronger libertarian elements; in 2001, 2003, and 2007, it had stronger conservative elements). Democrats used to be more ideologically diverse, but as their numbers shrank, they became more unified (liberal). When the Republicans were small in number but growing, they were solidly conservative; once they gained a majority, they exhibited a slightly more diverse membership, with a few liberals and populists.

Partisan differences have become more evident, often centering on government regulation of business, taxing and spending, and social issues (such as abortion and same-sex marriage). Anglo Democrats representing mostly rural, conservative districts often vote with the Republicans in order to reflect their constituents' views on issues such as the Defense of Marriage Act. This group, which included future party-switcher Chuck Hopson, came to be known as the "WD-40s"—white Democrats over forty years of age. The nickname, attributed to Representative Richard Raymond of Laredo, caught on and even provided comedic relief when the WD-40 company sent a letter to the group, complaining that the use of their trademark was illegal. These Democrats represent rural districts that are also swing districts, which normally vote Republican in statewide electoral contests. As a result, the WD-40s may be an endangered species.[27] As a Democrat, Hopson certainly felt endangered, which is why he switched parties.

Our ideology data demonstrate the party outliers (in terms of ideology) for the past few sessions. In the 1990s, some of the outlying Democrats switched to Republican; in 2007, for the first time, an outlying Republican (Kirk England, populist) switched to Democrat. Additional evidence of increased partisanship and ideological polarization is the willingness of Democratic Party leaders to campaign actively in primary elections against Democratic House incumbents who have been too supportive of the Republican leadership. Eighteen Democratic House incumbents were challenged in the March 2004 primary elections; seven lost their primary contest either in the first primary election or a runoff election, averaging 38 percent of the vote in the first primary. One of the losing Democrats was Ron Wilson, chair of the House Ways and Means Committee, who had supported Republican Speaker Craddick and the Republican redistricting effort. In 2008 and 2010, additional incumbents lost in the Democratic and Republican primaries. Thus, as party has become more dominant in the House, the voting has become more ideologically polarized, supplanting the old system of bipartisan conservative dominance in the House.

What does the future hold for partisanship in the Texas House of Representatives? According to political scientists Malcolm Jewell and Marcia Lynn Whicker, "strong party cohesion in the legislature depended on polarization of the state party: the two legislative parties should represent distinctly different types of constituencies with different interests."[28] In Texas, as in many southern states, as the number of Republican legislators grew, Democrats became less likely to draw their votes from conservative, rural voters and more likely to draw their votes from lower-income Hispanic, African American, and Anglo voters. If this trend continues, bipartisanship in the Texas House will cease to exist, and partisanship will increasingly provide the basis for political power and conflict.

How Is the Texas Legislature Organized?

⭐ **4.4** . . . Outline the structure of the Texas Legislature.

Political parties play key roles in the organization of the U.S. Congress. While parties are present in the Texas Legislature, they have not played the dominant role that they do in Congress (though as just discussed, with the recent Republican surge and the Democratic rebound, that appears to be changing). Rather, the institutional leaders and the committees are the key organizational units.

Leaders

president of the Texas Senate
The lieutenant governor of Texas, serving in his constitutional role as presiding officer of the Senate.

pro-tempore (pro-tem)
A legislator who serves temporarily as legislative leader in the absence of the Senate president or House Speaker.

The constitution declares that the lieutenant governor shall serve as the **president of the Texas Senate** and that the Senate shall elect a president **pro-tempore** (or **pro-tem**) to serve in the absence of the lieutenant governor. The constitution states that

Table 4.3 *What are the types of committees in the Texas Legislature?*

Standing Committee
A committee created at the beginning of a legislative biennium, which continues in existence throughout the biennium.

Substantive Committee
A committee that considers legislation as its primary duty; most are standing committees.

Procedural Committee
A committee that has jurisdiction over such things as legislative rules and calendars and administration of the House or Senate.

Special (or Ad Hoc) Committee
A committee created to study a specific problem or policy area; the committee is given a certain amount of time to complete its work, then it goes out of existence.

Interim Committee
A standing committee (or a commission, including some nonlegislative members), charged by the House Speaker and lieutenant governor to study high-profile issues during the interim between sessions; for instance, the Joint Select Committee on Windstorm Coverage reported to the legislature in 2007 on insurance issues related to Hurricanes Katrina and Rita.

Joint Committee
A committee created by both the House and the Senate, with members from both chambers, for a specific duty; examples include the Legislative Budget Board, the Legislative Council, and the Legislative Reference Library Board.

Conference Committee
A joint committee appointed by the House and the Senate for one specific bill passed by both chambers but with different provisions; it writes a common version of the bill and reports back to both chambers.

the House of Representatives shall choose its leader, the **Speaker of the Texas House,** from among its members. At the beginning of each regular session, the House elects a Speaker for the biennium. The Speaker appoints a Speaker pro-tem.

Speaker of the Texas House
The state representative who is elected by his or her fellow representatives to be the official leader of the House.

Committees

The legislature works through a system of committees. A **committee** is a subunit of the legislature appointed to work on designated subjects. Legislatures use committees because the full House or Senate could not possibly do all the work as one large body. Committees also help legislators develop subject specialties and thus, presumably, make better-informed public policies. (To learn more about types of committees, see Table 4.3.) *Standing committees* are the basic committees that do most of the work during legislative sessions. They can be either *substantive* (focusing on legislation) or *procedural* (focusing on legislative procedures). At the beginning of a regular session, the House and Senate create standing committees; the chairs of those committees appoint ad hoc subcommittees for specific bills. Some Senate committees also have permanent subcommittees.

In most sessions, the standing committees from the previous legislature are simply recreated. However, when there is turnover in leadership, the committee structure is changed. (To learn more about the standing committees and the number of members of each one for the 2009–2010 biennium, see Table 4.4.) House members typically serve on two or three committees. Senators serve on four standing committees and possibly an additional standing subcommittee.

Two of the most significant powers of the House Speaker and the lieutenant governor are the powers to appoint legislators to committees and to appoint the committee chairs. In the 1970s, the House created a weak seniority system for assignment to committees. Each member selects one committee that he or she wants to serve on, and the more senior requesters get the spots—a maximum of one-half of a committee's members (excluding the chair and vice chair) may be determined by seniority, with the other half completely within the power of the Speaker to name. Seniority does not apply on procedural committees. House committee chairs appoint subcommittee

committee
A subunit of the legislature, appointed to work on designated subjects.

Table 4.4 *What standing committees were created for the 2009 Texas legislative session?*

Senate Committees	Number of Members
Substantive Committees	
Agriculture and Rural Affairs	5
Business & Commerce	9
Committee of the Whole Senate	31
Criminal Justice	7
Economic Development	5
Education	9
Finance	15
Government Organization	7
Health & Human Services	9
Higher Education	5
Intergovernmental Relations (one subcommittee)	5
International Relations and Trade	7
Jurisprudence	7
Natural Resources	11
State Affairs	9
Transportation and Homeland Security	9
Veteran Affairs & Military Installations (one subcommittee)	5
Procedural Committees	
Administration	7
Nominations	7

House Committees	Number of Members
Substantive Committees	
Agriculture & Livestock	9
Appropriations (seven subcommittees)	27
Border and Intergovernmental Affairs	9
Business & Industry	11
Corrections	11
County Affairs	9
Criminal Jurisprudence	11
Culture, Recreation, and Tourism	9
Defense & Veterans Affairs	9
Elections	9
Energy Resources	9
Environmental Regulation	9
Federal Economic Stabilization Funding, Select	9
Higher Education	9
Human Services	9
Insurance	9
Judiciary & Civil Jurisprudence	11
Land & Resource Management	9
Licensing & Administrative Procedures	9
Natural Resources	11
Pensions, Investments & Financial Services	9
Public Education	11
Public Health	11
Public Safety	9
Regulated Industries	7
State Affairs	15
Technology, Economic Development & Workforce	9
Transportation	11
Urban Affairs	11
Ways & Means	11
Procedural Committees	
Calendars	13
General Investigating & Ethics	5
House Administration	11
Local & Consent Calendars	11
Redistricting	15
Rules & Resolutions	11

*There were also five select committees in the House of Representatives.

Source: www.capitol.state.tx.us/Committees. Texas Legislature Online, *Legislative Reports for the 81st Legislature, Regular Session,* 2009.

Table 4.5 *What special lingo do legislators use?*

Backscratching: Helping another legislator with a vote, with the expectation that he or she will return the favor.

Carrying water: Sponsoring a bill or an amendment at the request of a lobbyist or the administration.

Dog-and-pony show: Lengthy committee hearings, featuring scores of witnesses who tell emotional and personal stories to persuade legislators to vote a bill out of committee or to kill it.

Gerrymandering: Drawing redistricting lines to help or hurt either an incumbent or a group of voters, such as Democrats, Republicans, Anglos, African Americans, or Mexican Americans.

Gutting: Amending a bill in such a way that it severely weakens the bill or changes its original purpose, often resulting in the sponsor voting against his own bill.

Lite guv: The term *lieutenant governor* is often abbreviated as "lt. gov." In a verbal takeoff of this abbreviation, the office is humorously abbreviated, in comparison to the governor, of course, as the "lite guv."

Logrolling: Supporting and voting for another member's "local" bill (affecting only the author's district), with the assumption that he or she will then support you when you have a bill coming up.

Pork barrel: Appropriations of money to a project in a single legislative district.

Sine die: Legislators use this Latin phrase to describe the 140th day (the last day) of a regular legislative session.

Tag: Allows an individual senator to postpone a committee hearing on any bill for at least forty-eight hours, a delay that is often fatal in the crush of unfinished business during a session's closing days.

Taking a walk: Leaving a committee hearing or the floor to avoid voting on a controversial bill if such a vote would hurt the legislator with one group or another.

That dog won't hunt: A debating point suggesting that the legislator does not have a credible argument or proposal.

members and chairs; in the Senate, the lieutenant governor appoints chairs of the standing subcommittees.

Committee work can be a long, painstaking examination of policy matters, leading to markup or to redrafting and amending bills. Public hearings can be educational for the committee members, who may not know much about the subject, but who must become proficient enough in it to defend the committee's work. On the other hand, decisions are often made before the hearing, and public hearings can become what legislators derisively refer to as "dog-and-pony shows," with no real chance to affect the outcome. (To learn more about legislative lingo, see Table 4.5 for a glossary.)

Organizing for Power and Influence in the Legislature

In order to pass bills, legislatures must have vehicles for organizing the leadership and its supporting coalition; if the legislature is open and democratic, there will also be vehicles (and resources) for organizing opposition. In most legislatures and in the U.S. Congress, political parties serve as those vehicles, but not in Texas. In the absence of parties, strong factions and strong leaders rule. An organization of legislators who are all affiliated with the same political party is called a **legislative party caucus** (e.g., the House Republican Caucus). There were no party caucuses in Texas until the 1980s. The result is that a strong party system is now antithetical to the system of strong Speakers and lieutenant governors that has evolved in its absence.[29] It remains to be seen whether party caucuses will merely coexist in a subservient position with the leadership or will manage to become a new power center.

legislative party caucus
An organization of legislators who are all of the same party, and which is formally allied with a political party.

Leadership and Opposition in the House

The Texas Constitution requires that the representatives elect one of their members to be the leader of the House, and that person is called the Speaker. In the 1800s, by custom, a Speaker would serve one two-year term. A few served two terms, and one served three nonconsecutive terms. By the middle of the twentieth century, two terms was the norm.

Gus Mutscher's 1971 campaign for a then unprecedented three consecutive terms as Speaker, coupled with his role in the **Sharpstown scandal,** a bribery and fraud scandal that cost him his job, set the stage for the 1973 House reform session. (Mutscher resigned in 1971 and was convicted of bribery in 1973.) Believing that much of the source of the legislature's problems was concentration of power in the hands of the Speaker, the 1973 reformers proposed limiting Speakers to one term of office. They lost that battle, but in a move that reform advocates have since regretted, they won a vote to make the balloting for Speaker open and public. Now legislators vote publicly on a Speaker who is seeking reelection—with the fear of retaliation from a newly reelected Speaker and his or her allies against any who oppose them. Since the change to open balloting, we have witnessed the longest Speakerships in Texas history. Bill Clayton served four terms (1975–1982). Gib Lewis had five terms (1983–1992), as did Pete Laney (1993–2002). With Republicans winning a majority in 2002, Representative Tom Craddick won the Speakership in 2003, becoming the first Republican Speaker in more than 130 years. He won a second term in 2005, though there were already rumblings of discontent over his leadership. When Republicans lost six seats in 2006, those rumblings grew louder and exploded into a series of running battles. Craddick served a third term but was unseated at the beginning of the 2009 session by Republican Joe Straus.

THE SPEAKER'S RACE The campaign to determine the Speaker for the biennium, called the **Speaker's race,** is the cornerstone of the legislative process in the House. A representative who wishes to be Speaker announces his or her intentions and asks legislators to sign "pledge cards" of support. While this may seem a simple, in-house process, in reality it is a statewide campaign, with candidates now raising (typically from lobbyists) and spending huge amounts of money to get the required seventy-six votes. Much of the campaign money is spent to help elect legislators who will be pledged to the Speaker candidate; thus, in recent years, the Speaker's campaign has become a quasi-party organization.

In 2003, Travis County District Attorney Ronnie Earle (a former Democratic legislator) started an investigation of campaign activities involving the Texans for a Republican Majority political action committee (TRMPAC), the Texas Association of Business (TAB), U.S. House Majority Leader Tom DeLay, and Speaker of the Texas House Tom Craddick. Earle was trying to determine whether they had violated state laws by using (and hiding the source of) corporate money to support the election in 2002 of Republican legislative candidates who would then vote for Craddick for Speaker. TAB was later indicted by a Travis County grand jury on charges of violating state campaign finance laws. The investigation also resulted in related charges against DeLay and two associates who were involved with TRMPAC, a PAC organized by DeLay. TAB eventually pleaded guilty to a misdemeanor charge of unlawful campaign contributions and paid a $10,000 fine. The controversy also prompted DeLay's resignation from Congress.

The Texas House Speaker's race really never ends; instead, it becomes the center for organizing the House leadership, known as the **Speaker's lieutenants** and the **Speaker's team,** and wielding influence within the House. A Speaker who is running for reelection relies on help from lieutenants in circulating pledge cards and persuading legislators to support him or her. When a Speaker retires, the lieutenants vie among themselves for the office. Savvy lieutenants will seek pledge cards for the Speaker who is running for reelection and simultaneously for themselves for the future.

HOUSE LEADERSHIP AND THE POLITICAL PARTIES Until 2003, Republicans controlled the House during only one session, in 1870–1871. There were no Republican Party nominees for Speaker, and personal and factional groupings dominated the

---

Sharpstown scandal
The legislative scandal of 1971–1972 that resulted in a bribery conviction of the House Speaker and other officials and set the stage for the 1973 reform session.

Speaker's race
The campaign to determine who shall be the Speaker of the Texas House for a given biennium.

Speaker's lieutenants
House members who make up the Speaker's team, assisting the Speaker in leading the House, either informally, or in a role as a committee chair or other institutional leader.

Speaker's team
The leadership team in the House, consisting of the Speaker and his or her most trusted allies among the members, most of whom the Speaker appoints to chair House committees.

selection process, with the conservative Democratic faction almost always winning. In 1971, the *Dallas News* wrote that "the Texas House of Representatives, with minor exceptions, has been under conservative Democratic control since we first reported its happenings during the 1930s."[30]

House Democratic leaders often supported bipartisanship and eschewed efforts to create party caucuses. Speaker Laney was more open to party organization, especially after Republican legislators organized efforts to defeat him in his home district. He met with the House Democratic Caucus, though it still had not organized to influence the passage of legislation. When Republicans won sixteen additional seats in the 2002 elections, Craddick had enough pledges to replace Laney as Speaker.

THE SPEAKER'S INFLUENCE OVER COMMITTEES   Speakers have the ability to stack important committees with legislators from the faction that controls the House. Historically, there were no restraints on the Speaker's powers to assign representatives to their committees. Because of the perception that Speakers used these assignments to reward their friends (with appointment to the most important committees) and to punish their enemies (with appointment to the least desired committees), reformers in the mid-1970s won a limited seniority system that the Speaker must abide by in some appointments. Before the reforms, conservatives (reflecting the ideology of the Speakers) were substantially overrepresented on key committees. After the reforms, conservatives were still overrepresented on those committees, but to a lesser degree.[31]

Legislators say off the record that Speakers have extorted reelection pledge card signatures before making their committee assignments, one of the strongest powers that the Speaker has over House members. Such a practice certainly appears to violate democratic principles, but it is usually hidden from public view and does not give rise to a public reaction. This "extortion" system became so explicit in the Mutscher era that one of the reforms of 1973 was the adoption of a state law to legally define the promise of an appointment to a committee chair or vice chair position in exchange for a pledge in the Speaker's race as a bribe.

HOUSE OPPOSITION AND THE POLITICAL PARTIES   Opposition to the Speaker and the Speaker's team was traditionally not organized along party lines, though that is changing now. Even Republicans long resisted organizing, gaining greater leverage by being part of the conservative leadership coalition. In the early 1980s, Republican Representative Tom Craddick stated, "It's more to [our] benefit for us not to have" a caucus. Even when Republicans gained in numbers, they resisted organizing. One Republican said that a caucus would "polarize the members on party rather than on philosophy and issues."[32] A House Republican Caucus was not formally organized until 1989, with Craddick as its chair. He served as its chair until 1999.

Political scientists Malcolm Jewell and Marcia Lynn Whicker noted in the early 1990s that "the Speaker of the Texas House has controlled a bipartisan coalition of conservative Democrats and Republicans and has appointed members of both parties to committee chairmanships."[33] Since the mid-1970s, Democratic Speakers relied on Republicans as a part of their coalition to win office and rewarded them with committee chair positions.

THINKING NATIONALLY

Choosing a Speaker of the House

Congress and many state legislatures choose their legislative leaders through legislative party caucus mechanisms. Typically, for example, Republicans choose one of their legislators to run for House Speaker against a Democratic legislator chosen by the Democratic caucus. Where party discipline is strong, each party member votes for the party's candidate—and that can mean, as happened in 2007 in Congress, that a change in a party majority necessarily triggers a change in legislative leadership.

- Could the bloc of Democratic legislators who helped Republican Joe Straus secure the Texas House Speakership in 2009 have elected a Democrat as Speaker that year? Why or why not?

- What promises or commitments does a potential Speaker make to the other members for their support?

- Under what circumstances is a Speaker likely to be challenged for reelection?

When Republican Craddick announced for Speaker after the 2001 session, he said that were he to win, he would continue the practice of bipartisan committee leadership. He did, though with a different balance. In 2003, when Republicans gained control of the House by winning eighty-eight of the 150 seats, Speaker Tom Craddick appointed a disproportionate percentage of Republican committee chairs; Republicans constituted 59 percent of House members but 73 percent of the committee chairs (twenty-nine of forty). In 2005 and 2007, he continued that pattern, with thirty Republican chairs and ten Democratic chairs in both years, even though Democrats increased their proportion of the House. Republican Speaker Joe Straus, who unseated Craddick in 2009 with the key support of most Democrats in the House, appointed Democrats to chair 19 (or about 46 percent) of the House's 41 committees that year. But some Democrats complained that Straus named Republicans to chair most of the major committees.

ORGANIZING IN THE HOUSE THROUGH NONPARTY CAUCUSES   A **nonparty legislative caucus** is a group of legislators organized around some attribute other than party affiliation. In the absence of strong parties, opposition is usually ad hoc, with legislators who oppose the Speaker on one issue supporting him or her on others. In some sessions, nonparty caucuses (including county and regional delegations, ad hoc issue groups, racial and ethnic groups, and ideological groups) have served as opposition vehicles. There are now more than a dozen such caucuses in the House.

> **nonparty legislative caucus**
> An organization of legislators that is based on some attribute other than party affiliation.

A caucus called the House Study Group (HSG) formed in 1975 in opposition to Speaker Bill Clayton's team. The result was warfare between the two camps. For twenty years, the Speakers' teams tried to eliminate the HSG. While the repeated attempts failed, they did succeed in changing it from an opposition caucus to a staff-research office named the House Research Organization (HRO), which now serves all House members.

In 1985, Republicans and a few conservative Democrats formed the Texas Conservative Coalition (TCC). It helped defeat a health care proposal in 1985, triggering a special session to revise and pass it. By 1993, the TCC was using parliamentary points of order and staff research to effectively promote and oppose legislation. In 1996, the Texas Conservative Coalition Research Institute (TCCRI) was formed to provide information and promote conservative policies at all levels of government. In 1994, moderate and liberal Democrats formed a new caucus, the Legislative Study Group, to counter the influence of the Texas Conservative Coalition.

Leadership and Opposition in the Senate

The constitution designates a leader for the Texas Senate, though in a manner very different from the designation of the House Speaker. The constitution says that the lieutenant governor shall serve as the president of the Senate (though he or she is not a member of the Senate and may not vote except in the case of a tie vote). In 1999, anticipating Governor George W. Bush's run for the presidency, legislators and voters approved a constitutional amendment requiring the Senate, in the case of a vacancy in the office of lieutenant governor, to elect a lieutenant governor (and Senate president) from among its members until the next general election. When Rick Perry ascended to the governorship and vacated the lieutenant governorship in December 2000, the Senate convened a special session and elected Republican Senator Bill Ratliff as lieutenant governor. He served through 2002 but did not seek reelection. Voters elected Republican David Dewhurst to the office, effective January 2003. Dewhurst had served one term as land commissioner. He was reelected lieutenant governor in 2006 and 2010.

THE ROLE OF THE LIEUTENANT GOVERNOR   Many lieutenant governors use the post as a political stepping-stone. As a statewide elected official, the lieutenant governor gains more attention than the Speaker of the House and is more often mentioned as a possible candidate for higher office. Most of the early lieutenant governors served one term and went on to serve as governor. Three people have served as Speaker, lieutenant governor, and governor.[34]

Beginning in the 1890s, multiple two-year terms for lieutenant governors became the norm. The first three-consecutive-term lieutenant governorship occurred from 1907 to 1912. In 1974, the lieutenant governor's elected term in office was lengthened to four years. Except for Perry and Ratliff, the pattern is one of long tenure. Ben Ramsey served from 1951 through 1961, Bill Hobby served from 1973 through 1990, and Bob Bullock served from 1991 through 1998.

The lieutenant governor of Texas is one of the most powerful lieutenant governors in the states. Across the nation, twenty-six lieutenant governors preside over their senates, twenty-three can vote only in the case of a tie, and nine appoint committees.[35] The Texas lieutenant governor has all those powers and appoints Senate committee chairs. However, it is not the constitution that gives the lieutenant governor significant powers over the Senate. The senators themselves write the Senate rules, and historically they have written the rules to give the lieutenant governor real power over them—the power to appoint committee chairs, assign members to committees, and refer bills to committees. In the absence of a majority party leader in the Texas Senate, the Senate president is the most powerful force.

COALITION BUILDING IN THE SENATE   In the small Texas Senate, especially with weak political parties, leadership and opposition were historically organized on an ad hoc basis and heavily influenced by the personal relationships the senators and the lieutenant governor established with each other. Lieutenant governors are responsible for guiding legislation through the Senate, and they must appoint allies as key committee chairs, place allies on the important committees, and build a leadership coalition—recognizing that senators will also become leaders in the policy areas that are most important to them.

Partisanship was never a factor in this coalition building because there were no Republicans, and there was not a Republican lieutenant governor in the twentieth century until Rick Perry in 1999. As Republicans gained in numbers during Lieutenant Governor William Hobby's tenure, he included them in his coalition. In 1991, Lieutenant

---

How does the lieutenant governor influence the decisions of the Senate? Elected independently of the governor, the lieutenant governor has traditionally been the Senate's legislative leader. The power of this office comes not from the constitution but from the rules set by the senators.

Photo courtesy: Bob Daemmrich Photography, Inc.

Governor Bob Bullock adopted a more partisan approach, stripping Republicans of their committee chair positions. In 1993, when Republicans for the first time gained more than one-third of the Senate, Bullock reversed himself and appointed Republicans as committee chairs. In 1999, Perry appointed Republicans to eleven leadership positions and Democrats to eight. In 2001, Republican Lieutenant Governor Ratliff, reflecting the closeness of the party division in the Senate and the closeness of his election by the senators, appointed eight Democrats and seven Republicans to leadership positions. And, Republican David Dewhurst has continued the tradition of bipartisan committee chairs. Lieutenant governors know that their legislative powers depend on senators voting them those powers, and they cannot afford to have a large bloc of senators opposed to them.

How Does the Legislature Make Laws and Budgets?

⭐ **4.5** . . . **Summarize the process through which the Texas Legislature enacts laws and establishes the state budget.**

The legislative process is the method that the legislature follows in passing legislation. We look at the different kinds of legislative documents known as bills and resolutions, the significance of legislative rules, the step-by-step process in how a bill becomes a law, and special issues concerning the budgeting process.

What Is a Bill? What Is a Resolution?

When the legislature adopts or amends a state law, it is through a document called a bill. Other adoptions by the legislature are called *resolutions*. There are different kinds of resolutions. Thus, anything that the legislature considers will be labeled a bill, a joint resolution, a simple resolution, or a concurrent resolution.

When the legislature wants to create a law (called a *statute*) or amend an existing one, it must do so by passing a **bill.** The constitution specifies the form that every bill must take. It must have each component (e.g., an enacting clause), or it is subject to being ruled in violation of the requirements and thus thrown out, either by the legislature itself or by a court.

A **joint resolution** either proposes an amendment to the Texas Constitution or ratifies an amendment to the U.S. Constitution. A **simple resolution** goes through only one chamber (such as the resolution to adopt House rules or a resolution commending a citizen). A **concurrent resolution** expresses the will of both chambers (for instance, telling the U.S. Congress what the Texas Legislature thinks it should do), though there is no authority of the force of law behind it.

Rules, Procedures, and Internal Government

The rules adopted by the House and the Senate embody the constitutional limitations, plus more specific rules needed for smooth working (or for power wielding) in the legislature. The House and Senate also adopt "housekeeping" resolutions setting members' office budgets, policies for employees, the administrative authority of the leadership, and the governing of caucuses.[36]

How a Bill Becomes Law

In order to promote deliberation, the constitution requires that a bill be read on three separate days in each chamber of the legislature. It must also pass both chambers in the exact same form. A legislator files a bill or resolution and a clerk assigns it a number. The same bill might be introduced in the House and Senate with different

bill
A proposed law.

joint resolution
A legislative document that either proposes an amendment to the Texas Constitution or ratifies an amendment to the U.S. Constitution.

simple resolution
A legislative document proposing an action that affects only the one chamber in which it is being considered, such as a resolution to adopt House rules or to commend a citizen.

concurrent resolution
A legislative document intended to express the will of both chambers of the legislature, even though it does not possess the authority of law.

numbers—HB 357 and SB 823, for example, could be the same bill. Though there is no requirement that a bill be introduced in both chambers, it helps speed the process, allowing simultaneous House and Senate hearings. (To learn more about the basic steps by which a bill is enacted into law in the Texas Legislature, see Figure 4.3.)

Most committees get more bills referred to them than they can reasonably consider. Even when a legislator requests a hearing, there is no requirement that the chair

Figure 4.3 *What are the basic steps in the Texas legislative process?*
This figure shows the flow of a bill from the time it is introduced in the House of Representatives to final passage and transmittal to the governor. A bill introduced in the Senate would follow the same procedure in reverse.

Note: If the governor signs the bill or refuses to sign it, it becomes law. If the governor vetoes the bill, it takes a two-thirds vote of both the House and the Senate to override the veto and make the bill law.

Source: Legislative Budget Board, Texas Legislative Council, *Texas Fact Book, 2006* (January 2006): 14. Revised by the authors.

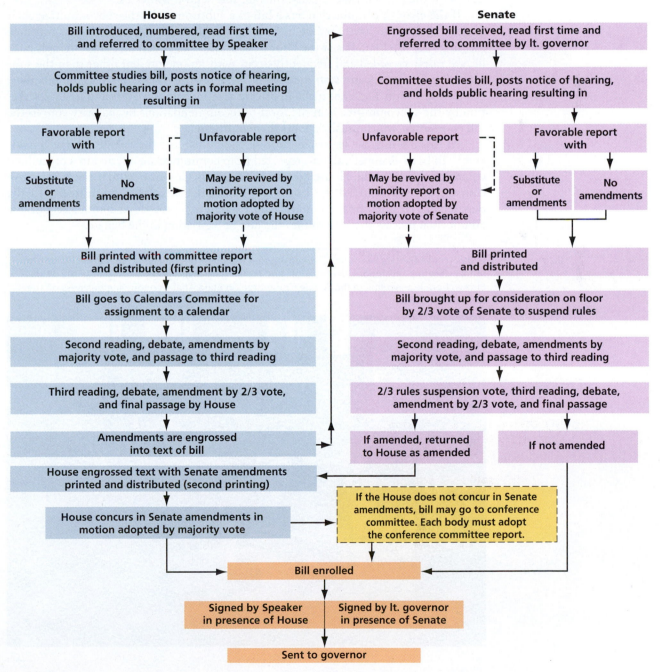

schedule the bill for one. While this practice in other states has led to revolts against the leadership, it has not been seriously challenged in Texas. When does a committee chair decide to let the committee consider a bill or decide to kill the bill by not setting it on the agenda? Such decisions are usually made privately, with no public discussion, and are influenced by the position (if any) of the Speaker of the House or the Senate president, by the lobbying of interest groups, and by the political needs of the chair and the bill's author.

Most bills are considered in public hearings, in which citizens may testify for or against the bill, but House committees may consider bills in formal meetings, in which testimony is usually not accepted. Because of the reforms following the 1971 Sharpstown scandal and the demand for a more open process, a House committee must post notice of a public hearing at least five days in advance of the hearing. Public hearings must be open to all, and votes must be taken in open meetings. The chair will lay out the bill and call on the author to explain it. The committee hears testimony from witnesses for the bill, witnesses against the bill, and neutral witnesses.

If the chair or committee refers a bill to a subcommittee, the subcommittee chair decides whether to have a public hearing or a formal meeting. Often, subcommittee meetings are brief huddles at the floor desk of the chair. Such meetings, though public, are rarely recorded and frequently occur with no one present other than the subcommittee members and staff members. There is little discussion, and the members often simply ratify decisions made in private meetings of legislators and lobbyists. Action by the subcommittee is in the form of recommendations by majority vote to the full committee, which usually adopts them as drafted.

At this point in the legislative process, the House and the Senate diverge considerably. In both chambers, all bills reported from committee are referred to a procedural committee. Bills in the House go to the Calendars Committee or, if the substantive committee requests it, to the Local and Consent Calendars Committee.[37] In the Senate, bills reported from committee are referred to a procedural committee, but it is an informal process that determines the fate of legislation in the Senate.

Is this where the work is done? The heavy, often tedious work of legislating is done in the committee. Hearings, testimony, deliberation, and marking up legislation are just part of the work. Shown here is a meeting of the Senate Committee on State Affairs conducting business on the floor of the Senate.

THE HOUSE CALENDARS COMMITTEE   The Calendars Committee sets the daily calendar for the House.[38] How a bill makes it onto—or is kept off—the daily calendar is one of the more controversial topics in the Texas House. Under 1993 reforms, several aspects of Calendars Committee operations changed. While the committee had been required to lay out the calendar at least twenty-four hours in advance, this requirement was sometimes violated. One reform requires the committee to distribute the daily calendar to each representative at least thirty-six hours in advance, and the committee has complied with the rule. Other reforms include requirements of advance public posting of the meetings and opening the meetings to the public and other members. Another reform requires the committee, within thirty days of receiving a bill, to take a public vote on whether to place it on a calendar. The committee circumvents this requirement by setting the bills that it wishes to set, then adopting a universal motion to not set all other bills on a calendar. Our review of the committee's minutes in the years after the reform revealed that the committee went through the formal procedures required to meet the new rules without changing the real decision-making process. The meetings typically lasted one to five minutes, as the members quickly ratified the list of bills brought in by the committee chair. Clearly, the real decision making was done behind the scenes.

THE SENATE SCHEDULING FUNCTION   The Senate Administration Committee sets a Local and Uncontested Calendar to consider noncontroversial bills, but for significant bills, there is no committee to advance or kill bills approved by the standing committees. Instead, as a means of controlling the flow of legislation, the **Senate two-thirds rule** requires every bill to win a vote of two-thirds of the senators to take up the bill out of the regular order of business. A senator whose bill has been approved by committee must give written notice of intent to move to suspend the regular order of business. This daily listing of notices is called the **intent calendar.**

By tradition, at the beginning of each legislative session, a senator will introduce a frivolous bill with no intention of ever asking for a vote on it in the full Senate. For example, in 2007 Senator Kim Brimer introduced SB 259, proposing a county park beautification and improvement program, as the bottleneck bill. The bottleneck bill is the first bill to be approved by any committee, so it is then placed at the top of the order of business. Thus, *every* bill except that one is always out of order, so long as the author of that bill does not request a vote on it. Therefore, before any other bill can be considered, the Senate must first vote to suspend the rule governing the regular order of business. That motion requires a two-thirds vote and must be made for each and every bill, both on second reading and on third reading.

The two-thirds rule is a method by which the Senate assures deliberation and compromise. It protects any minority that has at least one-third of the senators, because they can block passage of a bill. So, if an opposition bloc has at least one-third of the senators, the leadership bloc must bargain with it to get the bill passed. This rule makes the leadership–opposition blocs more fluid in the Senate. This protection of minority rights enhances pluralist democracy in the Senate, in stark contrast to the House. The 1979 Killer Bees incident, when twelve senators hid out in order to break the quorum and prohibit a vote, provides a colorful example of what can happen when that norm is violated.[39]

In recent years, however, Lieutenant Governor David Dewhurst and a Republican majority in the Senate have bypassed the two-thirds rule to force highly partisan issues backed by Republicans through the Senate. The first instance occurred during the 2003 special session on congressional redistricting, which was discussed earlier in this chapter. That decision prompted eleven Democratic senators to flee to New Mexico to shut down the Senate for more than a month. Eventually, the Republicans prevailed and passed the redistricting bill after Democratic senators returned to Austin. The second incident occurred in 2009, when Republican senators voted to bypass the two-thirds rule to allow the Senate to pass on a simple majority vote a

Senate two-thirds rule
The rule in the Texas Senate requiring that every bill win a vote of two-thirds of the senators present to suspend the Senate's regular order of business, so that the bill may be considered.

intent calendar
The Senate calendar listing bills on which the author or sponsor has given notice of intent to move to suspend the regular order of business in order that the Senate may consider them.

controversial bill requiring voters to have photo identification to vote. The bill, strongly backed by Republicans but opposed by most Democrats, won Senate approval that year but died in the House. Both these incidents prompted speculation that other efforts to suspend the two-thirds rule on highly divisive, partisan issues may become more prevalent in the future.

THE BILL REACHES THE FLOOR   Both chambers of the House and Senate are often referred to as the "floor" where legislative action occurs. At the beginning of each legislative day, the Speaker or president calls the members to order and the roll is called to ascertain whether a **quorum,** a required minimum of two-thirds of the members, is on the floor. After housekeeping measures (such as a prayer, announcements, introductions) and **first reading** of bills, the members consider the bills on **third** (final) **reading** (i.e., bills that have already been approved on second reading and require only the usually perfunctory final vote), then bills on **second reading** (when the real debate occurs).

In the House, the Speaker calls a bill from the calendar for second reading and recognizes the bill's author (or, in the case of a Senate bill, the House sponsor), who explains the bill from a podium at the front of the chamber. Any member may go to the microphone in the back of the chamber and ask the author questions. After the author's opening statement, any member may speak for or against the bill or offer amendments, and any other member may question that member. The author is limited to twenty minutes to open debate on the bill and twenty minutes to close it. All other members are limited to ten minutes, including any interruptions from questioners. Members take the full allotment of time only on major or controversial bills. Conceivably, debate on a bill could take days. In reality, this rarely happens. (To learn more about debate in the House, see Politics Now: Key Bills Left for Dead amid House Slowdown.)

In the Senate, the president recognizes a senator to suspend the regular order of business so that the Senate may consider a bill on second reading. The senator explains the bill, standing at his or her desk. There could be discussion at this point, if the bill is controversial. Otherwise, the rules-suspension vote is taken quickly, followed by further explanation, any amendments, and the second-reading vote. Unlike the House, the Senate has no time limits on debate, creating the **filibuster** as a tactical tool: a senator may hold the floor for an unlimited amount of time and thus can try to kill a bill by refusing to allow a vote on it.

An amendment must be **germane** to the bill—that is, related to the topic—but germaneness is a matter of interpretation by the Speaker of the House or Senate president. Amendments can drastically alter a bill and thus become powerful tools in the hands of opponents. The consideration of amendments is a critical part of the legislative process for both sides, and a controversial bill has the potential of lengthy debate and twists and turns in tactical victories and defeats.

In the chamber in which the bill originated, when the final vote on a bill on third reading is favorable, the bill is considered to be an **engrossed bill** and is then sent to the other chamber by a staff messenger. It then goes through the referral and committee process and may or may not ever make it to the floor of the second chamber.

TWO BILLS INTO ONE: THE FINAL STAGES   The Texas Constitution requires that, in order to become law, a bill must be adopted by both houses in exactly the same form. Many bills are amended in the second chamber, so an additional step is required to meet this requirement. The original chamber could simply vote to concur with the amendments placed on the bill by the other chamber, or it may vote to not concur and request a conference committee to adjust the differences between the two versions of the bill.

Conference committees have five House members appointed by the Speaker and five senators appointed by the lieutenant governor. If conferees cannot reach a compromise, the bill is dead. If they do reach a compromise, this new version of the bill is presented to each chamber, which must approve it with no further amendments by majority vote.[40] For instance, in 2007, the House passed HB 1, the state appropriations bill. The Senate

---

quorum

The minimum number required to conduct business (as in a legislative body).

first reading

The Texas Constitution requires three readings of a bill by the legislature; first reading is when the bill is introduced, its caption is read aloud, and it is referred to committee.

third reading

The Texas Constitution requires three readings of a bill by the legislature; third reading is the final reading in a chamber, unless the bill returns from the other chamber with amendments.

second reading

The Texas Constitution requires three readings of a bill by the legislature; the second reading is when debate and consideration of amendments occur before the whole chamber.

filibuster

A formal way of halting Senate action on a bill by means of long speeches or unlimited debate.

germane

Related to the topic.

engrossed bill

A bill that has been given final approval on third reading in one chamber of the legislature.

POLITICS **NOW**

| WORLD | NATION | LOCAL | **POLITICS** | OPINION | HEALTH & SCIENCE | ARTS | SPORTS | LEISURE |

Key Bills Left for Dead amid House Slowdown

By Jason Embry and Corrie MacLaggan

May 27, 2009
Austin American-Statesman
www.statesman.com

Texas House Democrats killed legislation Tuesday night that would have required voters to show more identification at the polls, winning—at least temporarily—the fiercest partisan battle of this year's legislative session. But the cost of victory was high. Their tactics put dozens of other proposals, some of them years in the making, in serious jeopardy with six days left in the legislative session.

Bills that would reform electric co-ops and the Texas Department of Insurance, make more families eligible for the Children's Health Insurance Program and give authorities more tools to fight transnational gangs were left in peril as the House reached a crucial bill-passing deadline at midnight Tuesday. The House did not take up those proposals and hundreds of others because Democrats used excessive debate to slow the movement of bills to a crawl, guaranteeing that there would not be time to debate the voter ID measure.

Legislators now have two ways of bringing proposals back to life. The first option is for senators to tack dying proposals onto other related bills that did not fall victim to the voter ID fight in the House.

The other option is for the House to take a two-thirds vote to bring up bills. That option has become the crucial point of contention between Democrats and Republicans.

Democrats say the House can use that option to keep important bills alive and limit the collateral damage from their slowdown strategy. They tried repeatedly in recent days to use that option to bring up key bills but were blocked by Republicans. . . .

But Republicans say that taking bills up out of order would reward Democrats' bad behavior by allowing them to seize control of the House schedule. . . .

At least one issue is already causing speculation about a special session of the Legislature this summer [which occurred on July 1, 2009]. . . .

The debate over voter ID has loomed over the entire session. In January, Republicans carved out an exception to the Senate's usual operating rules to make it almost impossible for Senate Democrats to block an ID bill.

The Senate later passed legislation requiring voters to show photo ID or two forms of nonphoto ID, which is more than what is now required. Democrats say beefed-up ID requirements would suppress voter turnout, but Republicans say they would ensure that only eligible voters are casting ballots.

That proposal was scheduled to come to the House floor Saturday. But Democrats stalled consideration of that measure and others by talking excessively about bills that normally would sail through the chamber without debate.

After a lengthy debate on the state's automatic admissions law for universities, some Democrats resumed the talk-a-thon Monday night and most of the day Tuesday.

> **Critical Thinking Questions**
> 1. Why do Democratic legislators oppose the voter ID requirement?
> 2. Why do Republican legislators favor the voter ID requirement?
> 3. Did this issue have any impact on the 2010 elections and the speaker's election in 2011?

then passed its appropriations bill, but with different amounts of money for many programs. The conference committee worked for weeks to adjust the differences. It finally produced a compromise bill, which the House and Senate then approved in floor votes.

If a bill achieves final approval, it is then an **enrolled bill** and is sent to the governor. The governor may sign the bill into law, ignore it (in which case it goes into effect without his or her signature), or veto it, as discussed in **chapter 5.**

enrolled bill
A bill that has been given final approval in both chambers of the legislature and is sent to the governor.

The Budgeting Process

Biennial legislative sessions necessitate biennial budgets, but some legislatures with annual sessions also adopt biennial budgets. Twenty-nine states prepare annual budgets, while twenty-one, including Texas, have biennial budgets.[41] The budgeting

Are they asking to be excused? Cue-giving and cue-taking are informal means of communicating with other members of the House on the hundreds of bills considered each session. Members, who often know little about a piece of legislation, are seen here providing information about their positions. One finger means yes; two fingers, no.

Photo courtesy: Bob Daemmrich Photography, Inc.

balanced budget

A budget in which the legislature balances expenditures with expected revenues, with no deficit.

deficit spending

Government spending in the current budget cycle that exceeds government revenue.

debt

The total outstanding amount the government owes as a result of borrowing in the past.

budget execution authority

The authority to move money from one program to another program or from one agency to another agency.

process is complex, largely because many of the numbers used to create the budget are projections and estimates, and state constitutional requirements limit what the legislature can do in Texas.

In 1931, the legislature designated the governor as the state's chief budget officer—but the same law gave the State Board of Control the responsibility of preparing the budget. The governor had no budget staff. Through the 1940s, the governor typically just gave the legislature the Board of Control's budget, with a few comments.[42] In 1951, the legislature and Governor Allan Shivers moved the budget function directly into the governor's office, where it has remained.[43] However, that was also the first session for the new Legislative Budget Board (LBB), and the legislature has consistently ignored the budget developed by the governor's office, in favor of the budget developed by legislative leaders in charge of the LBB.[44]

The LBB and the Governor's Budget Office prepare budgets for the legislature to consider. Before a regular session begins, the two offices hold joint hearings for state agencies to present their requests and for the public to comment. In the end, however, each prepares a separate budget proposal to submit to the legislature. For instance, for the 2008–2009 biennium, Governor Rick Perry proposed a budget of $167.3 billion, and the LBB proposed a $161.8 billion budget.[45]

In the budgeting process, legislators must adhere to a constitutional requirement for a **balanced budget**—balancing spending with expected revenues (as estimated by the comptroller of public accounts), and thus avoiding deficit spending. **Deficit spending** is spending in the current budget cycle (in Texas's case, the biennium) above and beyond incoming revenue, while **debt** is the total outstanding amount owed from past borrowing. Thirty-three states, including Texas, have a constitutional balanced-budget requirement.[46] In 1978, Texas adopted an additional constitutional spending limit. Article 8, section 22 of the constitution now imposes a limit on state spending, calculated by a complex formula tied to the state's economic growth. The legislature is prohibited from spending more state tax revenue (from funds not constitutionally dedicated) than a formula-calculated amount above the previous budget. The LBB determines the spending limit by estimating the rate of growth of the state's economy. This can be a subjective process, subject to much second-guessing and criticism. The LBB established the estimated rate of growth of the Texas economy at 13.11 percent for 2008–2009.

Thus, in the budgetary process, Texas legislators must consider the constitutional balanced-budget requirement, the comptroller's revenue estimate, proposed budgets submitted by the governor and the LBB, constitutional spending limits, and in the end, the governor's veto authority.

In 1985, voters approved a constitutional amendment (Article 16, section 69) creating **budget execution authority.** During an interim, the governor and the LBB are authorized to move money from one program to another or even from one agency to another. Because the lieutenant governor is the chair and the Speaker the vice chair of the LBB (and they appoint the members), this budget execution authority allows the governor, lieutenant governor, and Speaker the flexibility to handle some budget crises without having to call the legislature into special session.

How Do Legislators Make Decisions?

⭐ **4.6** . . . **Describe the factors that influence how legislators make decisions.**

In making decisions on how to vote, legislators interact with executive branch officials, judges, voters, lobbyists, reporters, staff members, party officials, and officials from the federal government and from other states. The legislature is also a social system and must be understood in the context of the norms of behavior and roles that legislators take with each other, from "backscratching" to "logrolling." (To learn more about legislative lingo, see Table 4.5).

The influences on how a legislator votes and provides leadership on policy issues are many and often conflicting. In deciding either how to vote on a particular bill or which bills to sponsor, a legislator asks such questions as these: Do I support it philosophically or in terms of good public policy? Which of my constituents will benefit from or be harmed by this bill? How much support will I get from them for the bill and in my reelection campaign? Will it generate opposition in my district? Whom can I gather into a coalition of support for the bill? Which lobbyists will support me, and which will oppose me? Will they be more or less likely to finance my campaign or an opponent's because of this bill? How will the media play the issue? Does the leadership support the bill? Can I win support from my fellow legislators? Will the bill help or hurt my reputation with them? What do I need to do to get the governor's support? Often, such legislative decision making must be made quickly and can come back to haunt a legislator later.

THINKING NATIONALLY

Governors and the Budget

Budgeting in Texas, as in most others states, is shared, but there are some governors with greater control over the state budget than others. Thad Beyle, a long-standing scholar of the American governor, studied the constitutional authority of governors and created an index that summarized each governor's budget power. For instance, the governor of Maryland was assigned a 5 on the basis that the governor has full responsibility, and the legislature may not increase the executive budget. New York, California, and Florida were assigned a 3 on the basis that the governor has full responsibility, and the legislature has unlimited power to change the executive budget. Texas was assigned a 2 because the governor shares responsibility, and the legislature has unlimited power to change the executive budget.[a]

- How do the Texas Legislature and governor cooperate, if at all, to develop the state's budget?

- Given the plural executive and the autonomy of these agencies from executive control, can these officials take their budget requests directly to the Texas Legislature, sidestepping the governor?

- If the budget powers of the Texas governor were increased with all budget requests submitted to his or her budget office, would this require a constitutional amendment?

[a] Thad Beyle, "Governors' Institutional Powers 2007," www.unc.edu.

Growth of Legislative Staff

Staffing and information have been focal points in institutional development of state legislatures. Legislators do not have the time or resources to do all the work required to conceive, develop, and pass legislation. Staff members can do much of the work in developing information. Deliberative democracy can be enhanced with increased availability of information, though a burdensome staff structure could also thwart access to lawmakers.

Some large states, such as Michigan and California, have significant party staff capabilities. In Michigan, most of the legislative staff is organized along partisan lines. In California, partisan professionals staff most of the committees.[47] In recent years, the Texas House Democratic Caucus had no staff members, and the Texas House Republican Caucus had only one; in the Senate, neither the Democratic nor the Republican caucus had staff members (though members' staff may serve the caucus).

The result of increased use of individual, institutional, and group staffing is that legislatures have much larger staffs than in the recent past (though Texas still has substantially fewer staff members than New York or California). However, there has been a political backlash against the larger staffing levels. As term limits took hold in

California in the 1990s, new legislators cut staffing substantially.[48] There are now just over 2,000 full-time-equivalent legislative staff members in Texas (including those in the representatives' and senators' offices, committees, and groups—the Legislative Council; the State Auditor's Office; the Legislative Budget Board; the Sunset Commission; and the Legislative Reference Library).

Staffing for Technical Assistance, Specialized Information, and Political Assistance

Early efforts at increasing legislative information were aimed at establishing state libraries, interim committees to gather information between sessions, and legislative councils. The councils were centralized staffing operations to provide bill drafting, policy research, and program evaluation services.

The Texas Legislature created its Legislative Council in 1949. It is a joint committee chaired by the lieutenant governor. The Legislative Council has ten representatives, five senators, and the lieutenant governor and Speaker as members. The council's attorneys and other staff members draft bills, conduct policy studies during the interim between sessions, produce documents such as committee schedules, legislative calendars, and bill-status information, and manage the legislature's computer systems. The legislature also established the Legislative Budget Board (LBB) in 1949. The LBB has four representatives, four senators, and the lieutenant governor and Speaker as members. The LBB's staff analysts prepare the state budget and conduct evaluations of agencies' programs.

By the 1960s, most state legislatures found centralized staffing inadequate. One staff office could not be specialized enough or attentive enough to the needs of individual legislators or committees, so legislatures began providing staff members for standing committees, individual legislators, and caucuses. By the 1970s, committees in the Texas Legislature were typically served by two or three staff members, hired by the committee chair. The expertise and duties of committee staff members vary considerably, with each chair having different priorities. In 2003, new Speaker Craddick abolished the four-year-old House Bill Analysis Office and returned to the committee staff members the job of analyzing bills.

Individual representatives did not have staff members—or offices—until the 1960s. Before then, they used a common pool of secretaries. Now legislators receive a monthly account to pay for office expenses, including staff. A typical representative hires three to five staff members in Austin plus one or two district staff members. Senators hire about five to ten Capitol staff members plus district staff. The staff provides constituent services (casework), administrative support, and assistance drafting legislation, negotiating with staff and lobbyists, and preparing support materials.

Relations with Lobbyists

A recurring issue in public policy is the proper role of lobbyists and their relationship with legislators. In the 1960s and 1970s, state legislatures passed many "open-government" measures, including stricter requirements for lobbyists to register, so that the public would know who was seeking to influence state government. In 2007, 1,629 lobbyists registered with the Texas Ethics Commission—more than nine for every legislator—representing more than 4,000 clients.[49]

Lobbyists legitimately approach the legislature to protect the interests of their clients or interest groups through public-policy changes. In trying to persuade legislators, they provide information that legislators need to evaluate—and thus lobbyists can be an invaluable resource to legislators in their quest for deliberative democracy. For instance, in the 2005–2006 battles over public education, the legislature got technical information from private groups such as the Texas Public Policy Foundation and the Equity Center, as well as from public officials and groups such as superintendents,

Why do they call it lobbying? Lobbyists and visitors, who are denied access to the floor of the Senate chamber while the body is in session, are seen mingling outside the chamber during a tax debate. One can often see lobbyists and legislators talking with each other in the lobby of the Capitol.

Photo courtesy: Courtesy of L. Tucker Gibson

teachers, and school boards. Everyone knew that the information came from groups with different goals, and thus had to be balanced, or compared with particular policy proposals that different legislators favored.

That role as an information source also makes lobbyists power players, and they can become protective of their influence with legislators by monopolizing access to legislators. One lobbyist justified his opposition to a stronger legislative staff by saying to one of the authors: "As long as the representative has analysis, he abdicates [decision-making responsibility] and doesn't need to talk to me." Party caucuses and leaders can also present competition for lobbyists. Upon the formation of the Senate Democratic Caucus in 1983, a senator said: "When the party starts taking positions on issues, lobby influence will be diminished."[50]

The Ethics of Lobbying

Most lobbyist–legislator contact happens with complete legitimacy, but the many questionable contacts and practices raise recurring questions about ethics.[51] Exposure of Frank Sharp's bribery of legislators in 1971 led to the largest wave of Texas government reforms in modern times. Since the Sharpstown scandal, a number of other cases have raised questions about ethical violations related to lobbying. The federal government attempted to ensnare corrupt legislators through its "Brilab" sting operation (Speaker Bill Clayton was accused of accepting a bribe but was acquitted in 1980). Stories circulated about outlandish spending by lobbyists on the "wining and dining" of legislators. Chicken magnate Lonnie "Bo" Pilgrim walked around the Capitol in 1989 handing out checks to senators after talking with them about his support of Governor Bill Clements's workers' compensation proposals. News reports described legislators creating and maintaining privately funded "officeholder accounts" for political and personal expenses.[52] Speaker Gibson Lewis garnered misdemeanor convictions for failure to report all his private financial holdings.

Often, the questionable activities concern blurring the line between lobbying activities and election and campaign activities. The same individuals who are the most successful lobbyists (primarily business representatives) are also deeply involved in raising and contributing money for legislative campaigns and for officeholder accounts. Legislators need money for the next campaign, and interest-group leaders want access to and influence with legislators, so the campaign-finance game is a symbiotic relationship. Legislators and lobbyists both get what they need.

Questions recur about whether campaign finances, wining and dining, and officeholder accounts taint public policy and political equality. In the wake of repeated news stories about lobby-paid junkets to Mexico, Las Vegas, and various resorts; stories about legislators paying their mortgages or buying cars with political funds; demands from public-interest groups for limits on lobbyists' expenditures; and Governor Ann Richards's successful 1990 campaign that capitalized on perceived unethical conduct, the 1991 legislature passed an ethics reform bill. The new law restricted the amount of money that lobbyists can spend on promoting legislation, increased their reporting requirements, and established the Texas Ethics Commission. But it didn't impose limits on campaign contributions to legislators and legislative candidates.

What is the Governor's Role in the Legislative Process?

⭐ **4.7** . . . Assess the governor's role in the legislative process.

Texas governors may be weak in their control of the executive branch (see **chapter 5**), but they are stronger players in the legislative process. Governors have leverage to push their agenda through the give-and-take of legislative politics because they have some things that legislators want—such as an emergency declaration for their bills (which allows the bills to be heard early in a legislative session), adding their bills to a call for a special session, or signing their bills into law.

The power to call special legislative sessions is a significant power of the governor because he or she may call one at any time for any purpose. The governor must specify what issues the legislature is being called to consider, although the governor can add subjects to the call of the session after it has begun. During special sessions, governors may refuse to add a bill to the agenda until or unless the legislative sponsor pledges support of the item that the governor is pushing the legislature to adopt. Thus, the governor is in complete control of the agenda of a special session. A special session may last no longer than thirty days. However, there is no limit on how many sessions a governor may call, and indeed they have been called back to back. Governor Ann Richards called four special sessions in the 1991–1992 biennium. There were none again until Governor Rick Perry called four special sessions during the 2003–2004 biennium, and he called three during the 2005–2006 biennium.

Party loyalty is a new factor in gubernatorial–legislative relations. During the long Speakership of Gib Lewis (1983–1992), opposition virtually disappeared except when Republicans left the leadership coalition on selected issues. When the legislature was fighting Republican Governor Bill Clements on tax or school-finance issues, Republican legislators would oppose the Speaker's bills. It put a strain on Lewis's leadership coalition, because seven committee chairs were Republicans.

At the end of the legislative process, the governor may sign the bill into law, veto the bill (nullify its passage), or ignore it, in which case it becomes law without his or her signature. In **chapter 5**, we examine governors' vetoes more closely. If the governor vetoes a bill, the legislature may consider a motion to override the veto, which requires a two-thirds vote. However, most vetoes happen late in the session or after the legislature has adjourned, so there is no chance to attempt an override. Vetoes of regular-session bills may not be overridden in a subsequent special session.

TOWARD REFORM: The Public and the Legislature

⭐ **4.8** . . . **Evaluate proposals to reform the legislature.**

Some element of the Texas citizenry is always agitating for reform of the political system—and those demands for change are often directed at the legislature. Such demands are often deflected or defeated, but sometimes they bear fruit. A change in leadership powers may change the role of party caucuses in the legislature. Such a push for reform at this level strikes at the very heart of the legislative process and the balance of power and, thus, is difficult. Toward the end of his speakership, Pete Laney championed campaign finance reforms, but those proposals, too, mobilized outside power centers that might be threatened by changes—and thus, the proposals died.

Other efforts at reform may have more strength. They are more likely to triumph if the public has been stirred up—as happened with the Sharpstown scandal and the ensuing reforms of legislative process and leadership powers in the 1970s. Over the past several years, the news media and public interest groups have stirred interest in the voting procedures in the legislature. They were frustrated at how many votes on the House and Senate floor were nonrecord votes. Thus, they—and their legislative allies—pushed measures to require more record votes.

In 2007, the legislature approved HJR 19, which voters then ratified as a constitutional amendment. This new constitutional rule requires a record vote on final passage of a measure. Proponents argued that such a requirement will help open up government to scrutiny, and thus encourage responsibility. Opponents argued that the legislative process could be slowed dramatically and, more significantly, that a record vote on final passage is often a charade—the real action on a bill is on the amendments and on second reading. Those votes can still be nonrecord votes. A member by a nonrecord vote could try to weaken a bill with amendments or to kill a bill on second reading. Then, if the bill survives, the member could cast a record vote for it on final reading and be able to claim support for it, despite his or her earlier efforts. Still, the new requirement became effective for the 2009 and future sessions.

The next push for reform may be over the phenomenon of "ghost voting"

How could a dead legislator cast a recorded vote? The House adopted electronic voting years ago, but there was a general practice for a representative to open the key and leave it on. If absent, a member would request a colleague to cast a vote, and if the legislator were not around, a colleague would cast a vote without any instructions. The practice came to public light when colleagues cast a vote for an absent colleague who was later found dead in his home. Finger-print identification voting machines, shown here, can combat the practice of "ghost-voting" but have yet to be used at the Texas Capitol.

·AYE·   ·PNV·   NAY

Photo courtesy: Ricardo B. Brazziell/Austin American-Statesman

in the House, where members vote by machine. Each member has a control device on his or her desk, by which the member hits a green button for yes, a red button for no, or a white button for present-not-voting. By House rule, each member may vote only from his or her own device (or by individually signaling the chair to record the desired vote). But what happens when a member is across the floor when a vote is called—or even out of the chamber? Often, a fellow member reaches over and votes for the neighboring member, even though the rules forbid it. The colleague might have been asked to do so and instructed which vote the member wanted, but it raises the possibility of one member casting a "yea" vote for other members when the absentees would have voted "nay." When that happens—and it does—a member can enter a statement in the *House Journal* stating that the voting machine "malfunctioned" and his or her intent was to cast a different vote—though the original vote still counts. The *Journal* is replete with such entries. Every once in a while, someone objects from the back microphone, and the Speaker will warn members not to do it—but the rule is not enforced, and everyone knows it.

In 2007, YouTube brought the issue to public attention. An Austin TV channel aired a news segment on the issue, and someone uploaded the segment to YouTube. Hits on the entry spiked and the issue burst into the open, increasing demands that the House stop the practice. Will the YouTube sensation trigger reform? Part of the answer may lie in whether the issue stays alive and whether some organized interest pushes it. A private citizen took the issue to a grand jury in 2008; the grand jurors issued a report calling for the House to enforce its rules, but did not issue an indictment.[53]

What Should I Have LEARNED?

Now that you have read this chapter, you should be able to:

⭐ **4.1 Trace the historical development of Texas's legislative branch, p. 101.**

When the Republic of Texas dissolved, the state legislature inherited many features of the former Congress, including its two-chamber structure. Few African Americans and Hispanics were elected to the legislature during the nineteenth century, and no African American was elected during the first part of the twentieth century. Throughout its history Anglos have dominated the legislature. The contemporary Texas Legislature looks much different from earlier legislatures with modernized and expanded facilities, an increased workload and staff, but it draws from the constitutional legacy of the earlier constitutions.

⭐ **4.2 Identify the provisions of the state constitution that apply to the Texas state legislative branch, p. 102.**

Under the provisions of the Constitution of 1876, the legislature is bicameral, and its membership is set at thirty-one senators and 150 representatives. In addition, the Texas Constitution sets terms of office and legislative sessions, qualifications for office, and compensation.

⭐ **4.3 Characterize the membership of the two houses of the Texas state legislature, p. 106.**

Legislators are more likely than the general population to be Anglos, male, lawyers and businesspeople, middle aged, and well educated. They are often conservative in political ideology. However, the composition of the legislature is changing to include more Hispanics, African Americans, and women, as well as a broader ideological array. For most of the years since the adoption of the 1876 Constitution, Democrats dominated the Texas Legislature, but the transformation of the state's party system has resulted in recent Republican control of both houses.

⭐ **4.4 Outline the structure of the Texas Legislature, p. 114.**

Like most states, the Texas Legislature has leaders and a committee system to structure its activities. Unlike most states, the Texas Legislature does not choose its leaders or create its committees in a partisan fashion. Consequently, conflicts are between the legislative leaders' teams and their opposition rather than between political parties—though partisanship is growing. Nonparty caucuses are also influential in the Texas Legislature.

⭐ **4.5 Summarize the process through which the Texas Legislature enacts laws and establishes the state budget, p. 122.**

The Texas Legislature makes laws and establishes the state budget during each biennial session, using a variety of resolutions and bills. The legislative process involves several stages, all of which provide an opportunity to halt or modify legislative proposals. Both bodies have an established set of rules, and those legislators who know how to adroitly use these rules can be successful in enacting their legislation or blocking measures that they oppose.

⭐ **4.6 Describe the factors that influence how legislators make decisions, p. 129.**

With over 1,500 measures enacted during most recent regular sessions, Texas legislators can't know everything about every bill. Thus, legislators turn to a variety of information sources to help them cast their votes. Legislators' votes are influenced by several factors, including the legislative leadership, committee chairs, staff members, lobbyists, members of the executive branch, and even their desk mates.

⭐ **4.7 Assess the governor's role in the legislative process, p. 132.**

The powers of the Texas governor include legislative powers (such as the veto, emergency declarations, and power to call and set the agenda of special sessions) and dictate that the governor and the legislature interact frequently and regularly during legislative sessions. Governors also use their personal resources, including direct contact with legislators, to move legislation through the process.

⭐ **4.8 Evaluate proposals to reform the legislature, p. 133.**

Recent efforts led to a new requirement for recorded votes, and public calls for an end to "ghost voting" may spark legislative debate over enforcement of rules. Other suggestions for reform have been raised over the years, including annual sessions, or a least a budget session in alternate years, lengthened legislative sessions, term limits, and increasing legislative salaries, to name a few.

Test Yourself: The Legislative Branch

⭐ **4.1 Trace the historical development of Texas's legislative branch, p. 101.**

Which of the following statements is inaccurate in its description of Texas Legislatures?
A. Since statehood, Texas has always functioned with a bicameral legislature.
B. Tejanos were members of the legislature under the early constitutions.
C. African Americans served for a brief period in the Texas Legislature after the Civil War.
D. Over most of its history, the members of the Texas Legislature have been fairly representative of the various populations of the state.
E. Even today, the Anglo population is disproportionately represented in the Texas Legislature.

⭐ **4.2 Identify the provisions of the state constitution that apply to the Texas state legislative branch, p. 102.**

Which of the following is NOT a constitutional provision related to the membership or structure of the Texas Legislature?
A. To serve in the House of Representatives, a member must be twenty-one years of age.
B. To serve in the Senate, a member must be twenty-six years of age.
C. A member receives $7, 200 a year in compensation.
D. A member is limited to a specific number of terms.
E. A member who is on active duty in the military can appoint someone to fill his or her place temporarily.

⭐ **4.3 Characterize the membership of the two houses of the Texas state legislature, p. 106.**

Under current provisions of the Voting Rights Act and decisions of the courts, the Texas Legislature cannot create new districts that

A. are equal in population.
B. cut across the boundaries of counties or cities.
C. pack minorities into a district to reduce their strength in another district.
D. gerrymander voters of a political party.
E. protect incumbents.

⭐ **4.4 Outline the structure of the Texas Legislature, p. 114.**

The power and influence of Texas legislative leaders stem from all but one of the following:
A. The power to appoint the members to standing committees.
B. The power to recognize members from the floor.
C. The right to determine salaries and per diem expenses.
D. The power to appoint chairs of key committees.
E. Their control over the scheduling of legislation.

⭐ **4.5 Summarize the process through which the Texas Legislature enacts laws and establishes the state budget, p. 122.**

The majority of bills introduced each session are "killed" at what stage of the process?
A. When the leadership assigns bills to hostile committees
B. At the committee stage when many bills never get a hearing.
C. When bills go to the Calendars Committee for scheduling.
D. On the third reading.
E. In the conference committees.

⭐ **4.6** **Describe the factors that influence how legislators make decisions, p. 129.**

Legislators are likely to
A. vote only on bills that they have read thoroughly.
B. require their staff to read and summarize every bill.
C. vote on a bill only after they have received a briefing from the legislator who sponsored the bill.
D. vote only on bills that the leadership has taken a position on.
E. look for a variety of cues, casting votes often on the basis of advice given by trusted colleagues.

⭐ **4.7** **Assess the governor's role in the legislative process, p. 132.**

A governor can usually exercise considerable influence in the Texas Legislature when
A. he or she has hand-picked the legislative leadership.
B. one house is controlled by one party and the other is controlled by the opposition party.
C. it is possible to pit conservatives against liberals in the legislature.

D. the lieutenant governor is of the opposition party.
E. when the ideological wing of his or her party controls both houses.

⭐ **4.8** **Evaluate proposals to reform the legislature, p. 133.**

Which of the following recommendations to restructure the Texas Legislature is the most radical?
A. No limits on the length of legislative sessions
B. Expansion of the number of seats in both the House and the Senate
C. The power of the legislature to call itself into session
D. A unicameral legislature with 200 seats
E. Six-year terms for the Senate and four-year terms for the House

Essay Questions

1. Would the Texas Legislature be more effective if it met in regular session every year? Why or why not?
2. Should the Texas Legislature be organized, like the U.S. Congress, along partisan lines? Why or why not?

Key Terms

balanced budget, p. 128
bicameral Texas legislature, p. 102
biennial legislature, p. 106
bill, p. 122
budget execution authority, p. 128
committee, p. 115
concurrent resolution, p. 122
debt, p. 128
deficit spending, p. 128
engrossed bill, p. 126
enrolled bill, p. 127
filibuster, p. 126

first reading, p. 126
germane, p. 126
intent calendar, p. 125
joint resolution, p. 122
legislative party caucus, p. 117
nonparty legislative caucus p. 120
per diem, p. 104
president of the Texas Senate, p. 114
pro-tempore (pro-tem), p. 114
quorum, p. 126
regular session, p. 106
second reading, p. 126

Senate two-thirds rule, p. 125
Sharpstown scandal, p. 118
simple resolution, p. 122
Speaker of the Texas House, p. 115
Speaker's lieutenants, p. 118
Speaker's race, p. 118
Speaker's team, p. 118
special (called) session, p. 106
term limits, p. 110
third reading, p. 126

To Learn More on the Legislative Branch

In the Library

Barnes, Ben, with Lisa Dickey. *Barn Burning, Barn Building: Tales of a Political Life, from LBJ Through George W. Bush and Beyond.* Albany, TX: Bright Sky, 2006.

Bickerstaff, Steve. *Lines in the Sand: Congressional Redistricting in Texas and the Downfall of Tom DeLay.* Austin: University of Texas Press, 2007.

Bowser, Jennifer D., Keon S. Chi, and Thomas H. Little. *Coping with Term Limits: A Practical Guide.* Denver, CO: National Conference of State Legislatures, 2006.

Deaton, Charles. *The Year They Threw the Rascals Out.* Austin, TX: Shoal Creek, 1973.

Herskowitz, Mickey, *Sharpstown Revisited: Frank Sharp and a Tale of Dirty Politics in Texas.* Austin, TX: Eakin, 1994.

Jones, Nancy Baker, and Ruthie Winegarten. *Capitol Women: Texas Female Legislators, 1923–1999.* Austin: University of Texas Press, 2000.

Kousser, Thad. *Term Limits and the Dismantling of State Legislative Professionalism.* New York: Cambridge University Press, 2005.

McNeely, Dave, and Jim Henderson. *Bob Bullock: God Bless Texas.* Austin: University of Texas Press, 2008.

Moncrief, Gary F., Peverill Squire, and Malcolm E. Jewell. *Who Runs for the Legislature?* Upper Saddle River, NJ: Prentice Hall, 2001.

Monmonier, Mark. *Bushmanders and Bullwinkles: How Politicians Manipulate Electronic Map and Census Data to Win Elections.* Chicago: University of Chicago Press, 2001.

Niven, David. *The Missing Majority: The Recruitment of Women as State Legislative Candidates.* Westport, CT: Praeger, 1998.

Squire, Peverill. *101 Chambers: Congress, State Legislatures, and the Future of Legislative Studies.* Columbus: Ohio State University Press, 2005.

Rosenthal, Alan. *Engines of Democracy: Politics and Policymaking in State Legislatures.* Washington, DC: CQ Press, 2009.

———. *The Decline of Representative Democracy: Process, Participation and Power in State Legislatures.* Washington, DC: CQ Press, 1998.

———. *Governors and Legislatures: Contending Powers.* Washington, DC: Congressional Quarterly Books, 1990.

On the Web

To learn more about the Texas Legislature Online, which provides legislative histories and access to bills, amendments, and statutes affected by proposed legislation, go to **www.capitol.state.tx.us**.

To learn more about the Texas Senate, including biographical information, committee assignments, and district data, go to **www.senate.state.tx.us**.

To learn more about the Texas House of Representatives, including information pertaining to the legislative process and live broadcasts of legislative proceedings, go to **www.house.state.tx.us**.

To learn more about the Texas Legislative Council, a state agency within the legislative branch that drafts bills and other legislative documents and provides informational publications for the Senate and the House, go to **www.tlc.state.tx.us**.

5

The Governor and the Executive Branch

During the 2009 session, the Republican-dominated Texas Senate, in major political rebukes of Governor Rick Perry, rejected his choice for chair of the State Board of Education and refused to confirm one of his appointees to the Board of Pardons and Paroles. This followed a contentious session in 2007, when Perry issued an executive order to the Health and Human Services Commission to require girls entering sixth grade to be vaccinated against human papillomavirus (HPV)—the most common sexually transmitted virus, and one that causes almost all cervical cancer.[1] His action created a classic case study of gubernatorial power engaged with executive agencies, legislators, interest groups, and the media.

In Texas alone, HPV causes nearly 400 deaths a year and thousands of illnesses. Gardasil, manufactured by Merck, is the first vaccine to protect against some (though not all) HPV strains. It is effective only if received before any potential infection. Governor Perry issued Executive Order RP-65 commanding the Health and Human Services Commission to require the Centers for Disease Control and Prevention-recommended vaccine (with some opt-out provisions) and to make it available immediately.[2] Perry's order would have cost about $29 million in state funds.

The reaction to the order was not what the governor had expected. Conservative interest groups spurred the legislature into action. The House Public Health Committee reviewed two bills to block the governor's action. Moreover, reporters and opponents quickly learned that Merck's lobbyist was none other than Mike Toomey, Governor Perry's former chief of staff, and that Merck had donated money to Perry's campaign on the same day that the governor's office initiated action to push forward on Gardasil.

Governor Perry insisted that his action had been proper. He brought in Heather Burcham,

Since 1846, the governor's office has been held by forty-five people. The majority were lawyers and had extensive careers in public life. But, in one way or the other, their actions as governors helped shape the office and the public's expectations of gubernatorial leadership. At left, Governor Beauford H. Jester signs a House bill in 1949 creating the State Youth Development Council. At right, Governor Rick Perry delivers the State of the State message in 2009.

a Houston woman who was gravely ill with cervical cancer, to urge acceptance of the program. But, newspapers across the state editorialized against the mandate, arguing that even if vaccination was a good policy, it should be debated by the legislature process and approved there—not mandated by an executive order. As the pressure mounted, Merck announced that it was ending its efforts to get states to mandate vaccinations.[3]

In the meantime, the attorney general ruled that a governor's executive order can only be a "suggestion" to an agency, not an order. The state legislature passed a bill forbidding the commissioner from requiring HPV vaccination with far more than the required two-thirds support for overriding a veto. So, Governor Perry let the law go into effect without his signature but expressed his regret that without the vaccination, women would be needlessly at risk. A few months after the 2007 session ended, Heather Burcham died.

What Should I Know About . . .

After reading this chapter, you should be able to:

★ **5.1** Trace the historical development of the structure of the executive branch in Texas, and state the reasons for the creation of the plural executive, p. 140.

★ **5.2** List the constitutional roles of the governor, p. 143.

★ **5.3** Identify the major powers assigned to the governor, and analyze how governors have interpreted and developed these powers, p. 144.

★ **5.4** Evaluate the effectiveness of Texas governors as policy makers and political leaders, p. 151.

★ **5.5** Outline the functions of the other elected administrative agencies within the plural executive, and evaluate their policy and administrative effectiveness, p. 158.

★ **5.6** Determine the role of the modern Texas bureaucracy in the formulation, implementation, and evaluation of public policy, p. 165.

★ **5.7** Explain how the legislature holds state agencies and public employees accountable, and evaluate proposals to reform the Texas executive branch, p. 170.

plural executive
An executive branch in which power and policy implementation are divided among several executive agencies rather than centralized under one person; the governor does not get to appoint most agency heads.

The top political leader and top official of the executive branch of Texas state government is the governor. However, power and policy implementation are not centralized in the Texas governor's office; rather, Texas has a **plural executive,** with power divided among several independently elected officials, appointed officials, and more than one hundred executive boards and commissions. The governor has little direct power over state agencies. This fragmented government is a double-edged sword: it increases the chance for conflicts over policy making, but it enhances the opportunity for policy innovation and experimentation.

Because Texas governors are not assured of control of state government, they must build strong outside support. That could consist of support from economic powers, popular support among voters, or both. In this chapter, we will explore the governorship and the executive branch, or bureaucracy, in Texas.

- First, we will examine *the roots of the executive branch in Texas,* indicating how the Texas governorship and division of executive authority developed.

- Second, we will describe *the constitutional roles of the governor,* emphasizing the roles of chief of state, chief executive, and commander in chief with a view toward the interpretation and development of these roles over time.

- Third, we will look at *the development of gubernatorial power,* comparing the powers of the Texas governor with those of other state governors and describing how governors use these powers in their various roles.

- Fourth, we will assess *the governor as policy maker and political leader,* describing how Texas governors use personal and political skills to achieve their policy goals.

- Fifth, we will explore *the plural executive in Texas,* describing the elected officials who make up the plural executive and their duties.

- Sixth, we will look at the *modern Texas bureaucracy* and examine its role in the formulation, implementation, and evaluation of public policy.

- Finally, we will examine the tools available to the legislature and the governor to *make agencies accountable* and also some of the ways in which the executive branch can be reformed.

ROOTS OF the Executive Branch in Texas

⭐ **5.1 . . . Trace the historical development of the structure of the executive branch in Texas, and state the reasons for the creation of the plural executive.**

The issue of how executive power should be organized and manifested in Texas has its roots in decisions made long ago, in the emerging political systems of the United States and Mexico. Spanish kings sent representatives of the crown to what is now Texas in the 1500s. In 1691, King Charles II designated the first *Governador de*

Tejas—Don Domingo Teran de los Rios—who, in addition to governing, drove cattle from interior Mexico and established the first herds in Texas.[4] After the Mexican Revolution against Spain, the Mexican Constitution of 1824 and the 1827 Constitution of the State of Coahuila y Tejas established an elected governor and an executive council and gave the governor the power to rule by decree.

Before the American Revolution, governors of the British colonies represented and served at the pleasure of the British monarch. Only two of the governors were elected. These early American governors were weak. They shared power with executive councils and with other statewide officials and were subordinate to the colonial legislatures.[5]

From President of the Lone Star Republic to Governor of Texas

After the Texas Revolution against Mexico, from 1836 to 1845, in the new Republic of Texas, the chief executive was the president, who ruled with a Cabinet (appointed by and responsible to him). When Texas joined the United States in 1845, it was with a relatively powerful governor. The first to serve in that office was James Pinckney Henderson. Texas governors, who were elected to two-year terms, appointed almost all state officials, including judges; the comptroller and the treasurer were elected by the legislature. By 1850, the constitution was amended to provide for the direct election of judges, the attorney general, comptroller, treasurer, and land commissioner. The state's Confederate Constitution of 1861 was similar to the 1845 one in terms of the governor's powers.[6]

The 1866 Constitution included a four-year term for the governor, with a limit of two consecutive terms, and gubernatorial (meaning of or by the governor) appointment of all officials but the comptroller and the treasurer. A new power for the governor was the line-item veto, which had been used in the Civil War. The 1869 Constitution retained a four-year term and allowed the governor to appoint local officials and state police and impose martial law. However, as one scholar of the Texas governorship wrote, "More disintegration of the executive power than ever was effected."[7] The lieutenant governor, comptroller, treasurer, land commissioner, and public instruction superintendent were all elected to four-year terms.

The 1876 Constitution further decentralized and limited state government. The governor's term was reduced to two years and the salary was reduced from $5,000 to $4,000. While Texans have amended this constitution many times since its adoption, the basic structure of executive power remains the same: a weak governor who must share power with other statewide elected officials and a strong legislature. Texas has had thirty-one governors under this constitution. (To learn more about the people who have served as governor of Texas, see Table 5.1.)

Who was the first governor of Texas? James Pinckney Henderson was elected Texas's first governor, serving from February 1846 to December 1847. When Mexico and the United States went to war, he persuaded the Texas Legislature to allow him to take personal command of a division of the Texas Rangers, who were being sent to fight in Mexico.

Photo courtesy: Briscoe Center for American History

Table 5.1 *What common characteristics do Texas governors share?*

Governor	Party	Age at Election	Years Served
Joseph D. Sayers	D	57	1899–1903
Samuel Lanham	D	56	1903–1907
Thomas M. Campbell	D	50	1907–1911
Oscar B. Colquitt	D	49	1911–1915
James E. Ferguson	D	43	1915–1917
William P. Hobby	D	39	1917–1921
Pat M. Neff	D	49	1921–1925
Miriam A. Ferguson	D	49	1925–1927
Dan Moody	D	33	1927–1931
Ross Sterling	D	55	1931–1933
Miriam A. Ferguson[a]	D	57	1933–1935
James V. Allred	D	35	1935–1939
W. Lee O'Daniel	D	48	1939–1941
Coke Stevenson	D	53	1941–1947
Beauford Jester	D	54	1947–1949
Allan Shivers	D	41	1949–1957
Price Daniel	D	46	1957–1963
John Connally	D	45	1963–1969
Preston Smith	D	56	1969–1973
Dolph Briscoe[b]	D	49	1973–1979
Bill Clements	R	61	1979–1983
Mark White	D	42	1983–1987
Bill Clements[a]	R	69	1987–1991
Ann Richards	D	57	1991–1995
George W. Bush	R	48	1995–2000
Rick Perry	R	50	2000–

[a]Miriam Ferguson and Bill Clements served nonconsecutive terms as governor.

[b]Dolph Briscoe served one two-year term and one four-year term. The governors after Briscoe served four-year terms.

Sources: Authors; Garland Adair, *Texas Pictorial Handbook* (Austin: Texas Memorial Museum, 1957); William Atkinson, *James V. Allred: A Political Biography* (Ph.D. diss., TCU, 1978); Biographical Files—Governors of Texas (Austin; Center for American History, University of Texas); Robert A. Calvert and Arnoldo DeLeon, *The History of Texas* (Arlington Heights, IL: Harlan Davidson, 1990); Council of State Governments, *The Governors of the States, Commonwealths, and Territories 1900–1980* (Lexington, K.Y: Council of State Governments, 1981); *Dallas Morning News* (March 7, 1991); Fred Gantt Jr., *The Chief Executive in Texas: A Study in Gubernatorial Leadership* (Austin: University of Texas Press, 1964), appendix 3; Ross Phares, *Governors of Texas* (Gretna, LA: Pelican, 1976); *Texas Almanac* (Dallas: A. H. Belo, 1992); Marquis Who's Who, *Who's Who in the South and Southwest,* 16th ed., 1978–1979, and 18th ed., 1982–1983 (Chicago: Marquis Who's Who).

Terms of Office

The state constitution sets the length of the term of office for the governorship, methods for removing a governor from office, and the line of succession in the event of a vacancy in the office. The constitution originally set the governor's salary, though the legislature does now.

LENGTH AND NUMBER OF TERMS   The length of the term of office for the governor is four years. It was established as a two-year term in the original 1876 Constitution and remained two years until it was amended, effective with the 1974 election.[8] There is no limit to the number of terms that the governor may serve.

Until the 1940s, no Texas governor served more than two terms. Virtually all governors won two terms when the terms were two years long. Then, from the 1940s to the 1970s, a three-term tradition was maintained. Democrat Dolph Briscoe was elected governor in 1972. When he won reelection in 1974, it was for the new four-year term. In 1978, he ran for another four-year term but was defeated in the Democratic primary—partly on an appeal by his opponent against having an unprecedented ten-year governor. Bill Clements served one four-year term and was defeated by Mark White, who served a single four-year term before being defeated by Clements. Clements then served another four-year term.[9] Ann Richards served a four-year term, then in 1994 lost to George W. Bush, who won reelection in 1998. He was the first governor to win back-to-back four-year terms, though he did not serve out his second term, as he resigned in December 2000 to become president. Rick Perry served out Bush's term, won election to a full term in 2002, then won reelection in 2006. In 2008, Perry became the longest serving governor in Texas history and won another term in 2010.

SALARY In all of Texas's constitutions until 1954, the governor's salary was set in the constitution. It was $4,000 in the 1876 Constitution.[10] Voters repeatedly defeated salary increases before a $12,000 salary was approved in 1935. In 1953, the constitution was amended to allow the legislature to set the governor's salary. It quickly became one of the highest governor's salaries in the nation. The salary level stagnated in the 1990s, and the comparative ranking slipped. In 2006, the governor was paid $115,345, which ranked twenty-eighth in the nation; the highest governor's salary was California's, at $206,500.[11] In 2007, the Legislature voted to raise the governor's salary to $150,000 a year, but Governor Perry refused to accept the raise and kept his salary at $115,345.

Was this a random act of criminal behavior or a political statement? The 154-year-old governor's mansion, located across from the Capitol building in Austin, was torched by an arsonist on June 8, 2008. The mansion, under renovation and unoccupied at the time, suffered extensive damage. Subsequently, it has undergone restoration and expansion.

Photo courtesy: Bob Daemmrich Photography, Inc.

The state also provides the governor with housing, a security detail, travel expenses, and access to state-owned planes and cars. The governor's mansion, which is located across the street from the Capitol, was torched by an arsonist on June 8, 2008, and it is undergoing massive renovations.

IMPEACHMENT Texas executive officials, like federal officials, are subject to impeachment by the legislative branch. One Texas governor has been impeached, convicted, and removed from office. In 1917, James E. Ferguson angered legislators and University of Texas (UT) alumni by vetoing UT appropriations in order to force changes that he wanted. Legislators resurrected old allegations that he had misused public money, impeached him, and convicted him. He was removed from office and barred from holding office again. Later, his wife, Miriam, successfully ran for governor under the slogan "Two Governors for the Price of One," becoming Texas's first woman governor.

SUCCESSION Article 4, section 17, of the constitution provides for succession. The lieutenant governor succeeds to the governorship if there is a vacancy. Voters approved a constitutional amendment in 1999 to assure that in the event of a vacancy in the governorship, the lieutenant governor would have to resign that office upon succeeding to the governorship, and the Senate would select a new lieutenant governor. Since 1876, five lieutenant governors have succeeded to the governorship: Richard Hubbard, William Hobby, Coke Stevenson, Allan Shivers, and Rick Perry.[12]

The Constitutional Roles of the Governor

⭐ **5.2** . . . **List the constitutional roles of the governor.**

The roles that the governor plays are set by constitutional and legislative mandates and by custom. Some of these roles encompass real powers and functions of the governorship; others appear to be little more than ceremonial.

chief of state

The governor in his or her role as the official head representing the state of Texas in its relationships with the national government, other states, and foreign dignitaries.

chief executive officer

The governor as the top official of the executive branch of Texas state government.

commander in chief

The governor in his or her role as head of the state militia.

chief budget officer

The governor, who is charged with preparing the state budget proposal for the legislature.

clemency

The governor's authority to reduce the length of a person's prison sentence.

governor's message

Message that the governor delivers to the legislature, pronouncing policy goals, budget priorities, and authorizations for the legislature to act.

veto

The formal, constitutional authority of the chief executive to reject bills passed by both houses of the legislative body, thus preventing their becoming law without further legislative action.

The Texas Constitution designates the governor as the **chief of state, chief executive officer,** and **commander in chief** of Texas. Article 4, section 9, of the constitution empowers the governor to conduct "all intercourse and business of the State with other States and with the United States," which is the function of chief of state. Article 4, section 7, designates the governor as the "commander-in-chief of the military forces of the State." Article 4, section 1, designates the governor as the chief executive officer, which is further defined in section 12, giving him or her the authority to appoint people to fill vacancies in state offices in certain circumstances. The fragmented organization of executive power, however, makes the position of chief executive officer one that depends largely on the political and personal skills of the governor.

The governor plays other roles that are alluded to in the constitution but not spelled out specifically. Article 4, section 9, requires the governor to "present estimates of the amount of money required to be raised by taxation for all purposes." In 1931, the legislature institutionalized this role by designating the governor as the state's **chief budget officer**—presumably the official responsible for preparing the budget proposal and for overseeing its implementation. However, the same law gave the State Board of Control the responsibility of preparing the budget, and in 1949, the legislature created the Legislative Budget Board, which prepares a budget proposal that becomes the basis for the state appropriations act (see **chapter 4**). Thus, the governor's role as chief budget officer is greatly circumscribed.

Because of the governor's limited constitutional powers over judicial vacancies (Article 5, section 28) and pardons, parole, and clemency (Article 4, section 11), he or she has a narrow role in law enforcement. The original 1876 Constitution gave the governor almost absolute power in **clemency,** the power to reduce prison terms. Governors received and granted thousands of requests for clemency and pardons, and there were recurrent rumors of bribery. The legislature created a Board of Pardons and Paroles in 1929, thus reducing the governor's powers, as well as the pressure on governors.[13] Article 4, section 11, gives the governor the power to grant reprieves and commutations of punishment and pardons "on the written signed recommendation and advice of the Board of Pardons and Paroles."

The governor has become a powerful figure in legislative politics. Article 4, section 8, of the constitution gives the governor the authority to call the legislature into special sessions and set the agenda for those sessions; section 9 requires the governor to deliver **governor's messages** to the legislature, such as the State of the State message and the budget message; section 14 creates the authority to **veto** (negate) acts of the legislature; section 15 empowers the governor to sign bills and resolutions. These constitutional powers, plus the ability to *threaten* to veto bills, make the governor an ever present force in legislative affairs.

The Development of Gubernatorial Power

★ **5.3 . . . Identify the major powers assigned to the governor, and analyze how governors have interpreted and developed these powers.**

How much power and what kinds of power a governor has depend on constitutional provisions, the era and political times in which a governor serves, and the relative power of other governmental officials. Regardless of how these factors have changed, Texas governors have always been weaker than governors in most other states.

Characteristics of Gubernatorial Power

Political scientist Joseph Schlesinger devised a scale to measure the power of governors, using data from 1960–1961. These data have been updated periodically since then. Schlesinger used four variables: *tenure* (length of term of office, limits on number of terms), *appointments* (power to appoint heads of executive agencies), *budget* (budget-preparation power), and *signing and vetoing of bills* (veto and line-item veto authority, time to consider legislation before signing or vetoing it, difficulty of legislative ability to override). Schlesinger found that strong governorships were typically in large, urbanized, wealthy, nonsouthern states, with a strong level of party competition.[14]

Restriction of Governors' Powers

Nationwide, distrust of government and governors in the eighteenth and nineteenth centuries led to restrictions on the power that governors could wield and on their terms of office. In the Jacksonian era, the powers of governors were increased somewhat: terms were extended to four years, and appointment, veto, and clemency powers were increased. Their powers were checked, though, by the increasing election of other executive officials.[15] Gradually, throughout the twentieth century, states lifted many of the gubernatorial restrictions and empowered their governors. Most governors now possess significant powers.

Texas was a practitioner of restrictions on gubernatorial power, especially in reaction to the strong government set up during Reconstruction. Under the 1869 Constitution, the governor had complete control over voter registration, the militia, and the state police, and could appoint the governing bodies of towns and cities. Under Republican Governor Edmund J. Davis, the militia and the state police were despised by some. (Of course, racial politics also influenced people's attitudes.) A much later historical analysis argued that "the police force was used so often to enforce the arbitrary will of the governor that it became an emblem of despotic authority."[16] In 1872, voters rebelled and elected an anti-administration legislature, which triggered adoption of a new constitution. The desire to punish Davis and to prohibit future governors from becoming powerful led constitutional convention delegates in 1875 to adopt provisions that reduced the governor's salary, elected a plethora of other officers independent from the governor, and restricted the governor's appointment and removal powers.[17]

Comparing the Texas Governor with Other Governors

Today, a comparison of the fifty governors around the United States reveals substantial differences among them, particularly some interesting contrasts with the Texas governorship. Whereas forty-one states have some kind of Cabinet system in which the major agency directors are selected by and responsible to the governor, Texas does not.[18] Rather, Texas has a plural executive: most agency directors are appointed by boards, rather than directly by the governor; some agency directors are elected; there is no systematic, ongoing process for the governor to coordinate executive policies; and it is virtually impossible for the governor to fire a board member or an agency head. (To learn more about this issue, see Join the Debate: Should the Texas Governor Have a Cabinet?)

Scholars of state government have developed institutional rankings of the governor to provide a basis for comparison and analysis. These scales provide state-by-state comparisons as well as comparisons over time as states change the powers of the governors. In his

Join the DEBATE | Should the Texas Governor Have a Cabinet?

As president of the Republic of Texas, Sam Houston governed with a Cabinet. In the ensuing decades, governors maintained significant control over the executive branch of state government in Texas, but the 1876 Constitution then stripped the governor of many powers, including controls over the executive branch. Attempts since then to reconvene Cabinet-style executive authority have been short-lived, often accompanied by high-profile clashes among executive officials. In 1931, the legislature created a committee to reorganize state government. Its reorganization plan suggested a Cabinet-style government to strengthen executive coordination, but the Cabinet proposal was killed.[a] The idea lives on with governors, though. Governor Allan Shivers (1949–1957) waited until his final Inauguration in 1955 to proclaim:

> I believe we should begin giving serious thought to reorganizing the executive branch. If the governor is to be held accountable for the conduct of the executive branch, future governors should have direct authority over—as well as responsibility for—the performance of administrative functions which are not policymaking in character, [including] appointment and removal.[b]

Today, forty-one states have some kind of Cabinet system in which the major agency directors are selected by and responsible to the governor. Texas does not.[c] The idea of a more unified executive in Texas, with a governor's Cabinet, is not dead—but such proposals have been defeated for more than a century. Should Texans reconsider the creation of a Cabinet?

To develop an ARGUMENT FOR the creation of a Cabinet, think about how:

- **The plural executive leads to conflict among members of the executive branch and policy deadlock.** If the general population perceives the governor as the state's chief executive officer, shouldn't the governor be assigned the authority and control over all of the administrative agencies? How would expanding the appointment powers of the governor and the creation of a Cabinet result in greater accountability of the governor?
- **Governors are limited in their abilities to coordinate and control the executive branch of government.** If independent department heads derive their powers from the constitution, how does a governor exercise oversight or reviews of what those agencies are doing? How can the governor control the budgets of these agencies or fire non-performing heads of independent agencies?
- **A Cabinet enables the governor to demand cooperation, coordination, and a high level of performance from those he or she appoints.** How would a Cabinet increase the efficiency of state government? In what ways would regular meetings of top government executives produce more informed discussions of pressing issues and expand considerations of solutions to state problems?

To develop an ARGUMENT AGAINST the creation of a Cabinet, think about how:

- **Texans have long valued the institution of the plural executive and a governor with limited powers.** Is there really any evidence that the majority of the public prefers a stronger institutional governor? How would the citizenry perceive a constitutional amendment to restructure the executive branch? In what ways might it be perceived as a grab for additional power with fewer checks on the governor?
- **Multiple, independent executive officers, elected by the people, serve to stimulate policy innovations.** How does the plural executive protect citizens from governors who refuse to respond to pressing issues or are just plain incompetent? In what ways can independent agencies lead to "cutting edge" policy innovation and reform?
- **The legislature and the voters have expanded gubernatorial power when it was needed.** What specific tools of authority have the legislature and voters given the governor in the past when they perceived a need? In what ways are these changes sufficient to permit the governor to carry out the functions of the office effectively? Doesn't the effectiveness of a governor really depend on his or her political skills and not the formal powers of the office?

---

[a]Joint Advisory Committee on Government Operations, "Final Report to the Governor of Texas and Members of the 65th Texas Legislature," January 1977.
[b]Fred Gantt Jr., *The Chief Executive in Texas: A Study in Gubernatorial Leadership* (Austin: University of Texas Press, 1964); *House Journal*, 54th Legislature, 70.
[c]Council of State Governments, *Book of the States 2005*, Table 4.6, 225, and Table 4.10, 233.

1960–1961 rankings based on tenure, appointments, budget power, and veto power, Joseph Schlesinger ranked Texas as tied for the weakest of the governors. When he updated his scale using 1968–1969 data, Texas ranked fiftieth, leading Schlesinger to comment that "Texas is the only populous state where the governor's formal strength is low."[19] Political scientist Thad Beyle has updated the rankings numerous times since then. In his rankings, Texas was always forty-eighth or forty-ninth, until he changed variables in 1999, which capped Texas's rank at 28th. Texas also has a weak governor using just the Schlesinger variables. Only the Texas and South Carolina governors have weak budget-making power, and only Texas, Georgia, Mississippi, and Oklahoma governors have weak appointment powers.[20]

The legislature and the voters have strengthened the Texas governorship in recent years. Today, the governor can appoint more high-level positions than ever before, and he or she has (limited) budget execution authority. Also, a 1980 amendment (Article 15, section 9) allows the governor, for the first time under the current constitution, to remove from office gubernatorial appointees—but only with a two-thirds vote of the Senate, and only his or her own appointees, not previous governors' appointees. No governor has yet used this power.

Constitutionally, it is apparent that the Texas governor is weak. However, governors may be able to amass and exercise more strength in the political arena, where appearance, charisma, and bluff may count more than constitutional reality. In 1994 and 1999, Beyle compared "personal power" of the governors. Texas's governor ranked significantly higher on personal power than on the institutional powers rankings. Indeed, when Beyle looked at ambition, future office possibilities, and electoral mandates, he concluded that the Texas governor ranked third, behind only Delaware and Kansas. When he then combined the personal rankings with the lower institutional rankings of the governors, he ranked the Texas governor ninth in the nation.[21]

The Governor's Power to Appoint Executive Officials

Article 4, section 12, of the constitution details the method for filling vacancies in the executive branch: "All vacancies in State or district offices, except members of the Legislature, shall be filled unless otherwise provided by law by appointment of the Governor." The governor appoints more agency heads today than ever before. Recent additions to the governor's appointment powers include education commissioner and health and human services executive commissioner. However, most appointments are to boards, commissions, and advisory panels. The governor makes several hundred appointments a year.[22]

A 1933 court case determined that the legislature may designate someone other than the governor to make an appointment, and no Senate confirmation would be required. However, if the legislature does not provide an alternative means, the governor appoints.[23] Some analysts argue that the legislature can specify a gubernatorial appointment without requiring Senate confirmation. Indeed, there are several positions that the governor fills without confirmation, though there are others that the Senate does confirm, without express provisions for confirmation.[24] Custom and the balance of political power seem to dictate on a case-by-case basis whether confirmation will be required.

While presidential appointment requires only a simple majority confirmation in the U.S. Senate, Texas gubernatorial appointments require consent of the Texas Senate in a vote of at least two-thirds of those present (Article 4, section 12c). Because most appointments are made while the legislature is not in session, when the Senate convenes in regular or special session, it may take up appointments made during the interim. Thus, some appointees may serve for a year or more before the Senate meets and confirms or rejects the nomination. **Senatorial courtesy** is a norm that requires the governor to preclear a nominee with the senator in whose district the nominee

senatorial courtesy

A process by which a governor, when selecting an appointee, defers to the state senator in whose district the nominee resides.

TIMELINE: Texas Governors and Structural Changes to the Executive Office

1846 **The First Governor of Texas**—James Pinckney Henderson (1808–1858) is elected the state's first governor after Texas joins the Union, taking office in February 1846.

1876 **Constitution Limits the Governor's Power**—In reaction to Reconstruction, a constitution is adopted that significantly limits the power of the governor.

1917 **Governor Impeached**—Governor James E. Ferguson is impeached by the Texas Legislature for vetoing appropriations to the University of Texas when the university refused to fire professors at his request.

1924 **First Woman Governor**—Miriam A. Ferguson is the first woman elected governor of the state of Texas.

resides. Senatorial courtesy and the recent growth of a two-party legislature mean that a governor must be sensitive to senatorial concerns or risk either embarrassment or a political battle.

A 1999 appointment attempt by Governor George W. Bush demonstrates how senatorial courtesy actually works. Bush wanted to reappoint Public Utility Commissioner Judy Walsh, who was from Austin. However, opponents of Walsh convinced Austin's Senator Gonzalo Barrientos to oppose the nomination. Governor Bush recognized the norm of senatorial courtesy and assumed that the Senate would then reject the nomination if he submitted it. However, since the legislature was not in session, the governor simply did not appoint anyone, which left Walsh in the position until the Senate convened next (and Governor Perry made a new appointment).[25]

The election of Republican Bill Clements provided the first test of how party clashes would affect appointments. Governor Clements made 105 lame-duck appointments after he was defeated in 1982, but early in 1983, new Democratic Governor Mark White and the Democratic Texas Senate found a way to negate most of the appointments. The Senate returned fifty-nine to White unconfirmed; two more were later rejected. White then reappointed eleven of Clements's picks but ignored the others and made his own nominations.[26] The legislature then approved, and voters ratified, a constitutional amendment shifting the dates of some appointments to take away the chance of so many lame-duck appointments. When George W. Bush became governor, the Senate Nominations Committee—chaired for the first time by a Republican—stalled several of Ann Richards's unconfirmed interim appointees, refusing them hearings, so Bush could fill those positions.

Analysis of appointees reveals that governors tend to appoint people like themselves and their allies. Because all but two governors have been male, all but three have been Democrats, and all have been Anglo, it should not be surprising that Anglo, male Democrats have historically dominated state boards and commissions.

1963 Governor John Connally Is Shot in Dallas— The shooting occurs at the same time that President John F. Kennedy is assassinated.

1978 First Republican Governor of Modern Times—Bill Clements is elected as Texas's first Republican governor of modern times.

1975 Terms Changed to Four Years—Governor Dolph Briscoe, who opposed the reforms of the 1974 Constitutional Convention, begins his second term, which was changed to four years by a constitutional amendment passed by voters in 1973.

2000 Longest Serving Governor—Rick Perry becomes governor after George W. Bush resigns to become U.S. president. Perry goes on to become the longest serving governor in the state's history.

Overrepresentation and underrepresentation are higher and lower numbers, respectively, than would be expected based on a group's numbers in the general population. For governors' appointees, those who have been overrepresented in appointments are Anglos and males, while women, African Americans, and Mexican Americans have been underrepresented (To learn more about the gender, race, and ethnicity of the appointments of the past five governors, see Table 5.2).

The pattern of appointments has changed only marginally in the past three decades, with the significant exception of Ann Richards (1991–1994). Governor Clements (1979–1982, 1987–1990) brought in more Republicans but reduced the number of minorities appointed. Governor White (1983–1986) appointed more women and minorities than

Table 5.2 *What gender, racial, or ethnic patterns can you discern in appointments made by recent Texas governors?*

	Texas Population	Appointees of Governor:				
	(2000)	White	Clements	Richards	Bush	Perry
Gender						
Male	49.5%	78%	82%	55%	63%	62%
Female	50.5	22	18	45	37	37
Race/ethnic group						
White	52.4	82	89	65	77	71
Mexican American	32.0	12	7	19	13	16
African American	11.5	6	3	14	9	11
Other	4.1	n/a	n/a	2	n/a	2

Sources: Clements, White, and Bush appointees from Peggy Fikae, "Bush Appointing Many Females, Minorities," *San Antonio Expression-News:* (July 9, 2000); Richards appointees from list supplied by Office of Governor Ann Richards, October 13,1994; Governor Perry's appointees from three years of data, Texans for Public Justice, "Governor Perry's Patronage," April 1, 2006, www.tpj.org; and from Office of Governor Rick Perry, May 19, 2006.

did his predecessors, though still in numbers far below their presence in the population.[27] Richards made a public issue of the gender and race of appointees. She is the only governor to appoint numbers of women and racial and ethnic minorities in approximate proportion to their presence in the population. By the end of her term, 45 percent of her appointees were women, 19 percent were Mexican American, and 14 percent were African American. Governor Bush did not appoint as many women and minorities; after four years in office, 37 percent of his appointees were women, 13 percent were Mexican American, and 9 percent were African American. Governor Perry's appointments pattern is in between Richards's and Bush's: in his first five years of office, about 37 percent of his appointees were women, 16 percent Mexican American, and 11 percent African American.[28]

When Ann Richards announced her gubernatorial campaign in 1989, she promised that her administration would "look like Texas." She and her supporters argued that a government truly responsive to the concerns of Texas must take into account the wide variety of groups in the population, and that one way of doing that is to have executive agency officials reflect that population diversity. Her pledge to do so gave a boost to her 1990 campaign. While in office, Governor Richards did appoint officials who more closely reflected the population demographics in the state. Those appointees not only provided new voices inside government but also served to break down barriers and expand public service opportunities for the broader groups from which they came.

Ron Kirk served as secretary of state, then became the first African American mayor of Dallas. In 2009, he was appointed U.S. Trade Representative by President Barack Obama. Susan Rieff served as the governor's environmental coordinator, became regional director for the Audubon Society, and later executive director of the Lady Bird Johnson Wildflower Center. Former legislative reformer Zan Holmes became the first African American to serve on the University of Texas Board of Regents. Lena Guerrero was appointed to the Texas Railroad Commission, which had previously been almost exclusively male and Anglo. While Guerrero lost her bid to win election to the seat, several Hispanics and women have served on the commission since then.

In addition to the significance of gender and race homogeneity or diversity of appointees, another issue has also dominated the debate over who gains a seat at the table of policy making and administration: the role of campaign donations. Often, key appointments go to the governor's largest campaign contributors. Of Governor Mark White's early appointments, 27 percent were campaign contributors.[29] Governor Richards appointed her largest contributor to the Parks and Wildlife Board. Another large contributor was appointed chair of the University of Texas (UT) Board of Regents. George W. Bush kept this tradition alive. In his gubernatorial campaigns, Bush collected about $2.4 million in contributions from people he appointed to state positions,[30] including Allan Polunsky (chair of the Board of Criminal Justice), David Laney (chair of the Transportation Commission), Donald Evans (chair of the UT Board of Regents, and later President Bush's secretary of commerce), Tony Sanchez (UT Board of Regents, and later Democratic candidate for governor), Tom Loeffler (UT Board of Regents), and Richard Heath and Mark Watson (Parks and Wildlife Commission).

Governor Bush's contributor-appointees typically gave about $25,000 to his campaigns, with Tom Loeffler giving the most at $141,000. Governor Perry's appointments continued this pattern at an even higher level, according to figures analyzed by the group Texans for Public Justice. For 2003–2005, one-third of Perry's appointees were campaign contributors, and seventeen gave more than $100,000. Texas Tech Regent Larry Anders gave the most at $220,304, followed by UT Regent Robert Rowling at $207,262 and Parks and Wildlife Commissioner Peter Holt at $206,000.

However, not all contributions in Texas are individual contributions. Texans for Public Justice also documented another dynamic: contributions from corporation political action committees (PACs) compared with gubernatorial appointment of corporate officials. PACs from Perry Homes, SBC, Pilgrim's Pride, Dell, Reliant Energy, TXU, Hance Scarborough, and H.E. Butt Grocery all gave more than $100,000 to Perry's campaigns, and executives from their companies were appointed to executive offices.[31]

The Power of Staff and Budget

The responsibilities of the governor's staff are broad: developing the governor's budget proposals and policy recommendations; performing public relations; serving as liaison with local, state, and federal agencies and with the legislature and party officials; answering correspondence and visiting with citizens who call on the governor; contacting and negotiating with lobbyists. These duties change with the priorities and organizational preferences of each governor.

Nineteenth-century Texas governors typically had two or three staff members. The growth in the number of boards and commissions, with the governor as an ex officio member of many of them, brought an increase in the governor's staff to about eight in the 1920s. Since the 1950s, the governor's staff has grown tremendously. Recent governors have had about 200 staff members. Measuring staff size, though, is difficult, because governors can persuade agency heads to pay for staff members that are then loaned to the governor and do not appear on the governor's payroll.

The amount of money that the legislature appropriates for the operations of the Office of the Governor depends on what functions the legislature and the governor choose to place under the office. While the governor's appropriations may exceed $100 million a year, usually less than $10 million is for the narrower Governor's Office (in 2009 it was $9.5 million), and the remainder is for discretionary funds, programs supported by trust funds, and suboffices included in the governor's budget, such as the governor's mansion, music and film industry marketing, information on disability policies, women's groups, criminal justice, and workforce issues. For fiscal years 2008 and 2009, the budget for the broad Office of the Governor was $754 million and $143 million, respectively—including large amounts for the Texas Enterprise Fund and bond proceeds.

The Governor as Policy Maker and Political Leader

★ **5.4 . . . Evaluate the effectiveness of Texas governors as policy makers and political leaders.**

If the Texas governor is constitutionally weak, then the governor's skill in wielding political power becomes even more important in his or her success at governing. As political scientist Fred Gantt points out in his study of the Texas governorship through the middle of the twentieth century, "Instead of the 'Chief Executive of Texas,' under existing laws he might more accurately be labeled the 'Chief Persuader of Texas.'"[32] In more recent years, an analysis of Ann Richards's governorship concluded that she "pushed the powers of a weak office to their limits,"[33] and George W. Bush was perceived as a governor with strong personal skills that made him a strong governor. The political leadership that a governor is able to provide flows from the governor's skills and previous experience, as well as similarity in party, philosophy, and ideology with other decision makers. (To learn more about governors' leadership styles, see Analyzing Visuals: Ideology and Governors.)

These skills must be honed in the electoral arena in order to win the governorship. All Texas governors have sought reelection; governors must, then, maintain those electoral connections while in office. Because Texas political parties have been weak, governors have had to build and sustain personal followings and organizations. Of course, campaign money is essential, and governors must raise money while they are in office, both to pay off any previous campaign debt and to prepare for the next campaign. These electoral linkages help build the visibility of the governor as well as an image of strength—which in turn helps him or her in wielding governmental power in battles with other officials and private interest groups.

Public Opinion Leadership

Because of their weak constitutional powers, Texas governors resort to public opinion leadership to increase their power with other office holders. Invariably, their opponents see such initiatives as public relations efforts to boost the governor's political fortunes. Governors have sometimes had their own television shows. When Governor Bill Clements developed a tense relationship with the media and stopped showing up for the taping of *The Governor's Report*, the show was renamed *Capitol Report*. Governor Mark White ran television commercials to build support for higher teacher salaries. (To learn more about governors and public opinion, see Politics Now: Rick Perry Strikes a Chord with Comments About Texas Secession.)

Governors hold news conferences either on a regular basis or whenever they believe such conferences will be beneficial to them. Sometimes they go outside Austin to try to stir up public support for their policies. Governor Clements tried an anti-tax

ANALYZING VISUALS

Ideology and Governors

This figure features four ideologies. It also identifies where several past governors fall in terms of their willingness to use governmental power to achieve equality or to limit personal freedoms. After studying the figure, answer the questions.

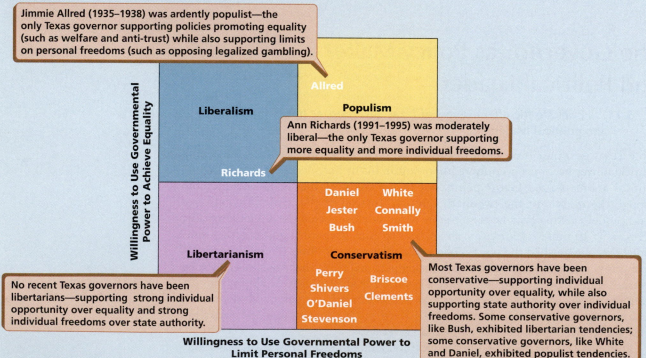

- Which governors have been most willing to use governmental power to achieve equality? To limit personal freedoms?
- What national events may have influenced the election of Ann Richards and James Allred, respectively?
- Why do you think so many of the state's past governors have been ideologically conservative? What does this suggest about Texans' views of the governor's role?

tour during a legislative session. Governor Mark White made trips during legislative sessions to key legislators' districts. Governor Ann Richards tried a "tour of state government" to promote dialogue between state officials and citizens in several locations across the state. Governors George Bush and Rick Perry spoke around the state about their tax and education proposals.

What happens if they don't get along? Under most circumstances, members of the plural executive cooperate, but sometimes intense philosophical, political, or personal differences can spill over into the legislative process. Shown here are Governor Rick Perry (center), Lt. Governor David Dewhurst (left), and House Speaker Joe Straus (right).

Photo courtesy: Bob Daemmrich Photography, Inc.

Relationship with the Legislature

To be a successful governor, one must succeed in pushing a program through the legislature and in killing unwanted legislative measures. To do so, a governor must develop good personal or working relationships with key legislators and must use the powers of the governorship to assist the legislative process and, sometimes, thwart it. As noted at the beginning of this chapter, this is sometimes easier said than done, particularly when the governor and legislators have serious policy or political differences.

A governor uses a grab bag of tools to win his or her legislative agenda, including direct appeals to voters, pleas from citizen study groups, pressure from lobbyists, breakfasts for legislators, entertainment (including evenings at the governor's mansion), individual legislative conferences, floor leaders, and staff representatives working the floor.[34] The State of the State message and budget message are the formal vehicles governors use to convey their wishes to the legislature. Governors also make emergency proclamations, which serve to put governors' favored bills ahead of others on the legislative schedule.

A hostile lieutenant governor or House Speaker could, of course, seriously damage the governor's chances of success. The governor has no role in the selection of the lieutenant governor because the office is elective. Governors can try to influence the 150 House members who select the Speaker, but to do so is politically risky. In the early twentieth century, governors sometimes became involved in House Speaker races. Governors Oscar Colquitt, Ross Sterling, and Jimmie Allred supported unsuccessful candidates for Speaker. As Miriam Ferguson began her term as governor in 1933, her husband, former Governor James Ferguson, successfully supported Coke Stevenson for Speaker.[35]

Since the 1930s, no governor has openly endorsed or campaigned for a House Speaker candidate, although they sometimes play a quiet and behind-the-scenes role in the Speaker's race. Governor John Connally used the ultimate gubernatorial power to influence the selection of a Speaker. When he had differences with Speaker Byron Tunnell, he appointed Tunnell to the Texas Railroad Commission in 1965, thus opening up the speakership. To ensure that he would get a new Speaker he liked, he tipped off young Representative Ben Barnes about the appointment. Barnes used the tip to gear up his ultimately successful campaign for the speakership.[36]

A key power of all U.S. governors is the ability to call special sessions of the legislature and to set the agenda for the special session (governors of thirteen states,

POLITICS**NOW**

WORLD | NATION | LOCAL | **POLITICS** | OPINION | HEALTH & SCIENCE | ARTS | SPORTS | LEISURE

Rick Perry Strikes a Chord with Comments About Texas Secession

April 18, 2009
Dallas Morning News
www.dallasnews.com

By Christy Hoppe

Gov. Rick Perry appears to have given new life to the state's two-decades-old tourism promotion—Texas: It's like a whole other country.

The empathy Perry has shown this week to those spitting-mad-at-Washington secessionists had newscaster Geraldo Rivera calling him "grossly irresponsible" and ripe for impeachment, while former U.S. House Majority Leader Tom DeLay said that Perry was being a righteous governor "standing up for the sovereignty of his state."

What is certain is that Perry has struck a chord. And it is aimed at Texas' ultimate mythology—that because it began as a country, by gum, it could go it alone again.

Unlike Texas, said state Rep. David Swinford, "other states know they don't have the right to secede. But that has been built into the Texas fabric, so we have the right to talk about it."

A poll of 500 Texans released Friday showed that 31 percent believe (incorrectly) the state retains the right to form an independent country. And another 18 percent said, given the opportunity, they would vote for Texas to secede.

The fact is, the treaty under which Texas joined the U.S. provides that it could be divided into five separate states. But it is not empowered to leave the Union, a question that the Civil War seems to have settled once and for all.

Perry has expressed bewilderment that his statements drew so much attention. And he did not, as some national media reports said, advocate secession. He did, however, assert Texas' right to leave the U.S., and he expressed sympathy for those so frustrated with the federal government's taxes, spending and mandates that they feel secession is an option.

Either way, he tapped into a go-it-alone mentality that has served Texas politicians well before. In 1991, Swinford, R-Dumas, filed a bill to allow the 28 counties in the Panhandle to secede from Texas. The new country was going to be called "Old Texas."

The bill went nowhere. . . .

No doubt, Perry is playing to his conservative base. Democrats, and quietly some Republicans, believe the frenzy Perry is whipping up is irresponsible. . . .

[State Democratic Party Chairman Boyd] Richie and others said that Perry is targeting a narrow base of enflamed Republican voters while preparing to run against U.S. Sen. Kay Bailey Hutchison in the 2010 Republican governor's primary.

"Clearly, he's playing their song," said political consultant Bill Miller. "And he was tone-perfect actually, for that group."

Critical Thinking Questions

1. Do you think Governor Perry simply made an "off-the-cuff" statement, or was this a carefully planned remark?
2. What was the governor's audience?
3. What political liabilities might the remarks produce for the governor?

including Texas, can set the agenda).[37] The Texas governor's ability to control the agenda of special sessions extends only to regular legislative acts and not to appointments or impeachments. In 1917, Governor James Ferguson vetoed the appropriations for the University of Texas, then called a special session to consider new appropriations. During that special session, the legislature impeached him. Ferguson claimed that the legislature could not act on impeachment because he had not added it to the agenda of the special session, but the Texas Supreme Court upheld the act of the legislature.[38]

The veto—the power to nullify bills passed by the legislature—is one of a governor's most potent legislative weapons. (To learn more, see The Living Constitution: Article 4, Section 14.) All of Texas's constitutions have given the governor the veto power, with the condition that the legislature may override (cancel) the veto by a vote of two-thirds in each chamber.[39] When the governor receives a bill passed by the legislature, he or she has ten days in which to sign or veto the bill. However, if the end of the legislative session occurs during that ten-day period, the governor then has twenty days from adjournment to consider the bills.

At the national level, if the U.S. Congress passes a bill and adjourns, and the president does not sign the bill, it dies. This is called a "pocket veto" (the president just pockets the bill and ignores it). In Texas, if the governor does not sign a bill, it becomes law anyway—Texas does not have the pocket veto.[40]

The mere existence of the veto power allows a governor to threaten to veto bills, which places the governor squarely in the middle of the negotiating, bargaining, and wheeling and dealing of the legislative process, as legislators seek to compromise in order to avoid a veto. Such threats can be made to legislators privately or in public.

Republican Governor Clements often resorted to vetoes and threats to veto in his dealings with the Democratic legislature. In his eight years as governor, Clements vetoed more bills and resolutions than any other governor—184— until Governor Perry surpassed his record in 2007, when Perry's career veto total hit 200. Although Ann Richards wanted to maintain good relations with her fellow Democratic leaders in the legislature, she nevertheless vetoed 36 bills and resolutions from the regular and two special sessions in 1991. And, she allowed 228 bills to become law without her signature. During her second legislative session in 1993, Richards publicly threatened to veto a bill allowing private citizens to be licensed to carry concealed handguns. She never had to veto the bill because her veto threats were enough to keep the legislature from passing it. Richards's opposition to the handgun bill was one of several factors in her loss the next year to Republican George W. Bush, who signed a handgun bill when the legislature approved one in 1995. Governor Bush vetoed twenty-four bills in 1995, thirty-six in 1997, and thirty-one in 1999—numbers typical of his predecessors. Then came Governor Perry's 2001 "Father's Day Massacre," when Perry vetoed seventy-eight bills in one day, to make his total of vetoes for the session eighty-two, a new record for one session. In so doing, he touched off a storm of protest. He vetoed forty-eight bills in 2003, nineteen in 2005, fifty-one in 2007, and thirty-five in 2009.[41]

In Texas, most bills are passed in the last ten days of the session. Consequently, most vetoes occur after adjournment, as did Governor Perry's Father's Day vetoes in 2001, and the legislature has no chance to vote to override. There have been only seventy-seven veto override attempts under the current constitution, and only twenty-six of these have been successful. Governor Bill Clements

What type of governor was John Connally? Politically adroit and a master of the political process, Connally, who served from 1963 to 1969, was perceived as a politically strong governor in spite of the constitutional limits of the office. After leaving the governorship, he went on to serve as Secretary of the Treasury under President Richard M. Nixon.

Photo courtesy: Bettmann/Corbis

Is this what they call "arm twisting"? Governor Rick Perry, as did most of his predecessors, visits with House members to advance his legislative proposals.

Photo courtesy: Bob Daemmrich Photography, Inc.

The Living Constitution

Every bill which shall have passed both houses of the Legislature shall be presented to the Governor for his approval. If he approve he shall sign it; but if he disapprove it, he shall return it, with his objections. . . . If . . . two-thirds of the members present agree to pass the bill, it shall be sent . . . to the other House . . . and, if approved by two-thirds of the members of that House, it shall become a law. If any bill shall not be returned by the Governor . . . within ten days . . . the same shall be a law . . . unless the Legislature, by its adjournment, prevent its return, in which case it shall be a law unless he shall file the same, with his objections, in the office of the Secretary of State. . . . If any bill presented to the Governor contains several items of appropriation he may object to one or more of such items, and approve the other portion of the bill.

—ARTICLE 4, SECTION 14

The Texas Constitution provides for gubernatorial vetoes in Article 4, section 14. The 1836 Constitution of the Republic of Texas is the basis for this provision. The provision has remained largely intact through the various Texas constitutions, with several notable exceptions. First, until the Constitution of 1876, the governor was allowed only five days to return vetoed bills. Second, under the Constitution of the Republic, the president could exercise a pocket veto (if the legislature adjourned during the five days allotted the president to sign or veto a bill, then the Texas president, by refusing to sign the bill, could exercise a veto). None of the constitutions of statehood have allowed the pocket veto. Furthermore, the constitutions of 1845, 1861, 1866, and 1869 did not allow post-adjournment vetoes. The current constitution extended the time to return objectionable bills to ten days and permitted the post-adjournment veto, giving the governor twenty days from adjournment to sign or veto bills. The line-item veto for appropriations measures originated with the 1866 Constitution.[a]

If the governor vetoes a bill and the legislature is in session, the provision requires that the chamber of origin must first consider the bill and that a two-thirds majority of the members present is necessary to send the bill to the other chamber. However, because the constitution does not specify whether the vote in the second chamber must be two-thirds of the members present or of the members elected, the chambers differ on their interpretations. According to Senate rules, "A vote of two-thirds of all members elected to the Senate shall be required for the passage of House bills that have been returned by the Governor with his objections, and a vote of two-thirds of the members of the Senate present shall be required for the passage of Senate bills that have been returned by the Governor with his objections."[b] In the House, on the other hand, a two-thirds vote of the members present is required, regardless of the bill's chamber of origin. The constitution is clear that on line-item vetoes, a two-thirds vote of the members present in each chamber is required.

The veto is the Texas governor's most significant constitutional power. The line-item veto, because the governor's budgetary powers are weak, is almost the only power that the governor has over the amounts and purposes of expenditures by the state.

CRITICAL THINKING QUESTIONS

1. How often you think the Texas Legislature overrides the governor's veto?
2. Against the background of their apprehension about the strong governor, why did the framers of the 1876 Constitution provide the Texas governor with a strong veto power?
3. Should the legislature be permitted to call itself into session to consider a governor's vetoes that were issued after adjournment of a session? Why or why not?

[a]George D. Braden, *The Constitution of the State of Texas: An Annotated and Comparative Analysis*, vol. 1 (Austin, TX: Legislative Council, 1977), 333.
[b]Texas Senate, *Rules of the 80th Legislature*, Rule 6.20.

had one veto overridden in 1979. There has been only one override attempt since then; in 1990, the Senate voted to override Governor Clements's veto of school finance legislation, but the House vote did not reach the required two-thirds.[42]

A variation of the veto authority is the line-item veto. For bills that appropriate money, this power allows the governor to select one or more lines of appropriations and veto them, while signing the rest of the bill into law. Line-item veto authority has been in the Texas constitutions since 1866. Forty-two governors now have this power.[43] The power is usually used to void a program that the governor opposes, but Governor Clements used it in 1989 to abolish an entire agency, the Advisory Commission on Intergovernmental Relations. In some legislative sessions, the governor vetoes only a handful of line items; in others, governors have vetoed up to twenty-six items. In 2005, Governor Rick Perry's line-item vetoes totaled a whopping $35.3 billion, as he vetoed all funds to the Texas Education Agency, in an (unsuccessful) attempt to force the legislature to overhaul school financing provisions.[44] In a special session that summer, the legislature reappropriated funding for the agency but was not able to reach agreement on substantive reforms to the school finance provisions.

Because the general appropriations bill is always passed at the end of a session, the legislature adjourns and then has no chance to override any line-item vetoes. Thus, the line-item veto can be a powerful weapon, and every recent governor has used it. However, the legislature has learned to mitigate against it by organizing material in the appropriations bills in such a manner as to limit the usefulness of such a veto. This includes lumping programs together and using "riders" to describe programs and funding levels, rather than line items for those programs.

Executive Orders

To exercise effective policy leadership, the governor must have significant influence over executive agencies. Presidents and governors in strong-governor states often steer executive agencies to act according to their will by issuing executive orders. Texas's weaker governors have used the executive order primarily for two purposes. The first is to force a gubernatorial voice in policy debates through the creation of governor's task forces, interagency councils, and so forth. The second is for emergency management. In fact, this latter area may be the only arena in which the governor has strong constitutional and statutory footing to order action by other executive officials. Section 418.012 of the Government Code states that under its emergency management provisions, "the governor may issue executive orders . . . [with] the force and effect of law." An executive order could declare a state of disaster, establish an emergency management council, or temporarily reassign resources.

Yet, modern governors have issued executive orders on a much broader array of policy issues, as noted at the beginning of this chapter. Governor Perry has made extensive use of them, generating controversy and litigation. In August 2005, he issued Executive Order RP-47, ordering the commissioner of education to establish a requirement that at least 65 percent of school districts' revenue be used for direct classroom instruction, riling superintendents, teachers, and legislators who argued that it was an arbitrary, damaging, and illegal initiative.

Under what authority do governors issue these orders? Whereas emergency management executive orders cite the specific statute that authorizes their issuance, other executive orders seem to have weaker legal footing. Bill Clements's Executive Order WPC-1, for instance, states that the governor is supposed "to be the chief spokesman for the State of Texas," and that the order is issued "under the authority vested in me." Ann Richards's Executive Order 92-1 also falls back on "under the authority vested in me." Rick Perry has expanded the language but not the specificity of the authority. For instance, Perry's Executive Order RP-65 for HPV vaccination was made "by virtue of the power and authority vested in me by the Constitution and laws of the State of Texas as the Chief Executive Officer." Yet, broad reference to the constitution and the laws masks the reality that the constitution deliberately created a weak governor and does not mention specific gubernatorial authority over the other executive officials.

The Plural Executive in Texas

⭐ **5.5** . . . **Outline the functions of the other elected administrative agencies within the plural executive, and evaluate their policy and administrative effectiveness.**

Americans place a high value on elections. We assume that elected officials are more responsive to citizens, and thus more democratic, than nonelected officials. Elected officials may not have any more authority than appointed officials, but election seems to give them more legitimacy in the eyes of citizens—and certainly being a part of the electoral process gives them more political power than appointed officials. (To learn more about the structure of the executive branch in Texas, see Figure 5.1.) Texas elects nine statewide executive officials[45] (plus the State Board of Education, whose fifteen members are elected from districts). Nearly half the states have reduced the number of elected state officials in recent decades. Texas reflected this trend in 1995, abolishing the position of state treasurer.

While most elected agency heads cooperate with the governor in policy implementation, there have been hostilities. Attorneys general are often seen as "governors-in-waiting," and many have feuded publicly with a governor, then run against the governor in the next election. Democratic Attorney General John Hill clashed with Governor Dolph Briscoe, then defeated Briscoe in the Democratic primary in 1978. Democratic Attorney General Mark White clashed with Republican Governor Bill Clements, then beat Clements for the governorship in 1982. Democratic Land Commissioner Garry Mauro and Governor George W. Bush squared off over coastal and other issues, then Mauro ran as the Democratic nominee against Bush in 1998 but lost. Comptroller Carole Keeton Strayhorn clashed repeatedly with Governor Rick Perry before running a losing race against him in 2006.

THINKING NATIONALLY

Elected State Officials

On the national level, we elect only the president (and his or her hand-picked vice president); the president appoints all the other highest-level executive officials. In Maine, New Hampshire, New Jersey, and Tennessee, only the governor is elected, and those governors have extensive appointment powers. Most other states elect a governor, a lieutenant governor, an attorney general, a secretary of state, and a treasurer/comptroller. Texas ranks fourth among the states in its number of elected state officials. In Texas, the land commissioner, agriculture commissioner, railroad commissioners, and State Board of Education members are elected, whereas other states' governors appoint officials like these.

- If an attorney general were elected with a much larger majority than the governor, which of them could claim a public mandate if the two disagreed on a policy? Why?

- Should the attorney general and comptroller be elected? Why or why not?

- How much do voters know about the various executive offices and the people who hold them?

Attorney General

Next to the governor and the lieutenant governor, the **attorney general** is the most significant elected state official. The attorney general serves as the chief counsel for the state of Texas. Because the attorney general is elected, he or she is independent from the governor (and, indeed, the governor has his or her own legal adviser). In about half of the years since 1978, governors and attorneys general have even been from different parties. Often, attorneys general have ambitions to run for governor, which can impede cooperation.

attorney general
The elected official who is the chief counsel for the state of Texas.

Figure 5.1 *What is the structure of the Texas executive branch?*

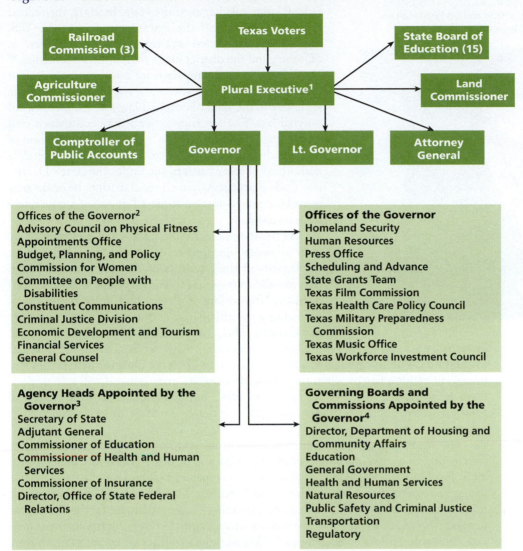

[1] Defined by the constitution or statutory law, the heads of these agencies are elected independently of the governor.

[2] The Offices of the Governor are created under statutory authority and serve to assist the governor in policy development, budgeting and planning, and coordination of policy among agencies and governments. Some 200 persons serve in these offices and are appointed by the governor.

[3] With the exception of the Secretary of State which is authorized under the Texas Constitution, these administrative positions were created under statutory law giving the appointment authority to the governor.

[4] Some two hundred state agencies, including universities, are assigned by statutory law the responsibilities for the administration of public policy in these areas. The members of the governing bodies are appointed by the governor with the approval of the legislature. In turn, the agency executives are appointed by the governing boards.

As chief counsel to state agencies, the attorney general and the hundreds of assistant attorneys general represent most agencies in litigation. When an agency sues a private individual or organization to force compliance with a state law or agency regulation, the attorney general's office usually provides the attorney for the agency. When someone sues a state agency, the attorney general must defend the agency. For example, in 1993, several mothers sued Medicaid officials from the Texas Department of Health and other state agencies, claiming that the agencies had denied their children Medicaid services that Congress had intended to be made available. The attorney general defended

Does the attorney general run one of the largest law offices in Texas? Attorney General Greg Abbott and his large staff are responsible for much of the civil legal affairs of the state.

Photo courtesy: AP/Wide World Photos

the state, arguing that its actions were legal. In 2000, a federal judge ruled against the state. In 2002, the federal appeals court upheld the state's actions, but the U.S. Supreme Court ruled against the state in *Frew* v. *Hawkins,* and the district judge then imposed remedies.[46]

While election campaigns for attorney general often focus on criminal issues, the attorney general has little authority in the field of criminal law and focuses instead on civil law. The attorney general may commence civil proceedings in areas where the legislature has given him or her jurisdiction. For instance, the attorney general is authorized in some cases to sue under the state's Deceptive Trade Practices Act. In criminal matters, he or she may assist local prosecutors on request, but only if a state interest is involved.

As the state's chief lawyer, the attorney general may issue advisory opinions to state and local officials on the legality of their actions, as Attorney General Dan Morales did in response to the *Hopwood* v. *Texas* (1996) decision, forbidding colleges and universities from enforcing some affirmative action plans,[47] and as Attorney General John Cornyn did in 2000, forbidding local governments from using public funds to provide health services to undocumented immigrants. Public officials request an Attorney General Opinion when they are uncertain about a law or when they think that the attorney general will rule in their favor in a dispute with private groups or other public officials. Attorney General Opinions have the force of law for agency officials, until or unless a court rules otherwise.

The attorney general has continuous opportunities to provide public policy leadership by deciding what kinds of cases to emphasize and by being pulled into public policy areas. Jim Mattox (1983–1991) sued numerous companies to force compliance with consumer safety, anti-fraud, and environmental statutes. Dan Morales (1991–1999) sued tobacco companies on health-related issues, winning a huge settlement for the state. Mattox and Morales devoted a massive amount of staff time to resolving the *Ruiz* v. *Estelle* case concerning prison management.[48] Also, Morales's staff members spent much time on redistricting issues, as a result of numerous lawsuits over the legislature's 1990s redistricting plans for the U.S. Congress and the Texas Legislature (see **chapter 4**).

In 1998, Jim Mattox won the Democratic nomination for attorney general in a comeback attempt but lost the general election to John Cornyn, the first Republican so elected. Cornyn served on the Texas Supreme Court from 1990 to 1998. In 1999, Attorney General Cornyn attacked the tobacco settlement that Morales had agreed to, trying to undo attorney fee provisions and trying to get courts to investigate the state's attorneys, including Morales. In 2002, the Texas Watch Foundation—a consumer public-interest group—published an analysis showing that Cornyn used the Deceptive Trade Practices Act far less than his predecessors.[49] Cornyn served only one term, choosing in 2002 to run for the U.S. Senate. Republican Greg Abbott, also a former Texas Supreme Court justice, won the office of attorney general in 2002, then won reelection in 2006 and 2010. Both Cornyn and Abbott elevated open records requirements as a public policy issue.

Comptroller of Public Accounts

comptroller of public accounts
The elected official who is the state's tax collector.

The **comptroller of public accounts** is the state's tax collector. The comptroller has offices across the state, and even in other states, to ensure that Texas collects what is due it. As of 1996, with the constitutional amendment abolishing the office of state treasurer, the comptroller is also the state's money manager. What makes the comptroller a powerful statewide official, though, is that he or she is responsible for estimating the amount of revenue that the state will have coming in, and the legislature may not appropriate more than that amount (except by a four-fifths vote). Thus, the comptroller becomes a significant legislative player.

The revenue forecasting function requires the comptroller to have a sophisticated economic analysis capability. The agency includes a large economic and policy research staff, which has become one of the state's most respected economic forecasting centers. Still, part of the comptroller's power in the legislative process is that the forecasts are built on assumptions, and those assumptions can be changed. For instance, the comptroller can increase or decrease the projected state revenues by increasing or decreasing the assumed price of a barrel of oil. Thus, if the comptroller wants to influence the amount of money available to the legislature, the revenue estimating process can accommodate those tactics.

Longtime Comptroller Bob Bullock (1975–1991) used the high-profile nature of the office to boost his standing with voters and then served as lieutenant governor (1991–1999). His comptroller's staff, known as "Bullock's Raiders," was aggressive in collecting overdue taxes from delinquent business taxpayers. Bullock was also an important voice in modernizing the tax laws in the 1980s.

John Sharp served as comptroller from 1991 to 1999, after service as state representative, state senator, and railroad commissioner. Governor Ann Richards and the legislature turned to him for assistance with a wide range of activities, demonstrating the scope, flexibility, and influence of this statewide elected office. Much of Sharp's energy was focused on performance evaluations of state agencies. His office was also given the task of starting up the state lottery, which was later reorganized under the new Lottery Commission.

In 1998, Republican Carole Keeton Rylander narrowly defeated Democrat Paul Hobby (son of former Lieutenant Governor Bill Hobby) to become the first Republican comptroller. She rose from local politics, having served on the Austin School Board and as mayor of Austin. She lost a race for Congress, was appointed to the Insurance Board, then won a seat on the Railroad Commission. As comptroller, she emphasized the school district audits that the office was responsible for. In 2002, she easily won reelection as comptroller. After her reelection, she remarried and changed her name to Strayhorn. In 2006, she ran unsuccessfully for governor as an independent candidate against Rick Perry. In 2007, she was succeeded by fellow Republican Susan Combs, who had served as a state representative, then for eight years as agriculture commissioner.

Who is responsible for keeping the budget and expenditure numbers straight? Susan Combs, a former state legislator and agriculture commissioner, was elected comptroller in 2006 and reelected in 2010. In addition to providing revenue estimates required to balance the budget, the comptroller is the state's primary tax administrator and accounting officer.

Photo courtesy: Texas Comptroller of Public Accounts

Land Commissioner

The **land commissioner** is more significant in Texas than in most states because the state owns so much land. The Republic of Texas validated all Spanish and Mexican

land commissioner
The elected official responsible for managing and leasing the state's property, including oil, gas, and mineral interests.

land grants, recognized existing property rights, established the General Land Office, and commissioned surveys of the state.[50] The 1845 terms of annexation to the United States gave to the state "all the vacant and unappropriated lands lying within its limits."[51] The land commissioner is responsible for managing and leasing the property.

As oil was discovered in the early twentieth century, the land commissioner enjoyed newfound importance—oil revenues from state-owned land pumped up funds for schools and universities, to which the land-generated revenues are constitutionally committed. Also, the land commissioner was given responsibility for the new Veterans Land Program in 1946, a program that loans money to veterans for the purpose of buying a homestead. Now the program includes loans for houses as well as land.

Recent land commissioners have enjoyed long tenures. Democrat Bob Armstrong served from 1971 to 1983. He later served on the Parks and Wildlife Commission, Governor Ann Richards appointed him as her energy adviser, and President Bill Clinton appointed him as assistant U.S. secretary of the interior. Garry Mauro, former executive director of the Texas Democratic Party, served as land commissioner from 1983 to 1999. Mauro expanded the scope of the office by focusing on natural gas resources. He promoted the use of natural gas, winning passage of a new state law requiring state and local vehicle fleets to purchase vehicles that can use multiple fuels, including natural gas. Mauro also aggressively turned the land-management responsibilities of his office into environmental protection programs, such as beach cleanups, corporate recycling programs, and coastal zone management. In 1998, Mauro won the Democratic nomination for governor but lost the general election to Governor George W. Bush.

In 1999, Mauro was succeeded by David Dewhurst, the first Republican to win the office. Dewhurst had served in the U.S. Air Force, the Central Intelligence Agency, and the State Department, then founded a Houston energy and investments company. He had not previously held an elective office. Dewhurst served as head of Governor Perry's Task Force on Homeland Security in 2001–2002 and was instrumental as a member of the Legislative Redistricting Board that redrew state legislative district lines in 2001. Dewhurst served only one term, choosing to run for lieutenant governor in 2002. He was replaced as land commissioner by fellow Republican Jerry Patterson, who won the office in 2002. Patterson had earlier been a state senator and in 1998 had lost to Dewhurst in the Republican primary for land commissioner. Patterson won reelection in 2006 and 2010. As land commissioner, he has pursued a major wind energy project off the Texas coast. In 2007 and 2008, he generated controversy by proposing to sell the state's 9,000-acre Christmas Mountain land in the Big Bend area.

Agriculture Commissioner

agriculture commissioner
The elected state official in charge of regulating and promoting agriculture.

The **agriculture commissioner** is the only statewide elected official whose job was created by the legislature instead of by the constitution. The job of the commissioner is to promote and regulate agricultural interests. The Texas Department of Agriculture administers promotion campaigns for Texas commodities and encourages use of Texas products through labeling them Texas made. Traditional regulatory programs include monitoring the accuracy of weights and measures, regulating the safety of grain warehouses, and ensuring compliance with pest control regulations and egg and seed labeling requirements.

In 1982, Jim Hightower defeated the incumbent commissioner in the Democratic primary and won the general election. Hightower had been head of an agricultural policy think tank in Washington, then had been editor of the *Texas Observer*, putting a populist voice to its coverage. Hightower was reelected in 1986, leading the Democratic ticket with more votes than any candidate received for any office. As agriculture commissioner, Hightower initiated and won legislative approval for new programs such as tighter regulation of pesticide use, a right-to-know law for farmworkers who use pesticides, organic food certification, revitalization of farmers' markets, and national promotion of Texas foods. He was narrowly defeated by Rick Perry in the general election in 1990, the first time that a Democrat other than governor had lost an executive office to a Republican; Hightower has gone on to become a nationally known speaker, radio show host, and author of several books on politics.

Perry, a Democratic state representative who had led an effort to limit Hightower's powers and his pesticide regulatory authority, switched to the Republican Party to run against Hightower. Perry deemphasized Hightower's new programs and reemphasized the traditional role of the department. He won reelection easily in 1994. In 1995, Perry and the Farm Bureau urged the legislature to repeal the farmworker right-to-know law, but they failed.

After Perry was elected lieutenant governor in 1998, he was succeeded as agriculture commissioner by Republican Susan Combs, a lawyer-rancher who had served in the Texas House from 1993 through 1996 from Austin. She co-authored the state's Private Real Property Rights Preservation Act. Combs then served as U.S. Senator Kay Bailey Hutchison's state director. She was the first woman to hold the post of agriculture commissioner. Combs won reelection in 2002. In 2006, she was elected state comptroller. Republican state Senator Todd Staples (R–Palestine) won election as agriculture commissioner; he was reelected in 2010.

Railroad Commissioners

The three railroad commissioners are elected in statewide elections. Whereas other state officials are elected to four-year terms, railroad commissioners are elected to six-year staggered terms, where one seat is up for election every two years. The **Railroad Commission** was the highest achievement of populists in the 1890s. Populists demanded regulation of railroads, and they insisted that the people have direct control over those regulators by electing them. Over the years, other regulatory duties have been added to the agency's responsibilities.

In the early twentieth century, oil companies wanted to produce, transport, refine, and sell oil and gas but were stymied by another populist victory, a state law forbidding monopoly market concentration.[52] A compromise allowed them an integrated business operation, but with regulation of the pipeline transportation of the oil and gas. Because the Railroad Commission already regulated a form of transportation, it was given authority over the oil and gas industry. Regulation of trucking and mining came later. Today, the federal government has usurped much of the agency's regulatory responsibilities for railroads and trucking, leaving oil and gas regulation as its primary function—and today, it is the oil and gas industry that has the most influence at the agency. In the 1960s, longtime Commissioner Ben Ramsey stated flatly that the Railroad Commission was "industry's representative in state government," and Commissioner Jon Newton stated in the 1970s that the commission was captive of the oil and gas industry.[53]

After the 1994 elections, for the first time in Texas history, all three railroad commissioners were Republicans, and that has remained the case since then. In 2008, the commission included Michael Williams, Elizabeth Ames Jones, and Victor Carrillo.

How much land does the state of Texas own? Republican Jerry Patterson is responsible for the 22 million acres owned by the state. One important responsibility assigned to the Commissioner of the General Land Office of Texas is the management of the state's mineral rights.

Photo courtesy: AP/Wide World Photos

Railroad Commission

A full-time, three-member paid commission elected by the people to regulate oil and gas production in Texas.

Is this agency as powerful as it was in the past? Created to regulate railroads within the state and subsequently given regulatory powers over oil and gas, the Texas Railroad Commission (shown here in the 1900s) was often seen as the most powerful state regulatory agency in the nation when the United States was energy independent.

Photo courtesy: Texas State Library and Archives Commission

Williams, who served President George W. Bush as assistant secretary of education for civil rights and had served as general counsel to the Texas Republican Party, is the first African American to serve as railroad commissioner. Governor Bush appointed him in 1998, and with his election to an unexpired term in 2000, he is the first African American elected to statewide executive office in Texas. In 2002, he won election to a full six-year term and won reelection in 2008 (for 2009–2014). In 2003, Governor Rick Perry appointed Victor Carrillo to fill a vacancy on the commission. Carrillo won a full term in 2004 (for 2005–2010) but was unseated by a challenger in the 2010 Republican primary. Carrillo, who had vastly outspent his little-known opponent, blamed his defeat on Republican voters who didn't want to vote for a Hispanic. In early 2005, Governor Perry filled another vacancy by appointing State Representative Elizabeth Ames Jones (R–San Antonio) to the position. In 2006, she won election to a new six-year term (for 2007–2012).

State Board of Education

State Board of Education
The fifteen-member elected body that sets some education policy for the state.

Texas Education Agency
The state agency that oversees local school districts and disburses state funds to districts.

The **State Board of Education** (SBOE) is an excellent example of the fragmentation of institutions and authority in Texas state government. Public education is governed by the elected fifteen-member SBOE, a commissioner of education appointed by the governor, a large bureaucracy called the **Texas Education Agency** (TEA), and a locally elected school board for each school district. Since the 1990s, those entities have sometimes warred with each other, with the legislature, and with interest groups.

Although the state has always had a presence in education, the nature of state leadership has evolved.[54] Beginning in 1866, Texas had a superintendent of public instruction, who was usually elected statewide. There was also an advisory Board of Education. Superintendent Annie Webb Blanton (1919–1923) was the first woman elected to statewide office in Texas. In 1949, the Board of Education was enlarged and made an elected board, with the new commissioner of education to be appointed by the board, with Senate confirmation. As a part of Governor Mark White's education reforms in the early 1980s, the board was reduced in size from twenty-seven to fifteen members. It was also changed to an appointed board, because elected board members were viewed as potentially hostile to the reforms. The legislature (and later the voters) required, though, that the board revert to an elected board (from districts) once the reforms were in place. The elected board recommended to the governor a person for appointment as commissioner of education. In 1995, the governor was given sole authority to appoint the commissioner, with Senate confirmation.

The elected structure of the State Board of Education was ripe for a takeover by special interest groups. With fifteen districts statewide, each board member represents twice as many people as a member of the U.S. House from Texas. Most voters know little, if anything, about candidates for the board, and races for board seats received little media attention until recently. In recent years, social conservative candidates backed by the Religious Right have been successful in using strong support in the Republican primary to capture several board seats. And, they have attempted to impose, with some success, their political and religious views on textbook and curriculum content. In 2010, a major fight over the history curriculum for Texas's public schools attracted national attention and much anger and ridicule from educators. A bloc of conservatives on the board succeeded in rewriting curriculum standards to, among other things, downplay the role of Hispanics in Texas history, diminish Thomas Jefferson's standing because of his strong belief in the separation of church and state, and ban the use of the word "capitalism" because it often was portrayed in a negative context. Several legislators, mostly Democrats, announced that they would file legislation during the 2011 session to abolish the board or greatly restrict its authority. Several bills attacking the board were filed in the 2009 session, but none made it out of committee.

Modern Texas Bureaucracy

⭐ **5.6** ... **Determine the role of the modern Texas bureaucracy in the formulation, implementation, and evaluation of public policy.**

The purpose of government bureaucracy is implementation—to put into effect, to execute legislative policy, hence the term executive branch. Legislatures are chiefly responsible for creating public policies (policy making). Bureaucracies are supposed to translate legislative intent into actual, working public policy—that is, to implement the wishes of the legislature. Agencies do so by rule making (adopting standards and processes by which they operate and make decisions), regulation of private activities, and provision of services and products. However, as they attempt to understand and to implement legislative intent, agency officials often must fill out the details that are missing in legislation and thus sometimes also make policy. Texas's rule-making process, spelled out in the **Administrative Procedures Act,** requires agency officials to seek written public comments, and agencies sometimes have public hearings before adopting rules and regulations.

Legislatures create executive agencies to respond to particular problems. How they organize the agencies is determined by the nature of the problem, the personalities and political dynamics at work, and the organizational structure that is in vogue at the time. The ongoing question of how much power the governor should have over executive agencies is often entwined with questions of reorganizing the executive branch. Though the Texas governor is chief executive, he or she has little direct authority over executive agencies and may not reorganize them. Texas executive agencies

Why is the State Board of Education ridiculed by some people? The State Board of Education, whose fifteen members (one of whom is shown here) are elected from districts, has been the stage of intense ideological conflict. In 2010, the board's decisions in rewriting the state's history curriculum brought anger and ridicule from across the nation.

Photo courtesy: Bob Daemmrich Photography, Inc.

Administrative Procedures Act
A statute containing Texas's rule-making process.

Figure 5.2 *What variations exist within the administrative structures of Texas agencies?*

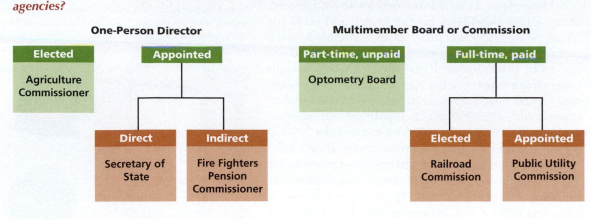

are organized in a host of ways, but there are two basic patterns: agencies are headed either by one person or by a multimember board or commission. (To learn more about the organizational schemes, see Figure 5.2.)

Of the agencies following the first pattern, eight are headed by someone the governor appoints, such as the secretary of state. Five agencies have directors elected by the people, as noted earlier: Office of the Attorney General, Office of the Comptroller of Public Accounts, General Land Office, Texas Department of Agriculture, and the Texas Railroad Commission. Those statewide elected officials are significant because of their prominent role in policy making and in public opinion leadership. Though the governor appoints few directors of state agencies, the number has grown in recent years. Agency heads appointed directly by the governor are generally seen as more powerful than those appointed by boards or commissions, by virtue of access to the governor and of being part of the governor's political team. However, the distribution of elected versus appointed officials is not based on rational assumptions as much as it is on political power and personalities in power at the time the decisions are made.

Following the second pattern are agencies run by multimember boards or commissions—the two terms are used interchangeably. About one hundred agencies are run by a part-time, unpaid board or commission.[55] The members of most governing boards and commissions are appointed by the governor. In most cases, the board or commission hires a person to run the agency. The Texas Alcoholic Beverage Commission is an example of such an agency. The commission's members, appointed by the governor, make policy and hire an administrator.

Five agencies are run by a full-time, paid commission. These are the governor-appointed Public Utility Commission (PUC), Texas Commission on Environmental Quality (TCEQ), Texas Workforce Commission, the Board of Pardons and Paroles, and the elected Texas Railroad Commission. Commission members usually hire an executive director to assist them in running the agency.

Secretary of State

Texas secretary of state
The state official appointed by the governor to be the keeper of the state's records, such as state laws, election data and filings, public notifications, and corporate charters.

The first appointment usually made by an incoming governor, and a key one, is the **Texas secretary of state.** This officer is the keeper of state records. Election data, state laws and regulations, public notifications through the *Texas Register,* and corporate charters are managed by the secretary of state.

The secretary of state serves as the state's chief elections officer—registering voters, making sure that counties conduct elections properly, and collecting and certifying election results. In this capacity, the secretary is one of the most important political officials inside state government. The secretary is a key liaison between the governor, political parties, and elected officials across the state.

Secretaries of state have a golden opportunity to create a political base. In fact, many secretaries run for elective office after serving the governor. After stints as secretary of state, Crawford Martin, John Hill, and Mark White ran successfully for attorney general, and Bob Bullock ran successfully for comptroller and lieutenant governor. Ann Richards's Secretary of State Ron Kirk ran successfully for mayor of Dallas, then won the Democratic nomination for U.S. Senate, losing in the November 2002 election. President Barack Obama later appointed him U.S. Trade Representative. George W. Bush's Secretary of State Tony Garza ran successfully for railroad commissioner, and Bush, as president, appointed him U.S. ambassador to Mexico. Bush appointed Secretary of State Alberto Gonzales to the Texas Supreme Court; Gonzales won election to that seat in 2000 but resigned to become President Bush's chief counsel, then U.S. attorney general.

Rick Perry has had a series of secretaries of state, including Democratic State Representative Henry Cuellar, Republican State Representative Gwyn Shea, Geoffrey Connor, Roger Williams, Phil Wilson, and Esperanza "Hope" Andrade. Williams, a Weatherford businessman, is a longtime associate of George W. Bush and a key Republican fundraiser, and he is often mentioned as a possible candidate for elective office. Cuellar later was elected to Congress.

Public Utility Commissioners

The **Public Utility Commission** (PUC) has jurisdiction over telephone and electric power companies, while the Texas Railroad Commission retains authority over gas companies. The three members of the PUC are appointed to staggered six-year terms by the governor. The public utility commissioners have a role that is largely **quasi-judicial.** They have the authority to hold hearings and issue rulings. The agency was created in 1975 in a storm of public sentiment to limit rapidly rising utility rates.

Governor Rick Perry appointed several members who served only briefly. Former investment banker and local prosecutor Barry Smitherman was appointed to the commission in 2004 and became chair in 2007. In 2008, Perry appointed Kenneth Anderson Jr. and Donna Nelson as commissioners.

In 1995, the legislature redrafted the PUC's statute. Technological developments and congressional support for deregulation framed the debate. In 1995, the legislature passed a bill deregulating telecommunications, and in 1997 passed a bill deregulating public utilities. Under the 1997 bill, most monopoly electric utilities were split into transmission and distribution companies, power-generating companies, retail providers, and independent-system operators. One goal is to guarantee residential customers choice of providers (though the PUC must maintain a no-call list for customers who don't want telephone solicitation about electric service). The PUC still regulates transmission and distribution, but rates for power generating and retail are deregulated. The PUC also oversees some activities of ERCOT—the Electric Reliability Council of Texas.

Public Utility Commission
A full-time, three-member paid commission appointed by the governor to regulate public utilities in Texas.

quasi-judicial
Partly judicial; authorized to conduct hearings and issue rulings.

Texas Commission on Environmental Quality

In 1991, the legislature combined many of the state's environmental programs into a new agency, the Texas Natural Resource Conservation Commission (TNRCC), and abolished the Air Control Board and the Water Commission. In 2002, TNRCC assumed a new name, the **Texas Commission on Environmental Quality** (TCEQ). Its three commissioners are appointed by the governor to staggered six-year terms.

Commissioners have a quasi-judicial role in contested cases, but they have significant policy roles that make them the real powers in running the agency. Businesses

Texas Commission on Environmental Quality
A full-time, three-member paid commission appointed by the governor to administer the state's environmental programs. (Formerly the Texas Natural Resource Conservation Commission.)

that will be emitting pollutants into the air or water must seek permits from the commission and must comply with regulations to limit the amount of those emissions. Thus, the commission becomes a lightning rod when environmental and neighborhood groups seeking to restrict activities that could pollute are in conflict with businesses seeking to keep costs down while using modern industrial techniques and expanding or beginning new operations supplying products to the marketplace.

The legislature has considered scores of bills to scale back the environmental authority of the agency, and some of them were adopted. A 1995 "property rights" law requires state agencies to evaluate the costs of environmental regulation to property owners, and it could force the state to abandon regulations that might lower private-property values. The legislature also scaled back the public participation provisions that the agency must follow. A 1999 bill would have abolished contested case hearings but was passed in a modified version that keeps most contested case hearings and changes public-comment provisions. Another significant change in legislative policy requires the agency to now consider not just the environmental impacts of a specific business that is applying for a permit but also the cumulative impact of concentrated facilities in an area.

Insurance Commissioner

insurance commissioner
The official appointed by the governor to direct the Department of Insurance and regulate the insurance industry.

Because of the need to know whether insurance companies have assets sufficient to pay their claims, and because out-of-state companies proved difficult to pursue if customers had complaints of fraud, Texas has long had a public official or public body to oversee or regulate the insurance industry. The legislature has periodically reorganized the state agency, sometimes having a multimember body of commissioners and sometimes a single commissioner. In 1993, the three-member State Board of Insurance was replaced by a single commissioner, appointed by the governor. The **insurance commissioner** runs the Department of Insurance and is one of the few single executive heads appointed directly by the governor, but the commissioner has a high level of independence because the governor can remove the commissioner only under extraordinary circumstances. The commissioner's job is to monitor the health of the insurance industry and, within new confines voted in by the legislature, to regulate insurance rates. In 2005, Governor Rick Perry appointed Mike Geeslin as insurance commissioner. Geeslin, a former Perry budget and policy adviser, had been serving as deputy insurance commissioner.

Between 1997 and 2002, homeowner's insurance premiums increased by more than 100 percent in Texas, stoking a major battle over the role of the department. In 2003, the legislature authorized the insurance commissioner to force insurance companies to lower their rates on homeowners' insurance. However, two of the largest insurers in Texas, State Farm and Farmers, fought the commissioner's attempt to lower their rates 12 percent and 17.5 percent, respectively. The companies insisted that their rates were fair and contested the commissioner's attempt to force lower rates in court. In December 2004, after extended negotiations, Farmers agreed to lower its future rates and agreed to a $117 million settlement with ratepayers. Ratepayers and policyholders, however, argued that they were due $1 billion and refused the settlement. They got a court to agree and throw out the settlement the commissioner had negotiated.[56] The case continues to drag on in court. Meanwhile, policy holders' $117 million refunds remain in limbo.

Health and Human Services Commission

Health and human service programs are administered in Texas by numerous state agencies. Governor Ann Richards proposed consolidating and merging these services into one agency, using the slogan "one person, one trip." Comptroller John Sharp, in urging consolidation, wrote: "This fragmentation produces well-documented agency-wide problems such as a failure to maximize federal funds, inconsistency in rate-setting and contracting and a failure to coordinate client transportation services."[57] In 1991, the legislature partially agreed by creating the commissioner of health and human services. The commissioner did not run the agencies but was supposed to oversee the massive health and human services programs scattered across the agencies. The commissioner was appointed directly by the governor. In 1999, voters rejected a constitutional amendment that would have increased the tenure and powers of the commissioner and allowed the governor to fire him or her.

In 2003, the legislature completely reorganized the health and human services agencies to create a new system. The legislation merged twelve agencies into four new departments under the Health and Human Services Commission (HHSC), which is headed by an **executive commissioner of health and human services** appointed by the governor and confirmed by the Senate. The HHSC also was given additional duties, such as centralizing eligibility requirements for several programs, including Medicaid, Temporary Assistance for Needy Families (TANF), and the Children's Health Insurance Program. In addition, HHSC is responsible for consolidating administrative services for all health and human services agencies. The four new departments, each headed by a commissioner who is selected by the executive commissioner with the governor's approval, are:

executive commissioner of health and human services
The official appointed by the governor to oversee the state's multi-agency health and human service programs.

- Department of Family and Protective Services, which reconstitutes the Department of Protective and Regulatory Services.
- Department of Assistive and Rehabilitative Services, which assumes the powers and duties of the Texas Rehabilitation Commission, Commission for the Blind, Commission for the Deaf and Hard of Hearing, and Interagency Council on Early Childhood Intervention.
- Department of Aging and Disability Services (DADS), which consolidates mental retardation and state school programs of the Department of Mental Health and Mental Retardation (MHMR), community care and nursing home services programs of the Department of Human Services, and aging services programs of the Texas Department of Aging.
- Department of State Health Services, which takes over programs from the Texas Department of Health, the Texas Commission on Alcohol and Drug Abuse, and the Health Care Information Council. It also assumes the community and state hospital programs from MHMR.

By merging the agencies, the legislature hoped to improve services, enhance accountability, increase efficiencies, and reduce costs.

Public Counsels

In recent years, as conflicts grew over regulatory policies, public-interest groups charged that regulatory agencies had become **captured agencies.** They were seen as consistently making decisions favorable to business interests and not adequately protecting consumers. A concept that gained some acceptance is that of **public counsels** to serve as advocates for the public before governmental agencies. The legislature gave the governor power to appoint a public insurance counsel and a public utility counsel. These attorneys are heads of small agencies separate from the Department of Insurance and the Public Utility Commission. The counsels and their staffs examine rate-hike requests and other regulatory matters before the agencies. Then they go before the regulators to argue for their position, which is usually for rate reductions or for lower rate increases than the private companies have requested or the regulatory agency staff has recommended.

captured agency
A government regulatory agency that consistently makes decisions favorable to the private interests that it regulates.

public counsels
Officials appointed by the governor to represent the public before regulatory agencies.

Boards and Commissions

Most state agencies are organized with a multimember policy-making body and a staff under the direction of the policy-making body. Some of these bodies are called boards, some are called commissions, and a very few are called councils or authorities. Collectively, these bodies are often referred to as the "board and commission" system of government. Some boards or commissions govern more than one agency. For instance, the ten boards of trustees of the state's colleges and universities run thirty-seven general academic institutions, nine medical schools, and nine major services.

Boards and commissions are used for large and small agencies. Most have three or nine members, although a few have more. A board or commission may have no staff, a handful of staff members, or a large bureaucracy. The Board of Criminal Justice, for instance, hires a full-time, well-paid, and powerful executive director, who oversees a staff of more than 40,000.

In almost all cases, members of these policy-making bodies are appointed by the governor, with Senate confirmation. (A few have statutorily designated membership from agency heads or elected officials.) These appointments to boards and commissions constitute the bulk of the governor's appointments. However, for most boards, the terms of members are six years, and the terms are staggered, so a governor is not usually able to gain control of a majority of a board until late in his or her first term of office. Even then, there is no assurance that members will do as the governor wishes. The governor may request the removal of an official that he or she appointed, but it requires approval of two-thirds of the Senate, and no such removal has ever occurred.

Other than the full-time, paid members of the PUC, TCEQ, Workforce Commission, Board of Pardons and Paroles, and Texas Railroad Commission, the members of these boards and commissions are not paid. They are volunteer, part-time positions. Members' expenses are reimbursed when they travel to meetings. Most boards or commissions meet monthly or quarterly. They may work through smaller committees of members, with additional meetings of those committees.

TOWARD REFORM: Making Agencies Accountable

⭐ **5.7** . . . Explain how the legislature holds state agencies and public employees accountable, and evaluate proposals to reform the Texas executive branch.

Legislatures may delegate decision-making authority to executive agencies—a practice long recognized by courts. In creating agencies and programs, and in delegating authority to agencies, legislatures do not then wash their hands of responsibility for those programs. Rather, they have a duty to oversee what they have created and delegated. Legislative oversight of the bureaucracy includes review of expenditures, review of rules and regulations, performance reviews, audits, sunset review (in which the continuing need for an agency is evaluated), review of staff sizes and functions, and response to constituent complaints about agencies. Although Texas has not done so, some states have adopted legislative vetoes of administrative rules and regulations (though several state courts have thrown them out as unconstitutional violations of separation of powers).[58]

The Sunset Process

A **sunset law** establishes a date for programs or regulations to expire (the sun will set on them) unless the legislature renews them. The sunset concept is used in Texas to force a review of executive agencies and programs. It was first adopted in Colorado in 1976 and is now in use in about two-thirds of the states.[59] The Texas Sunset Act was adopted in 1977. While the motivation for the movement was to review and abolish some agencies, ironically the first step was to create a new agency—the Sunset Advisory Commission. It consists of five state senators, five state representatives, one public member appointed by the lieutenant governor, and one public member appointed by the House Speaker. Under the Texas system, each state agency is given a twelve-year life span. If the commission recommends continuation of an agency, it drafts legislation, usually with changes in the structure or procedures of the agency.

In addition to agency-specific recommendations, the first commission adopted a set of across-the-board good government recommendations for all agencies to open themselves up to public participation and scrutiny and to minimize conflicts of interest. Early Sunset Advisory Commission analyses clearly reflect that the staff, and perhaps commission members, believed that agencies had been captured by private interests. The first two commissions, appointed in 1977 and 1979, focused on breaking the hold that trade associations had over professional licensing agencies and reestablishing an arms-length relationship between the regulated and the regulators. The commission recommended imposing controls on agencies that for years had escaped serious legislative oversight. Commission actions to impose these controls were fiercely opposed by lobby groups and trade associations surrounding the agencies.[60]

Sunset has become a target for those wary of the repeated battles that ensue as interest groups, agencies, and their defenders and detractors clash over how programs will be organized and implemented. In 2009, the commission reviewed twenty-five agencies, recommending that seventeen be continued in some form, two abolished outright, two abolished with their functions transferred to other agencies, and four have no sunset date.[61] By the end of the legislative session, the legislature abolished the Board of Tax Professional Examiners and the Polygraph Examiners Board, transferring these agencies' functions to another agency.[62]

A sunset battle erupted in 2009 over the Texas Residential Construction Commission, an agency created several years earlier with the strong support of homebuilders. The idea behind the agency was to set uniform building standards and weed out bad builders in exchange for giving the homebuilding industry legal protections against lawsuits from unhappy buyers. But consumer advocacy groups complained that the agency was little more than a homebuilder protection agency, and that perception was reinforced by reports that Houston homebuilder Bob Perry, one of the state's biggest political contributors, had played a major role in the agency's creation. Lawmakers refused to extend the agency's life after it came up for sunset review in 2009. In this case the legislature reversed the

THINKING NATIONALLY

Legislative Review of Agencies

State legislatures along with Congress have the responsibility of keeping the ever-expanding administrative agencies accountable and effective in carrying out policies enacted by lawmaking bodies. Congress first incorporated the practice of the legislative veto in the Reorganization Act of 1932 by permitting either house to reject or nullify any plan adopted by the president. Kansas adopted a general legislative veto in 1939, which permitted the legislature to reject any administrative regulation by concurrent resolution, and by the 1980s approximately 20 states had adopted some form of legislative veto.

The legislative veto poses a constitutional issue in terms of separation of powers. And, when the legislative veto has been challenged in state and federal courts, it generally has been declared unconstitutional. Legislative review or oversight of administrative agencies is tedious work with limited appeal to many legislators, but the skillful and persistent use of oversight with the tools of the budget and financial and program audits can serve to keep agencies in line.

- Were the courts correct in declaring the legislative veto unconstitutional?

- Why might many legislators avoid taking on the task of review and assessment of the actions of administrative agencies?

- Are there other ways legislatures attempt to control the actions of administrative agencies?

Sunset Advisory Commission, which had recommended that the agency be re-created with new consumer reforms added.

The Growth of Public Employment

For most of the past 50 years, growth in public employment has been at the state and local level—not with the national government. In 1972, all governments in Texas employed some 504,000 people. Within thirty-five years, this number increased to over 1.3 million. State employment increased by 134 percent while local employment in the state increased by 177 percent. (To learn more about the growth in the state's public employment, see Table 5.3.)

Bureaucrat bashing and threats to reduce the number of public employees are a favorite ploy of many candidates running for public office. Governor Bill Clements vowed to cut 25 percent of the state workforce; when he left office, it was larger than when he took office. More recently, the legislature has adopted caps on numbers of employees that an agency may employ. One result of this policy is increased outsourcing of services; the state is currently contracting with thousands of private entities. Once programs are enacted by the legislature, it is difficult to reduce or eliminate them. In practice, the state's expanding population means a corresponding increase in many public programs.

The legislature adopts pay scales, titled the Classification Salary Schedule and the Exempt Salary Schedule, as a part of the appropriations bills. The bottom of the salary schedule for fiscal year 2008–2009 was $16,176, while the top was $203,935. The top earners are physicians, highest-level investment managers and actuaries, and the deputy comptroller. Some top officials, however, are also allowed to accept private pay supplements. While such a policy raises questions of conflicts of interest, state leaders have decided that they will not get qualified people for some positions without extremely high pay levels, and they do not want to pay extremely high salaries with tax dollars. So they authorize officials to use private money as pay supplements. Typically, college football coaches, physicians at state hospitals and medical facilities, university chancellors, university presidents, some professors in endowed chairs, and the heads and investment officers of pension funds get supplements from private funds, making them the highest-paid state employees.

Regulating the Revolving Door

Over the years, many regulatory agencies had become training grounds for young attorneys and other professionals taking their first jobs out of college or law school.

Table 5.3 *How has the number of people employed by the Texas bureaucracy changed since 1972?*

Unit of Government	Full-Time Equivalent Employees				
	1972	1982	1992	2002	2007
State	**124,560**	**175,660**	**238,974**	**269,674**	**290,451**
Total Local	**380,038**	**557,082**	**744,325**	**979,164**	**1,053,991**
Counties	37,302	67,228	94,145	120,885	133,722
Municipalities	93,107	127,794	147,812	172,846	175,635
School Districts	223,646	335,855	460,212	634,589	690,712
Special Districts	25,983	26,205	42,156	50,844	53,922
Total for Texas	**504,598**	**732,742**	**983,299**	**1,248,838**	**1,344,442**

Sources: U.S. Department of Commerce, Bureau of the Census, *Census of Governments, 1972,* vol. 3, no. 2, table 14; *Census of Governments, 1982,* vol. 3, no. 2, table 13; *Census of Governments, 1992,* vol. 3, no. 2, table 14; *Census of Governments, 2002,* vol. 3, table 9; *Census of Governments, 2007, Texas Government Employment and Payroll Data, Build-a Table,* www.census.gov.

They would work for state agencies for a few years for relatively low pay while gaining valuable experience in a particular regulatory area and making influential contacts in the state bureaucracy. Then they would leave state employment for higher-paying jobs in the industries they had regulated and would represent their new employers before the same state boards and commissions for which they had once worked. Alternatively, they might become consultants or join law firms representing regulatory clients. Former gubernatorial appointees to boards and commissions—not just hired staffers—also participated in this **revolving door** phenomenon, which raised ethical questions about possible insider advantages.

revolving door
An exchange of personnel between private interests and public regulators.

An early step in restricting the revolving door was the 1975 law that created the Public Utility Commission (PUC). This law prohibited PUC members and high-ranking staffers from going to work for regulated utilities immediately after leaving the agency. An ethics reform law in 1991 expanded the restrictions to other agencies.

Regulating the Relationship Between Agencies and Private Interests

Executive agencies have the primary role of implementing decisions made by the legislature. However, they also play key policy-making roles, and their freedom to interpret legislative intent makes them policy powerhouses. In the 1950s, political scientist Marver Bernstein described the evolution of agencies, from their creation in an atmosphere of public outrage at perceived abuses by private industry, to their original role as independent watchdogs over the industry, to an unintended role as an agency captured by the private interests, consistently making decisions favorable to those interests. This final stage "is marked by the commission's surrender to the regulated. Politically isolated, lacking a firm basis of public support, lethargic in attitude and approach, bowed down by precedent and backlogs, unsupported in its demands for more staff and money, the commission finally becomes a captive of the regulated groups."[63]

The Texas Railroad Commission fits Bernstein's model. Born as the fruit of populists' anger at railroad company rates and practices, the commission at first responded to the public's demand for lower rates. By the time the agency's largest role was to regulate the oil and gas industry, it was so fully captured by that industry that it ran an ad (sponsored by two industry associations) claiming, "Since 1891 the Texas Railroad Commission has served the oil industry."[64] The Public Utility Commission has had a history similar to that of the Texas Railroad Commission. Attempts at creating a new state agency had stalled for years. In the 1970s, the populace was stirred up over high utility rates and the appearance of favoritism to utility companies by government institutions. This popular agitation, triggered by economic crisis, brought about political change and the creation of the PUC. Years later, however, many consumer advocates were viewing the PUC as sympathetic to utilities.

The Texas Residential Construction Commission, which the legislature decided to "sunset" in 2009, was another example of an agency believed to have been compromised by the industry—in this case, homebuilding—it supposedly was created to regulate.

The iron triangle (see **chapter 3**) is a model that includes the role that agencies play in the policy process. The closeness of private interests in Texas to legislators (through lobbying and campaign contributions) and to executive agencies (through influence on gubernatorial appointments and through the revolving door) lends strength to the iron triangle model. If one follows the proposed rules and regulations as first published by agencies in the *Texas Register*, the written comments received, and the revisions and final rules, it appears that in many cases the agencies merely go through the motions of including the public. The decisions have already been made or are made in consultation with key private interests, out of the public eye. Indeed, that is what a Texas court ruled in 1999 in a case invalidating some rules of the Texas Natural Resource Conservation Commission.[65]

Gubernatorial and Executive Power

The 1990s was a decade of extensive executive branch reorganization in Texas. Since then, agency structures have generally been left alone, except for the major restructuring of health and human services agencies in 2003. The changes have given the governor more appointments to make but have not expanded the office's constitutional authority.

A recent reform effort has attempted to address the issue of gubernatorial vetoes that are issued late in a legislative session or after the legislature has adjourned. The large number of vetoes that Governor Rick Perry has signed in his long tenure has prompted some legislators to try to expand their opportunities to override those vetoes. The constitutions of 1845, 1861, 1866, and 1869 did not allow post-adjournment vetoes, but the current constitution does. In 2007, Representative Gary Elkins introduced HJR 59, proposing a state constitutional amendment for a legislative session to override governor's vetoes that are issued at the end of or after a regular session. The resolution was approved by the House by the requisite two-thirds vote but died in a Senate committee. A similar proposal also died in 2009.

What Should I Have LEARNED?

Now that you have read this chapter, you should be able to:

⭐ **5.1 Trace the historical development of the structure of the executive branch in Texas, and state the reasons for the creation of the plural executive, p. 140.**

During the Republic, the executive branch had a structure similar to that of the national government. The president of the Republic was a strong executive who appointed other executive officials, much like the president of the United States appoints a Cabinet. In subsequent constitutions, the executive branch went through a series of modifications, and the unified executive of the Republic was replaced by a plural executive designed to minimize the power of any one office or individual.

⭐ **5.2 List the constitutional roles of the governor, p. 143.**

Explicit or implicit in the provisions of the constitution and legislation are roles assigned to the governor. These include chief of state, commander in chief, and chief budget officer. The governor's legislative role is based, in part, on constitutional provisions pertaining to the call of special sessions, a governor's message to the legislature, and the veto. When judicial vacancies occur, the governor is charged with filling the vacancies with the approval of the Senate, but the governor's other judicial powers are severely limited. The plural executive and the independent agencies significantly limit the administrative role of the governor as well.

⭐ **5.3 Identify the majors powers assigned to the governor, and analyze how governors have interpreted and developed these powers, p. 144.**

Historically, the Texas governor is one of the weakest in the nation. The framers of the 1876 Constitution intentionally limited the powers of this office. The more restrictive two-year term has been expanded to four years, and the legislature has given the governor more appointive powers over non-constitutional agencies and some budgetary powers. But, core aspects of the budgetary process are shared with the legislature. The governor has no control over the administrative functions of the other constitutional agencies, and there is no personnel system under the control of the governor. Hence, the office remains weak today.

⭐ **5.4 Evaluate the effectiveness of Texas governors as policy makers and political leaders, p. 151.**

The political and policy leadership that a governor is able to provide flows from the governor's skills, previous experience, and similarity in party, philosophy, and ideology with other decision makers. At the base of that leadership is electoral skill. Texas's governors resort to public opinion leadership to increase their power with other officeholders. Still, to be successful, a governor must succeed in pushing a program through the legislature and in killing unwanted legislative measures. To do so, a governor must use a grab bag of tools and must develop good personal or working relationships with key legislators. It is the adroit use of both formal and informal powers coupled with timing and political persuasion that produces an effective governor.

⭐ **5.5 Outline the functions of the other elected administrative agencies of the plural executive, and evaluate their policy and administrative effectiveness, p. 158.**

Texas elects nine statewide executive officials—more than most states. These include governor, lieutenant governor, attorney general, comptroller of public accounts, land commissioner, agriculture commissioner, and three railroad commissioners, as well as fifteen education board members elected from districts. The responsibilities of the agencies headed by these individuals are extensive, and as state government has expanded, these agencies have expanded their roles in policy formation and administration.

⭐ 5.6 Determine the role of the modern Texas bureaucracy in the formulation, implementation, and evaluation of public policy, p. 165.

The Texas Legislature creates executive agencies to bring solutions to problems faced by Texas citizens. Upon close inspection of the activities of the personnel working in these agencies, it becomes clear that agencies are involved in every stage of the policy process. Agencies consult with the state legislature on the drafting of laws and creation of programs. They carry out the programs that are created, and they help the legislature evaluate the effectiveness of laws and programs affecting the agencies.

⭐ 5.7 Explain how the legislature holds state agencies and public employees accountable, and evaluate proposals to reform the Texas executive branch, p. 170.

It takes thousands of people to implement or administer programs that have been enacted by the Texas Legislature, and the number of state employees has steadily increased over the past five decades as the state's population has increased, along with public demands for increased services. Questions about the performance of state agencies and individual employees are inevitable, and it primarily is the responsibility of the legislature to control the bureaucracy. This process is called legislative oversight, and the resources used by the legislature to carry out this responsibility include control of expenditures, review of rules and regulations, performance reviews, audits, sunset review, and review of staff sizes and functions. While there has been some reorganization of state agencies and a modest expansion of gubernatorial appointment powers, it will take a major rewrite of the executive article of the constitution to significantly expand the powers of the governor and address complaints about the plural executive.

Test Yourself: The Governor and the Executive Branch

⭐ 5.1 Trace the historical development of the structure of the executive branch in Texas, and state the reasons for the creation of the plural executive, p. 140.

Which of the following terms best describes the structure of the executive branch of Texas government?
A. Cabinet government
B. Commission government
C. Unified executive
D. Plural executive
E. Committee executive

⭐ 5.2 List the constitutional roles of the governor, p. 143.

Which of the following is NOT a function or role assigned to the Texas governor by the state's constitution?
A. Chief of state
B. Commander in chief of state's military
C. Chief budget officer
D. Legislative message and veto
E. Chief executive officer

⭐ 5.3 Identify the major powers assigned to the governor, and analyze how governors have interpreted and developed these powers, p. 144.

From a constitutional perspective, the Texas governor's weakest power is
A. influence and control over the budget.
B. the veto.
C. appointments.
D. tenure of office.
E. calling special sessions of the legislature.

⭐ 5.4 Evaluate the effectiveness of Texas governors as policy makers and political leaders, p. 151.

Texas governors have been successful because
A. they have been willing to strong-arm or threaten the legislature.
B. they have assembled the support of the other elected officials in common causes.
C. they have been able to influence the selection of the leaders of the legislature.
D. they have mobilized public opinion and the resources of interest groups.
E. they have brought pressure to bear on the legislature or state agencies from the national political party.

⭐ 5.5 Outline the functions of the other elected administrative agencies within the plural executive, and evaluate their policy and administrative effectiveness, p. 158.

Excluding the governor and lieutenant governor, which statewide elected office is perceived to be the most significant?
A. Land commissioner
B. Comptroller of public accounts
C. Attorney general
D. Agriculture commissioner
E. Railroad commissioner

⭐ **5.6 Determine the role of the modern Texas bureaucracy in the formulation, implementation, and evaluation of public policy, p. 165.**

Which statement does NOT apply to state commissions?
A. Most members are appointed by the governor with Texas Senate confirmation.
B. They generally cannot be reorganized by the governor.
C. Most of the day-to-day functions are carried out by an executive hired by the commission.
D. Most commissions have unpaid members.
E. Membership on a commission or board is for the duration of the governor's term in office.

⭐ **5.7 Explain how the legislature holds state agencies and public employees accountable, and evaluate proposals to reform the Texas executive branch, p. 170.**

In the language of public administration, "revolving door" refers to
A. the rapid movement of state employees up the agency's organizational structure.
B. the movement of a state employee from one agency to another.
C. the movement of a state employee from a legislator's staff to an agency position.
D. the movement of a state employee to a private sector business regulated by the agency in which that employee served.
E. the movement back and forth between employees working for the governor, the legislature, and the agencies.

Essay Questions

1. With the constitutional limitations placed on the office of governor, how have governors compensated for these restraints and demonstrated considerable success in pursuing their legislative agendas?
2. What case can you make for the elimination of the plural executive and the creation of the executive branch much like the U.S. presidency?
3. Should the Texas governor and lieutenant governor run for election together as a ticket, much like the president and vice president of the United States? Why or why not?

Key Terms

Administrative Procedures Act, p. 165
agriculture commissioner, p. 162
attorney general, p. 158
captured agency, p. 169
chief budget officer, p. 144
chief executive officer, p. 144
chief of state, p. 144
clemency, p. 144
commander in chief, p. 144

comptroller of public accounts, p. 160
executive commissioner of health and human services, p. 169
governor's message, p. 144
insurance commissioner, p. 168
land commissioner, p. 161
plural executive, p. 140
public counsels, p. 169
Public Utility Commission, p. 167
quasi-judicial, p. 167

Railroad Commission, p. 163
revolving door, p. 173
senatorial courtesy, p. 147
State Board of Education, p. 164
sunset law, p. 171
Texas Commission on Environmental Quality, p. 167
Texas Education Agency, p. 164
Texas secretary of state, p. 166
veto, p. 144

To Learn More on the Governor and the Executive Branch

In the Library

Barta, Carolyn. *Bill Clements: Texian to His Toenails.* Austin, TX: Eakin, 1996.

Beyle, Thad, ed. *Governors and Hard Times.* Washington, DC: CQ Press, 1992.

Davis, J. William. *There Shall Also Be a Lieutenant Governor.* Austin, TX: Sterling Swift, 1976.

Duncan, Marilyn, and Shirley Beckwith. *Guide to Texas State Agencies,* 11th ed. Austin, TX: LBJ School of Public Affairs, 2001.

Forsythe, Dall W., ed. *Quicker, Better, Cheaper? Managing Performance in American Government.* Albany, NY: Rockefeller Institute, 2001.

Gantt, Fred, Jr. *The Chief Executive in Texas: A Study in Gubernatorial Leadership.* Austin: University of Texas Press, 1964.

Hendrickson, Kenneth, Jr. *The Chief Executives of Texas: From Stephen F. Austin to John B. Connally Jr.* College Station: Texas A&M Press, 1995.

Lauderdale, Michael. *Reinventing Texas Government.* Austin: University of Texas Press, 1999.

Lipson, Leslie, with an introduction by Marshall E. Dimock. *The American Governor from Figurehead to Leader.* Chicago: University of Chicago Press, 1939.

McNeely, Dave, and Jim Henderson. *Bob Bullock: God Bless Texas.* Austin: University of Texas Press, 2008.

Morris, Celia. *Storming the Statehouse: Running for Governor with Ann Richards and Dianne Feinstein.* New York: Scribner's, 1992.

Prindle, David. *Petroleum Politics and the Texas Railroad Commission.* Austin: University of Texas Press, 1981.

Reston, James, Jr. *The Lone Star State: The Life of John Connally.* New York: Harper and Row, 1981.

Texas General Land Office. *The Land Commissioners of Texas.* Austin: Texas General Land Office, 1986.

Tolleson-Rinehart, Sue, and Jeanie R. Stanley. *Claytie and the Lady.* Austin: University of Texas Press, 1994.

On the Web

To learn more about the Texas governor's office and the programs associated with the governor, go to **www.governor .state.tx.us.**

To learn more about the National Governor's Association, go to **www.nga.org.**

To learn more about the Texas executive agencies, go to the Texas Records and Information Locator (TRAIL) Web site at **www.tsl.state.tx.us/apps/lrs/agencies.**

To learn more about the Sunset Advisory Commission, which analyzes state agencies and recommends reforms, go to **www.sunset.state.tx.us.**

6

The Judicial Branch

At 9:30 p.m. on September 25, 2007, the state of Texas executed Michael Richard, who had been convicted of the 1986 rape and murder of Marguerite Dixon. His execution was not unusual—Texas leads the nation with more than 400 executions in the past thirty years—but the decision by the Texas Court of Criminal Appeals to let the execution proceed stirred a nationwide controversy.[1]

On the same day, September 25, 2007, the U.S. Supreme Court halted a planned execution in another state while it considered the legality of lethal injections. The legal community presumed that the two actions constituted a *de facto* moratorium on executions.

Upon hearing the news of the Supreme Court's action, Michael Richard's attorneys immediately prepared a request to stop his execution, which was planned for later that

day. They had to file with the highest Texas court—the Texas Court of Criminal Appeals. When the attorneys tried to print out their appeal, their computer malfunctioned. As the clock was nearing the 5 p.m. closing time for the Texas Court of Criminal Appeals, they quickly called to explain their problem and request that the court stay open for twenty minutes.

The clerk who answered the phone asked presiding Judge Sharon Keller what to do about the request. Keller instructed the clerk to tell the appellate lawyers, "We close at 5," and Richard was executed.

Sharon Keller had been a Dallas prosecutor before being elected as a Republican to the Texas Court of Criminal Appeals in 1994. She had campaigned as a law-and-order candidate and, as a judge, she gained a reputation of siding consistently with

The courts of last resort—the Texas Supreme Court and the Texas Court of Criminal Appeals—have come a long way from their original chambers (on the left) in the capitol with three members to their current chambers (on the right) in the supreme court building with nine members. In addition, the state has established new courts and extended or redefined jurisdiction of courts throughout Texas.

prosecutors. Keller led the court to support policies speeding executions.

When the Richard execution—and the phone call—made the news, civil rights activists angrily denounced what they saw as her callous disregard of due process. Richard's family filed a wrongful death suit against Keller. The National Association of Criminal Defense Lawyers, hundreds of Texas lawyers, and Texas State Representatives Lon Burnam and Harold Dutton filed complaints with the State Commission on Judicial Conduct, arguing that Judge Keller had violated Richard's constitutional rights and damaged the reputation of the judiciary.

In 2008, the Supreme Court ruled that the chemicals used in lethal injections did not amount to cruel and unusual punishment and hence did not violate the U.S. Constitution.[2] The legal and political case against Judge Keller, however, took a while longer to resolve.

The complaint against Keller could have led to her removal from office. However, the State Commission on Judicial Conduct did not make that recommendation. Instead, in July 2010, the Commission sharply rebuked Keller in a public warning, but she was allowed to retain her position as a judge.

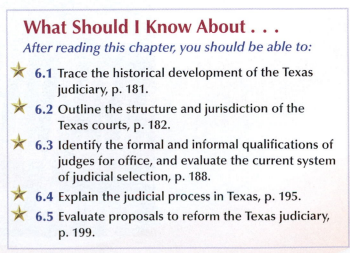

What Should I Know About . . .

After reading this chapter, you should be able to:

⭐ **6.1** Trace the historical development of the Texas judiciary, p. 181.

⭐ **6.2** Outline the structure and jurisdiction of the Texas courts, p. 182.

⭐ **6.3** Identify the formal and informal qualifications of judges for office, and evaluate the current system of judicial selection, p. 188.

⭐ **6.4** Explain the judicial process in Texas, p. 195.

⭐ **6.5** Evaluate proposals to reform the Texas judiciary, p. 199.

The judiciary differs from the other branches of Texas government—the legislative and the executive—in two respects. First, the judiciary is the least familiar branch of Texas government. Most Texans have little knowledge of the structure and operation of the courts and even less knowledge of the judges who hold positions on them. The election of judges may ask too much of Texas voters. Second, unlike the other branches, the judiciary cannot initiate action. It must wait for an individual or group to seek its assistance by initiating a lawsuit. Even then, the court must determine whether it is an issue that can be settled by the application of state law or is a matter that must be considered by another branch of government.

As in other states, the principal function of courts in Texas is to settle disputes by applying the law. The dispute may involve the state's acting on behalf of the community to prosecute suspected criminals or it may involve individuals who disagree about the terms of a contract. In both kinds of disputes, the courts examine the facts, interpret the law, and attempt to settle the conflict.

In this chapter, we will examine the Texas judiciary to understand how the courts apply and interpret the law to settle disputes.

- First, we will examine *the roots of the Texas judiciary,* describing how the structure and operation of the judiciary has evolved since the early 1800s.
- Second, we will describe *the structure of the Texas judiciary*, indicating the various types of courts and their responsibilities.
- Third, we will describe *judges and judicial selection* in Texas, indicating who settles disputes in Texas and how they are chosen.

Can Texas judges be held accountable for their actions or decisions? Judicial misconduct "is an action by a judge that brings discredit upon the judiciary or the administration of justice. It could be a violation of the Texas Constitution, the Texas Penal Code, the Code of Judicial Conduct, or other rules established by the Supreme Court of Texas." Presiding Judge Sharon Keller's actions in the efforts of Michael Richard's attorneys to file a plea for a stay of execution resulted in disciplinary proceedings by the State Commission on Judicial Conduct.

Photo courtesy: Erich Schlegel/Dallas Morning News

- Fourth, we will describe *the judicial process in Texas,* examining how criminal cases and civil cases are handled.
- Finally, we will explore *reforms for changing the Texas judiciary,* analyzing persistent problems that affect the ability of the judiciary to settle disputes fairly and impartially as well as proposals for solving those problems.

ROOTS OF the Texas Judiciary

6.1 . . . Trace the historical development of the Texas judiciary.

The first courts in Texas were established in the Austin colony when Stephen F. Austin appointed a provisional justice of the peace for the province of Texas in 1822. Since Texas was a part of Mexico, the Mexican governor subsequently replaced the justice of the peace with three elected officials who applied Spanish law in Austin's colony. The judiciary was a point of contention between the Anglo settlers and the Mexican government.

As an independent republic, Texas created a judiciary that primarily reflected English tradition, although some features of Spanish law were retained. Under the 1836 Constitution, the Republic of Texas created a supreme court, which had appellate jurisdiction only, and allowed Congress to create inferior courts. Judges were elected by Congress. Counties also had county and justice of the peace courts, whose judges were popularly elected.

In subsequent constitutions, Texas retained the basic judicial structure established in the 1836 Constitution. Almost every constitution provided for the popular election of judges. As caseloads increased, additional courts were created, especially at the appellate level. In the 1876 Constitution, the judiciary consisted of the supreme court, with appellate civil jurisdiction; the court of appeals, with criminal jurisdiction and limited civil jurisdiction; and an array of district, county, and justice of the peace courts. In 1891, the constitution was amended to provide an intermediate level of courts of civil appeals. The amendment also changed the name of the court of appeals to the court of criminal appeals and limited its jurisdiction to criminal cases. With the addition of the intermediate courts, whose numbers could be increased by the legislature, the Texas Supreme Court was allowed to exercise discretion in accepting appeals. However, the additional civil appeals courts did not affect a growing caseload for the Texas Court of Criminal Appeals. (To learn more about the constitutional basis for the judiciary, see The Living Constitution: Article 5, Section 1.)

A constitutional amendment in 1945 increased the number of justices on the Texas Supreme Court from three to nine, and amendments in 1966 and 1978 increased the number of judges on the Texas Court of Criminal Appeals, but it still could not keep up with the growing number of criminal appeals. In 1980, the courts of civil appeals became courts of appeals, and their jurisdiction was extended to criminal cases. Thus, the remedy that had cured the supreme court's caseload difficulties was applied to the court of criminal appeals.[3]

Over the years, constitutional amendments and legislative acts have added courts and changed the structure of the Texas judiciary, creating a system that is among the most complicated and confusing in the United States, if not the world. In the next section, we describe the current array of courts and their responsibilities.

The Living Constitution

The judicial power of this State shall be vested in one Supreme Court, in one Court of Criminal Appeals, in Courts of Appeals, in District Courts, in County Courts, in Commissioners Courts, in Courts of Justices of the Peace, and in such other courts as may be provided by law.

—ARTICLE 5, SECTION 1

The Texas judicial system reflects both Spanish and Anglo-American traditions. The earliest courts were based on Spanish traditions. The 1836 Constitution of the Republic of Texas provided for a supreme court, which consisted of a chief justice and all of the district judges, who served as associate justices. Subsequent constitutions, including the 1876 Constitution, provided for one supreme court. However, the 1876 Constitution, unlike other constitutions, stripped all criminal jurisdiction from the Texas Supreme Court and gave it to a Texas Court of Appeals. In 1891, an amendment created an intermediate court of civil appeals and a separate court of criminal appeals with criminal jurisdiction. The court of criminal appeals, which originally consisted of three judges, was enlarged to five members in 1966 and to nine members in 1977. In 1980, a constitutional amendment extended intermediate appellate jurisdiction in criminal cases to the courts of civil appeals and renamed them courts of appeals. Only one other state, Oklahoma, has two supreme courts.[a]

There are several criticisms of Texas's system of two supreme courts. Some critics stress the inefficiency of having two highest state courts and the possibility of conflicting rulings from the courts. Others argue that judges who deal exclusively with either civil or criminal law are unlikely to possess the broad perspective that judges who deal with both types of law develop. Supporters of the two supreme courts counter that the two courts have rarely disagreed or issued conflicting opinions and that specialization in criminal or civil law is a benefit because judges cannot be experts in both types of law.[b]

CRITICAL THINKING QUESTIONS

1. How are the appellate functions divided between two courts?
2. Are two courts of last resort necessary and advisable, or would the merger of the two courts into one supreme court, exercising both criminal and civil jurisdiction, be better? Explain your answer.
3. What problems might result from the merger of the Texas Supreme Court and Texas Court of Criminal Appeals?

[a]George D. Braden, *The Constitution of the State of Texas: An Annotated and Comparative Analysis* (Austin: Texas Advisory Commission on Intergovernmental Relations, 1977), 363–8; "Texas Court of Criminal Appeals," *Handbook of Texas Online*, October 6, 2010, www.tsha.utexas.edu/handbook/online/articles/view/TT/jpt1.html.
[b]See William L. Willis, "The Evolution of the Texas Court of Criminal Appeals," *Texas Bar Journal* (September 1966); and Paul Burka, "Trial by Technicality," *Texas Monthly* (April 1982).

The Structure of the Texas Judiciary

⭐ **6.2 . . . Outline the structure and jurisdiction of the Texas courts.**

The Texas judiciary incorporates five levels of courts, some created by the constitution and others created by the legislature. (To learn more about the courts at each level, see Figure 6.1.)

Local Trial Courts

At the lowest level are local trial courts of limited jurisdiction, which include municipal courts and justice of the peace courts. By statute, the legislature allows each incorporated city in Texas to create a municipal court. Some larger cities are allowed several courts. In 2010, 915 cities had established municipal courts, employing 1,490 judges. **Municipal courts** exercise original jurisdiction over traffic misdemeanors, such as speeding, failure to wear a seat belt, and parking on a sidewalk. The maximum penalty in these cases is a fine or sanction that does not include confinement to jail or imprisonment. Municipal courts also have original jurisdiction over Class C misdemeanors, such as public intoxication and simple assault. The penalty in these cases cannot exceed $500. In addition, municipal courts have exclusive original jurisdiction over criminal violations of city ordinances—which may include a maximum fine of $2,000 for violations of fire safety, zoning, and public heath ordinances. Finally, municipal courts exercise civil jurisdiction in cases involving dangerous dogs, and municipal judges perform magistrate functions. Magistrate duties include conducting examining trials (preliminary hearings for county and district courts to determine whether sufficient evidence exists to hold someone for trial), issuing search and arrest warrants, and providing statutory warnings.

municipal court
City court with limited criminal jurisdiction.

In 2009, more than 7.8 million new cases were filed in Texas municipal courts. Of those cases, more than 82 percent involved traffic and parking offenses—thus, the name "traffic courts," which is often given to municipal courts. The remaining cases involved violations of municipal ordinances and state laws. Eighteen percent of the cases disposed of in 2009 involved a trial and a decision by a judge or jury, and less than 1 percent of those cases were appealed.[4]

The other local trial court in Texas is the justice of the peace court. Most states have eliminated justice courts, but there were 822 justice of the peace courts in Texas in 2010. Each of Texas's 254 counties, depending on its population, must create between one and eight justice precincts. Depending on the population of the precinct, each justice precinct in a county has one or two judges.

justice of the peace court
Local county court for minor crimes and civil suits.

Justice of the peace courts have both civil and criminal jurisdiction. They exercise exclusive original jurisdiction in civil cases involving less than $200, and concurrent original jurisdiction with district and county courts in civil cases involving less than $10,000. The justice of the peace courts function as small claims courts: the parties in a civil suit present their sides in the case before a judge, who decides the case based on the evidence and testimony provided by the parties. Neither party needs to be represented by an attorney. Because small claims courts provide an inexpensive method of resolving disputes involving small amounts of money, they are often called the "people's courts."

Justice of the peace courts have original jurisdiction over Class C misdemeanors throughout the county. However, if municipalities within a county have municipal courts, the justice courts usually only hear

Shouldn't justices of the peace be required to have law degrees? Rooted in a time when the state was rural and laws were limited, this court functioned on a part-time basis, was accessible to those in sparsely settled areas of the state, relied on fees or fines for funding, served to adjudicate a range of limited issues, and required no legal training. Times have changed. Today, the law and issues are more complex, but proponents of the justice of the peace courts have successfully resisted most changes to the required qualifications of the judges. Seen here is the "court building" of the justice of the peace in Bronte, Texas, located in sparsely populated Coke County.

Photo courtesy: Photo by H B GIBSON

Figure 6.1 *What is the structure of the Texas court system?*

Source: Texas Office of Court Administration

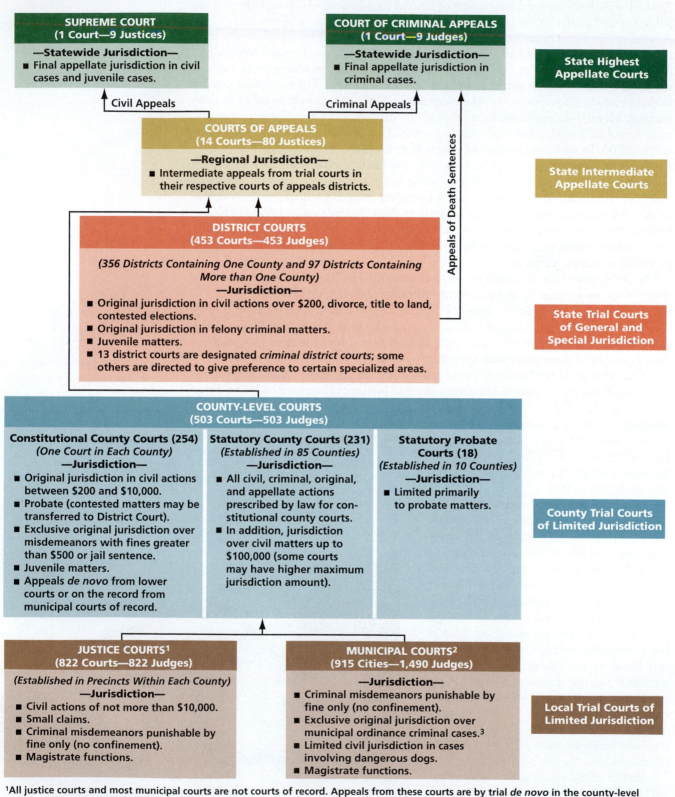

cases that occur within the unincorporated areas of the county. Justices of the peace also perform magistrate duties—such as issuing search and arrest warrants, conducting preliminary hearings, performing marriages—and have jurisdiction over forcible entry and detainer actions, which are usually attempts by landlords to remove tenants. Despite these extensive responsibilities, justices of the peace are not required to be licensed attorneys, and that situation has generated some criticism.

County Courts

At the next level of the Texas judiciary are county courts of limited jurisdiction. There are two major categories of county courts: constitutional county courts and county courts at law.

The Texas Constitution establishes a constitutional county court in each of the state's 254 counties. **Constitutional county courts** have concurrent original jurisdiction in civil matters with justice of the peace courts (suits between $200 and $10,000) and with district courts (suits between $200 and $10,000). They also have jurisdiction over probate cases (legal matters primarily involving wills and estates), unless the probate is contested, in which case they are transferred to a district court. Constitutional county courts exercise original jurisdiction over misdemeanors with fines greater than $500 and/or a jail sentence.

Constitutional county courts also exercise appellate jurisdiction over cases from municipal and justice of the peace courts. Since few municipal courts and no justice of the peace courts are courts of record, there is no transcript of the trial. Without a transcript, there is no record of the proceedings for the county court to review for procedural errors. Consequently, appeals from most municipal courts and all justice of the peace courts take the form of a completely new trial—termed a **trial *de novo*.**

Statutory county courts—**county courts at law**—were created to relieve county judges in urban counties of their judicial functions so that they could concentrate on their duties as presiding officer of the commissioners court (see **chapter 7**). In 2010, there were 249 county courts at law, including probate courts, in more than eighty counties. Some counties have several county courts at law.

The state legislature has created county courts at law to meet the needs of each county's court system. Since the courts cost the state nothing, if the state legislators from a county want a court at law created, the legislature will probably accommodate them. Since each court is established by statute, a county court at law may have concurrent jurisdiction with other statutory county courts or may exercise original subject-matter jurisdiction in a limited field—such as civil, criminal, or probate—or appellate jurisdiction. The original civil jurisdiction of these courts varies greatly, although most exceed the $10,000 limit placed on the constitutional county courts, and at least one court has no limit.[5]

The effect of these statutes is a bewildering array of county courts at law, making meaningful generalizations about these courts and their jurisdictions difficult. Nevertheless, most county courts at law have limited original jurisdiction in civil cases, usually in those cases that involve less than $100,000. They also have limited original jurisdiction in criminal cases involving Class A and B misdemeanors, and they handle many drunken driving cases. Most county courts at law have the same appellate jurisdiction as constitutional county courts. County court at law judges must be licensed attorneys, but judges of the constitutional county courts don't have to be lawyers. They are required only to be "well informed in the law."

County courts of all types disposed of more than 786,000 civil and criminal cases during the 2009 fiscal year but saw more than 860,000 cases added to their dockets. At the beginning of the reporting period, there were approximately 920,000 civil and

constitutional county court
Constitutionally mandated court for criminal and civil matters.

trial *de novo*
New trial, necessary for an appeal from a court that is not a court of record.

county court at law
Statutory county court to relieve county judge of judicial duties.

Can they ever catch up with the workload? There are currently 453 district courts, such as the 331st District Court in Austin, which is presided over by Judge Bob Perkins. New district courts are created by the legislature, but with the increase in the state's population, the district courts usually end the year with more cases than they had at the beginning of the year.

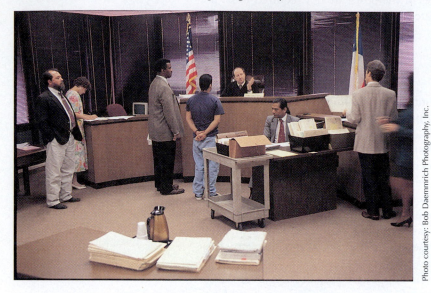

Photo courtesy: Bob Daemmrich Photography, Inc.

district court

Court of general jurisdiction for serious crimes and high-dollar civil cases.

court of appeals

Intermediate appellate court for criminal and civil appeals.

criminal cases pending from the previous year. At the end of 2009, more than 900,000 cases were carried over into 2010.[6]

District Courts

The state courts of general and special jurisdiction are the district courts, which numbered 453 in 2010. The **district courts** have original civil jurisdiction in cases involving more than $200 or $500, all suits over the title to land, divorce proceedings, election contests, and contested probate matters. The district courts also have original criminal jurisdiction in all felony cases.

Most district courts exercise both criminal and civil jurisdiction. However, in metropolitan areas, the district courts tend to specialize in criminal, civil, juvenile, or family matters.

The district courts disposed of 860,000 civil and criminal cases during the 2009 fiscal year, but more than 870,000 new civil, criminal and juvenile cases were added. Despite a clearance rate of more than 98 percent, the courts ended the year with 906,000 cases carried over into 2010.[7]

The district courts reported that only 3,500 cases went to trial in 2009. Criminal cases can be dismissed for a number of reasons, including conviction in another case or insufficient evidence, and a person can avoid trial through deferred adjudication. Very few criminal defendants go to a full trial. Most criminal cases are resolved through plea bargaining. A criminal defendant, through a lawyer, negotiates with prosecutors a guilty plea that will get a lesser sentence than he or she could expect to receive if convicted in a trial. Many civil lawsuits are resolved through negotiations between the opposing parties, but those that are tried and appealed can take several years to be resolved. Without plea bargains and negotiations, the caseload would simply overwhelm district courts.

Intermediate Courts of Appeals

There are fourteen **courts of appeals** in Texas with a total of eighty justices. Other than the 1st and 14th Courts of Appeals, which are located in Houston and serve the same area, each court serves a distinct geographic region. Each court includes a chief justice, who is elected as chief justice by the voters in a general election, and between two and twelve justices. Cases are usually heard by a panel of three justices. Certain cases, however, are heard *en banc,* which means that all of the justices assigned to the particular court of appeals participate. Since the courts are reviewing the record of the trial court, no testimony is taken, and no juries are involved. Decisions are rendered by a majority of the justices participating in the case. These courts exercise appellate jurisdiction over civil and criminal appeals from district and county courts in their respective regions. Only death penalty cases, which go directly from a district court to the court of criminal appeals, escape the courts' jurisdiction.

Combined, the courts of appeals disposed of more than 11,000 cases during fiscal 2009, but approximately 8,000 other cases were still pending on their dockets at the end of that year.[8] Disparities, however, exist in the sizes of caseloads between individual courts, with those in Houston and Dallas handling the lion's share. The Texas Supreme Court partially balances the load by transferring cases among courts.

The Courts of Last Resort

The state's highest appellate courts include the **Texas Supreme Court,** for civil matters, and the **Texas Court of Criminal Appeals,** for criminal matters. Both courts have limited original jurisdiction; most of their cases involve appeals from the courts of appeals. Both are courts of last resort, meaning that they are the last state courts to which a person can appeal a case. Of course, a person who claims that a "federal question" is involved may petition the U.S. Supreme Court for a writ of *certiorari.*

The Texas Supreme Court includes a chief justice and eight justices. The Texas Court of Criminal Appeals also has nine members, a presiding judge and eight judges. The Texas Supreme Court always hears cases *en banc,* with all nine justices participating in the case. The constitution allows the Texas Court of Criminal Appeals to sit in panels of three judges, except for capital murder cases, but it almost never does. For both courts, decisions are reached by a majority vote. Both courts are located in Austin, but they are allowed to hear cases in other locations in Texas. The Texas Supreme Court, only recently given the authority to hear cases outside Austin, has traveled to several other cities to hear cases.

The operations of the two highest state courts in Texas are similar. Each court exercises some discretion in reviewing cases, although the Texas Court of Criminal Appeals is required to review all capital cases from the district courts. To secure a review by the Texas Supreme Court, a party in a suit files a **petition for review**—a request for the supreme court to review the decision of the court of appeals. In conference, the nine justices consider the request, and if four justices agree, the petition is granted. The case is then scheduled for oral argument before the court, and the parties to the suit submit legal briefs.

In 2009, the Texas Supreme Court received 835 petitions for review and granted 85. A refusal to grant a petition for review allows the ruling of the lower court to stand. The court also processed more than 2,000 other writs and motions[9] and issued 165 opinions.[10]

The Texas Court of Criminal Appeals reviews **applications for discretionary review,** following the same procedure as the Texas Supreme Court in reviewing its petitions for review. If four judges concur, the petition is granted. In 2009, the Texas Court of Criminal Appeals considered 1,569 petitions for discretionary review and granted 125. The workload of the court also included direct appeals (223), applications for writs of *habeas corpus,* and original proceedings.[11]

After the courts hear the oral arguments in a case, they decide the case in conferences. When the court has reached a decision, one of the justices is assigned the

Texas Supreme Court
Court of last resort in civil and juvenile cases.

Texas Court of Criminal Appeals
Court of last resort in criminal cases.

petition for review
Request for Texas Supreme Court review, which is granted if four justices agree.

application for discretionary review
Request for Texas Court of Criminal Appeals review, which is granted if four judges agree.

TIMELINE: The Constitutional Evolution of the Texas Supreme Court and Court of Appeals[a]

1836 **Origins of Texas Court System**—The constitution of the Republic provides for "one supreme Court and such inferior courts as the Congress may establish."

1850 **Popular Election of Texas Supreme Court**—A constitutional amendment passes providing for the popular election of Texas Supreme Court justices.

1891 **Court of Criminal Appeals**—To manage the increasing workload, the court of appeals is limited to only hearing criminal cases. Intermediate courts of civil appeals are created for different geographical regions of the state.

1845 **Appointed Three-Member Supreme Court**—The first constitution of the state of Texas reduces its supreme court membership to three justices; all are appointed by the governor with the consent of the Senate.

1876 **Structure of Courts in Post-Reconstruction Era**—The 1876 Constitution provides for a three-member elected supreme court and establishes a three-judge court of appeals with appellate jurisdiction in criminal cases. Subsequently, a commission of appeals is created to hear appellate cases.

[a]Information for timeline taken from several sources including Adrienne Sonder, Tarlton Law Library, The University of Texas at Austin, "Timeline of the Texas Supreme Court and Court of Criminal Appeals," November 2006, tarlton.law.utexas.edu/justices/timeline.html.

task of writing the court's opinion. The Texas Supreme Court justices wrote 165 opinions in 2009, an average of more than eighteen per justice. These opinions included majority opinions, *per curiam,* or unsigned opinions, concurring opinions, and dissenting opinions. During this same period, the Texas Court of Criminal Appeals judges issued 534 opinions, of which 29 percent were signed opinions and 47 percent were *per curiam.* The remaining opinions were concurring and dissenting opinions.

The Texas Supreme Court performs several administrative duties in addition to its judicial responsibilities. It is responsible for establishing the rules and procedures that govern trials and appeals in civil and juvenile cases in Texas. It also establishes the rules for the operation of state agencies in the judicial branch, such as the Office of Court Administration, Commission on Judicial Conduct, and State Bar of Texas.

Judges and Judicial Selection

★ **6.3** . . . **Identify the formal and informal qualifications of judges for office, and evaluate the current system of judicial selection.**

There are more than 3,300 judges in Texas. Except for municipal judges, they are selected in partisan elections. Trial judges—justices of the peace, constitutional and statutory county court judges, and district court judges—serve four-year terms, while appellate judges and justices—courts of appeals, supreme court, and court of criminal appeals—serve six-year terms. After describing the qualifications for Texas judges, we will examine judicial selection.

1945 **Texas Supreme Court Expanded to Nine**—Membership of the supreme court is increased to a chief justice and eight associate justices in an effort to relieve the workload of the appellate courts.

1985 **Judicial Districts Board**—The Judicial Districts Board is created to redraw judicial districts in order to equalize the workload. Changes in the district boundaries require legislative approval, but few changes have been implemented.

SUPREME COURT
(1 Court—9 Justices)
—Statewide Jurisdiction—
■ Final appellate jurisdiction in civil cases and juvenile cases.

COURT OF CRIMINAL APPEALS
(1 Court—9 Judges)
—Statewide Jurisdiction—
■ Final appellate jurisdiction in criminal cases.

State Highest Appellate Courts

COURTS OF APPEALS
(14 Courts—80 Justices)
—Regional Jurisdiction—
■ Intermediate appeals from trial courts in their respective courts of appeals districts.

State Intermediate Appellate Courts

1977 **Changes in the Court of Criminal Appeals**—The court of criminal appeals is increased from five to nine members, and the court is authorized to sit in panels of three to hear noncapital cases.

Civil Appeals / Criminal Appeals

Appeals of Death Sentences

DISTRICT COURTS
(453 Courts—453 Judges)
(356 Districts Containing One County and 97 Districts Containing More than One County)
—Jurisdiction—
■ Original jurisdiction in civil actions over $200 or $500,¹ divorce, title to land, contested elections.
■ Original jurisdiction in felony criminal matters.
■ Juvenile matters.
■ 13 district courts are designated criminal district courts; some

State Trial Courts of General and Special Jurisdiction

Judicial Qualifications and Personal Characteristics

The Texas Constitution establishes the qualifications for most Texas judges, which vary by judicial office. (To learn more about judicial qualifications, see Table 6.1.) Consequently, Texas judges vary greatly in education and training. In personal characteristics, however, the judges are quite similar.[12]

Table 6.1 *What are the qualifications for Texas judges?*

Court	Term of Office	Salary in 2009*	Qualifications for Office
Municipal courts	2 or 4 years	Set by city, highly variable	Determined by the city; varies by city
Justice of the peace courts	4 years	Set by county, highly variable	None
Constitutional county courts	4 years	Set by county, highly variable	Must be "well informed in the law"
County courts at law	4 years	Set by county, highly variable	25 years of age, county resident for 2 years, licensed attorney in Texas, served as judge or practiced law for 4 years
District courts	4 years	$125,000–$173,000	Age 25 to 74, citizen, district resident for 2 years, licensed attorney in Texas, practicing lawyer or judge for 4 years
Courts of appeals	6 years	Chief justice: $140,000–$147,500 Justices: $137,500–$145,000	Age 35 to 74, citizen, practicing attorney or judge of a court of record for at least 10 years
Texas Court of Criminal Appeals	6 years	Presiding judge: $152,500 Judges: $150,000	Same as courts of appeals
Texas Supreme Court	6 years	Chief justice: $152,500 Justices: $150,000	Same as courts of appeals

*There is a base state salary the district courts and higher. Presiding judges are allocated higher salaries, and there are provisions for additional compensation for extra judicial services.
Source: Office of Court Administration, "Annual Statistical Report for the Texas Judiciary," December 2009, www.courts.state.tx.us/pubs/AR2009/AR09.pdf and "Judicial Qualifications, Selection, and Terms of Office."

Has the diversity on the Texas Supreme Court increased? Chief Justice Wallace Jefferson of the Texas Supreme Court, seen here delivering his State of the Judiciary in Texas address before the 81st Legislature, is one of two African Americans on the court. The Texas Supreme Court also includes two Hispanics and two women.

Photo courtesy: Bob Daemmrich Photography, Inc.

For municipal courts, the municipality's legislative body or the city charter establishes the qualifications for its judges. These qualifications vary widely among the municipalities in Texas. In 2009, some 58 percent were graduates of law schools, and 52 percent were licensed to practice law. In ethnicity, 77 percent were Anglo, 15 percent were Hispanic, and 5 percent were African American. Two-thirds of the judges were males.

Justices of the peace are required to be registered voters, but there are no educational, age, or experience requirements. As a result, in 2009 few (9 percent) had graduated from law school, and even fewer (8 percent) were licensed attorneys. Seventy-seven percent of the judges were Anglos, 19 percent were Hispanic, and 4 percent were African American. Sixty-seven percent of the justices of the peace were males.

As noted above, the Texas Constitution requires constitutional county judges to be "well informed in the law of the State," but no law degree or license to practice law is required. However, county judges who perform judicial duties are required to complete at least thirty hours of instruction in the administrative duties of the office and in substantive, procedural, and evidentiary laws. Among the county court judges in 2009, 14 percent had graduated from law schools, and 12 percent were licensed attorneys. Approximately 90 percent of the judges were Anglo males.

A statutory county court judge must be at least twenty-five years old and a licensed attorney with a minimum of four years experience either as a judge or a practicing attorney. In 2009, 73 percent of the judges were Anglos, 22 percent were Hispanic, and 4 percent were African American. Sixty-nine percent were males.

A district court judge must have resided in the judicial district for two years and have been a licensed attorney in Texas or served as a judge for four years. In 2009, 77 percent of these judges were Anglos, 17 percent were Hispanic, 4 percent were African American, and 72 percent were males.

The constitution requires all appellate court judges—those on the courts of appeals, supreme court, and court of criminal appeals—to be at least thirty-five years of age and no older than seventy-four and have been a practicing attorney or a judge of a court of record for at least ten years. In 2009, judges for Texas's fourteen courts of appeals were predominately middle-aged (average age of fifty-five), Anglo (82 percent), and male (59 percent). The judges had served on the court for an average of about eight years. Although some of these judges came to the court directly from private practice, others had served on lower courts or as prosecutors.

The members of the state's two highest courts also share similar personal characteristics. In 2010, there were seven males and two females on the Texas Supreme Court and five males and four females on the Texas Court of Criminal Appeals. The average age of those serving on the Supreme Court was 53, and on the Court of Criminal Appeals the average age was 66. All nine members of the court of criminal appeals were Anglo, while on the supreme court, Justices David Medina and Eva Guzman are Hispanic and Justice Dale Wainwright and Chief Justice Wallace Jefferson are African American. Average tenure on the supreme court was nearly eight years; on the court of criminal appeals, it was more than ten years.

Judicial Selection

For more than a century, Texas has chosen its judges in partisan elections and is currently one of only eight states that elect all or most of their judges through partisan elections. There are two exceptions to partisan elections: municipal judges and filling vacancies in other judicial offices. Municipal judges may be elected or appointed by the city council. If vacancies occur in statutory county judgeships, the county commissioners court appoints a judge. For district courts, courts of appeals, and the Texas Supreme Court and Texas Court of Criminal Appeals, vacancies are filled by gubernatorial appointment. Appointed judges serve until the next general election, when they must compete in a partisan election (except for municipal judges) to retain their positions. In 2009, one-third of the eighteen top judges were initially appointed to the courts, as were 54 percent of the eighty courts of appeals judges and 36 percent of the district court judges.

Most scholarly work on judicial selection classifies Texas as one of eight states that elects all or some of its state judges in partisan elections.[13] Yet, a significant number of judges are initially appointed by the governor or the county commissioners courts. In practice, this means that the state functions with a combined system of judicial selection—partisan elections with appointments. Many Hispanic and African American jurists initially gained seats on courts through appointments, and the governor's judicial role is expanded through this appointment process. Additionally, well-publicized appointments by the governor are used to cultivate political support among different parts of the electorate.

Most of the time, however, potential judges have to compete in partisan contests. First, one must win the nomination of a political party in a primary election or state convention, which requires a political campaign. For the appellate courts in Texas, where the judges are selected in large districts or statewide, a primary election campaign can be time consuming and costly. Then, another campaign must be waged in the general election. Again, getting voter attention requires more campaign contributions. Opinion polls indicate that a majority of Texans favor an electoral system and the accountability of judges that it promotes. But many voters repeatedly have demonstrated that they know little, if anything, about the judges and judicial candidates on the ballot—particularly in urban areas with long ballots—and often cast their votes in judicial races on the basis of party labels or familiar-sounding names. (To learn more about the arguments for and against election of judges, see Join the Debate: Should Texas Elect Its Judges in Partisan Elections?)

Over the past few decades, several incidents have raised questions about to whom the judges are accountable and whether judges who depend on campaign contributions to get elected can remain fair and impartial. Since the early 1970s, when the Texas Legislature passed a strong Deceptive Trade Practices–Consumer Protection Act, a battle for control of the Texas Supreme Court has raged between plaintiffs' lawyers, who represent injured parties in civil suits, and defense lawyers and the businesses, doctors, and insurance companies that they represent. During the late 1970s and early 1980s, plaintiffs' lawyers and their association, the Texas Trial Lawyers Association, were the presumptive winners, electing judges who sided with plaintiffs in medical malpractice and product liability suits. Although the Texas Supreme Court did not always decide for the plaintiffs, trial lawyers were more likely to be successful than defense lawyers. In 1985, for example, the supreme court decided for the plaintiffs in 69 percent of the court's cases and for the defendants in only 28 percent of the cases.[14]

In 1986, two justices who had received campaign contributions from trial lawyers were the subjects of investigations. The House Judicial Affairs Committee investigated Justices C. L. Ray and William Kilgarlin, both Democrats, for alleged improper contact with attorneys. The House panel made no recommendations concerning the allegations against Ray and Kilgarlin, but the State Commission on Judicial Conduct,

Join the DEBATE | Should Texas Elect Its Judges in Partisan Elections?

Judges are expected to be well qualified, fair in making their decisions, and independent from political and public pressures. In a democratic system, we also expect some degree of judicial accountability to the public, though some judicial systems stress accountability more than others. Texas selects its judges in partisan elections—a system intended to stress accountability.

Especially with the growth of party competition in Texas, judicial campaigns have become high-dollar affairs, requiring judicial candidates to solicit funds. But, some campaign contributions raise concerns about future undue influence. For example, among the major contributors to judicial campaigns are lawyers and clients who are the same people coming before the courts asking for favorable decisions in cases. Such campaign finance dynamics have fueled movements in Texas, as well as across the nation, to reform state-level judicial selection processes in an attempt to increase judicial independence. Should judges in Texas be elected in partisan elections, or are there other ways to hold Texas judges accountable?

To develop an ARGUMENT FOR partisan judicial elections think about how:

- **A majority of Texans support the election of judges.** Why did the framers of the 1876 Constitution return to judicial elections after earlier constitutions provided for the appointment of judges? In what ways does the selection of judges through elections reflect the will of the Texas people?
- **Electing judges promotes accountability.** How do you eliminate a bad judge who is appointed for a long term or life? In what ways does election of judges serve to produce responsibility from the courts?
- **Texans want their judges to be competent, qualified, and—especially—fair.** How does election of judges help ensure that judges will be fair? Is there any conclusive empirical evidence to indicate that merit selection or appointment results in more competent and better-qualified judges than elections?

To develop an ARGUMENT AGAINST partisan judicial elections, think about how:

- **Judicial campaigns in Texas cost a lot of money.** Should a judge have to rely on his or her own wealth to run for an office that is a public service? In what ways does political campaigning and fund-raising detract from the judge's work on the court?
- **Texans want their judges to be impartial, fair, and above politics.** In what ways do judicial elections have the potential to turn judges into partisan politicians rather than impartial judges? How can judges be independent on the bench if they receive monetary support from partisan voters and organizations?
- **Historically, Texans have expressed intense apprehension over "secretive" power.** Who are the people who contribute to judicial campaigns? Why do they contribute? What do they expect in return? In what ways is justice for sale in Texas?

How is judicial campaigning similar to campaigning for other offices in Texas? Judicial campaign signs such as these can be found on many stretches of road in Texas.

Photo courtesy: Courtesy of L. Tucker Gibson

the state agency responsible for disciplining judges, also investigated the charges and issued public sanctions against both justices in 1987. Ray received a reprimand for multiple violations of the Code of Judicial Conduct. Kilgarlin received an admonition, the commission's mildest punishment.

The Texas Supreme Court received national attention in 1987 when journalist Mike Wallace devoted a segment of a CBS-TV *60 Minutes* program to the question "Is Justice for Sale?" Wallace focused on the campaign contributions of Houston trial lawyer Joe Jamail, who won an $11 billion judgment against Texaco for interfering with Pennzoil's attempt to purchase the Getty Oil Company in 1984. Jamail, who contributed $10,000 to the original district court judge assigned to the case, gave thousands more to supreme court justices. Wallace questioned the ethics of a judicial system that allowed lawyers to contribute to the political campaigns of judges before whom they appear. Later in 1987, Democratic Chief Justice John Hill and Democratic Justices Robert Campbell and James Wallace resigned from the supreme court. Republican Governor William Clements appointed three Republicans to fill the vacancies on the court, including Thomas R. Phillips as chief justice. (To learn more about how Texas courts of last resort compare to those of other large states, see Table 6.2.)

While a cloud of suspicion hung over the supreme court, a group pushing tort reform, the Texas Civil Justice League (TCJL), initiated an attack on the Deceptive Trade Practices–Consumer Protection Act in the Texas Legislature. In the 1987 and subsequent legislative sessions, TCJL and other tort reform groups, including Texans for Lawsuit Reform, convinced the legislature to limit punitive damages, change the state's workers' compensation program to limit civil damage lawsuits, limit the liability of manufacturers of products, and protect firearm manufacturers against suits. The groups would be particularly successful in the 1995 legislative session, following Governor George W. Bush's support for tort reform in his gubernatorial campaign.[15]

With six supreme court positions on the ballot in 1988—the three midterm appointees plus the three justices whose terms were up for election—business interests saw an opportunity to reverse the supreme court's preference for plaintiffs, and judicial campaigns became more expensive as the competition increased. Twenty candidates seeking the six positions on the supreme court in 1988 raised more than $10 million for their primary and general election campaigns. Two supreme court candidates raised more than $2 million each.[16] Also, nonlawyer special-interest groups, especially the Texas Medical Association, became major contributors to judicial candidates through their political action committees (see **chapter 3**). The Texas Medical Association supported a slate of four Republicans and two conservative Democrats. Only one candidate, Paul Murphy, was defeated by a plaintiff-backed candidate, Lloyd Doggett, who now serves in the U.S. House of Representatives.

Table 6.2 *How do Texas courts of last resort compare to those in other large states?*

	Number of Prisoners on Death Row (2008)	Courts of Last Resort (2008)
Texas	370	2, Supreme Court and Court of Criminal Appeals, 9 justices each, partisan election
California	669	1, Supreme Court, 7 justices, appointed by governor, retention election
New York	0	1, Court of Appeals, 7 justices, appointed by governor from Judicial Nomination Commission, Senate confirmation
Florida	388	1, Supreme Court, 7 justices, appointed by governor with nomination commission

Source: American Judicature Society, "State Judicial Selection," www.ajs.org/selection/sel_stateselect.asp, and Office of Court Administration, "Annual Report for the Texas Judiciary, Fiscal Year 2009," www.courts.state.tx.us/pubs/AR2009/Ar09.pdf.

Tort Reform

Texas, along with every other state and the U.S. government, has struggled with the contentious issues of tort reform for more than thirty years. A tort is a civil wrong—bodily injury, unsafe products, job discrimination, wrongful death, and medical malpractice to name a few—and the civil codes of governments provide remedies through the courts for relief for persons who have suffered harm by the actions of others.

If a person is killed on the job due to unsafe conditions, how much should his or her family be compensated? If a person slips in a restaurant and suffers permanent injury requiring round-the-clock care, how much money is the individual entitled to? If a person is driving under the influence of alcohol and crashes because of a design flaw in the accelerator, does the driver have a basis for compensation from the car manufacturer?

These are just a few of the types of questions courts must answer as a result of numerous lawsuits filed for a wide range of perceived grievances. Torts involve many players, including insurers, lawyers, professional and trade associations, and a range of advocacy groups representing diverse segments of the population. And the economic stakes are extremely high.

Advocates for tort reform argue that there are extensive abuses of tort laws that can only be controlled by legislation. However, those who argue against tort reform assert that changes in tort law will provide immunity for those engaging in harmful practices.

- Are there a large number of frivolous civil suits filed claiming harm or damages?

- Should legislatures place caps on the amount of money a judge or jury can award in tort cases?

- Should there be limits on punitive damages that can be awarded?

During the early 1990s, the cost of judicial elections continued to rise. In 1990, six candidates for three seats on the court spent $6 million. A study of fundraising by Texas Supreme Court justices during the 1994 and 1996 election cycles indicated that a significant percentage of campaign contributions came from lawyers, law firms, and PACs with interests before the court. The seven justices raised more than $9 million in contributions over $100 for their most recent reelection campaigns, and 40 percent of the contributions came from lawyers and parties who had cases on the court's docket between 1994 and 1997. The report concluded that "today's justices continue to sully the court's reputation by raising millions of dollars from parties and lawyers who have business before the court."[17]

The 1994 election was also the last time that Democratic candidates were able to mount competitively financed campaigns for the Texas Supreme Court. Democrat Jimmy Carroll actually raised more money than his Republican opponent, Priscilla Owen, but he lost anyway. Democrat Alice Oliver-Parrott raised over $1.5 million, but her Republican opponent, incumbent Nathan Hecht, raised more than $2 million. Conservative Democrat Raul Gonzalez, who was backed by doctors and business interests, also raised more than $2 million. He faced two opponents in the Democratic primary and barely defeated Rene Haas in the runoff primary, but he easily won the general election. In 1998, three Republican incumbent justices raised an average of $1 million to their Democratic opponents' average of $96,000. Incumbent Democratic Justice Rose Spector raised $563,931 to her Republican opponent's $1,214,450.[18]

As Republicans replaced Democrats on the Texas Supreme Court, the court became more likely to rule in favor of defendants. Between 1995 and 1998, 70 percent of the supreme court cases that pitted consumers, patients, and crime victims as plaintiffs against corporate, professional, and government defendants were won by the defendants. In 2005–2006, defendants won 83 percent of the cases, with conservative Republicans in firm control and consistently making decisions in support of insurance companies and other defendants in civil suits.[19]

CBS newsman Mike Wallace and *60 Minutes'* cameras visited the Texas judiciary again in 1998. The segment suggested that justice may still be for sale in Texas, but with different people—the business community—now wielding the influence.

The large sums of money necessary to compete in judicial races and the sources of those contributions have created an image problem for Texas judges. As Chief Justice Thomas R. Phillips told the Texas Legislature in 1999, "Neither party label nor campaign war chests necessarily compromise a judge's ability to be fair and impartial. . . . But these attributes of Texas justice do compromise the appearance of fairness. When judges are labeled as Democrats and Republicans, how can you convince the public that the law is a judge's only constituency? And when a winning litigant has contributed thousands of dollars to the judge's campaign, how do you ever persuade the losing party that only the facts of the case were considered?"[20]

Indeed, in a poll of Texans, 83 percent thought that campaign contributions had a significant effect on judges' decisions. Only 7 percent said that the contributions had no effect on their decisions. Furthermore, nearly half of the state judges and 79 percent of Texas attorneys stated that campaign contributions had a significant influence on judicial decisions. Only 14 percent of the judges and 1 percent of the attorneys believed that campaign contributions had no influence on judicial opinions.[21]

The high cost of judicial campaigns, racially polarized voting in statewide and countywide contests, and the small numbers of Hispanics and African Americans who are licensed attorneys mean that one consequence of Texas's judicial selection process is that minorities have had only limited success in gaining representation in the judiciary. With increasing Republican strength in judicial elections, minority candidates, most of whom are Democrats, may become even less likely to win judicial contests.

Xavier Rodriguez's case illustrates a problem that minorities face in judicial elections even when they are members of the Republican Party. Governor Rick Perry appointed Rodriguez to the Texas Supreme Court in 2001. In the 2002 Republican primary election, he had the support of state Republican leaders, endorsements from major newspapers, and a $700,000 war chest, yet he lost to a little-known Anglo lawyer, Steven Wayne Smith. As political scientist Richard Murray noted, "In a primary where there are so many white voters who know little about either candidate, the default goes to the Anglo over the Hispanic. . . . He might have survived if his parents had named him Billy Bob."[22] In district court contests in large urban counties, where all district judges compete in countywide elections, straight-ticket Republican voting in judicial elections has virtually eliminated any minority judges who were appointed or elected. In 2010, however, two of the nine Republican Supreme Court justices, including Chief Justice Wallace Jefferson, were African Americans, and one was Hispanic.

The effect of partisan preferences has been dramatic. In 1997, among the eighty judges on the courts of appeals, forty-four were Republicans and thirty-six were Democrats. Of the fourteen courts of appeals, six courts had a Republican majority, six courts had a Democratic majority, and two courts were evenly divided. On the state's top courts, seven of the nine supreme court justices were Republican, and six of the nine court of criminal appeals judges were Republicans. In 2010, all eighteen members of the two highest courts were Republicans, and about three-fourths of the courts of appeals judges were Republicans.[23]

The Judicial Process in Texas

⭐ **6.4** . . . **Explain the judicial process in Texas.**

Most Texans will experience the judicial system as a potential juror or in municipal court for a traffic offense. Others, however, may experience the criminal or civil justice process as a plaintiff or defendant. For every Texan, a general understanding of the judicial process is helpful. We start by describing the criminal justice process and then consider the civil justice process.

The Criminal Justice Process

In Texas, the legislature has established a graded penalty system, classifying criminal offenses into eight categories: capital murder, four degrees of felonies, and three classes of misdemeanors. (To learn more about these graded penalties, see Table 6.3.) The legislature also adopted the code of criminal procedure, which regulates how criminal trials are conducted.

ARRESTS AND SEARCHES   In many cases, an individual will be arrested after an arrest warrant has been issued by a magistrate. To issue the warrant, a magistrate will

Table 6.3 *What punishments do Texas courts give for different offenses?*

Offense	Maximum Punishment	Examples
Capital felony	Execution	Capital murder
First-degree felony	5–99 years or life; $10,000 fine	Aggravated sexual assault; theft of property valued at $200,000 or more
Second-degree felony	2–20 years; $10,000 fine	Tampering with a consumer product; theft of property valued at $100,000 or more but less than $200,000
Third-degree felony	2–10 years; $10,000 fine	Drive-by shooting without injury; theft of property valued at $20,000 or more but less than $100,000
State jail felony	180 days to 2 years; $10,000 fine	Credit-card or debit-card abuse; theft of property valued at $1,500 or more but less than $20,000
Class A misdemeanor	1 year; $4,000 fine	Burglary of a vehicle; abuse of a corpse; theft of property valued at $500 or more but less than $1,500
Class B misdemeanor	180 days; $2,000 fine	Silent or abusive calls to a 911 service; DWI; theft of property valued at more than $20 but less than $500
Class C misdemeanor	$500 fine	Assault without bodily injury; attending a dog fight; theft of property valued at less than $20

require sufficient information in the form of a complaint. The officer seeking the arrest warrant must satisfy the requirements of probable cause: tangible evidence that a crime was committed and that the person named in the complaint committed the offense. In most cases, however, police officers arrest an individual without a warrant but based on probable cause because the officer sees an offense being committed or receives a credible report of the commission of a felony and the officer does not have time to procure a warrant. Upon arrest, a person and his or her possessions may be searched. Again, a search warrant is usually necessary, but there are conditions under which a warrantless search is reasonable and evidence seized may be admissible in court. In Texas, search warrants are not required for searches pursuant to a lawful arrest and for seizures of evidence in plain view of an officer. Of course, searches conducted with the consent of the person under arrest are considered reasonable.

BOOKING   Booking establishes an administrative record of a suspect's arrest. At this time, the suspect is usually fingerprinted and photographed, has the charges explained, and is allowed to make a phone call. For minor offenses, a suspect is usually released on "station house bail." For serious offenses, a suspect is placed in a holding cell until his or her appearance before a magistrate.

MAGISTRATE APPEARANCE   If the district or county attorney decides to charge the suspect, he or she becomes a defendant and is brought before a magistrate. The magistrate informs the defendant of the charges, his or her rights under *Miranda* v. *Arizona* (1966), and his or her right to an examining trial. An examining trial is conducted by a magistrate to determine if there is sufficient evidence to continue the criminal proceedings. If the magistrate decides that there is not sufficient evidence, the defendant is released. The examining trial is also used to set bail and take the testimony of witnesses. If the defendant is able to post bail, he or she will be released until the trial.

GRAND JURY INDICTMENT   Unless defendants waive their right, a grand jury review will be held. In Texas, grand juries consist of twelve people, chosen by a judge from a list provided by a jury commission. The prosecutor presents the evidence to the grand jury, and if nine members are convinced that sufficient evidence exists to justify a trial, the grand jury issues a "true bill." In that case, an indictment accusing the defendant is prepared by the prosecutor and signed by the grand jury foreperson. Otherwise, the grand jury issues a "no bill," and the defendant is released. The indictment is filed with the court's clerk, and a copy is delivered to the defendant, notifying him or her of the court date. If the defendant is free on bail, the judge may issue a warrant for the defendant's arrest.

ARRAIGNMENT   After an indictment in felony cases and in misdemeanor cases that can result in a jail sentence, an arraignment is required. If the defendant is indigent and requires a court-appointed attorney, the judge will either appoint one or a public defender will be provided. After the defendant is represented by counsel, the judge will again read the charge and take the defendant's plea. At this time, the defendant may plead guilty as a result of a plea-bargain agreement. The prosecutor provides the court with a victim's impact statement, which indicates how the defendant's acts have affected the victim's life and which may be used by the judge or jury during sentencing.

PRETRIAL MOTIONS   Pretrial motions establish the scope of the trial, determining, for example, what evidence is admissible, what witnesses may testify about, and what issues can and cannot be raised. Pretrial motions can also be used by the defense attorney to request a jury trial or bench trial, request a continuance, determine if the defendant is competent to stand trial, change the trial's location, or discover evidence held by the prosecution that could prove the defendant's innocence.

JURY SELECTION   Defendants have a right to a jury trial but can waive that right unless the charge is capital murder. If either the prosecution or defense requests a jury trial, a group of potential jurors, known as the *venire* or jury pool, is assembled. The potential jurors are assigned numbers randomly and seated in the courtroom. The prosecution and the defense question the potential jurors in a process known as *voir dire*. Each side gets a number of peremptory challenges, depending on the seriousness of the offense, which allow the attorneys to dismiss jurors without cause. The only limitation is that neither side may use their peremptory challenges to exclude potential jurors based on their race or gender. Any potential juror may be challenged for cause, such as prejudice against the defendant, but the judge must agree to eliminate the potential juror from the jury pool. After *voir dire,* if the case involves a felony, the first twelve potential jurors will constitute the jury; if the case involves a misdemeanor, the first six will form the jury. Jury verdicts must be unanimous.

TRIAL   In Texas, trials are conducted in two distinct phases—a guilt determination phase and a sentencing phase. There are seven stages in the guilt determination phase. First, the prosecution reads the indictment or information. Then the defense attorney, acting for the defendant, responds by entering a plea. Second, the prosecution provides opening remarks, telling the jury the nature of the offense, the facts that it plans to establish, and how it plans to prove the charges against the defendant. The defense attorney may deliver opening remarks or wait until the prosecution has presented its case to make remarks. Third, the prosecution presents the state's case, calling witnesses and entering evidence in an attempt to prove the defendant guilty beyond a reasonable doubt. Fourth, after the prosecution has presented its case, the defense presents its case. In rebuttal, the prosecution can call additional witnesses to discredit the defense's witnesses. The defense is also given an opportunity to rebut the state's rebuttal witnesses. Fifth, the judge reads the jury its charge, a set of instructions for reaching a verdict. Sixth, the prosecution and defense are given a last chance to convince the jury during final arguments. Finally, the jury retires to the jury room to deliberate and reach a verdict. If the jury cannot reach a unanimous verdict, the judge may declare a mistrial. If the jury finds the defendant not guilty, he or she is released from custody. If the defendant is found guilty, the second phase begins—the sentencing phase.

During the sentencing phase, the defendant's prior convictions are admitted as evidence. The stages are similar to the guilt phase but abbreviated into five steps. In capital murder cases, the sentencing phase involves the jury considering whether the defendant is likely to commit further violent crimes and is a threat to society and whether the defendant actually caused, intended, or anticipated that a human life would be taken. If the jury answers both questions affirmatively, then the jury must consider whether mitigating circumstances warrant a sentence of life imprisonment rather than the

ANALYZING VISUALS

Is This Cruel and Unusual Punishment?

The U.S. Supreme Court's early decisions pertaining to "cruel and unusual punishment" focused on who was executed. Increasingly, the issue is turning to how people are executed. Texas has used lethal injections for executions since 1982. A condemned prisoner is strapped to a gurney, two needles are inserted, and the inmate is injected with three solutions that produce an anesthetic overdose and respiratory and cardiac arrest. In 2008, the U.S. Supreme Court ruled that the chemicals used in lethal injections did not amount to cruel and unusual punishment. Examine the photo below, and then answer the questions.

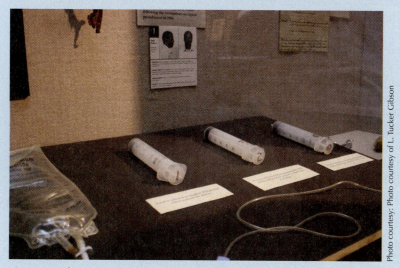

Photo courtesy: Photo courtesy of L. Tucker Gibson

- Is death by lethal injection more humane than hanging or electrocution? Explain your answer.
- Should a condemned prisoner have the right to choose the form of execution—hanging, electrocution, firing squad, or lethal injection?
- Do you think painful deaths constitute cruel and unusual punishment? How might a defined execution date constitute cruel and unusual punishment, regardless of the method of execution used?

death penalty. The jury's responses determine whether the defendant receives life in prison without parole or death by lethal injection.[24] (To learn more about what constitutes cruel and unusual punishment, see Analyzing Visuals: Is This Cruel and Unusual Punishment?)

APPEALS   Except in capital murder cases, which are automatically reviewed by the Texas Court of Criminal Appeals, convicted criminals may appeal the trial court's decision to a court of appeals. The court of appeals will review the records of the trial to determine if a reversible error was committed and consider the bases for the appeal in written briefs by attorneys and oral arguments before the court. A further appeal is possible, but the court of criminal appeals determines whether to accept an application for discretionary review and hear the appeal.

The Civil Justice Process

The Texas Supreme Court establishes civil procedures, which tend to be less formal than criminal procedures.

PRETRIAL PROCEDURES   To initiate a civil suit, the plaintiff, the person who has been injured, files a petition with the clerk of the court that will hear the case. The petition indicates the plaintiff's complaints against the defendant and the remedy sought in the case, usually a monetary award. The court clerk informs the defendant of the charges filed and indicates that the defendant can provide a written answer to the complaint, indicating why the plaintiff is not entitled to the requested remedy. Before the judge sets a trial date, if the parties have not settled the suit out of court, the parties file their petitions, answers, and other documents pertinent to the case. Either party to the suit may request a jury trial; otherwise the judge conducts a bench trial, determining the facts and applying the applicable law.

TRIAL   As in a criminal trial, a civil trial begins with the plaintiff's attorney presenting the evidence and witnesses to prove the bases of the complaint. The defendant's attorney may challenge the evidence presented and cross-examine the plaintiff's witnesses. The defendant's attorney then presents evidence, which may be challenged by the plaintiff's attorney, and witnesses, who may be questioned by the plaintiff. If a jury is deciding the case, the judge will issue a charge to the jury, instructing the jury on how to conduct its deliberations and specifying the relevant law in the case. After the charge, the lawyers make their final arguments. The judge then issues the jury a set of questions that the jury will answer. The jury's answers will provide the basis for the judgment in the case. In district courts, ten of the twelve jurors must agree on the answers. In county and justice of the peace courts, five of the six jurors must agree. Based on the jury's answers or verdict, the judge issues a judgment, indicating the remedy to the complaint.

APPEALS   Appeals in civil cases, as in criminal cases, involve the record from the trial court, written briefs by the attorneys, and oral arguments before the judges. Appeals from district and county courts are reviewed by a court of appeals and possibly by the Texas Supreme Court.

TOWARD REFORM: Changing the Texas Judiciary

⭐ **6.5 . . . Evaluate proposals to reform the Texas judiciary.**

The Texas judicial system is often the recipient of criticism—from lawyers and judges, politicians and criminal justice specialists, businesses and public-interest advocates, and victim advocates and prisoner advocates. Often these criticisms result in attempts to reform court structure, judicial selection, or campaign finance. We consider each criticism and the possible reforms in turn.

Reforming the Court Structure

As indicated earlier, the Texas judicial system is complex and confusing, consisting of five layers of courts. Numerous proposals for judicial reform advocate simplifying and unifying the court structure.

Because of the addition of courts over the years, Texas trial courts present a tangle of mixed jurisdictions in which overlapping jurisdiction is the rule rather than the exception. For example, a civil suit involving more than $200 but less than $10,000 falls within the jurisdiction of the justice of the peace courts, the constitutional county court, the statutory county courts, and the district courts. Moreover, the statutory county courts' jurisdiction often overlaps the civil jurisdiction of the district courts.

This allows an attorney to shop for justice, seeking a judge who is more likely to decide favorably for a client.

The constitutional revision efforts in 1974 and 1975 (see **chapter 2**) included a proposal for a new structure for the court system, based on the work of the Texas Chief Justice's Task Force on Judicial Reform.[25] In the early 1990s, the Texas Research League studied the Texas judiciary and published an extensive report with recommendations for a new court structure.[26] The constitutional revision efforts of Representative Rob Junell (D–San Angelo) and Senator Bill Ratliff (R–Mt. Pleasant) in 1999 also included changes in the Texas judiciary, which were endorsed by Republican Chief Justice Phillips.

Although the proposals vary, all would simplify and unify the court structure. (To learn more about one such proposal, see Figure 6.2.) At the local level, municipal courts would operate as they do currently. Constitutional county courts and statutory courts would be eliminated. Consequently, jurisdiction of the justice of the peace courts would be expanded to cover the current jurisdiction of the county courts, and the judges would be required to be licensed attorneys.

The district courts would be the state's only trial courts, except for the specific jurisdiction assigned to justice of the peace courts. The state would be divided into judicial districts, each of which would have one district court but could have more than one judge. Specialization could be retained so that some district judges could handle specific cases, such as family cases or criminal cases. The advantage of one district court with several judges would be in equalizing caseloads among the judges. The courts of appeals would be retained, but the geographic districts would be redrawn to equalize the courts' caseloads and prevent the necessity for shifting cases from one court to another, as is the current practice.

Figure 6.2 *Would this proposal for a unified, simplified judicial structure address most of the concerns about the state's judiciary?*

Under this proposal there would be only one court of last resort; court of appeals districts would be restructured to equalize the workload; and rather than have a large number of different numbered district courts allocated to a county, a district court would be defined in terms of a geographic area with multiple judges.

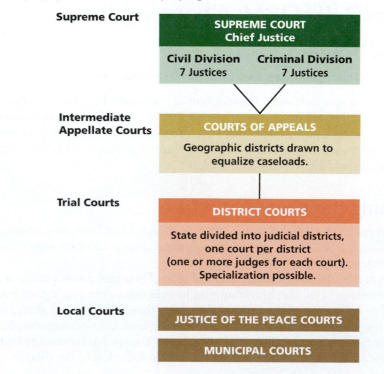

Most reforms would merge the Texas Supreme Court and the Texas Court of Criminal Appeals into one supreme court. However, a Texas Research League study argues that the two courts should be retained.[27] The proposal by Junell and Ratliff contemplated one supreme court consisting of a chief justice and fourteen justices, who would be divided equally between a civil division and criminal division. The chief justice could, by court rule, sit with either or both divisions. The most recent effort for reforming the court structure, with many of the provisions discussed here, was Republican Senator Robert Duncan's SB 1204, which passed the Senate in 2007, only to die in the House.[28]

Reforming Judicial Selection

Since at least 1946, various groups, including the Texas State Bar and a series of task forces on judicial selection, have recommended that Texas adopt a merit system for selecting judges. The election of Steve Mansfield, who misrepresented his judicial experience and qualifications, to the court of criminal appeals in 1994 revived talk of reform. Mansfield was a little-known insurance lawyer from Houston with little experience in criminal law. He beat an equally unknown lawyer in the Republican primary and then, thanks to heavy straight-ticket Republican voting, unseated a 12-year Democratic veteran of the court in the 1994 general election.

Lieutenant Governor Bob Bullock appointed a committee of state senators and judges to study judicial selection and make a recommendation for reform. After many meetings, the committee produced a compromise that attempted to accommodate the conflicting interests involved in judicial selection—the political parties, lawyers for plaintiffs and defendants, ethnic minorities, and judges. The compromise called for a mixed nonpartisan election and appointment system. The Texas Senate easily passed the proposal in 1995, but opposition in the House surfaced from Hispanics and Republicans.

A major hurdle in these battles to reform the judicial selection process has been that Hispanics and African Americans have never been represented on the Texas courts in proportion to their percentages of the population. In the 1980s, minority plaintiffs challenged the method of selection of district court judges in countywide elections as violating the U.S. Voting Rights Act, which prohibits states from using voting procedures that dilute minority voting strength (see **chapter 3**). In late 1989, U.S. District Court Judge Lucius Bunton ruled that the countywide election of judges in nine counties violated the act. However, after several appeals, the case was finally settled in 1993, when the U.S. Supreme Court refused to review a U.S. Court of Appeals ruling that the results in Texas's countywide, partisan elections were more a reflection of the partisan affiliations or preferences of voters than the race or ethnicity of judicial candidates. The court also indicated that because the judges could hear cases from anywhere in the county, the state had an interest in maintaining a link between the court's jurisdiction and the at-large electoral base by allowing all voters in the county to vote for each judge in the county.[29]

In 1996, a Texas Supreme Court task force considered judicial selection but was unable to agree on a substitute for the current system. In every legislative session since 1997, legislators have considered major proposals for judicial selection reform, but none has been adopted. In 1997, Senator Rodney Ellis, an African American Democrat from Houston, proposed that appellate judges be appointed and trial judges be elected in nonpartisan elections.[30] In more recent sessions, Senator Robert Duncan, an Anglo Republican from Lubbock, proposed that judges of appellate and district courts be appointed by the governor and confirmed by a two-thirds Senate vote. After serving one term, the judges would run in retention elections.[31] The three most recent chief justices of the Texas Supreme Court, including the current chief justice, Wallace Jefferson, all have urged the legislature to scrap the partisan election system for judges. But a compromise that accommodates the varied interests in judicial selection has not proven possible so far.[32] (To learn more about the judicial elections in Texas, see Politics Now: Justice: End Judicial Elections.)

POLITICS NOW

| WORLD | NATION | LOCAL | **POLITICS** | OPINION | HEALTH & SCIENCE | ARTS | SPORTS | LEISURE |

Justice: End Judicial Elections

February 12, 2009
Austin American-Statesman
www.statesman.com

By Chuck Lindell

The chief justice of the Texas Supreme Court, in a passionate plea for reform Wednesday, asked the Legislature to abolish the state's 133-year tradition of partisan judicial elections, saying the influence of politics and money has destroyed public confidence in justice.

In his biennial State of the Judiciary speech to a joint session of the Legislature, Chief Justice Wallace Jefferson also asked lawmakers to create a commission to examine wrongful convictions. At least 36 Texans, including one on death row, have been exonerated in recent years, many due to advances in DNA testing.

The commission should determine what went wrong in such cases and recommend reforms to limit recurring problems, Jefferson said, thanking Sen. Rodney Ellis, D–Houston, for taking a leading role in seeking the change.

An Ellis bill to create a Texas Innocence Commission died last session and has been reintroduced.

Jefferson reserved the bulk of his speech for what he called "the corrosive influence of money" in judicial elections. Polls show that more than 80 percent of Texans believe campaign contributions influence courtroom events, he said.

"That's an alarming figure—four out of five," Jefferson said. "If the public believes that judges are biased toward contributors, then confidence in the courts will suffer." The chief justice advocated a merit selection system, with appointed judges running for re-election without opposition and without party identification. These "retention elections" let voters choose between keeping the judge in office or not.

Such a change would require amending the Texas Constitution.

The Legislature has shown little inclination to scrap judicial elections. Former Chief Justice John Hill called for their abolition 23 years ago, and his successor, Tom Phillips, was an aggressive advocate for reform to no avail.

About half of states use some form of appointment system, Jefferson said, but only seven employ partisan judicial elections, with candidates listed on the ballot by party affiliation.

States with appointed judges commonly use nominating committees to screen applicants and forward a slate of candidates to the governor, said Seth Andersen, executive vice president of the American Judicature Society, a nonprofit reform group based in Iowa. Many committees are a mix of lawyers and nonlawyers chosen by different constituencies to promote diversity, he said . . . .

Critical Thinking Questions

1. Do you agree with Chief Justice Jefferson that the Texas judicial election system is broken? Why or why not?

2. Why do you think there has been little "legislative traction" or support for alternatives to the partisan election of judges in Texas?

3. Given the number of executions Texas has carried out since 1982 and the number of persons now on death row, should a commission be established by the legislature to review "wrongful convictions?"

Reforming Judicial Campaign Finance

Faced with the cost of judicial campaigns and its effect on the judiciary's imputed fairness, the legislature enacted a Judicial Campaign Fairness Act in 1995. The act limits contributions to judges and judicial candidates and restricts the periods during which they can raise money.

For supreme court justices, individuals can contribute $5,000 per election under the act. Thus, an individual can give a supreme court candidate $5,000 for the primary election, $5,000 if there is a runoff primary, and another $5,000 for the general election. However, a candidate who is unopposed either in the primary or in the general election faces reduced contribution limits. Law firms and their political action committees can contribute $30,000 to a supreme court candidate, which includes individual contributions from the firm's attorneys. Candidates are also limited in the amount of contributions that they can accept from general political action committees not affiliated with law firms. For supreme court candidates, the PAC limit is $300,000.

There are several loopholes in the act. Most importantly, there is no requirement that a judge who has received a large contribution from a lawyer or party to a suit before the court recuse himself or herself from the case. Also, the penalties for violating the contribution limits apply only to the candidate who accepts the contribution and not to the contributor. Incumbent judges who face little or no opposition in primary or general elections can still amass large war chests that intimidate potential candidates in future elections.[33] The 1996 races for the Texas Supreme Court—the first conducted under the law—demonstrated how weak the new reforms were. Four Republican incumbents still raised a combined $4 million, easily swamping fund-raising efforts by their unsuccessful challengers.

In 1997, Texans for Public Justice (TPJ), a self-proclaimed judicial watchdog group, formed to spotlight the role of money in Texas judicial campaigns and to press for stronger campaign finance reforms. To influence public opinion, TPJ analyzes public campaign finance reports and unleashes press releases. TPJ argues that Texas Supreme Court justices raise money from court litigants and that their decisions are tainted as a result.[34] A 2009 U.S. Supreme Court decision may strengthen some of the provisions of the Judicial Campaign Fairness Act. In *Caperton* v. *Massey*, the Supreme Court held that a justice acted improperly when he failed to recuse himself from a case in which one of the parties had donated three million dollars to his judicial campaign. However, states are given leeway in determining what constitutes a significant donation.[35]

What Should I Have LEARNED?

Now that you have read this chapter, you should be able to:

⭐ **6.1 Trace the historical development of the Texas judiciary, p. 181.**

Texas's first courts were established in the Austin colony but were replaced by Mexican courts under Spanish law. Over the years, the court system has evolved through several constitutions, moving back and forth between judicial appointment and judicial election. Since the adoption of the 1876 Constitution, courts have been added through constitutional amendments or legislative actions. The addition of courts to meet the needs of a growing and diverse population has produced a state court structure that is complex and confusing.

⭐ **6.2 Outline the structure and jurisdiction of the Texas courts, p. 182.**

Five levels of courts now make up the Texas judiciary. At the lowest level are local courts of limited jurisdiction, municipal courts, and justice of the peace courts, which handle less serious criminal cases and some small civil suits. The county trial courts include constitutional county courts in every Texas county and statutory courts in many counties. These courts exercise original jurisdiction and some appellate jurisdiction. District courts are trial courts that have original jurisdiction in serious criminal cases and higher-dollar civil suits. The courts of appeals are intermediate appellate courts for criminal and civil cases.

Texas has two courts of last resort: a supreme court for civil cases and a court of criminal appeals for criminal cases. This structure raises questions about who is responsible for bringing some degree of uniformity and consistency throughout the judicial system.

⭐ **6.3 Identify the formal and informal qualifications of judges for office, and evaluate the current system of judicial selection, p. 188.**

The qualifications necessary to be a judge vary by court and are prescribed by the constitution or statutes. The qualifications for justice of the peace and constitutional county courts are minimal, and no significant legal training is required. For appellate courts, a license to practice law and experience as an attorney or judge are required. The composition of the courts does not reflect the demographic composition of the state. Most judges in Texas are middle-aged, Anglo males. Unlike most other states, Texas uses partisan elections to select most of its judges. Within the past several decades, judicial campaigns have become more expensive and highly contentious, reflecting deep differences in judicial philosophies. As judges from the lowest to highest courts come to rely on contributions from lawyers and groups that have cases before the court, the public has come to question whether those judges can be fair and impartial in deciding cases.

⭐ **6.4** **Explain the judicial process in Texas, p. 195.**

The procedures in a criminal case are more formal and rigorous than in a civil case, but the process is similar. If no pre-trial settlement occurs, the trial moves through the presentation of opening arguments by the opposing attorneys, examination and cross-examination of witnesses, presentation of evidence, rebuttal, and summation followed by a verdict.

⭐ **6.5** **Evaluate proposals to reform the Texas judiciary, p. 199.**

Many suggest that the judicial structure could be unified and simplified so the public could understand the judiciary and its operation. The Texas Legislature has considered establishing some variation of merit selection for judges. In addition, several groups have sought reforms to increase the number of Hispanic and African American judges and limit the role of campaign contributions in judicial races. The legislature passed the Judicial Campaign Fairness Act of 1995 to limit campaign contributions to judges and judicial candidates and require greater public disclosure of contributions, and the U.S. Supreme Court decision in *Caperton* v. *Massey* (2009) may further strengthen campaign contribution provisions.

Test Yourself: The Judicial Branch

⭐ **6.1** **Trace the historical development of the Texas judiciary, p. 181.**

Which of the following best describes reasons for the complex structure of the Texas judiciary system?
A. Texans can't agree on the selection of judges—appointment or election.
B. Texans intentionally planned a system of courts with varied and overlapping jurisdiction.
C. It is difficult to amend the Texas Constitution to change the structure of the courts.
D. Courts were added or expanded on a piecemeal basis to respond to immediate problems without a comprehensive plan for the court system.
E. Lawyers and jurists have been the primary beneficiaries of this complex structure and have worked continuously to block efforts to bring order to the system.

⭐ **6.2** **Outline the structure and jurisdiction of the Texas courts, p. 182.**

The Texas courts that handle the largest number of cases are
A. the supreme court and the court of criminal appeals.
B. the 14 courts of appeals.
C. the 453 district courts.
D. the 254 constitutional county courts and the 249 statutory county courts.
E. the municipal and justice of the peace courts.

⭐ **6.3** **Identify the formal and informal qualifications of judges for office, and evaluate the current system of judicial selection, p. 188.**

The most significant obstacle to obtaining a judgeship on one of the state's courts is
A. obtaining the necessary education.
B. securing a political party's nomination.
C. raising sufficient campaign funds.
D. overcoming gender bias.
E. acquiring sufficient job experience.

⭐ **6.4** **Explain the judicial process in Texas, p. 195.**

If a person is convicted of capital murder in a district court,
A. the case automatically goes to one of the 14 courts of appeals for review.
B. the case automatically goes to the Texas Supreme Court for review.
C. the case automatically goes to the U. S courts for review.
D. the case automatically goes to the Texas Court of Criminal Appeals for review.
E. the case is tried *de novo* in the court with original jurisdiction.

⭐ **6.5** **Evaluate proposals to reform the Texas judiciary, p. 199.**

Of the various alternatives advanced for judicial reform in Texas, the most far-reaching is
A. limits on campaign contributions coupled with partial public financing of judicial campaigns.
B. appointment of all state and county judges by the governor with senate confirmation.
C. nonpartisan election of all judges.
D. selection of judges by the state legislature.
E. judicial appointments by the governor from a nominating commission coupled with retention elections.

Essay Questions

1. Why are so few jury trials held in Texas courts?
2. On what basis might a member of the Hispanic or African American community argue that the Texas court system is discriminatory?
3. New courts are added by the legislature with almost every session, but the number of pending cases increases from one year to the next. Why? What could be done to lessen the courts' workload?
4. How can one measure and compare the performance of elected judges and appointed judges?
5. If the current system of partisan election of judges is retained, should all campaign contributions be limited to $500.00?

Key Terms

application for discretionary
      review, p. 187
constitutional county court, p. 185
county court at law, p. 185
court of appeals, p. 186

district court, p. 186
justice of the peace court, p. 183
municipal court, p. 183
petition for review, p. 187

Texas Court of Criminal Appeals,
      p. 187
Texas Supreme Court, p. 187
trial *de novo*, p. 185

To Learn More on the Judicial Branch

In the Library

Anderson, Ken. *Crime in Texas,* rev. ed. Austin: University of Texas Press, 2005.

Annual Statistical Report for the Texas Judiciary, Fiscal Year 2009 (Austin, TX: Office of Court Administration, 2009), 57–59.

Cheek, Kyle and Anthony Champagne. *Judicial Politics in Texas: Partisanship, Money, and Politics in State Courts.* New York: Peter Lang Publishing, 2004.

Champagne, Anthony, and Judith Haydel, eds. *Judicial Reform in the States.* New York: University Press of America, 1993.

Cook, Kerry Max. *Chasing Justice: My Story of Freeing Myself After Two Decades on Death Row for a Crime I Didn't Commit.* New York: William Morrow, 2007.

Dow, David R. *Executed on a Technicality: Lethal Injustice on America's Death Row.* Boston: Beacon, 2005.

Dow, David R., and Mark Dow, eds. *Machinery of Death: The Reality of America's Death Penalty Regime.* New York: Routledge, 2002.

Horton, David M., and Ryan Kellis Turner. *Lone Star Justice: A Comprehensive Overview of the Texas Criminal Justices System.* Austin, TX: Eakin, 1999.

House Research Organization. *Focus Report: Should Texas Change Its Laws Dealing with Sex Offenders?* (October 18, 2006).

Marquart, James W., Sheldon Ekland-Olson, and Jonathan R. Sorensen. *The Rope, the Chair and the Needle: Capital Punishment in Texas, 1923–1990.* Austin: University of Texas Press, 1994.

Office of Court Administration, *Public Trust and Confidence in the Courts and Legal Profession in Texas* (Austin, TX: Office of Court Administration, 1998).

Office of Court Administration, *The Courts and the Legal Profession in Texas—An Insider's Perspective: A Survey of Judges, Court Personnel, and Attorneys* (Austin, TX: Office of Court Administration, 1998).

Provine, Marie. *Judging Credentials: Nonlawyer Judges and the Politics of Professionalism.* Chicago, IL: University of Chicago Press, 1986.

Texans for Public Justice. *Supreme Spending: Political Expenditures by Texas' High-Court Justices.* Austin: Texans for Public Justice, 2008.

Texas Research League. "Texas Courts: A Study by the Texas Research League." Austin: Texas Research League, 1990–1992.

On the Web

To learn more about the Texas courts, go to the official Texas judicial Web sites at **www.courts.state.tx.us.**

To learn more about Texas courts and judges, go to the Office of Court Administration Web site at **www.courts.state.tx.us/oca.**

To learn more about two organizations that advocate for policy changes to reduce litigation against business interests, go to the Texas Civil Justice League and Texans for Lawsuit Reform Web sites at **www.tcjl.com** and **www.tortreform.com.**

To learn more about two organizations that advocate for policy changes to reduce the influence of money in judicial selection and decision making, go to the Texans for Public Justice and the Texas Watch Foundation Web sites at **www.tpj.org** and **www. texaswatch.org.**

7 Local Governments

On September 13, 2008, Hurricane Ike bore down on the upper Texas coast, slamming directly into Galveston Island. Many Texas coastal residents were still recovering from a 2005 hurricane, Rita, and state and local officials were still working to improve hurricane preparedness and evacuation procedures when more than seven feet of water flooded Galveston.[1] The storm made its way toward Houston, causing major damage and leaving some sections of the city without power for many days. More than 100 people in the United States, including about forty in Texas, were killed. But the death toll and damage could have been worse. Galveston City Manager Steve LeBlanc and other local and state officials had issued timely evacuation warnings. Fortunately, most Galveston and many Houston residents had heeded these warnings to evacuate.

Soon, some local government officials in the Houston-Galveston area began to consider another form of hurricane preparedness—construction of a multibillion-dollar "Ike Dike" to protect the heavily populated and heavily industrialized area from storm surges. The project would include a fifteen-mile extension of Galveston's existing seawall, construction of a similar structure along the Bolivar Peninsula, and construction of massive floodgates at the entrance to Galveston Bay. Some local officials liked the idea. Others were reluctant to endorse it because of its intimidating cost, uncertainty over how much of the cost could be picked up by the federal government through the U.S. Army Corps of Engineers, and how much might be left to local governments. Some environmentalists, meanwhile, feared such a huge construction project would disrupt the fragile ecosystem of Galveston Bay.[2]

Devastating hurricanes repeatedly ravage the Texas coast, killing people, destroying property, and creating nightmarish problems for local governments. Galveston's 1900 hurricane, at left, is still the deadliest natural disaster in U.S. history, and resulted in the creation of the commission form of city government. In 2008, Hurricane Ike, at right, killed scores of people and caused billions of dollars of damage.

Hurricanes obviously pose bigger challenges than even a large city government can handle alone. But local governments often are the first governments to whom people turn during times of emergency. Even during more normal times, local governments are likely to have the most direct effect on most people's lives.

Local governments across the state struggle to keep up with the demands of increasing populations. New schools must be constructed and more teachers hired. New roads and streets must be paved and old, worn-out bridges replaced. New waste landfills must be developed that meet stringent environmental laws. New sources of water must be acquired, and new sanitation systems must be expanded and upgraded. More police and emergency personnel must be hired, and new medical facilities for low-income populations must be built. And the list of demands for new or expanded government services and functions goes on.

Local governments are responsible for an expanding range of services and are often given little credit for what they do. They are often described as the governments closest to the people, but constitutional and legislative restrictions often hamper them in their efforts to carry out their basic responsibilities, and voter disengagement robs them of the popular support essential in a democratic system.

What Should I Know About . . .

After reading this chapter, you should be able to:

★ **7.1** Trace the historical development and constitutional roots of local government in Texas, p. 208.

★ **7.2** Outline the general structure of county governments and the responsibilities of elected officials, p. 210.

★ **7.3** Differentiate among the various forms of city governments and how they are governed, p. 216.

★ **7.4** Identify the functions of special districts and the reasons for their creation, p. 227.

★ **7.5** Assess the prospects for reforms of local government and politics in Texas, p. 230.

Texas has three basic categories of political subdivisions that can be characterized as local governments. There are 1,209 city governments, 254 county governments, and 3,372 "special district" governments, including 1,082 school districts.[3] These are all local governments, though some are also connected to state government (e.g., counties), and some are regional (e.g., hospital authorities) rather than strictly local in nature. Texas also has twenty-four regional planning councils, or Councils of Governments—COGs—that are consortiums of local governments designed to provide planning and coordination of government services. Some local governments are established directly in the Texas Constitution, while some are established in statute. The voluminous Local Government Code creates some political subdivisions and establishes rules for all of them.

In this chapter, we will discuss the forms and roles of local government and politics in Texas:

- First, we will examine *the roots of local government in Texas,* including historical and constitutional influences.

- Second, we will describe the structure, role, and function that *counties* play as local governments and administrative arms of the state government in Texas.

- Third, we will look at the governance of *cities* in Texas and how institutional structures, powers, and politics of city government have changed.

- Fourth, we will explore myriad *special districts* in Texas, with an emphasis on water districts and school districts.

- Finally, we will look at proposals for *reform* of *local government and politics in Texas,* including structures, interactions, and policies.

ROOTS OF Local Government in Texas

★ **7.1 . . . Trace the historical development and constitutional roots of local government in Texas.**

The roots of governance for counties, cities, and schools in Texas go back to the colonial period. Few people lived in Texas when Spain and then Mexico governed the area, and there certainly were no settlements of any size. Thus, local governments that were created were expected to govern vast rural territories. Twenty-three large districts, or municipalities, were governed by a council, a judge, an attorney, a sheriff, and a secretary.[4] The 1827 Constitution of the State of Coahuila y Tejas also directed these local governments to establish schools to educate the young.[5]

When the Republic of Texas was formed, it continued using the local districts (municipalities) that Mexico had established, but it called them *counties.* In nineteenth-century rural America, including Texas, counties were the governmental point of contact for most people.[6] Texas copied the form of county government that was then prevalent in southern states of the United States. The Congress of the republic also enacted laws creating cities as **municipal corporations.** By the end of the republic, the Texas Congress had created thirty-six counties and incorporated fifty-three cities.

These county and city governments became involved in protracted battles over the politics of education. Until the middle of the nineteenth century, education of

municipal corporation
A city.

children was a private or even church matter in the United States. Texas was forming its political structures and policies at the time that the idea of public education was gaining hold. One of the grievances cited by Texans in 1836 was that the Mexican government had failed to establish a system of public education. The 1836 Constitution of the Republic of Texas required the Texas Congress to establish a general system of education, though little was done.

When Texas joined the United States, the republic's form of government for counties was brought forward with few changes. As Texas's population grew in the 1840s and 1850s, so did demands for smaller counties. The legislature obliged, passing laws carving the large counties that had originated with Spanish and Mexican governments into smaller counties and requiring that county courthouses be so centrally located that each citizen could travel to the seat, vote, and return home in a day. By 1861, there were 122 counties.[7] During those early days of statehood, the legislature continued to incorporate cities; it also wrote a new general state law providing rules for the incorporation of small cities, though the legislature still wrote their charters.[8]

Texas's early state constitutions carried forward the republic's constitutional support for public education through local governments. The 1869 Constitution mandated a strong public education system, but the taxes levied to support the system generated intense opposition, fueling the fires against the Reconstruction Constitution.[9]

Texas's statutory Constitution of 1876 (see **chapter 2**) spells out powers and policies for various local governments. Article 9 of the Texas Constitution of 1876 is "Counties." Yet, in Article 11, "Municipal Corporations," the first section is "Counties as Legal Subdivisions. The several counties of this State are hereby recognized as legal subdivisions of the State." Through statutes passed under this constitution, the legislature also has filled in additional details for local governments.

The Constitution of 1876 continued the basic form of county government but increased the number of county officers. The legislature continued to expand the number of counties until 1931, when Loving County (along the New Mexico border) was organized as the 254th county. As the number of counties grew, disputes over boundaries inevitably arose, pitting one county against another. The legislature responded by passing specific bills affixing the boundaries of counties in dispute and by passing new laws in a (futile) attempt to avoid future boundary disputes.[10]

Under the Constitution of 1876, a general state law still allowed local incorporation of small cities, but the legislature found itself writing numerous municipal charters for growing cities. As a result of a nationwide municipal **home-rule** movement, Texas adopted a constitutional amendment in 1912 that allowed some cities to govern themselves and to decide their own structure and, with some limits, their powers.[11] In 1933, the constitution was amended to allow *counties* home-rule authority also, but the conditions under which a county could qualify for home-rule status were so stringent that no county successfully converted to home-rule status.

Finally, the 1876 Constitution required the legislature to establish a system of free public schools. In the late nineteenth century, first county commissioners were empowered to run the schools, then cities, then separate school districts. What resulted was a patchwork of systems around the state.[12]

In constitutional terms, local governments are the creation of the state. Although many people may think local governments have aspects of independence or sovereignty, they do not. They are not mentioned in the U.S. Constitution, and their relationship to the state is based on the unitary principle, not the federal principle. The prevailing constitutional view of local governments is expressed as Dillon's rule: local governments "owe their origin to, and derive their powers and rights wholly from, the legislature."[13] (To learn more about how local governments in Texas compare to local governments in other large states, see Table 7.1.)

home rule

The right and authority of a local government to govern itself, rather than have the state govern it.

TIMELINE: Development of Local Government in Texas

1821 First Major Settlements—Four major settlements are established in San Antonio, Goliad, Nacogdoches, and the Rio Grande Valley.

1836 First Official Counties—In the first year of the Constitution of 1836, the 23 municipalities become counties.

1858 Incorporation of Cities—The first statute is enacted allowing incorporation of cities under the general laws of Texas.

1901 Commission Form of Government—In the aftermath of the Galveston Hurricane of 1900, the city adopts the commission form of government, establishing a precedent for urban reforms in Texas.

Counties

⭐ **7.2** ... Outline the general structure of county governments and the responsibilities of elected officials.

Texas has by far the largest number of counties of any state: 254. Brewster County, the largest with 6,204 square miles, is larger than Connecticut, Delaware, or Rhode Island. Harris County is the most populous, with more than 4 million people. It also is the third most populous county in the nation—behind Los Angeles County, California, and Cook County (Chicago), Illinois. The population of Harris County is larger than the population of twenty-four states. Loving County is the least populous, having dropped to only 57 residents in 2009.[14] (To learn more about the population patterns in Texas counties, see Analyzing Visuals: The Texas Urban Triangle.) Texas's counties have formed an organization to facilitate communication and to represent their interests. The **Texas Association of Counties**, with headquarters in Austin,

Texas Association of Counties
Professional association that provides information, training, and other services for Texas county officials. The group also lobbies the legislature on behalf of county governments.

Table 7.1 *How do local governments in Texas compare to local governments in other large states?*

	Number of Cities	Number of Counties	Number of Special Districts	Largest County (population in millions)	Largest City (population in millions)
Texas	1,209	254	3,372	Harris (4.1)	Houston (2.2)
California	478	57	3,809	Los Angeles (9.8)	Los Angeles (3.8)
New York	618	57	1,799	Kings (2.6)	New York City (8.4)
Florida	411	66	1,146	Miami-Dade (2.5)	Jacksonville (0.8)

1913 Home-Rule Charters—Cities over 5,000 in population are permitted to adopt home-rule charters.

1933 County Home-Rule Authority— Counties are given home-rule authority by constitutional amendment.

1969 County Home-Rule Rescinded—No county has been successful in restructuring its government due to the complexity of the process.

1995 Revisions to Education Code—The legislature fundamentally revises the state education code.

provides information, training, and other services for Texas county officials. The group also lobbies the legislature on behalf of county governments.[15]

County governments are multifunctional. Their primary areas of responsibility include roads, public safety, jails, public health, and elections. In Texas, counties are both administrative arms of the state government and locally elected governmental bodies. The state needs to perform some functions—such as elections, public health initiatives, and automobile registration—throughout the state but cannot staff state offices in every county. So, counties serve as local offices to administer some programs for the state. At the same time, counties perform many functions that are strictly local, so their officers are selected locally.

Structure of County Government

When delegates met in the constitutional convention in 1875, a primary goal was to limit government's power. **Chapter 2** discussed how they limited state government power by fragmenting it, and they did the same with county government. County authority is fragmented into offices consisting of a county judge, commissioners, county attorney, district attorney, sheriff, treasurer, auditor, tax assessor-collector, county clerk, judges, district clerk, justices of the peace, constables, and other offices.

County officers (except for the auditor) are elected to four-year terms. The county runs the state's elections, so county offices are on the general election ballot at the same time as state elections, with officials elected in partisan elections. All are elected countywide, except for the four commissioners, the justices of the peace, and constables.

ANALYZING VISUALS

The Texas Urban Triangle

The Texas urban triangle is an emerging triangular megalopolis of 66 counties (out of 254) that is now home to more than 72 percent of the state's population. Through 2030, over 75 percent of the state's growth will occur here. Examine the map of the Texas urban triangle based on a study conducted by students and faculty at Texas A&M University for the Texas Department of Transportation, and then answer the questions.

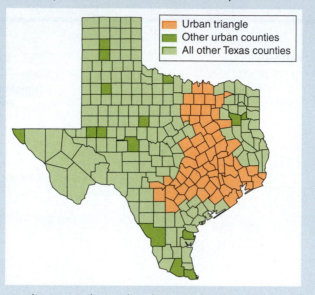

- Which of the three major metropolitan areas located in the triangle—Houston, San Antonio, Dallas—will likely experience the most growth over the next two decades? Why?
- What do you anticipate to be the environmental impact of this concentrated population growth in the Texas urban triangle?
- Is the state's current transportation infrastructure (roads, rail, and air) sufficient to support the anticipated growth in the urban triangle?

(To learn more about the structure of county governments, see The Living Constitution: Article 5, Section 18.)

COUNTY COMMISSIONERS COURT   The primary governing entity for the county is the commissioners court,[16] whose form is prescribed by the constitution as consisting of one county judge and four county commissioners. The **county judge** is formally the judge for court cases heard in the county (through the "constitutional county court"), but modern-day county judges have turned over many judicial functions to district courts and county courts-at-law (see **chapter 6**). Some county judges, primarily in rural counties, retain non-litigation judicial matters, such as wills. Despite the name, though, today's county judge is actually the chief executive officer of the county. He or she also serves as a voting member and the chair of the commissioners court.

The **commissioners court,** as the legislative body for the county, is responsible for adopting the budget for all county offices, setting tax rates, overseeing county programs, and redistricting. The four **county commissioners** perform both legislative and executive functions and are elected from single-member districts called precincts. Commissioners serve four-year, staggered terms. Every two years at the general election, two commissioners are elected. Each commissioner is responsible for building

county judge

Elected official who is the chief administrative officer of county government, serves on the commissioners court and may also have some judicial functions.

commissioners court

The legislative body of a county in Texas.

county commissioner

Elected official who serves on the county legislative body, the commissioners court.

and maintaining county roads in his or her precinct. Throughout much of the twentieth century, the commissioners' primary job was to provide roads for farmers to get to and from town. In fact, they are still known in some areas as "road commissioners."

The commissioners court must perform redistricting functions for county commissioner precincts. Since counties have historically been governments for rural Texans, and since commissioners wanted to divide up the road duties equally among the four precincts, commissioners courts often drew precinct district lines to produce four districts that were geographically fairly equal in size. Thus, each commissioner had a sizeable rural area in his or her precinct. After the U.S. Supreme Court declared that congressional and state legislative district lines must be drawn to produce equal population districts,[17] a resident of Midland County sued the county, arguing that equal representation should also apply to this local legislative body. In 1968, the U.S. Supreme Court agreed, in *Avery* v. *Midland County,* declaring that the one-person, one-vote standard applied to counties.[18] Since then, Texas county commissioners courts have had to base their redistricting on the population count in the decennial U.S. Census. As a result, in Texas's metropolitan areas, county commissioners courts are now elected by the majority of urban residents, rather than by rural residents.

Are counties outgrowing their courthouses? Across the state, there are courthouses such as the Jones County Courthouse with distinguished architectural features. Constructed when the state had a much smaller population, many of these courthouses are inadequate to house all of the functions now assigned to the counties. Courthouse annexes can be found in a large number of the counties.

Photo courtesy: Courtesy of L. Tucker Gibson

DISTRICT ATTORNEYS AND COUNTY ATTORNEYS   Counties elect district attorneys, county attorneys, and/or criminal district attorneys. There is no uniform system applied across the state. The chief prosecutors for violations of state laws are usually district attorneys. A **district attorney (DA)** is an elected official who prosecutes criminal cases. He or she may be elected from and serve one county, but in rural areas, the DA may be elected from and serve a judicial district that includes several counties. Most counties also elect a **county attorney,** who provides legal advice and services to the county government. If there is no district attorney serving the county, the county attorney also prosecutes criminal cases and represents the county in civil cases. If there is a district attorney, the county attorney usually prosecutes less serious criminal cases (misdemeanors), though again, the practices are not uniform across the state.

SHERIFF   The **sheriff** serves as the chief law enforcement officer in the county. While sheriffs' departments have countywide jurisdiction, generally they operate in the unincorporated areas of the county and leave law enforcement in the cities to municipal police departments. Sheriffs also may contract to provide law enforcement for small cities. The sheriff hires deputies, and together they provide general public safety protection for citizens, serve warrants and civil papers, conduct criminal investigations, arrest offenders, and operate the county jail (which holds alleged and convicted county offenders, and where alleged felons who are not released on bond await trial in district courts).

COUNTY CLERK AND DISTRICT CLERK   The **county clerk** keeps records for the county commissioners court and for county courts. He or she is also the official keeper of records such as real estate titles and marriage licenses. County clerks are responsible for conducting county and state elections, unless the county has a separate elections administrator. **District clerks** keep records for district courts. In urban counties, the district clerk may serve several courts; in rural areas, the district clerk may serve one

district attorney (DA)
Elected official who prosecutes criminal cases.

county attorney
Elected official serving as the legal officer for county government and also as a criminal prosecutor.

sheriff
Elected official who serves as the chief law enforcement officer in a county.

county clerk
Elected official who serves as the clerk for the commissioners court and for county records.

district clerk
Elected official who is responsible for keeping the records for the district court.

The Living Constitution

Each county shall . . . be divided into four commissioners precincts in each of which shall be elected by the qualified voters thereof one County Commissioner, who shall hold office for four years. . . . The County Commissioners . . . , with the County Judge as presiding officer, shall compose the County Commissioners Court, which shall exercise such powers and jurisdiction over all county business, as is conferred by this Constitution and the laws of the State, or as may be hereafter prescribed.

—ARTICLE 5, SECTION 18

The Texas Constitution establishes the structure for county government and its powers in Article 5. The principal problems for counties are a constitutionally mandated structure required of all counties regardless of size and a lack of power to enact local laws. Many argue that the answer to these problems is home rule for Texas counties.

Texas voters approved a constitutional amendment in 1933 that gave counties home-rule authority, the power of county voters to choose a different structure of local government than prescribed by the constitution. But no county established home rule before the amendment was repealed in 1969. The home-rule amendment offered a progressive change for county governments, but it was the subject of contradictory interpretations, and procedures for a county to adopt home rule were excessively restrictive. The approval process required a majority of qualified electors in the county, a majority of those voting in the incorporated areas of the county, and a majority of those voting in the unincorporated areas of the county. Even if a majority of a county's voters approved, a small part of the electorate was able to defeat home rule.[a]

El Paso County attempted to adopt home rule in 1934. Initiated by a citizens group and endorsed by the *El Paso Herald-Post* in a series of articles preceding the charter election, the proposed change failed. Countywide, the proposal carried by 295 votes. The voters in the city of El Paso approved the charter by 1,143 votes, but voters outside the city defeated the charter by a margin of 848 votes.

Travis County initiated a home-rule campaign in 1934, but legal questions about the charter commission's authority ended the movement. Tarrant County's home-rule efforts failed in 1934 because the county commissioners court ignored the home-rule charter convention's proposal. Home-rule movements in Bexar, Dallas, and Harris Counties in 1934 failed for various reasons.[b]

Home rule for Texas counties would permit each county's residents to create a government that would fit the residents' specific needs. A merger of county and city governments and offices could occur. Counties also could make and enforce local ordinances, as home-rule cities do now. As a result, the legislature would no longer be required to solve individual county problems with amendments to the Texas Constitution or state laws.[c]

These arguments were revived in 1997 and 1999, when several urban counties pushed for constitutional amendments that would permit counties to hold elections on home rule. But opposition from a variety of state and local interests defeated the efforts.

CRITICAL THINKING QUESTIONS

1. Texas has adopted home rule for cities, but why has it been so difficult to implement a workable form of home rule for county governments?
2. Which people, groups, or interests are most likely to oppose county home rule?
3. If a workable amendment allowing Texas counties to establish home rule were adopted, what changes would you anticipate in your county? Would governments (city, county, and special districts) be merged?

---

[a]George D. Braden, *The Constitution of the State of Texas: An Annotated and Comparative Analysis*, vol. 1 (Austin: Texas Legislative Council, 1977), 448.
[b]Robert E. Norwood, *Texas County Government: Let the People Choose* (Austin: Texas Research League, 1970), 72–74.
[c]Braden, *The Constitution of the State of Texas*, 652.

district court that covers several counties in a judicial district. In some small counties, one person may perform the duties of both the county and the district clerk.

JUDGES AND CONSTABLES District judges, county court-at-law judges, justices of the peace, and constables provide judicial and court services. The number of each varies from county to county, as the legislature has adopted a crazy-quilt pattern of institutions and officials, county by county, depending on population size and on local initiatives asking the legislature for special consideration. (These officials are discussed more in **chapter 6**.)

COUNTY TAX ASSESSOR-COLLECTOR The **county tax assessor-collector** is responsible for an array of functions. These include collecting local property taxes, registering voters, registering automobiles, and collecting motor vehicle sales taxes and registration fees. Because the legislature created county central appraisal districts in the 1970s, tax assessor-collectors do not actually assess property values anymore. Instead, the central appraisal district assesses the value of property for all taxing entities in the county, and the tax assessor-collector collects the taxes.

Do all county commissioners courts have five members? The Texas Constitution requires all counties to have a commissioners court comprised of a county judge and four commissioners. In the small counties, the job requires a limited amount of time, but in the urbanized areas such as Bexar County, the job has become full time.

Photo courtesy: Courtesy of L. Tucker Gibson

TREASURER AND AUDITOR The **county treasurer** is the county's money manager. The treasurer deposits revenue collected by the county, signs checks, disburses funds, keeps accounts of receipts and expenditures of county funds, and invests county funds. All but the smallest counties are also required to have a **county auditor** who audits records of all county officers and departments, helps prepare the county budget, and sets up and administers the accounting systems. Unlike other county officials, the auditor is appointed for a two-year term by the district court. Because auditor and treasurer functions are similar, many counties have decided that they do not need both. Several counties have asked the legislature for constitutional amendments to abolish the requirement that they have a treasurer. The legislature and voters have obliged—amending the constitution to repeal the requirement for some specific counties but not for others.[19]

county tax assessor-collector
Elected official who collects taxes for the county (and perhaps for other local governments).

county treasurer
Elected official who serves as the money manager for county government.

county auditor
Official appointed by a district judge to audit county finances.

Authority of County Governments

County authority is established, in excruciating detail, both in the Texas Constitution and in the **Local Government Code.** Counties are limited to the specific grants of power and areas of responsibility spelled out in the constitution and statutes. Consequently, when new problems arise, or when counties have difficulty administering existing laws, they must seek new or clarified authority from the legislature. Another way to respond to county-level problems is to grant them **general ordinance-making authority,** the legal right to adopt ordinances covering a wide array of subject areas—an authority that some cities have. The Texas Association of Counties has lobbied the legislature in favor of expanded authority numerous times, but developers and realtors have opposed the counties, and the legislature has repeatedly defeated the effort. In 1999, however, in the wake of the boom of suburban and rural development and the court decision in *Elgin Bank* v. *Travis County,* the legislature approved a new law that allows

Local Government Code
The Texas statutory code containing state laws about local governments.

general ordinance-making authority
The legal right to adopt ordinances covering a wide array of subject areas—an authority that some cities have but counties do not.

counties significant authority to regulate subdivisions. The law requires platting and drainage in new subdivisions and gives counties authority to enforce those requirements.[20] Since then, numerous counties have begun using the new powers.[21]

A key function of county governments is administering elections. As the whole nation learned from Florida's 2000 election, counties have independent authority to make many election decisions, and uniform election procedures do not always exist from county to county. Following the 2000 Florida fiasco, in which confusing butterfly ballots and faulty punch-card systems made some votes invalid, the Texas Legislature in 2001 revamped county election authority and procedures: punch-card ballots would be phased out; any new voting system must meet accessibility needs of disabled voters; butterfly ballots are prohibited; ballots must be hand inspected; ineligible-voter lists must be verified by the county.[22] In response to Congress's Help America Vote Act of 2002, the Texas Legislature adopted additional measures in 2003 to ensure compliance with the act, including the creation of a statewide voter registration list and the provision of at least one direct recording electronic (DRE) voting device at each polling place.[23]

Finances of County Governments

While most property tax revenues go to school districts (see the section on special districts), counties have relied heavily on the property tax to fund myriad services they provide. Skyrocketing taxes have led the legislature to impose more and more requirements on counties for hearings, notice, and reports of votes on actions that raise the effective tax rate—even prescribing the exact words that a county commissioner must recite in a motion to change taxes.[24] In 1987, the legislature allowed counties to collect a sales tax, but only if the county is not part of a metropolitan area with a metropolitan transit authority that collects a sales tax. The effect of this arrangement is that rural counties and those with medium-sized cities can collect sales taxes, but metropolitan counties cannot.

In recent years, counties have increased their reliance on fees. Some fee revenues (for instance, motor vehicle registration fees) are pass-through: counties collect the state-imposed fees and send the money to Austin, retaining a small portion allowed for county overhead. Counties are authorized to collect other fees that are totally county revenues. The legislature has created numerous new fees in recent years, especially in the area of criminal justice. These include jury fees, processing fees, hot check fees, crime-stopper fees, video fees, witness summons fees, breath-testing fees, courthouse security fees, and others. The collection and distribution system for these fees is complicated and confusing for offices throughout the courthouse. Moreover, the 2005 legislature mandated that counties implement a court fee collection program.[25] Counties collect more than thirty different fees for state government, plus about thirty fees for local services.

Cities

★ **7.3** . . . **Differentiate among the various forms of city governments and how they are governed.**

Texas has 1,209 cities. Three of the nation's ten largest cities are in Texas—Houston (2 million), San Antonio (1.3 million), and Dallas (1.2 million). Thirty-one cities have populations that exceed 100,000, and of these, nine exceed 250,000. Most cities, however, are small, and size matters in the type of government that the city may have. As Texans moved off the farms and into cities in the late nineteenth and early twentieth centuries, burgeoning cities found it difficult to manage the new growth and to respond to social, economic, and infrastructure problems that the growth brought. They turned to the state legislature for new authority and new governmental forms.

As rural populations dwindled, the rural-dominated legislature sometimes violated requirements to redistrict, thus keeping rural incumbents in power. Cities often could not get what they wanted from the hostile state legislature.

Other states faced similar dynamics. In 1875, Missouri decided to allow cities to adopt their own charters and decide how to govern themselves, thus triggering a movement across the nation for municipal home rule. Home-rule proposals became a part of the agenda of the Progressive movement in the early 1900s. In 1912, Texas passed a constitutional amendment for municipal home rule. In 1913, the legislature stipulated in the enabling legislation that home-rule cities may adopt any provisions that are not inconsistent with the Texas Constitution or statutes. Today, forty-eight states have some form of municipal home rule.[26]

When the municipal home-rule amendment was added to the constitution in 1912, it authorized cities with more than 5,000 people to write their own city charter and decide what structure and authority to give their city government. Today, 329 cities are home-rule cities. The others are called **general-law cities,** because they are governed by the general state laws regarding municipalities, rather than by a locally adopted charter.[27] For small general-law cities, the Local Government Code spells out the form and powers of the city government, and even specific actions that the city must follow.

general-law cities
Cities with fewer than 5,000 residents, governed by a general state law rather than by a locally adopted charter.

The idea behind home rule is that city leaders need tools to address their local problems, and that one-size-fits-all state provisions deny cities the flexibility they need. For any city that qualifies for home rule, the Local Government Code stipulates that the city "may adopt and operate under any form of government" and that "the municipality has full power of local self government." Thus, some home-rule cities decide, for instance, to operate their own electric company, while others do not; some allow citizens to recall city officials from office, while others do not. The city of Austin decided (via a voter initiative) to place limits on local campaign finances.

Home-rule municipalities sometimes see state laws passed to restrict their authority to govern themselves or to give them special authority. For instance, the Local Government Code stipulates that if the city of Houston does not adopt a voter-approved local ordinance providing for some single-member districts for city council members, then it must follow a specific form spelled out in the statute. (The city responded to the pressure and adopted its own system.) Other sections of the law apply only to the city of Austin. The legislature, however, must be careful. Laws aimed at one specific local government are unconstitutional,[28] so legislators devise laws that apply to cities in a particular population bracket. Of course, they can try to create a population bracket that encompasses only one city, so long as no one challenges it in court.

Why does the legislature pass laws seemingly at odds with home-rule provisions of the Texas Constitution and Local Government Code? When local battles become unresolvable or some people don't like a decision of the city council, some parties will seek help from the legislature. The legislature then has to decide between the opposing groups. In some cases, it may be fights between local developers lobbying for new restrictions on municipal authority and city officials trying to restrict development. (To learn more about local and state authority, see Join the Debate: Should Texas Cities Be Allowed to Photograph Red-Light Runners?)

Forms of City Governments

A group of people can live in somewhat close proximity to each other in an unincorporated area of a county, but they are not required to form a city. Cities are formed when residents of an area express a desire for ongoing public or governmental services assigned to cities under state law. The number of residents living in a proposed city largely determines the form of government that can be used. Most new cities incorporate as a Type B general-law city, which requires a minimum population of 201 people. If the city grows to 600 or has one manufacturing plant, this city can switch to Type A general-law status.

General-law cities do not have individual charters. A community that meets the population requirements petitions the county judge, who then calls for an election of voters who are affected by the proposed city incorporation. Once incorporated, the city follows complex provisions of the Local Government Code for its authority, structure of government, and election system.

Approximately 75 percent of Texas cities are general-law cities, but the distinctions among Class A, B, and C cities have become blurred over time with continued revisions in the Local Government Code. As state law has evolved, it has permitted one class of city to "borrow" or use the powers of a different class of city unless limited by specific statutes.

For most general-law cities, the Local Government Code mandates a mayor–council or commission form of government, depending on the class of the general-law city.[29] But with increased options available to general-law cities, there are a wide range of permutations in the specific structures of city governments.

Cities with more than 5,000 population may change to the home-rule form of government by adopting a form of government through a charter election of the voters. There is a formal process for the adoption of a home-rule charter prescribed in the code, but a city has four general options: **weak mayor–council, strong mayor–council, council–manager,** and **city commission.** The details of these forms, however, vary from city to city. About 290 Texas home-rule cities have chosen the council–manager form of government, fifteen have chosen weak mayor–council, and four have chosen strong mayor–council.[30]

WEAK MAYOR–COUNCIL   The mayor could be elected at large or by the city council from among its members. The mayor has authority to preside over city council meetings, is the symbolic head of government, and presides at ribbon-cutting ceremonies, but is essentially equal in power to other city council members. The collective council hires, manages, and fires city staff. (To learn more about weak-mayor cities, see Figure 7.1, which shows the city organizational chart for White Oak, a weak-mayor home-rule city in Gregg County, bordering Longview.)

STRONG MAYOR–COUNCIL   The strong mayor is distinguished from a weak mayor by his or her executive powers. The mayor is elected citywide, presides at city council meetings, hires, manages, and fires city staff, and may have the power to veto actions of the city council. Most large American cities have strong mayors. In Texas, few cities have strong mayors, and among Texas's ten largest cities, only Houston uses the strong mayor–council form; Dallas defeated strong-mayor proposals twice in 2005. (To learn more about strong-mayor cities, see Figure 7.2, showing the city organizational chart for the city of Houston.)

COUNCIL–MANAGER   Progressive-era reforms led to this government form, in which a professional manager, hired by the city council, to run the city (hire, manage, and fire staff), while the city council and mayor set policy, adopt budgets and tax rates, and oversee the manager. Most home-rule cities in Texas have city managers. (To learn more about the city manager form of government, see Figure 7.3.) The mayor and city council hire their own staff as well as the municipal judges, court clerk, city clerk, city auditor, and city manager. The city manager hires all other city employees and directs their activities.

CITY COMMISSION   On September 8, 1900, the deadliest natural disaster in U.S. history devastated Galveston, the wealthiest city in Texas at the time. A hurricane killed an estimated 8,000 to 10,000 people and wiped out three-fourths of

weak mayor–council

A form of city government in which the mayor has no more power than any other member of the council.

strong mayor–council

A form of city government in which the mayor has strong powers to run the city by hiring, managing, and firing staff and controlling executive departments; the mayor also serves on the council.

council–manager

A form of city government in which the city council and mayor hire a professional manager to run the city.

city commission

A form of city government in which elected members serve on the legislative body and also serve as head administrators of city programs.

Figure 7.1 *What does a weak mayor–council form of government look like?*

When White Oak reached a population of 5,000, it was entitled to convert to a home-rule city, which it did. During this change of status, the city chose to retain its weak mayor–council form of government, illustrated by the city's organizational chart.

Source: City of White Oak

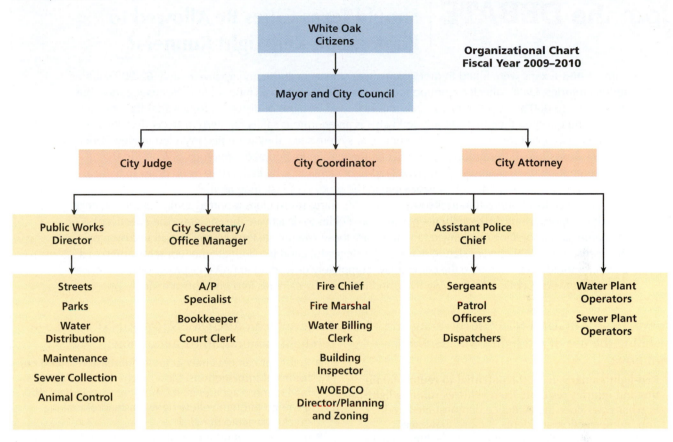

the city. Human remains were still being found five months later. In attempting to cope with the disaster, the legislature allowed Galveston to revamp its city government, giving authority to specific individuals (commissioners) to govern particular policy areas (such as public health, public safety, public improvements). The city managed to build a major sea wall, prop up houses and buildings, and clean up and rebuild the city.[31] In this form of government, the commissioners meet as a body to adopt budgets, set tax rates, and perform other communal functions, but each individual member has authority in the specified functional area. After Galveston's experience, the commission form of government spread quickly to nearly 500 cities across the nation, but the form has since fallen into disuse amid charges of turf battles and lack of coordination among the officials. Today, no Texas city uses the commission form of government.[32] Some cities use the term "commission" rather than "council" for the governing body, but they do not have the commission form of government.

Authority and Functions of City Governments

Cities are multifunctional governments, providing police, fire, public works, recreation, health, and other services. Cities have wide authority to provide services directly to citizens. Some decide to give franchises to private companies to provide services in the city. For instance, you may live in a city where a private company picks up your garbage, or you may live in a city where the city itself runs the garbage pickup service.

Join the DEBATE | Should Texas Cities Be Allowed to Photograph Red-Light Runners?

Some 3,468 Texans were killed in motor vehicle accidents in 2008, and approximately 62,000 suffered serious injuries. Data collected from police reports are based on a number of violation categories, but more than 28,000 accidents and 158 fatalities occurred because of disregard for a signal light or sign.[a] There is no question then that running red lights is an enormous safety concern in Texas. Twenty-one states have adopted some type of red light camera system since they were first installed in New York City in 1993. Texas joined this group in 2003, when the legislature adopted a photographic traffic signal enforcement system (commonly known as "red-light cameras"). By early 2010, more than sixty local governments were using the cameras or were in the process of installing them.[b]

However, local opposition to the fines—in 2009, thirty-seven cities reported some 1.3 million tickets with fines approaching $100 million—has led some cities to deactivate the cameras. The effectiveness of the cameras is also being challenged, and there are those who allege the cameras are an intrusion on their privacy. In 2009, the legislature made an unsuccessful effort to eliminate the red-light cameras altogether.[c] Should Texas eliminate the camera law completely or work to improve its provisions? Is there a tradeoff between public safety, saving lives, and intrusion by cameras into one's private life?[d]

To develop an ARGUMENT FOR retaining and expanding the use of red-light cameras, think about how:

- **Red-light cameras have the potential to reduce fatalities and injuries resulting from vehicles running lights.** In what ways does the evidence demonstrate a reduction in intersection accidents in cities that have installed cameras? Shouldn't mechanisms that increase safety be the primary concern of local governments?
- **Red-light cameras are more accurate and can lead to more efficient use of the law enforcement capacity of a local government.** In what ways would the recording of a traffic violation by a camera be more accurate than an officer's observation? How does use of these cameras free up police officers to deploy throughout the community to increase safety elsewhere?
- **Legal and constitutional safeguards can be built into the camera system.** Is the right to drive a car a constitutional right? How can cameras be used in a way that ensures citizens' legal rights and privacy are protected?

Have you ever been "red lighted?" Cameras are being used by cities across Texas to reduce serious accidents at intersections.

To develop an ARGUMENT AGAINST the use of red-light cameras, think about how:

- **Red-light cameras may actually increase rear-end collisions at intersections.** How might driver behavior lead to more accidents, if other motorists expect drivers to go through yellow lights, instead of braking quickly to avoid fines?
- **Red-light cameras are used by cities to generate income and not to achieve safety goals.** In a period of budget cuts and reductions in city personnel, aren't the fines really a form of a tax? Are cities shortening yellow lights to increase the number of red-light violations?
- **Red-light cameras are an intrusion into our privacy rights.** How is the camera another example of "big brother" watching citizens? In what ways have cities opened themselves up to a quagmire of litigation based on constitutional arguments?

Photo courtesy: Bob Daemmrich Photography, Inc.

---

[a] Texas Department of Transportation, "Texas Motor Vehicle Crash Statistics, 2008," www.dot.state.tx.us.
[b] House Research Organization, "Red-light Cameras in Texas: A Status Report," *Focus Report* July 31, 2006; Governors Highway Safety Association, "Speed and Red Light Camera Laws," May 2010, www.ghsa.org; Insurance Institute for Highway Safety, "Communities Using Red Light and/or Speed Cameras," May 2010, www.iihs.org.
[c] "Texas Red Light Cameras Generate $100 Million Worth of Tickets," December 12, 2009, www.thenewspaper.com; "Texas House Votes to Sunset Red Light Cameras," May 17, 2007, www.the newspaper.com.
[d] National Safety Commission, "Red Light Cameras: Are They Worth the Legal Problems," September 24, 2009.

Figure 7.2 *What does a strong mayor-council form of government look like?*
As reflected in the organization chart of Houston, the mayor has responsibilities for
appointments and the oversight of day-to-day administration.
Source: City of Houston, www.houstontx.gov.

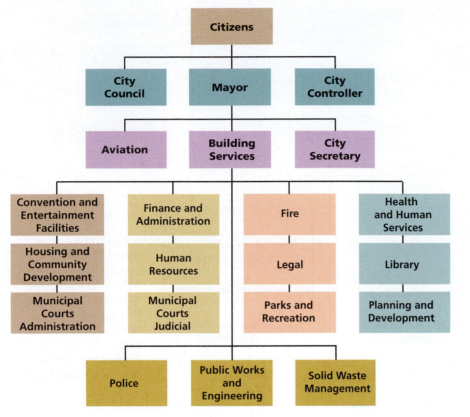

Municipalities have broad regulatory authority. When cities use regulatory authority in the areas of zoning, buildings, signs, nuisances, and subdivision development,
public needs and private property rights often collide. The **Texas Municipal League**
serves as the voice of cities in the capital, lobbying to defend cities' authority and powers. Sometimes, of course, cities do not agree with each other or choose not to join in
an effort to protect a city. Other times, cities and their association fight battles against
counties and the Texas Association of Counties.

Finances of City Governments

Although faced with growing populations and increased demands for public services,
Texas cities have limited financial options. Unlike counties and school districts, they receive no state appropriations. City governments are disproportionately dependent on
regressive taxes, such as property taxes and a one-cent sales tax. Other revenue sources
include franchise fees, court fines, hotel occupancy taxes, taxes on amusements, fees on
various permits, and transfers from funds generated by locally owned utilities.[33] Cities
also receive funding from a variety of federal grant-in-aid programs. Federal stimulus
funds allocated to Texas under the American Recovery and Reinvestment Act of 2009
went to local governments across the state, but such funding usually is for a short period
and subject to change. (To learn more about sources of city revenue, see Figure 7.4.)

Texas cities have been given considerable discretion to determine what taxes they
will impose, and to a large extent the state has not depended on the cities to fund state
programs. But cities are continually threatened by legislative proposals to place caps or

Texas Municipal League
Professional association and lobbying arm for city governments.

regressive tax
The tax level increases as the wealth
or ability of an individual or business
to pay decreases.

Figure 7.3 *What does a council–manager form of government look like?*

In a council-manager form of government, such as the one found in Austin, the mayor and city council hire their own staff, municipal judges, court and city clerks, city auditors, and city manager. The manager then hires and oversees all other city employees.

Source: City of Austin, www.ci.austin.tx.us.

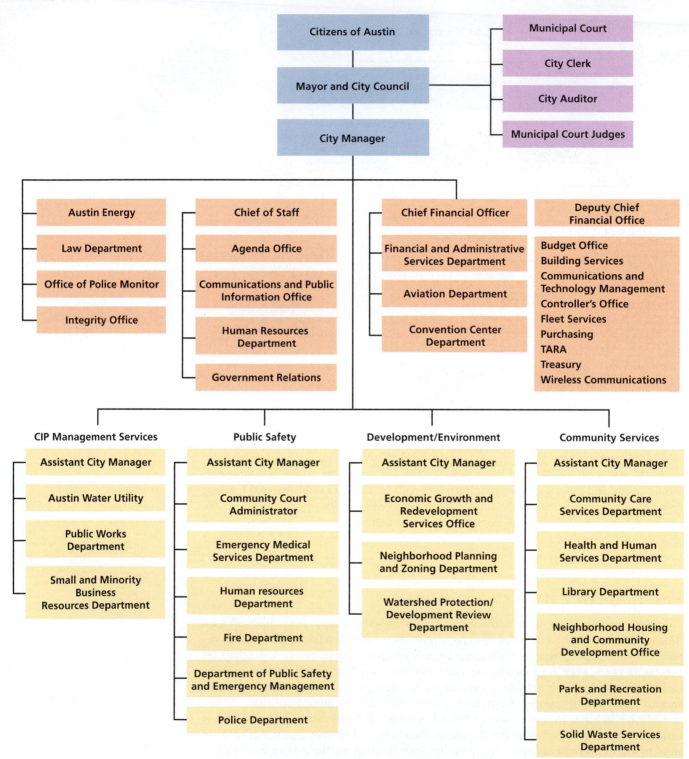

Are all city council chambers this ornate? City councils vary in size, and so do the chambers in which they meet. All have the primary responsibility of establishing city policies and enacting budgets. Most of the councils across the state have very modest and often informal facilities. In contrast, the San Antonio City Council meets in the renovated lobby of a historical bank located in the central business district.

Photo courtesy: Courtesy of L. Tucker Gibson

general obligation bonds
A method of borrowing money to pay for new construction projects such as roads, drainage, and physical facilities of a city. Generally requires citizen approval and repaid from general tax revenue.

revenue bonds
Bonds sold by governments that are repaid from the revenues generated from income-producing facilities.

other restrictions on their taxing authority.[34] Through their associations and lobbyists, cities work hard to thwart such restrictions.

Raising taxes to meet budget shortfalls is an option but often with severe political consequences. Citizens can challenge a tax increase of more than 8 percent a year through a *rollback* election, and homeowners have the right to appeal appraisal rates. Vociferous and strident opposition to taxes are often a sufficient threat to elected officials to avoid a tax increase. (To learn more about how tax freezes are affecting cities, see Politics Now: Tax Freezes for the Elderly are Costing Cities.)

City revenues tend to track the state's economy. When the economy is robust and expanding, city revenues usually grow. A strong economy eases the pressure for cities to raise property taxes, increase fees, lay off city workers, freeze the hiring of new employees, or reduce services. Conversely, when the state's economy sours, as it did in the late 1980s, 2001, and again in 2008, the opposite occurs.[35]

Sales taxes were down in 2009 over the previous year, as was the hotel-motel tax. The unemployment rate as of early spring 2010 was over 8 percent. Texas did not experience the home real estate problems of other states, but its housing market with new construction was stagnant. New construction translates into new tax revenue, a key part of cities' financial planning.

Although cities are required by law to balance their operating budgets, many municipal construction projects are financed by loans through the issuance of **general obligation bonds,** which are subject to voter approval. These bonds are secured by the city's taxing power. The city pledges its full faith and credit to the lender and, over a number of years, repays the bonds with tax revenue. Cities also fund various projects through **revenue bonds** that are payable solely from the revenues derived from an income-producing facility. The poor economy of the late 1980s made it more difficult

Figure 7.4 *Where do cities obtain their revenue?*

Texas cities derive approximately 58 percent of their funds from two regressive taxes—the sales and property taxes.

Source: Texas Town & City 97 (January 2009) p. 22.

Court Fines 3.9%
Permits/Fees 5.5%
Interest Earnings 1.6%
Transfers from Other Funds 5.8%
Franchises 9.9%
Other Services 15.7%
Property Tax 28.8%
Sales Tax 28.8%

Strong Mayor Government

New York City, Los Angeles, Chicago—the great (and large) cities of the United States—are governed by strong mayors who hire, direct, and fire city staff and sometimes have veto authority over city council actions. Of the ten largest U.S. cities, six function under the strong mayor system, including Houston, the fourth largest city. San Diego, California, went from the council–manager form of government to the strong mayor in 2006 for a five-year trial period.

In city governments from the Northeast and Midwest to the South and West Coast, there has been a shift from the use of the strong mayor to the council–manager form of government. With the exception of Houston, all the major cities in Texas use the council–manager form of government, and there does not appear to be much interest or support for changing to the strong mayor form.

■ Why is the strong mayor form of government unpopular in Texas?

■ Are cities headed by a strong mayor more likely to respond quickly and decisively to major catastrophes than cities with a council–manager form of government?

■ Is the choice of the form of government related to underlying social, economic, and political factors? Explain your answer.

annexation

Enlargement of a city's corporate limits by incorporating surrounding territory into the city.

extraterritorial jurisdiction (ETJ)

The area outside a city's boundaries over which the city may exercise limited control.

for cities to borrow money. And with a pent-up demand for improving infrastructure (streets, waste disposal systems, libraries, and other facilities), cities have entered an era of bond financing that has been radically altered by the performance of Wall Street and changes in state and federal tax laws.[36] Although city finances had improved by 2008, cities continued to postpone capital spending for streets, water systems, and a variety of other infrastructure improvements. Additionally, there were concerns about the crisis in the mortgage markets that increased home foreclosures across the state. A significant decline in home values had a direct impact on revenues generated from the property tax.

Municipal Annexation

One of the most controversial and tortuous areas of municipal government and politics is the issue of municipal boundaries and **annexation** of territory to expand those boundaries. The unilateral power of home-rule cities to annex dates back to the 1912 Home-Rule Constitutional Amendment. Absent any state restrictions, cities could decide on their own whether and how to grow. In 1963, the legislature passed the Municipal Annexation Act to restrict home-rule cities' leeway in annexing. The 1963 act is an arena for legislative battles nearly every session, sometimes with minor changes, sometimes, as in 1999, with major changes.[37] The most significant areas of controversy in annexation policies include how the annexation occurs, services that cities must provide in newly annexed areas, and the status of areas beyond the city limits known as **extraterritorial jurisdictions (ETJs)**.

Under the Municipal Annexation Act, a city may expand its municipal boundaries by an area up to 10 percent of its geographic area in any one year.[38] The city is not required to obtain the consent of anyone for annexation, though it must hold public hearings. A city also controls an ETJ of up to five miles from its city limits, depending on its population size.[39] The act states that the purpose of limited municipal controls in areas beyond city limits is "to promote and protect the general health, safety, and welfare."[40] For instance, if developers were allowed to build a subdivision immediately outside city limits without complying with local street and sewer standards, then the costs of upgrading the area to city standards could be expensive when the city later annexed the area. A city's authority to set minimal development standards for areas within its ETJ lessens the city's costs after annexing the area. When a city decides to annex territory, it may not include any area within the existing ETJ of another municipality. When cities annex territory, they must provide services to those areas within timelines specified in the state law.

To complicate matters, some cities use what is called limited-purpose annexation. A home-rule municipality with a population greater than 225,000 may annex an area for the limited purposes of applying its planning, zoning, health, and safety ordinances in the area, without the consequences of full annexation. In essence, limited-purpose annexation provides stronger municipal controls than ETJ restrictions but less than full annexation. Still another variant is called strip annexation. Some cities have used annexation powers to annex narrow strips along highways in order to rapidly extend city boundaries (and ETJs) to outlying areas. In 1973, the act was amended to

Tax Freezes for the Elderly Are Costing Cities

By Aman Batheja

May 2, 2010
Fort Worth Star-Telegram
www.star-telegram.com

As Tarrant County cities try to deal with budget shortfalls, the impact of generous property tax freezes adopted several years ago for elderly and disabled homeowners is starting to be felt. Government entities in Tarrant County—19 cities along with the county government and the community college—lost nearly $6.6 million in tax revenue last year because of the freezes, according to county records.

In Texas, reliable data on the impact of the local-option caps isn't available, but it's clear that billions of dollars in taxable values have been kept off the tax rolls since voters approved a constitutional amendment in 2003 allowing them. And, that amount is certain to grow higher in the coming years as a wave of baby boomers reaches retirement age.

"As the city's population continues to age, and it will, more people will qualify for that benefit, which challenges how much the city can raise in revenue," said Horatio Porter, a Fort Worth budget officer.

Property tax appraisal notices will begin reaching mailboxes this week, and thousands of homeowners under the freeze could learn that the value of their property has changed but that their tax bill is staying the same. . . .

Senior citizens in Texas have enjoyed frozen property taxes for school districts since 1993. The thinking among many proponents is that most senior citizens don't have school-age children and therefore deserve a break on helping cover the costs of public education.

State Rep. Fred Brown, R–Bryan, proposed a constitutional amendment in 2003 allowing cities and counties to choose also to freeze their property taxes for elderly and disabled homeowners. Rising property values were raising concerns that older Texans were going to be priced out of their homes. . . .

The Legislative Budget Board predicted that the yearly loss to cities and counties would grow to $20.3 million by 2008. Last year, Tarrant County's coffers lost $1.7 million because of the tax freeze. Of local cities that adopted it, Fort Worth missed out on the most: $1.6 million.

The percentage of elderly or disabled homeowners who took advantage of a tax freeze last year ranged from roughly 7 to 25 percent per city, according to Tarrant Appraisal District records. The differences depend largely on a city's demographics, various city officials said. . . .

Critical Thinking Questions

1. What is the relationship between the appraised value of a home or other property and the tax rate?
2. Should all persons over a specific age be entitled to a tax freeze, or should such freezes be means tested or based on income or liquid assets? Explain your answer.
3. If you were a homeowner, would you resent the cost-shifting to you that occurs as a result of tax freezes? Explain your answer.

prohibit the annexation of strips less than 500 feet, and in 1987 the minimum permissible width was increased to 1,000 feet.[41]

In 1998, a Senate interim committee made several recommendations for amendments to the Municipal Annexation Act.[42] The committee's bill was designed to provide protection for those to be annexed. The 1999 legislature amended numerous provisions of the proposal, then passed it. As a result of those 1999 amendments, in order to annex, a city must now take the following steps:

- Develop a three-year plan for annexation, and not annex the targeted area during that three-year period.
- Make an inventory of the current services in the area.
- Provide to the annexed area all services currently provided in its full-purpose boundaries no later than two and one-half years (or four and one-half years in some circumstances) after annexation.
- Require negotiations and arbitration regarding services.

- Conduct at least two public hearings.
- Not reduce level of services in the area from what they were before annexation.

Newly annexed citizens may enforce a service plan by asking a court for a writ of *mandamus* (an order to perform a certain act). If the court finds that the city is not implementing a service plan, it must provide an option of disannexation, or it must order compliance, a refund of taxes, or civil penalties. The law grandfathers existing land uses or planned land uses at the time of annexation.[43]

Politics and Representation in City Governments

Unlike county elections, municipal elections in Texas are nonpartisan, and they are held on election dates separate from state and county elections. With political parties absent from the nominating process, who then is influential in the socialization, recruitment, and financing of city candidates? The answer to that question is different today from what it was up to the 1970s.

at-large-by-place

An election system in which all positions on the council or governing body are filled by city-wide elections, with each position designated as a seat, and candidates must choose which place to run for.

single-member districts

Election system in which a legislator runs from and represents one district rather than the entire geographic area encompassed by the government.

Traditionally, city council elections in Texas tended to be at-large or **at-large-by-place** elections, where all candidates had to run for office across the entire city. The general pattern of competition was that the business community in the city would coalesce, plan strategy for the elections, recruit candidates, keep other candidates out of the race if possible, and fund the candidates. Some of the business coalitions created formal organizations, while others operated informally. They included such groups as the Dallas Citizens Charter Association/Citizens Council, San Antonio Good Government League, Committee for a Greater Fort Worth, Austin Citizens League, and Houston's "8-F Crowd."[44] Because it was difficult to mount a serious citywide campaign in a large city without substantial resources, these business coalitions held nearly monopoly power on municipal politics for decades. Not surprisingly, the candidates that they recruited to fill city council and mayoral seats typically came from the business community and reflected business community leadership: they were white, male, and conservative politically.

The business monopoly over municipal politics in Texas was weakened in the 1970s with the coming of **single-member districts,** in which an officeholder runs from and represents one district rather than the entire geographic area encompassed by the government. The League of United Latin American Citizens (LULAC), the Mexican American Legal Defense and Educational Fund (MALDEF), the National Association for the Advancement of Colored People (NAACP), and Texas Rural Legal Aid began using the federal Voting Rights Act (see **chapter 3**) as a basis for lawsuits challenging the validity of at-large municipal elections that usually resulted in all-white city councils. As courts handed down decisions overturning at-large elections, and as some cities responded to the pressure by making changes on their own, most large cities in Texas abandoned at-large elections in favor of either single-member districts or a mixed system of some single-member districts and some at large. Not all have done so. (To learn more about a variety of elections systems, see Table 7.2.)

With the advent of single-member districts, candidates who previously could not mount an effective

Partisan Ballots for City Offices

Cities in California have often been governed by officials who were leaders in their political parties and elected on partisan ballots. Sometimes they have even been state officials who went back down to the local level and continued their electoral careers there. House Speakers Willie Brown and Antonio Villagarosa, both Democrats, became mayors of San Francisco and Los Angeles, respectively, and Governor Jerry Brown, also a Democrat, became mayor of Oakland before being reelected governor of California in 2010. In Texas, city officials are elected on a nonpartisan ballot. Party officials can—and do—run for local office, but they may not run as party leaders, with party nominations. A former chair of the Texas Democratic Party, Bill White, was elected mayor of Houston. Travis County Democratic Party Chair Kirk Watson was elected mayor of Austin before winning a seat in the state Senate.

- Why does Texas use a nonpartisan ballot for city offices but a partisan ballot for county offices?
- Would it make a difference if city officials in Texas were elected on a partisan ballot?
- Which system do you think Texas cities should use, and why?

Table 7.2 *What type of government and election system do the ten largest cities in Texas have?*

	Type of Government	City Council Election System	Estimated Population (2008)
Houston	Strong Mayor–Council	9 single-member districts, 5 at-large, mayor at-large	2,023,601
San Antonio	Council–Manager	10 single-member districts, mayor at-large	1,292,997
Dallas	Council–Manager	14 single-member districts, mayor at-large	1,227,082
Austin	Council–Manager	6 at-large-by-place, mayor at-large	777,783
Fort Worth	Council–Manager	8 single-member districts, mayor at-large	677,897
El Paso	Council–Manager	8 single-member districts, mayor at-large	602,422
Arlington	Council–Manager	5 single-member districts, 3 at-large, mayor at-large	355,641
Corpus Christi	Council–Manager	5 single-member districts, 3 at-large, mayor at-large	285,147
Plano	Council–Manager	4 single-member districts, 3 at-large, mayor at-large	259,045
Garland	Council–Manager	8 single-member districts, mayor at-large	234,003

Source: Compiled by authors from city sources.

campaign throughout the entire city became viable. Neighborhood groups, ethnic and racial groups, and other community groups joined the business community in recruiting, endorsing, funding, and socializing candidates to run for city council. The most visible result of the change in election systems has been the ethnic and racial make-up of city governments. Whereas it was difficult to find any minority city council members in Texas up through the 1960s, by the 1990s, African Americans and Mexican Americans constituted majorities or near majorities of the city councils in some of the largest cities. Minorities also have been winning citywide races, such as mayoral races and at-large city council seats. The best known has been Henry Cisneros, who served as mayor of San Antonio from 1981 to 1989 and then served in President Bill Clinton's Cabinet. Recent Mexican American mayors include Ed Garza (San Antonio), Gus Garcia (Austin), and Raymond Caballero (El Paso). Former mayors Lee Brown (Houston), Ron Kirk (Dallas), and Elzie Odom (Arlington) are African American.

Of course, the selection of single-member districts as a means of addressing imbalance in city politics is not the only option. Both cumulative voting and proportional representation would likely yield results that more closely reflect a city's population than is the case with at-large elections, without the redistricting dilemmas that single-member districts raise. **Cumulative voting** allows a voter in a multimember or at-large system to cast a number of votes equal to the number of seats being filled; the voter may cast his or her votes all for one candidate or split them among candidates in various combinations. Some small Texas cities and some school districts are experimenting with cumulative voting. Under a cumulative voting system, if six candidates are running for three seats on a city council, the three candidates who receive the most votes would be elected. **Proportional representation** awards seats based on the proportion of the vote that a political party receives for a legislative body. This system is used in some European countries but is rare in the United States.

Additionally, women have won considerable support in recent city elections. Women winning mayoral elections in recent decades include Dallas Mayors Laura Miller and Annette Strauss, Houston's Kathy Whitmire, San Antonio's Lila Cockrell, Austin's Carole Keeton Strayhorn (later elected Texas railroad commissioner and state comptroller), and Fort Worth's Kay Granger (now U.S. representative).

cumulative voting

A method of voting in which voters have a number of votes equal to the number of seats being filled, and voters may cast their votes all for one candidate or split them among candidates in various combinations.

proportional representation

A voting system that apportions legislative seats according to the percentage of the vote won by a particular political party.

Special Districts

⭐ **7.4** . . . **Identify the functions of special districts and the reasons for their creation.**

Not only does the Texas Constitution set up the state, county, and city governments, it also sets up some political subdivisions of the state that are collectively known as special districts. The constitution allows the legislature, counties, and cities to establish

Table 7.3 *What are the different kinds of special districts in Texas?*

Constitutional Special Districts	Example
Road district	Travis County Road District No. 1
School district	Lubbock Independent School District
Junior college district	North Harris Community College District
Hospital district	Tarrant County Hospital District
Airport authority	Dallas–Fort Worth Airport Authority
Tax appraisal district	Erath County Appraisal District
Conservation and reclamation district	Southeast Texas Agricultural Development District

Statutory Special Districts	Example
Sports facility district	Nueces County Sports Facility District
Crime control and prevention district	Fort Worth Crime Control and Prevention District
Municipal utility district (MUD)	Westlake Municipal Utility District No. 1
Metropolitan transit authority	Dallas Area Rapid Transit Authority
Soil conservation district	Webb County Soil and Water Conservation District
Waste disposal authority	Gulf Coast Waste Disposal Authority
Municipal power agency	Texas Municipal Power Agency
Groundwater subsidence district	Harris–Galveston Coastal Subsidence District
River authority	Brazos River Authority
Underground water district	High Plains Underground Water Conservation District
Water conservation and improvement	Harris County WCID No. 91 district
Flood control district	Harris County Flood Control District

Source: Authors; Virginia Marion Perrenod, *Special Districts, Special Purposes: Fringe Government and Urban Problems in the Houston Area* (College Station: Texas A&M Press, 1984).

additional special districts. Based on the 2007 *Census of Governments*, Texas has 3,372 special districts, far outstripping the number of counties and cities. Harris County alone has more than 434.[45] Although state, county, and city governments are multifunctional, most special districts are established by the state constitution or by a government to perform just one function. (To learn more about types of special districts, see Table 7.3.)

Why not simply let the multifunctional counties and cities perform these duties? There are different reasons, of course, for each type of special district. Some policy areas (such as river management) must be addressed on a regional basis rather than by individual counties or cities. The constitutional tax limitations placed on counties and cities have made it difficult or impossible for those governments to take on new tasks, so some special districts have been created to circumvent the constitutional tax ceiling. And, independent school districts were created out of a belief that an issue as important as public education would be better addressed by a government focusing on that one need, rather than having to compete with the other needs that counties and cities must address. The legislature creates many municipal utility districts (or MUDs) to provide water and other utility services to new subdivisions and other developments outside of a city's limits. These districts often are created at the request of developers, who reap substantial financial benefits from the suburban population growth the districts help generate.

Water Districts

Growing population pressures and recurrent droughts make water management a hot button issue in Texas politics and policy. The state and local governments often address water policies by creating and empowering special districts. The constitution authorizes the legislature to create special districts for water management (Article 3, section 52) and for conservation and development of natural resources (Article 16, section 59). The legislature also creates other types of water districts. For instance, water issues were at the top of the legislative agenda in 1999, and the legislature created thirteen water districts in that session.[46] The Water Code regulates the creation of groundwater conservation districts and the election of their local boards. A district may be composed of all or part of other political subdivisions, such as counties or cities. If the district encompasses several counties, voters in each county must approve it. In cases where there is no local action to create a district, the Texas Commission on Environmental Quality (TCEQ) can designate a priority groundwater management area and force hearings and elections to create a district. If voters still do not approve it, the TCEQ could manage the priority area itself or ask the legislature to create a district. For instance, the TCEQ designated part of Comal County as a priority area.[47]

School Districts

The most common type of special district is a school district. Texas has 1,081 local school districts, second only to California's 1,102.[48] Elected school trustees are unpaid government officials. They set the policies for the districts (within federal and state guidelines and requirements), set the district property-tax rate, decide where and when to build new schools, and hire the superintendents to run the schools.

All of Texas is divided among the school districts. There is no uniformity in either geographic size or population size of the districts. Some districts are small—San Vicente Independent School District in Brewster County had thirty-three students in 2009—while the largest, Houston Independent School District in Harris County, had 200,225 students.[49] Texas has more than 8,300 public elementary and secondary schools, second in the nation to California, and the number grows every year.[50] Almost all of those schools are operated by local school districts. Local schools and school districts operate under a shifting degree of state oversight and regulation. The State Board of Education, the commissioner of education, and the Texas Education Agency (TEA) have some jurisdiction over school districts. In 1995, the Texas Legislature enacted an entirely new education code, recreating the TEA, the State Board of Education, and the commissioner of education, but abolishing some state policies and allowing school districts more leeway in deciding policies.

The 1995 act also set out a process for creating home-rule school districts, free from many state requirements and TEA guidance, if local voters so choose. So far, no districts have attempted to convert to home rule. However, the act also authorized the creation of **charter schools,** which are public schools operating under a contract granted by the state (with the intention of trying different educational methods) rather than under the control of the local school district. By 2009, Texas had 437 public charter schools.[51] There is both strong support for and strong opposition to charter schools. More than a dozen charter schools have failed, some experience rapid teacher turnover, and some have operated with no school transportation and no school lunches.

Just as at-large elections in cities have been challenged under the Voting Rights Act, so have at-large elections in school districts. In 1983, the legislature authorized, but did not mandate, local school districts to use single-member districts. More than one hundred school districts were sued or threatened with a suit in the 1980s and 1990s. By 2008, 161 school districts elected at least some trustees from single-member districts.[52]

On being challenged, some districts entered into negotiated agreements with plaintiffs, and some of those districts approved cumulative voting systems rather than single-member districts. As a result of lawsuits and negotiated settlements, Texas has more governments that use cumulative voting systems than any other state in the nation. By 2008, thirty-five school districts (as well as a community college district and seventeen small cities) had held elections with cumulative voting.[53]

For more than three decades, the big policy issue in Texas concerning school districts has been school finance. Texas relies heavily on the local property tax collected by school districts to fund public education, with additional money from the state. As a result of this heavy reliance, Texas in some recent years has led the nation in local property tax increases. After protracted court battles in which property poor districts sought more equity in school funding, the legislature—under a Texas Supreme Court order to enact a constitutional school finance system—adopted a revised finance system in 1993. Dubbed the Robin Hood plan, it requires school districts with above average property wealth to share tax revenue with poorer districts. In 2006, the legislature modified the system, after the courts had again declared the system unconstitutional.[54]

charter schools
Public schools that have flexibility from state regulations in order to encourage innovation in educational programs.

TOWARD REFORM: Local Government and Politics in Texas

★ **7.5 . . . Assess the prospects for reforms of local government and politics in Texas.**

This chapter has examined the roots of local government in Texas, how the governments are structured, and how the politics have worked. The state legislature, the state's voters (through constitutional amendments), and local governments and voters are constantly considering reforms of local government structures, politics, and policies. Should counties be granted greater powers to respond to suburban and ex-urban sprawl? Does Texas need all the county officials that the constitution mandates? What taxing authority should special districts be allowed? Reform debates, though, are usually focused on specific governments and specific problems, rather than general reforms.

At-Large Versus Single-Member Districts

In Austin, the city council is elected in an at-large-by-place system. As other cities shifted to single-member districts (often by court order) in an attempt to provide more equal (and diverse) representation, Austin successfully resisted such reforms. It did so by an informal "gentleman's agreement" to reserve one seat for African American candidates and one for Mexican American candidates. Indeed, for thirty years, the council has had one African American and one Mexican American member. On several occasions, pressure built to the point of triggering charter-revision elections to force a single-member district system. Each time, voters defeated the proposals. In 2008, city council member Mike Martinez spearheaded an effort to again call an election on a single-member district plan. This time, however, the African American community was divided over such a reform proposal. By 2008, the Hispanic population of Austin had grown proportionally, while the African American population was a smaller percentage of the total population (and more diffuse); thus, it might be difficult to draw district lines in a way to create a majority African American district. Conceivably, single-member districts could result in the loss of any African American representation on the council. Austin's charter revision proposals for single-member districts failed to come to a vote in 2008.

Land-Use Regulation

The 1990s reforms of land-use regulation led to marginally greater county power to pass ordinances for platting and subdivision controls. Marginal change in county powers is likely the most change that will happen, given the power dimensions in land-use policies. In another arena affecting counties, recent efforts to abolish some county offices for specific counties may continue. In 2007, though, the legislature and the state's voters went further by amending the constitution to abolish the position of hide inspector that had been in place since the adoption of the constitution in 1876.

Public School Funding

The question of how best to fund public schools in Texas also often triggers heated political and policy debates over what changes are truly reforms of the system and what changes are patchwork efforts to fix an immediate problem without altering the overall picture. Inevitably, these debates involve school districts. The most recent legal battle involving the wealthier districts, the poorer districts, and state government in 2005–2006 resulted in legislators reducing local property taxes without increasing overall education funding. And, they didn't fix the basic school funding problem. Many experts expect still another lawsuit over school funding to be filed in the near future.

E-Government

For many contemporary Texans, accessing their governments by the Internet is commonplace and expected, but it wasn't too long ago that a citizen had to go to the courthouse or city hall to learn about the agenda of a governing body. Tax and property records could only be reviewed at the courthouse. Information about public projects or public services often required direct contact with an employee of a public agency. It was difficult to determine who was in charge of a particular program and responsible for its implementation. In some jurisdictions, record keeping was manual and often poorly organized. Fires had devastating effects, with many government records being destroyed.

Computer technology has changed much of this, and the buzzword for many of the applications of technology in the public sector is e-government, the expanded use of technologies in government operations and the disbursement of information to the general public. Local governments, encouraged by their professional associations, quickly latched on to these new technologies to improve their performance and provide greater access to their citizens. Not only can bills, fees, or fines be paid over the Internet, information about public services is more accessible.

In some instances, public employees are losing their jobs or being deployed to perform expanded functions. While this has led to some cost savings, there has also been a change in the attitude of many government employees toward citizens. Some city leaders now speak of citizens as customers, and an underlying dimension of the use of new technologies is greater accessibility, responsiveness, and accountability.

What Should I Have LEARNED?

Now that you have read this chapter, you should be able to:

⭐ **7.1 Trace the historical development and constitutional roots of local government in Texas, p. 208.**

The local governments formed in Texas by Spain and Mexico influenced the creation of the first counties under the Republic of Texas. Municipal governments in the early period of the state were shaped by the English legacy of local governments. Local governments are the creation of the state and derive their authority and powers from the state. They are not autonomous or sovereign. The provisions of the Constitution of 1876 along with extensive provisions in the Local Government Code provide for the varied structures of local governments.

⭐ **7.2 Outline the general structure of county governments and the responsibilities of elected officials, p. 210.**

The general structure of county government is spelled out in the state's constitution, which was adopted at a time when less than 10 percent of the population lived in urban areas. Designed to serve the needs of a rural population, county government has been difficult to refocus on the urban needs of the state. In part, county governments are the administrative arms of the state, assigned specific functions by the state government. Local issues or problems also fall under the jurisdiction of the counties, but the counties have no power to address many of these

issues. Reflecting the concerns of the constitutional framers, county government is complex and highly fragmented with a number of elected officials.

⭐ **7.3 Differentiate among the various forms of city governments and how they are governed, p. 216.**

Texas is a highly urban state, with more than 1,200 cities. Most of these cities are small, but three are among the ten largest cities in the nation. Cities with fewer than 5,000 residents, called general-law cities, are limited to exercising the authority granted them by the state, while the constitution grants larger cities home-rule authority. A home-rule city chooses a form of government based on local conditions or perceived needs. Election systems vary across the state, but one distinguishing feature is nonpartisanship—candidates running for city councils do not run as Democrats or Republicans. Most cities still use at-large elections with a number of variations, but armed with the federal Voting Rights Act, minority plaintiffs have filed lawsuits forcing many cities to adopt single-member districts. In recent years, changes in election systems have increased the number of Hispanics and African Americans serving on city councils.

⭐ **7.4 Identify the functions of special districts and the reasons for their creation, p. 227.**

Approximately 3,400 special districts have been created in Texas to provide functions or services not assigned to counties or cities. In some instances, a special district is created to perform a single function. In other instances, special districts have multiple government functions. There are also special districts that serve multiple counties. The best-known type of special district is the school district.

⭐ **7.5 Assess the prospects for reforms of local government and politics in Texas, p. 230.**

Across the state, cities continue to revisit the issue of their forms of government. With increased population, a city has additional options for its governmental structure.

Whether precipitated by lawsuits or state legislation, there are ongoing changes in local election systems. Periodically, the issue of county home rule is raised, and with increased urbanization, the issue is likely to come up again. Increased financial pressures coupled with a limited number of tax sources have prompted local governments to seek new revenue sources. Often, cities need to rely on permissive legislation enacted by the state.

Test Yourself: Local Governments

⭐ **7.1 Trace the historical development and constitutional roots of local government in Texas, p. 208.**

The prevailing legal theory upon which the status of local government is derived is known as

A. the unified doctrine of local government.
B. the dispersal theory of local government.
C. Dillon's rule.
D. the Marshall rule.
E. the Local Government rule.

⭐ **7.2 Outline the general structure of county governments and the responsibilities of elected officials, p. 210.**

Which of the following is not a constitutionally defined county office?
A. County judge
B. Sheriff
C. District or county attorney
D. County administrator
E. County treasurer

⭐ **7.3 Differentiate among the various forms of city governments and how they are governed, p. 216.**

If a city's population exceeds 5,000, it can choose to become a
A. general-law city with no limits on its taxing authority.
B. type A city limited to a mayor-council form of government.
C. home-rule city with the authority to choose whatever form of government it wants.
D. special district with multiple functions.
E. type C city with unlimited powers except those that conflict with state law.

⭐ **7.4 Identify the functions of special districts and the reasons for their creation, p. 227.**

The most significant problem facing public school districts in Texas today is
A. their size.
B. the patchwork of irregular boundaries.
C. funding.
D. a declining school population.
E. the retirement of large numbers of teachers.

⭐ **7.5 Assess the prospects for reforms of local government and politics in Texas, p. 230.**

Minority representation on local governing bodies is most likely to increase when
A. cumulative voting is used.
B. place elections are held in lieu of at-large elections.
C. single-member districts are used.
D. partisan elections are used.
E. nonpartisan elections are used.

Essay Questions

1. Why do you think the Texas Constitution and the state legislature place so many restrictions on local governments?
2. What arguments can you advance for the consolidation of cities and counties in the highly urbanized areas of the state?
3. Why do most Texas cities prefer the weak mayor form of government to the strong mayor option?
4. Is the proliferation of special districts an inevitable by-product of the current structure of city and county governments in Texas?
5. Should school districts remain independent? Or, would schoolchildren and taxpayers be better served if city or county governments operated their local schools? Explain your answer.

Key Terms

annexation, p. 224
at-large-by-place, p. 226
charter schools, p. 229
city commission, p. 218
commissioners court, p. 212
council–manager, p. 218
county attorney, p. 213
county auditor, p. 215
county clerk, p. 213
county commissioner, p. 212
county judge, p. 212
county tax assessor-collector, p. 215

county treasurer, p. 215
cumulative voting, p. 227
district attorney (DA), p. 213
district clerk, p. 213
extraterritorial jurisdiction (ETJ),
   p. 224
general-law cities, p. 217
general obligation bonds, p. 223
general ordinance-making authority,
   p. 215
home rule, p. 209
Local Government Code, p. 215

municipal corporation, p. 208
proportional representation, p. 227
regressive tax, p. 221
revenue bonds, p. 223
sheriff, p. 213
single-member districts, p. 226
strong mayor–council, p. 218
Texas Association of Counties,
   p. 210
Texas Municipal League, p. 221
weak mayor–council, p. 218

To Learn More on Local Governments

In the Library

Blodgett, Terrell. *Texas Home Rule Charters.* Austin: Texas Municipal League, 1994.

Brooks, David B. *Texas Practice: County and Special District Law,* 2d vols. 35, 36, and 36A. St. Paul, MN: West, 2010.

Collier, Ken, Steven Galatas, and Julie Harrelson-Stephens. *Lone Star Politics: Tradition and Transformation in Texas.* Washington, D.C. CQ Press, 2008.

Halter, Gary. *Government and Politics of Texas.* 6 ed. New York: McGraw-Hill, 2004.

Hanson, Royce. *Civic Culture and Urban Change: Governing Dallas.* Detroit, MI: Wayne State University Press, 2003.

Hill, Patricia E. *Dallas: The Making of a Modern City.* Austin: University of Texas Press, 1996.

Orum, Anthony. *Power, Money, and the People: The Making of Modern Austin,* rev. ed. Houston: Gulf, 1991.

Perrenod, Virginia Marion. *Special Districts, Special Purposes: Fringe Governments and Urban Problems in the Houston Area.* College Station: Texas A&M Press, 1984.

Rosales, Rodolfo. *The Illusion of Inclusion: The Untold Story of San Antonio.* Austin: University of Texas Press, 2000.

Saxe, Allan A. *Politics of a Texas City: Arlington, Texas, an Era of Continuity and Growth.* Austin, TX: Eakin, 2001.

Scarbrough, Linda. *Road, River, and Ol' Boy Politics: A Texas County's Path from Farm to Supersuburb.* Austin, TX: Texas State Association, 2005.

Sibley, Joel. *Storm over Texas: The Annexation Controversy and the Road to Civil War.* New York: Oxford University Press, 2005

Tannahill, Neal. *American and Texas Government: Policy and Politics.* 10 ed. New York: Longman Publishing, 2010.

Texas Association of School Boards. *A Guide to Texas School Finances.* Austin, TX: TASB, 2010.

———. *Guide for School Board Candidates.* Austin, TX: TASB, 2010.

On the Web

To learn more about the Texas Association of Counties, located in Austin, go to **www.county.org.**

To learn more about the Texas Municipal League, which advocates before the Texas Legislature and state agencies on behalf of Texas cities, go to **www.tml.org.**

To learn more about the Texas Association of School Boards, which represents the 1,000-plus school boards in Texas, go to **www.tasb.org.**

To learn more about the National Civic League, which has long been an advocate for reforms of local government and increased participation of citizens, go to **www.ncl.org.**

8

Public Policy in Texas

After five months of slogging through 6,000 pieces of legislation; countless hours meeting with constituents, lobbyists, and staff; and thousands of hours of committee work, the Texas Legislature adjourned in 2009.

In many ways, the governor and legislators had conducted business much like they always had. The governor had announced his policy proposals in his State of the State message to the legislature, and individual legislators had filed bills (proposed laws) on hundreds of subjects. In between all the committee hearings and debates on the House and Senate floors, the governor and legislators were being lobbied privately by special interest groups trying to pass or kill specific pieces of legislation and by state agency heads seeking new authority and increased funding. Much of the activity, particularly the most controversial wrangling, was covered in the media, but most of

the decision making happened behind closed doors.

By the end of the session, the vast majority of the proposed laws had died. But some 1,700 bills had been enacted, including hundreds of local bills that had generated little controversy, and the new state budget, which determined the state's spending priorities for the next two years. There were some clear winners and losers among state agencies, local governments, and interest groups.

The public policy challenges Texas faces today related to poverty, pollution, crime, education, a clogged transportation system, and an outdated tax structure are similar to challenges faced by other states. With much difficulty, Texas survived the collapse of its traditional oil-based economy and then the collapse of its real estate industry in the 1980s. As the economy diversified and the

There is expanding evidence of Texas government in public policy making. Numerous state agencies have been created by the Texas Legislature in recent years to implement new policies. Many are housed in office buildings near the state Capitol. The Capitol in the 1920s is shown at left and from the present-day at right.

state emerged as a major player in the global economy, state government spent billions of taxpayer dollars on major improvements in prison and mental health facilities and a more equitable distribution of public education dollars. Reluctantly, Texas political leaders finally accepted the scientific evidence that the state faces major environmental problems, and with a population now over 25 million, Texans across the state are playing a hard-scrabble game for access to finite sources of water.

Decisions made decades ago to invest in alternatives to an energy-based economy have helped transform the economy of Texas into the third largest in the nation. Economic diversification across the state has served as a buffer to economic downturns. Texas has not avoided recessions, but it has been able to weather economic downturns better than most states. While perceived regressive by many of its critics, the state's tax system has served to attract new industries.

Policy making is often associated with the Texas Legislature, but all branches of the government—including the courts—share some role in the process. The governor shapes policies through the proposals submitted to the legislature. Bureaucracies make policy when they write procedures to implement the actions of the legislature. They also shape policy in the day-to-day administration of programs. And the courts shape policy in their interpretation and application of laws.

What Should I Know About . . .

After reading this chapter, you should be able to:

★ **8.1** Trace the evolution of public policy in Texas, p. 236.

★ **8.2** Identify the multiple approaches to public policy analysis, p. 237.

★ **8.3** Analyze the state's budget-setting process and its central role in all public policy, p. 241.

★ **8.4** Evaluate current policies affecting funding, equity, and access to quality education in the areas of both public and higher education, p. 248.

★ **8.5** Describe the policy challenges Texas faces in the areas of criminal justice, health and human services, and the environment, p. 255.

★ **8.6** Characterize public policy reforms Texas has implemented to address contemporary challenges, p. 265.

S ystematic analysis of the decisions of policy makers can give the impression that policy making is a rational, thoughtful process. In some respects, it is. But the more cynical observer might argue that policy making is analogous to making sausages or hot dogs—they might taste good, but you don't want to see what goes in them or how they are made.

In this chapter, we will look at contemporary public policy in Texas from a number of perspectives.

- First, we will explore *the roots of public policy in Texas*.

- Second, we will examine *approaches to policy analysis*.

- Third, we will analyze *the budgetary process* and its central role in public policy in Texas.

- Fourth, we will explore current *educational policies and politics* in Texas.

- Fifth, we will examine several *other policy challenges facing Texas today* in the areas of criminal justice, health and human services, and the environment.

- Finally, we will turn our attention to *prospects for reform in the policy-making process* to address contemporary challenges.

ROOTS OF Public Policy in Texas

⭐ **8.1** . . . Trace the evolution of public policy in Texas.

Texans expect their governments to solve many of the problems they and their communities face, as do citizens across the nation. During the state's formative period, governments performed limited functions, with security—protecting Texans from potential military incursions and hostile American Indians—a top priority. As settlers put down roots, property ownership became important, and laws were required to define ownership, the means of disposing of land, and water and mineral rights. For these laws to be effective, courts and courthouses had to be authorized and funded. With an ever-increasing population and the emergence of a complex economy, governments inevitably expanded their functions.

Some elements of earlier Spanish and Mexican law still can be found in the present day Texas Constitution and state laws, including community property laws. A woman retains the right to property owned prior to marriage and retains a legal right to property acquired during a marriage. In the case of a divorce, one-half of the community property is hers.

All Texas constitutions have included homestead provisions. As early as 1829, when Texas was still part of Mexico, the legislature of Coahuila and Texas enacted a law that exempted one's domicile from seizure by a creditor. Expanded to apply to many new circumstances, the homestead principle has shaped a great deal of property law in Texas.[1]

With Texas's population now exceeding 25 million, water has taken on increased significance as a policy issue, and old laws and traditions are being challenged. Groundwater, or water below the ground, now provides about 60 percent of the water used by Texans. But the "rule of capture," a holdover from the rural era, still governs access to this limited resource. Simply stated, this rule provides that "landowners have the legal right to capture and pump unlimited quantities of water beneath their land, without liability to surrounding landowners."[2] Some wonder how long a growing state with competing water needs can afford to keep this policy.

Many issues the state now faces already have been confronted by policy makers but must be readdressed as conditions and circumstances change. For example, public education was an issue leading to the War of Independence from Mexico in 1836, and it surfaced again in the Reconstruction period. It resurfaced in 1949 with legislation for state funding of local school districts, and it has been a recurring policy controversy since the late 1960s. There also are new issues—such as global warming, toxic waste, and terrorism.

Approaches to Policy Analysis

★ **8.2** . . . Identify the multiple approaches to public policy analysis.

Political scientists and policy analysts, rooted in many different academic disciplines, spend a lot of time defining public policy and all its critical elements. But we will use the definition developed by Thomas Dye, who defined public policy as "whatever governments choose to do or not to do."[3]

Except for an occasional federal judge, individuals acting alone haven't forced many changes in public policy. The political power necessary to shape policy is exercised through groups and organizations—both in the private and public sectors. As noted throughout this book, some groups or interests have been more influential than others. Within the framework of policy analysis, there often are winners and losers when public officials act or refuse to act.

We have chosen to organize our discussion of policy issues using a perspective of policy-making as a process. There is logic and simplicity to this model, in that it tracks policy making in terms of a chronology of actions, from problem recognition and definition through the evaluation of a policy. Moreover, the concept of policy making as an ongoing process provides for the possibility of future action, even after a policy has been adopted. Policies often have unintended consequences that may present additional problems, funding may be inadequate, or in some cases, it takes time for policy makers—or the citizens a policy affects—to realize that the wrong solution has been applied to a particular problem.

Models of the Policy-making Process

In earlier chapters, we also introduced iron triangles and policy networks, two concepts that have been used by political scientists to analyze the many players in policy making. Just as is true at the national level, there are "relatively stable relationships and patterns of interaction"[4] that occur among state agencies, legislative committees and subcommittees, and interest groups—the so-called iron triangles. Given the limitations of this concept, policy analysts have turned to "policy networks," a concept developed by Hugh Heclo, in which policies are developed and implemented in a complex arena of players, including interest groups, think tanks, foundations, policy specialists, academics, government agencies at all levels, and the mass media.[5] From this perspective, public policies occur in a fluid, less well-defined environment with players moving in and out of the process. The policy network concept is more difficult to observe and measure, but it can provide a more comprehensive assessment of what occurs.

The Policy Process

THE ELEMENTS OF PUBLIC POLICY   Setting public policy usually involves questions of costs and benefits. The ultimate political problems to resolve are who will benefit from specific policy decisions and who will pay the bill.[6] Certain groups, businesses, or individuals receive direct benefits from governmental decisions—benefits that are paid for by other individuals through taxes. In this process there is, in effect, a transfer of money from one segment of the population to another. Critical decisions must be made on the allocation of the tax burden, which will inevitably produce intense political conflict.

Public policies also provide indirect benefits. Although low-income Texans may receive the direct benefits of welfare assistance, job training programs, and subsidized housing and health care, the entire population eventually stands to gain if the poverty cycle is interrupted. Similar arguments can be made for funding equity between poor and rich school districts. The state's economic growth and future prosperity will be adversely affected and its crime rate will rise if serious problems of illiteracy and school dropouts aren't successfully addressed now.

Public policy also includes regulation of the private sector. Indiscriminate use of land, water, and other natural resources has been curtailed by environmental policies seeking to protect the best interests of the state as a whole. But those policies often conflict with property rights and spark angry responses from some businesses and other private property owners, who threaten political retaliation against public officeholders.

Additionally, public policy affects the governmental process itself. Decisions on political redistricting, revisions in election laws, and changes in the structure and organization of state and local governments ultimately address the issue of how power is distributed. They help determine how many people will be able to achieve their personal and collective objectives and improve their lives.

Another dimension of public policy is rooted in the notion of the general good of the community. Related to the concept of indirect benefits, it reflects the values upon which a political culture is based. Whether defined in terms of "it's the right thing to do" or a more systematic theory of the bonds that create the political community, there are elements of public policy that reflect the common needs or interests of those who live in the state.

THE STAGES OF PUBLIC POLICY   There are many activities in the private sector that bear on public policy, such as a decision by a large corporation to close its operations in a city. But the following discussion focuses on the governmental institutions that make binding and enforceable decisions affecting all those who live in the state.[7]

A number of scholars have approached policymaking as a sequential process (Table 8.1). Although this approach may suggest artificial start and stop points, the process is dynamic and continuous.

People have to identify a problem before they can expect the government's help in resolving it.[8] Subsequent steps in the policymaking process include gaining access to public officials, getting a solution drawn up and adopted, seeing it carried out, and evaluating its effectiveness.

People in a particular neighborhood, for example, may experience an increase in respiratory problems. Right away, they suspect a nearby chemical plant, and their suspicions are reinforced every time winds blow across the neighborhood from the direction

Table 8.1 *Stages of the Policy Process*

Stages of the Process	Actions Taken
Identification and Formation of an Issue	Defining a common problem and building coalitions to force the issue on the public agenda.
Access and Representation	Gaining access to elected or administrative officials and getting them to see the problem.
Formulation	Getting those in government to initiate action on the problem by sifting through alternative solutions.
Adoption or Legitimation	The government's specific solution to the problem, including the authorization of programs and allocation of funds.
Implementation	The application of the government's policy to the problem.
Evaluation	Assessing the effects of the policy and determining if its objectives were achieved.

Sources: Charles O. Jones, *An Introduction to the Study of Public Policy,* 2nd ed. (North Scituate, MA: Duxbury Press, 1977), and James E. Anderson, David W. Brady, Charles S. Bullock III, and Joseph Stewart Jr., *Public Policy and Politics in America,* 2nd ed. (Monterey, CA: Brooks/Cole Publishing Company, 1984).

of the plant. After complaints to the plant manager bring no satisfaction—or relief—the unhappy neighbors turn to government. To make sure they are heard, they identify others affected by the same problem and join forces in a citizens' group. Such groups are central to the policymaking process. By banding together, people increase their financial resources, leadership capabilities, and political strength.

Their next step is to find the governmental body or agency that can address the problem and then convince it to do so. They may first approach the city council, only to learn that state laws and regulations govern emissions from the plant. They may then turn to the Texas Commission on Environmental Quality, which may determine that the plant is violating its state permit and may impose an administrative fine or seek legal action by the attorney general. Or the commission may find its hands tied by a loophole in the state's anti–pollution laws. In that case, the concerned citizens need help from the legislature, where they have to convince their elected representatives to translate their concerns into a change in policy.

Simply identifying a problem and getting a large number of other people to share your concerns is not a solution. Solutions must be developed and enacted through specific laws, regulations, or other policy changes. Philosophically, there is little disagreement that every child in Texas should have access to a quality education. But what does that mean in practical political terms? Proposed solutions have been extremely diverse. Legislative staffs, blue ribbon committees, independent research organizations, academicians, and consultants from various points on the political spectrum have all contributed studies and opinions. The resolution of their differences is essentially a political process. In the final analysis, "successful policy formulations must deal with the question of selecting courses of action that can actually be adopted."[9]

The legislature is primarily responsible for sifting through proposed alternatives and setting policy at the state level. But the separation of powers doctrine under which our government operates gives the judiciary important scrutiny over legislative action—or inaction. In recent years, several major federal and state court decisions have forced the legislature to make far-reaching changes in education, criminal justice, and mental health and mental retardation programs. Those court orders have prompted some lawmakers and other critics to complain that the judiciary overstepped its authority and was attempting to preempt the legislature. Others believe, however, that the legislature had neglected its responsibilities and needed some prodding.

Virtually every public policy has a cost. It is not enough for the legislature to create a program. Programs have to be funded, or they are meaningless. Sometimes, the legislature requires local governments to pick up the tab, but most programs have to compete with hundreds of other programs for a limited number of state tax dollars. Thus, the state's complex budgetary process is at the heart of policymaking and is closely monitored by individuals and organizations interested in policy development. Conflicts over the budgetary process can be very intense.

Once legislation has been enacted and funded, its specific provisions must be implemented, or carried out. Much of this activity is the responsibility of state and local agencies that have been created to carry "a program to the problem."[10] Earlier political scientists referred to this stage of the policy process as public administration, and much of it falls within the domain of administrative agencies and departments. But government bureaucrats aren't the only ones involved in carrying out policy. So are legislators, judges, interest groups and nonprofit organizations. The activities in this implementation phase include:

Interpretation—the translation of program language into acceptable and feasible directives;

Organization—the establishment of organizational units and standard operating procedures for putting a program into effect; and

Application—the routine provision of services, payments, or other agreed-upon program objectives or instruments.[11]

Governments spend a lot of time evaluating the effects of public policy. In Texas, this is called performance review (see **chapter 5**). An enormous amount of information is gathered to determine if programs have met stated goals and, if not, what changes or adjustments are required. Legislative committees, in their oversight function, demand information from agencies to help determine whether to continue to fund programs, expand them, or change them. With an eye on future funding, agencies also spend considerable resources assessing the impact of their own activities and performance. Program evaluation also is part of the broader issue of accountability of public officials and their responsiveness to the needs, demands, and expectations of their constituents. Interest groups, think tanks, scholars, and the news media also actively participate in this phase of the policy process.

Program assessment and evaluation become the basis for future policy and funding decisions. We have found some comprehensive solutions to a limited number of problems, including some diseases, but most governmental policy produces only limited or partial solutions. Problems and issues are ongoing, and policymakers often have to adjust or redirect their efforts at problem-solving. A solution enacted today can produce additional problems requiring further attention tomorrow. As we will discuss later in this chapter, for example, recent changes in public education policies and funding are part of a long history of efforts to improve the quality of education in Texas.

Players in the Policy Process

Any individual can participate in the policy process through any number of channels. There are thousands of players in the policy arenas of state and local governments, including bureaucrats, the courts, interest groups, businesses, the news media, and policy specialists. Although some of these have a broad perspective on state policy and a wide range of policy interests, most have narrow and highly specialized interests. One way to think about the relationships among policy participants is to "identify the clusters of individuals that effectively make most of the routine decisions in a given substantive area of policy."[12]

issue networks
The loose and informal relationships that exist among a large number of actors who work in broad policy areas.

There are hundreds of these subsystems or policy **issue networks** in state government, and it is often difficult to sort out how policy decisions were made and who was most influential in the final outcome. For example, there are individuals such as James Leininger, a San Antonio physician who made a fortune from his design of a hospital bed, and Bob Perry (no relation to Governor Rick Perry), a wealthy builder, who have given millions in campaign contributions to influence public policy. Leininger also started the Texas Public Policy Foundation, an organization committed to conservative policy issues. Although inferences can be drawn, it often is difficult to demonstrate their specific role or impact in policy decisions.

The policy process also is increasingly dominated by specialists who may be identified with interest groups, corporations, legislative committees, or administrative agencies. These experts, or "technopols," understand the technical nature of a problem and, more importantly, the institutional, political, and personal relationships of those involved in trying to solve it.[13] Yet, these individuals do not seek publicity or credit for their work, and much of their influence in policy decisions goes unreported.

Federal policies directly impact the policies of Texas through mandates, preemptions, and grants-in-aid, and state policy makers are in ongoing conversations with employees of federal agencies as well as members of Congress. Add to this mix a number of organizations such as the National Governors Association, the Council of State Governments, and the U.S. Conference of Mayors. Not only do these organizations actively seek to influence federal policies that affect state and local governments, they assist states in formulating public policy and developing interstate cooperation. Hence changes in tax law, health care, public education, and other public policy areas are generally a product of a "kaleidoscopic interaction of changing issue networks."[14]

The Budgetary Process

⭐ **8.3** . . . Analyze the state's budget-setting process and its central role in all public policy.

Balancing a new state budget in the face of a $10 billion revenue shortfall was the legislature's most difficult task in 2003, and that regular session of the legislature was the most difficult budgetary session in a dozen years. With Republicans in charge of the statehouse, the new budget was written without increasing state taxes, but fees for numerous state services were increased and funding was cut for health care and many other important programs. Lawmakers for the first time also allowed university regents to raise tuition without legislative approval, and the costs of attending public universities in Texas soon began to soar. The Republican approach to bridging the revenue shortfall differed from how the legislature had resolved the most significant, previous budgetary crisis in 1991, when Democrats still held the governor's office and a majority of both legislative houses. The legislature balanced the 1991 budget with some cuts and other cost-savings steps plus a $2.7 billion package of tax and fee increases. The legislature, with voter approval, also created the Texas lottery that year as a future revenue source. With the exception of 2003, Texas lawmakers wrote state budgets from 1993 through 2009 without raising state taxes, but they put more stress on an already strained budget and tax system. Moreover, it took several billion dollars in federal economic stimulus funds to help lawmakers avoid higher state taxes or significant cuts in services in 2009 and 2010.

Like most other states and unlike the federal government, Texas operates on a pay-as-you-go basis that prohibits **deficit financing**. The comptroller must certify that each budget can be paid for with anticipated revenue from taxes, fees, and other sources. And, like other states, Texas greatly increased its spending on state government programs in the 1970s, 1980s, and 1990s. Population growth and inflation were major factors, in addition to federal mandates and court orders for prison and education reforms.

The biggest share of state expenditures (including federal funds appropriated by the legislature) is for education, which accounted for approximately 41 percent of the 2010–2011 budget. Health and human services, which has seen a significant boost in recent years from increased Medicaid spending but suffered other cuts in the 2003 session, was second at 33 percent. Business and economic development accounted for 11 percent. (To learn more about general categories of state spending, see Figure 8.1.)

The two-year 2010–2011 state budget totaled $182 billion, an increase of about $94 billion over the 2000–2001 budget. Legislative budget experts say increases in federal programs and mandates and federal court orders have accounted for much of the recent increase in state spending.

deficit financing
Borrowing money to meet operating expenses. It is prohibited by the Texas Constitution, which says that state government must operate on a pay-as-you-go basis.

Two-Year Budgets

The Texas Legislature's budget-writing problems are compounded by the length of the budget period and the structure of the budget itself. Because the Texas Constitution provides that the legislature meet in regular session only every other year, lawmakers must write two-year, or biennial, budgets for state government. That means state agencies, which begin preparing their budget requests several months before a session convenes, have to anticipate some of their spending needs three years in advance.

The governor and legislative leaders have the authority between legislative sessions to transfer funds between programs and agencies to meet some emergencies. The governor proposes transfers to the Legislative Budget Board (LBB), a ten-member panel that includes the lieutenant governor, the speaker, and eight key legislators. The LBB can accept, reject, or modify the governor's proposal and can propose budgetary changes to the governor.

Figure 8.1 *What were the state appropriations for the 2010–2011 biennium?*

Source: Legislative Budget Board, *Summary of Conference Committee Report for Senate Bill 1,* May 2009.

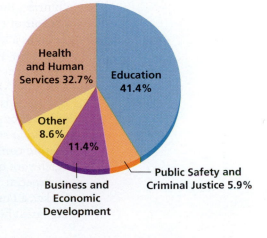

Education 41.4%
Health and Human Services 32.7%
Other 8.6%
11.4%
Business and Economic Development
Public Safety and Criminal Justice 5.9%

Agencies submit their biennial appropriations, or spending, requests to the Legislative Budget Board. After its staff reviews the requests, the LBB normally recommends a budget that the full legislature uses as a starting point in its budgetary deliberations.

Dedicated Funds

The legislature's control over the budget-setting process is further restricted by legal requirements that dedicate or set aside a major portion of state revenue for specific purposes, leaving legislators with discretion over only about one-half of total appropriations. These required expenditures include federal funds earmarked for specific purposes by the federal government or monies dedicated to specific uses by the state constitution or state law. The state treasury has more than 500 separate funds, including many that are dedicated to highways, education, parks, teacher retirement, and dozens of other specific purposes. These restrictions hamper the legislature, particularly during lean periods. But the dedicated funds are jealously guarded by the interest groups that benefit from them, and many funds have become "sacred cows" that most legislators dare not try to change.

dedicated funds
Constitutional or statutory requirements that restrict some state tax or fee revenues to spending on specific programs.

One of the major **dedicated funds** is the Highway Trust Fund, which automatically gets three-fourths of the revenue from the motor fuels tax. Under the Texas Constitution, revenue in that fund can be spent only to purchase right of way for highways or to construct, maintain, and police highways. The remainder of the motor fuels tax revenue goes to public education. Any legislative proposal to tap into the highway fund for other state needs would be fought by a strong lobbying effort from highway contractors as well as business leaders, mayors, and county judges with local road projects they wanted completed.

Other major dedicated funds include the Permanent School Fund and the Permanent University Fund, land- and mineral-rich endowments that help support the public schools and boost funding for the University of Texas and Texas A&M University systems. In 1991, the legislature, working with the comptroller, began consolidating and eliminating many funds, but constitutionally dedicated funds cannot be changed without voter approval.

The State's Regressive Tax System

A 2009 study by Citizens for Tax Justice and the Institute on Taxation and Economic Policy ranked Texas's tax system among the ten most regressive in the country. Texas's system is based largely on the sales tax, the local property tax, and fees that consume a larger portion of the incomes of the poor and the middle classes than the upper class. (To learn more about the regressive impact of the state's tax system, see Table 8.2.) Based on this study's calculations, state and local governments in Texas taxed poor families at 12.2 percent of their incomes and middle-class families at 7.6 percent. By contrast, the wealthiest Texans (the richest 1 percent of the families) paid only 3.3 percent of their incomes in state and local taxes. Political leaders have long touted Texas as a low-tax state, but, according to this study, that is only from the perspective of wealthy Texans.[15]

STATE TAXES   The legislature enacted a hybrid corporate income tax in 1991, but Texas is one of only nine states without a personal income tax, and public and political opposition to that revenue source remained high.[16] Each budgetary crisis seemed to stretch the existing tax structure to the breaking point, only to see the legislature come up with another patch. Critics compared the tax structure to an ugly patchwork quilt that had been stitched together over the years to accommodate various special interest groups and cover an assortment of emergencies. Senator Carl Parker, a Port Arthur Democrat, argued in Senate floor debate in 1991: "They (existing taxes) hit the poor people worse than they do rich folks. They let some people off

Table 8.2 *What are the ten most regressive state tax systems?* *

State	State Taxes as a % of Income on		
	Poorest 20%	Middle 60%	Top 1%
Washington	17.3%	9.5%	2.9%
Florida	13.5	7.8	2.6
South Dakota	11.0	6.9	2.1
Tennessee	11.7	7.6	3.3
Texas	**12.2**	**7.6**	**3.3**
Illinois	13.0	9.7	4.9
Arizona	12.5	8.5	5.6
Nevada	8.9	6.1	2.0
Pennsylvania	11.3	8.9	5.0
Alabama	10.2	8.6	4.8

Note: States are ranked by the ITEP Tax Inequality Index. The ten states in the table are those whose tax systems most increase income inequality after taxes compared to before taxes.
Source: Carl Davis, et al., *Who Pays? A Distributional Analysis of the Tax Systems of All 50 States,* 3rd. ed. (Washington, DC: Institute on Taxation and Economic Policy, 2009).
*Ranking reflects the composite of the ratios of the taxes paid by the poor to those of the rich.

scot-free, while they tax others heavily. And the direction we seem to be going is worse, not better."[17]

SALES TAXES   In 1961, the legislature, over the objections of Governor Price Daniel, enacted the state's first **sales tax.** Its initial rate was 2 percent of the cost of purchased goods. The rate has since been increased several times, and in 2010, the statewide sales tax rate was 6.25 percent, lower than rates in nine other states, including California.[18] In the Texas metropolitan areas, where city and mass transportation authority taxes of 1 percent each are added to the state tax, the total sales tax is 8.25 percent. The sales tax generated $21 billion in 2009, which was 25 percent of the state's major taxes.[19]

sales tax
A tax charged as a set percentage of most retail purchases and many services. It is the main source of tax revenue for state government in Texas and an important source of revenue for many cities and metropolitan transit authorities.

With each financial crisis, it becomes more difficult politically for the legislature to raise the sales tax rate. And even though groceries and medicine are tax-exempt, critics charge that the sales tax is regressive because it affects low-income Texans disproportionately more than wealthier citizens. Moreover, the sales tax is heavily weighted toward products and leaves many services—including legal and medical fees and advertising—untaxed. Thus, sales tax revenue doesn't automatically grow with the state's economy, because the Texas economy is becoming more and more service-oriented.

BUSINESS TAXES   The franchise tax, which was overhauled in 1991 and became a hybrid corporate income tax, for many years was the state's major business tax. It applied only to corporations, which were taxed on their income or assets, whichever was greater. The tax didn't cover partnerships or sole proprietorships and was paid by fewer than 200,000 of the state's 2.5 million businesses. At the urging of Governor Rick Perry, the legislature in a special session in 2006 replaced the franchise tax with a broader-based business tax, which applied not only to corporations but also to professional partnerships, such as law firms, for the first time. The new business tax, which produced $4.3 billion in 2009, was part of a trade-off for lower school property taxes and was enacted in response to a Texas Supreme Court order for a new way of paying for public education. Although the smallest businesses were exempted from the tax, the new levy still raised taxes for many companies that had been paying little, if any, taxes under the franchise tax. In response to heavy criticism from small businesses, the legislature in 2009 raised the exemption even more.

PROPERTY TAXES   The biggest source of taxpayer dissatisfaction and anger in Texas in recent years has been the local property, or ad valorem, tax, the major source of revenue for 3,800 cities, counties, schools, and special districts. Total **property tax** levies

property tax
A tax on homes, businesses, and certain other forms of property that is the main source of revenue for local governments. The tax is based on the assessed value of the property.

increased by 246 percent between 1989 and 2008, from $11.3 billion to $39 billion, according to the state comptroller's office.[20] The largest increases have been in local school taxes, which have been significantly raised to pay for state-mandated education reforms and school finance requirements, including a law ordering the transfer of millions of dollars from wealthy to poor school districts (discussed later in this chapter).

SEVERANCE TAXES   Oil and gas severance taxes helped the legislature balance the budget with relative ease when oil prices were high in the 1970s. But energy-tax revenue slowed considerably after the energy industry crashed in the 1980s. Severance taxes accounted for 28 percent of state tax revenue in 1981, but only 5 to 6 percent in recent years.[21]

sin tax

A common nickname for a tax on tobacco or alcoholic beverages.

OTHER TAXES   State government also has several volume-based taxes, such as taxes on cigarettes, alcoholic beverages, and motor fuels. They have set rates per pack or per gallon and don't produce more revenue when inflation raises the price of the product. These taxes, particularly the so-called **sin taxes** on cigarettes and alcohol, have been raised frequently over the years and produced $2.4 billion in revenue in 2009.[22] The legislature raised the cigarette tax from 41 cents per pack to $1.41 per pack in 2006, but twenty states had pushed the tax higher by 2010.[23]

GAMBLING REVENUES   For years, Texas government maintained a strong moralistic opposition to gambling. Charitable bingo games were tolerated and eventually legalized. But the state constitution prohibited lotteries, and horse race betting was outlawed in the 1930s. After the oil bust in the 1980s, however, many legislators began to view gambling as a financial opportunity rather than a moral evil, and in key elections most Texas voters indicated they agreed.

lottery

A form of gambling, conducted by many states, in which participants purchase tickets that offer an opportunity to cash in on a winning number or set of winning numbers. Voters legalized a state lottery in Texas in 1991.

In a special session in 1986, when spending was cut and taxes were raised to compensate for lost revenue from plummeting oil prices, the legislature legalized local option, pari-mutuel betting on horse and dog races. Voters approved the measure the next year. In 1991, under strong pressure from Governor Ann Richards, the legislature approved a constitutional amendment to legalize a state **lottery,** which voters also endorsed that year. Limited casino gambling on cruise ships operating off the Texas coast also has been legalized by the legislature.

Gambling, however, has not been a panacea for the state's financial needs. Years after pari-mutuel betting had been approved, the horse and dog racing tracks still had not produced any significant revenue for the state treasury. Although the lottery began impressively, with sales of $4 billion in tickets in its first two years of operation, revenues since have lagged behind projections. Supporters of the game warned that the lottery couldn't necessarily be depended upon as a reliable, long-term revenue source, but in 1997, lawmakers dedicated lottery revenue to public education. The new law also ordered shortfalls in school funding from the lottery to be made up with tax dollars.[24] The lottery generated $1.6 billion for public education in 2009.[25]

All but two states permit some form of public or legalized gambling, which includes commercial casinos and Indian casinos. In Texas, however, there are no commercial casinos in the state, and the efforts of the state's three American Indian tribes to run casinos on their reservations have been challenged by state officials (see **chapter 1**).

Bonds: Build Now, Pay Later

Although the Texas Constitution has a general prohibition against state government going into debt to cover operating expenses, the state had about $34.1 billion in state bonds outstanding at the end of fiscal 2009. About $3.1 billion of the total would have to be paid off with tax dollars, while approximately $31 billion of the state debt was in the form of self-supporting revenue bonds.[26] Taxpayer-supported debt ballooned during tight budgetary periods when the legislature, prompted by federal court orders, used **general obligation bonds,** which are backed by state taxes, to finance the construction of prisons and mental health and mental retardation facilities. These expenses were submitted to the voters for approval in the form of constitutional amendments.

Some legislators have become increasingly uneasy about increasing the tax liability on future taxpayers. Interest on bonds can double the cost of a construction project, experts say. Debt service paid from taxes totaled $1.27 billion in the 2006–2007 biennium, according to the Legislative Budget Board.[27] Bond issues, however, have been widely supported by Democrats and Republicans, liberals and conservatives alike. In promoting a prison bond issue in 1989, Governor Bill Clements said, "If there ever was anything that was proper for us to bond, it's our prison system, where those facilities will be on-line and in use for a twenty-five or thirty-year period."[28]

Over the years, the state also has issued billions of dollars in bonds for such self-supporting programs as water development and veterans' assistance. Those programs use the state's credit to borrow money at favorable interest rates. The state lends that money to a local government to help construct a water treatment plant or to a veteran to help purchase land or a house, and the debt is repaid by the loan recipients, not by the state's taxpayers.

The state of Texas has increased its overall debt by 158 percent in the past ten years. Although the state's debt has grown at a faster clip than that of cities, there has been a similar pattern of increased debt of local governments, which now have a debt load of $160 billion.[29]

general obligation bonds

A method of borrowing money to pay for new construction projects, such as prisons or mental hospitals. Interest on these bonds, which require voter approval in the form of constitutional amendments, is paid with tax revenue.

Failed Efforts in the Pursuit of Tax Reform

Various liberal legislators and groups seeking more funding for state services have long advocated a state **income tax.** But until fairly recently, no major officeholder or serious candidate for a major office dared even hint at support for such a politically taboo alternative. Finally, in late 1989, then–Lieutenant Governor Bill Hobby broke the ice for serious discussion of the issue in a speech to the Texas Association of Taxpayers, whose members included executives of many of the major businesses in Texas. Hobby, who had already announced that he wouldn't seek reelection in 1990, proposed the enactment of a personal and corporate income tax, coupled with abolition of the corporate franchise tax and reductions in property and sales taxes. Hobby also told his audience that it would take the business community to convince the legislature to pass an income tax.

Lieutenant Governor Bob Bullock then shocked much of the political establishment by announcing in March 1991, less than two months after succeeding

income tax

A tax based on a corporation's or an individual's income. Texas is one of only a few states without a personal income tax.

Why are bonds popular in Texas? Bonds are popular because they enable Texas to pay for projects with projected state taxes. In 2007, voters—encouraged by Governor Rick Perry and cycling champion Lance Armstrong, a cancer survivor—approved $3 billion in bonds to boost state funding for cancer research.

Photo courtesy: AP/Wide World Photos

Hobby, that he would actively campaign for a state income tax. Bullock, a former state comptroller, said it was the only way to meet the state's present and future needs fairly and adequately while also providing relief from existing unpopular taxes. Bullock proposed making local school property taxes deductible from the income tax, and he recommended the repeal of the franchise tax.

But Bullock did not receive much support from interest groups. And the Texas House, which must initiate legislative action on tax bills, remained strongly opposed to an income tax, as did the governor, Democrat Ann Richards. Eventually, the legislature that year changed the corporate franchise tax to include the hybrid corporate income tax described earlier in this chapter, while holding the line against a personal income tax.

During the 1993 legislative session, Bullock pulled another surprise and proposed a constitutional amendment, which won easy legislative approval, to ban a personal income tax unless the voters approved one. Bullock probably had more than one reason for his apparent about-face. One obvious factor was that his 1994 reelection date was approaching, and he needed to defuse any political problems caused by his endorsement of an income tax two years earlier. Whatever Bullock's motivations, the amendment was overwhelmingly approved by Texas voters in November 1993, leaving many people convinced that a major revenue option had been removed from the state's budget picture for years to come. (To learn more about the debate over the income tax, see Join the Debate: Should Texas Adopt an Income Tax?)

Alternatives to Finding New Revenues

Recent recessionary periods in the state's economy have placed enormous pressures on governments as they address declining or interrupted revenues coupled with an increased population with expanding demands. Few citizens really like new taxes, but the conservative anti-tax, anti-government ethos of the state's political culture makes it extremely difficult to resolve the budget problems of the state and local governments. If new taxes are excluded as an option, where do government leaders look to find revenues to provide public services? State leaders throughout the country have been reexamining their delivery of public services to assure taxpayers they were getting the best possible return on their dollars. Texas was in the forefront of these efforts.

GOVERNMENT EFFICIENCY   In 1991, the Texas Legislature, facing a large revenue shortfall, instructed the state comptroller to supervise periodic performance reviews of all state agencies and programs with an eye toward eliminating inefficiency and mismanagement and producing savings. The comptroller also reviewed the budgets and operations of some local school districts. Billions of dollars in potential savings were identified over the next several years, and a number of the comptroller's recommendations were adopted by the legislature and school boards. The legislature transferred those programs from the comptroller's office to the Legislative Budget Board in 2003 after a series of budgetary disputes with Comptroller Carole Keeton Strayhorn. Performance reviews along with the sunset process (in which the continuing need for an agency is evaluated) continue to be used by the legislature.

INCREASING FEES INSTEAD OF TAXES   User fees and permits charged for public services plus licenses, fines, and other penalties generate some $7 billion over two years or more than 4 percent of the state's budget. Some—including the increased use of toll roads and higher tuition at state universities—are controversial, but most generate little opposition. Only campers, for example, are affected by higher fees for camping in state parks. Most people don't notice the higher water quality fees imposed by the

Join the DEBATE | Should Texas Adopt an Income Tax?

Texas is one of only a handful of states without a personal income tax. Although the tax system is touted as business-friendly and attractive to new investment, it also is regressive, falling disproportionately on lower income groups. With pressures building on the financing capacity of all governments in the state, the lucrative income tax seems to be a potential solution.

But political opposition to an income tax remains high. An additional hurdle is a constitutional requirement that any personal income tax be approved by voters, as well as by the legislature. If the legislature does decide to try to sell an income tax to voters, support from the business community will be crucial.

State government's ability to provide quality education, highways, and other public support systems is essential to the business community's long-term success. The sales tax was first adopted after the business lobby got behind it, but the state's new franchise tax is unpopular with many businesses, and business interests remain influential. Would adopting an income tax solve any of the state's financial woes? Would the business community support such a tax?

To develop an ARGUMENT FOR adoption of a state income tax, think about how:

- **Available tax sources are inadequate to meet current and future budget needs.** In what ways are current policies underfunded due to limited financial resources? How would the income tax allow the state to provide for the needs of new and expanding sectors of the economy?
- **Existing taxes are particularly susceptible to economic downturns, reducing revenues to governments.** How do recessionary periods impact sales tax revenue? What happens to tax revenues when property values decline? In what ways would an income tax be a more stable source of revenue?
- **The current tax system is regressive.** Is it fair that lower income Texans pay a higher percentage of their incomes in taxes than wealthier Texans? How would an income tax be more equitable?

To develop an ARGUMENT AGAINST adoption of a state income tax, think about how:

- **Opposition to an income tax in Texas historically has been strong.** If citizens have demonstrated their opposition to the personal income tax in the past, how likely is it that they will favor one now? If an income tax is adopted, won't citizens expect reductions in other taxes?
- **Texas is advertised as a low tax state.** How would introducing an income tax affect the decisions of new businesses considering relocation to Texas? In what ways would an income tax increase the costs of doing business, thus reducing the state's ability to attract new industries?
- **An income tax could result in more government spending.** What have numerous performance reviews shown about government waste and inefficiencies? In what ways would an income tax encourage government agencies to spend more?

What is this cartoonist trying to say?
In 1991, Lieutenant Governor Bob Bullock startled state political and business leaders when he proposed a state income tax. It was a proposal unpopular with most Texans.

Photo courtesy: John Branch, San Antonio Express-News

TIMELINE: Milestones in Contemporary Texas Public Policy

1949 Gilmer-Aikin Law—Texas enacts legislation to create the first systematic statewide funding of public schools.

1968 *Rodriquez* v. *San Antonio Independent School District*—This case, filed in federal court, initiates the battle over school funding.

1961 Sales Tax—Texas adopts a state sales tax.

1980 *Ruiz* v. *Estelle*—In this federal case conditions in the Texas prison system are declared unconstitutional.

Texas Commission on Environmental Quality on cities. The list of user fees is long, but it can be argued that such fees target people who benefit from specific public services. And many Texans prefer that approach to general tax increases.

Educational Policies and Politics

⭐ **8.4 . . . Evaluate current policies affecting funding, equity, and access to quality education in the areas of both public and higher education.**

More tax dollars are spent on education than any other governmental program in Texas. In 1949, the legislature enacted the Gilmer-Aikin law, which made major improvements in the administration of public education and significantly boosted funding for public schools, but it was soon outdated. By the 1970s, it was obvious that quality and equity were lacking in many classrooms. Thousands of functional illiterates were graduating from high school each year, and thousands of children in poor school districts were being shortchanged with substandard facilities and educational aids.

Public Education

Public elementary and secondary education in Texas is financed by a combination of state and local revenues, a system that produced wide disparities in education spending among the state's approximately 1,050 school districts. The only local source of operating revenues for school districts is the property tax. Districts with a wealth of oil production or expensive commercial property had high tax bases that enabled them to

1984 Major School Reforms—A new law passes, which includes new taxes, class size limits in the lower grades, and the "no pass, no play" rule for extracurricular activities.

2003 Tuition Deregulated—Tuition is deregulated at state universities, resulting in a significant increase in student costs at public institutions.

1996 Temporary Assistance for Needy Families—A federal law creates a new public assistance program that results in a significant reduction in people on welfare in Texas.

2011 Revenue Shortfall—The Texas Legislature faces a large revenue shortfall, which threatens cuts in funding for many state programs.

raise large amounts of money with relatively low tax rates. Poor districts with low tax bases, on the other hand, had to impose higher tax rates to raise only a fraction of the money that the wealthy districts could spend on education.

In many cases, educational resources varied greatly between districts within the same county. But, many of the poorest districts were in heavily Hispanic South Texas, and ethnicity became a significant factor in a protracted struggle between the haves and have-nots. Hispanic leaders played major roles in the fight to improve the futures of their children.

In 1968, a group of parents led by Demetrio P. Rodriquez, a San Antonio sheet metal worker and high school dropout, filed a federal lawsuit (*Rodriguez v. San Antonio Independent School District*) challenging the system.[30] The plaintiffs had children in the Edgewood Independent School District, one of the state's poorest. A three-judge federal panel agreed with the parents and ruled in 1971 that the school finance system was unconstitutional. But, the state appealed, and the U.S. Supreme Court in 1973 reversed the lower court decision. The high court held that while the Texas system of financing public education was unfair it did not violate the U.S. Constitution. As a result, the Texas Legislature started pumping hundreds of millions of dollars in so-called equalization aid into the poorer school districts. But lawmakers did not change the system, and the inequities persisted and worsened.

By the early 1980s, there was a growing concern among Texas leaders about not just the financing of public education but also the quality of education. Their concerns were shared by leaders in other states in the wake of a national study called *A Nation at Risk* that had sharply criticized the nation's educational systems as inadequate. In 1983, newly elected Democratic Governor Mark White tried to raise school-teachers' salaries to keep a campaign promise to the thousands of teachers who had been instrumental in his election. When the legislature refused to increase taxes for higher teacher pay without first studying the educational system with an eye toward reform, White joined Lieutenant Governor Bill Hobby and House Speaker Gib Lewis in appointing the Select Committee on Public Education. Computer magnate Ross Perot of Dallas—who several years later would become better known as an independent candidate for president—was selected to chair it. In an exhaustive study, the panel found that high schools were graduating many students who could barely read and write and concluded that major reforms were necessary if the state's young people were to be able to compete for jobs in a changing and highly competitive state and international economy.

With Perot spending some of his own personal wealth on a strong lobbying campaign, the legislature in a special session in 1984 enacted many educational reforms in a landmark piece of legislation known as **House Bill 72** and raised taxes to boost education spending. The bill raised teacher pay, limited class sizes, required prekindergarten classes for disadvantaged four-year-olds, required students to pass a basic skills test before graduating from high school, and required school districts to provide tutorials for failing students. It also replaced the elected State Board of Education, viewed as anti-reform by state leaders, with a new panel appointed by the governor. The new board became an elected body four years later, after the appointed panel had time to oversee the initial implementation of the new law.

The two most controversial provisions in the 1984 education reform law, however, were a literacy test for teachers and the so-called **"no pass, no play" rule,** both of which were to contribute to White's reelection defeat in 1986. Most teachers easily passed the one-time literacy—or competency—test, a requirement for keeping their jobs, but many resented it as an insult to their abilities and professionalism. The no-pass, no-play rule, which prohibited students who failed any course from participating in athletics and other extracurricular activities for six weeks, infuriated many coaches, students, parents, and school administrators, particularly in the hundreds of small Texas towns where Friday night football was a major social activity and an important source of community pride. Education reformers, however, viewed the restriction as an important statement that the first emphasis of education should be on the classroom, not on the football field or the band hall.

The 1984 law, however, still did not change the basic, inequitable finance system, and the state was soon back in court over that issue. A lawsuit, filed in 1984 in a state district court in Austin by the Edgewood Independent School District, twelve other poor districts, and a number of families represented by the Mexican American Legal Defense and Educational Fund (MALDEF), contended that the inequities in the finance system violated the Texas Constitution. Dozens of other districts and individuals joined the case as plaintiff-intervenors, and, in 1987, state District Judge Harley Clark of Austin ruled the school finance system violated the state constitution.

The Texas Third Court of Appeals reversed Clark in December 1988. But in October 1989 in *Edgewood* v. *Kirby,* the Texas Supreme Court unanimously, struck down the finance system and ordered lawmakers to replace it by May 1, 1990, with a new law that gave public school children an equal opportunity at a quality education.

Funding Problems Persist

Governor Bill Clements called the legislature into special session in February 1990 to address the Texas Supreme Court order. But the issue was so divisive it took four special sessions and an extension of the court's deadline for the governor and the legislature to agree on a new finance plan, which included a small increase in the state sales tax to boost funding to poor districts. But the Edgewood plaintiffs called the new law inadequate and promptly took the state back to court.

After a trial on the new law, state District Judge Scott McCown allowed the new law to remain in effect for the 1990–1991 school year, but ruled in September 1990 that the plan was, like its predecessor, unconstitutional because it did not narrow the huge gap

---

House Bill 72

A landmark school reform law enacted in 1984. Among other things, it reduced class sizes, required teachers to pass a literacy test to keep their jobs, and imposed the no pass, no play rule, which restricts failing students from participating in extracurricular activities.

"no pass, no play" rule

A provision of Texas House Bill 72 that restricts a student failing a course from participating in extracurricular activities.

Edgewood v. *Kirby*

A unanimous and landmark decision by the Texas Supreme Court in 1989 that ordered the Texas Legislature to devise a more equitable school finance system.

in wealth between rich and poor school districts. The Texas Supreme Court agreed. Lawmakers had to enact two more school finance plans before finally meeting the Supreme Court's approval. Acting in 1993, the legislature approved a law, signed by Governor Ann Richards, that gave wealthy school districts several options for sharing revenue with poor districts.

In the late 1990s, the legislature increased funding for public education but failed to keep up with the increasing needs of a growing school enrollment. A number of school districts joined a suit in state district court, arguing that the 1993 law was unconstitutional because many districts had been forced to raise their property tax rates to or near the limit allowed by the state for school maintenance and operations, $1.50 per $100 valuation. The districts argued that the situation amounted to, in effect, a state property tax, which was prohibited by the Texas Constitution. The districts also sought more state aid.

Ruling in the latest lawsuit in 2005, the Texas Supreme Court held that the heavy reliance on property taxes for school funding amounted to an unconstitutional statewide property tax and gave the state until June 1, 2006, to correct the problem.[31] Governor Rick Perry called the legislature into special session and won approval of a proposal to cut school maintenance tax rates by as much as one-third over the next two years. To replace the lost revenue, legislators used part of a budgetary surplus, enacted the new, broad-based business tax described earlier in this chapter, and raised the state cigarette tax by $1 per pack. The legislature, however, did not increase state funding for the public schools, and the local school tax savings touted by Perry soon were eroded by rising property values. As property values increased, tax bills increased without any change in the tax rate. The property tax burden continued to increase, and by 2009, local property taxes were paying for about 47 percent of public education costs. (To learn more about the sources of revenue for local school districts, see Figure 8.2.)

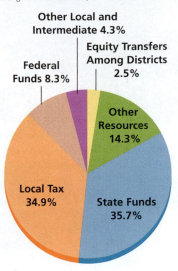

Figure 8.2 *How much of the cost of public education was paid by Texas local governments from 2008–2009?*

Source: Texas Education Agency, *2008–2009 Budgeted Financial Data,* www.tea.state.tx.us.

- Other Local and Intermediate 4.3%
- Equity Transfers Among Districts 2.5%
- Federal Funds 8.3%
- Other Resources 14.3%
- Local Tax 34.9%
- State Funds 35.7%

Other Issues Affecting the Public Schools

TEACHER PAY AND WORKING CONDITIONS   The school districts' financial problems and other work-related stresses were taking their toll on schoolteachers. Thirty-eight percent of teachers were seriously considering quitting the profession in 1994, according to a survey by the Texas State Teachers Association (TSTA). Teachers complained of low pay, excessive paperwork and other administrative hassles, and poor student discipline.[32] The legislature raised the minimum teacher salary in 1995 and gave teachers an across-the-board pay increase in 1999. But according to the National Education Association, Texas still ranked only thirty-second in the country, with average teacher pay of $39,232 in 2001–2002.[33] After numerous pay raises, salaries still lagged behind the national average in 2010, and by the end of that school year, budgetary problems were prompting some school districts to consider teacher layoffs.

STANDARDIZED TESTS AND "ACCOUNTABILITY"   For years now, students in the public schools have been required to take standardized tests to be promoted to higher grades, graduate from high school, and help measure a school's effectiveness. But the tests—most recently called the Texas Assessment of Knowledge and Skills (or TAKS)—and the so-called school accountability system to which the results of these tests contributed have been controversial. There have been accusations that teachers were pressured to concentrate on teaching students how to pass the test—in order to attain a favorable rating for their schools—rather than to present a more enriching educational curriculum. The testing and accountability systems have been revised several times, including in 2009, as legislators and educators struggled to balance political and educational concerns.

Are charter schools solution for low-performing students? National charter schools such as the KIPP Aspire Middle School, located in central San Antonio, were authorized and funded under the leadership of George W. Bush in 1995 to provide alternatives to public schools for low-performing students.

CHARTER SCHOOLS   Upon taking office in 1995, Governor George W. Bush advocated more innovation for local schools and less red tape for teachers and administrators. The legislature responded with a major rewrite of the education law to allow school districts and other groups to create charter schools that would be free of some state regulations. The charter school movement got off to a mixed start. Several of the charter schools had financial problems or were mismanaged and had to shut down after only brief periods of operation. But others flourished, strongly supported by parents and students who believed their innovative techniques enhanced the learning experience. By 2009, there were 437 charter schools with approximately 100,000 students operating in Texas.[34]

VIRTUAL SCHOOL NETWORK   The legislature enacted a law in 2007 that authorized the Texas Education Agency to create and administer a state Virtual School Network to provide supplemental education for high school students over the Internet. In participating districts, students can enroll in required courses, including those with dual credit, for which a student receives both high school and college credit. Courses are structured to provide extensive communication between a student and a teacher and among participating students. Students do not have to be located on the physical premise of an educational facility.[35]

PRIVATE SCHOOL VOUCHERS   For several years, a number of legislators, primarily Republicans, have advocated a voucher program that would allow some public school children to attend private schools at state expense. The idea, supporters say, is to allow disadvantaged children from failing schools to have a chance at a quality education. But opponents, including public education groups, say such a program would unfairly divert money from the public schools at a time when public classrooms need more funding. Voucher bills have failed during several recent legislative sessions.

HOME SCHOOLS   In 1994, the Texas Supreme Court upheld the right of parents to educate their own children at home, ending a ten-year legal battle over the home school issue in Texas. The court said a home school was legitimate if parents met "basic education goals" and used a curriculum based on books, workbooks, or other written materials. It was reported at the time that nearly one million American families, including 100,000 in Texas, educated their children at home.[36] The U.S. Department of Education reported that there were 1.5 million home schooled students in 2007.[37] A recent estimate by the Texas Home School Coalition placed the number of home schooled children in the state at 300,000, but there is no way to verify this number under existing state regulations.[38]

Higher Education

Texas has thirty-five state-supported, general academic universities; eight medical schools and health science centers; four public law schools; fifty community (or junior) college districts; and four campuses of the Texas State Technical College System.

These institutions of higher learning serve more than 1 million students. They are governed by numerous policy-setting boards appointed by the governor or, in the case of community colleges, elected by local voters. The Texas Higher Education Coordinating Board, which is appointed by the governor, has oversight over university construction and degree programs.

The state makes no pretense that all its universities were created equal. The University of Texas at Austin and Texas A&M University at College Station are the state's largest universities, have higher entrance requirements than other schools, fulfill important research functions, and, thanks to a constitutional endowment, have some of the state's best educational facilities. They receive revenue generated by the land- and mineral-rich **Permanent University Fund (PUF).** The University of Texas receives two-thirds of the money in the Available University Fund, which includes dividends, interest, and other income earned by the PUF, and Texas A&M receives one-third. University of Texas and Texas A&M regents can also pledge revenue to back bonds issued for land acquisition, construction, building repairs, purchase of capital equipment, and purchase of library materials for other campuses within the two university systems. Universities outside the two largest systems share in a separate building fund to which the legislature appropriates about $175 million a year.

Responding to a federal desegregation lawsuit, the state in the 1980s made a commitment to improve higher educational opportunities for minority students and employment opportunities for minority faculty members. More funding was provided for predominantly African American Texas Southern University in Houston and Prairie View A&M University in nearby Waller County. Prairie View, which is part of the Texas A&M System, was guaranteed a special share of Available University Fund revenue in a constitutional amendment adopted in 1984. Texas agreed to a five-year desegregation plan with the U.S. Department of Education in 1983 and subsequently created the Texas Educational Opportunity Plan, under which traditionally Anglo schools, including the University of Texas at Austin and Texas A&M, increased minority recruitment efforts.

Residents of heavily Hispanic South Texas, however, challenged the state's distribution of higher education dollars. In a lawsuit filed in state district court in Brownsville in 1987, several Hispanic groups and individuals represented by the Mexican American Legal Defense and Educational Fund contended the state's higher education system discriminated against Mexican American students by spending less on universities in the border area. The plaintiffs pointed out that there were no state-supported professional schools south of San Antonio and only one doctoral program—in bilingual education at Texas A&I University in Kingsville.

After the lawsuit was filed, Texas A&I, Laredo State University, and Corpus Christi State University were made part of the Texas A&M System, and Pan American University campuses in Edinburg and Brownsville were added to the University of Texas System. But efforts to negotiate a settlement of the suit failed, and it went to trial in late 1991 as a class action on behalf of all Mexican Americans who allegedly suffered or stood to suffer discrimination in higher education in the Mexican border area of Texas. In January 1992, state District Judge Benjamin Euresti Jr. of Brownsville ruled the higher education funding system unconstitutional because it discriminated against South Texas, but his ruling later was overturned by the Texas Supreme Court.[39]

HOPWOOD: A TEMPORARY SETBACK TO AFFIRMATIVE ACTION Texas's efforts to increase minority enrollments in its universities suffered a setback in 1996 when the Fifth U.S. Circuit Court of Appeals in New Orleans ruled that a race-based admissions policy previously used by the University of Texas School of Law was unconstitutional. The U.S. Supreme Court refused to grant the state's appeal and let the appellate court's decision stand. The so-called *Hopwood* case was named after lead

Permanent University Fund (PUF)

A land- and mineral-rich endowment that benefits the University of Texas and Texas A&M University systems, particularly the flagship universities in Austin and College Station.

plaintiff Cheryl Hopwood, one of four white students who sued after not being admitted into the law school.[40]

Then-Texas Attorney General Dan Morales held in 1997 that the *Hopwood* ruling went beyond the law school and prohibited all universities in Texas from using race or ethnicity as a preferential factor in admissions, scholarships, and other student programs. The Texas Legislature, meeting in 1997, enacted a new law that guaranteed automatic admissions to state universities for high school graduates who finished in the top 10 percent of their classes, regardless of their scores on college entrance examinations. The law was designed to give the best students from poor and predominantly minority school districts an equal footing in university admissions with better prepared graduates of wealthier school districts. The new law also allowed university officials to consider other admissions criteria, including a student's family income and parents' education level.

There was little change in minority enrollments at many Texas universities after the *Hopwood* decision, because many universities hadn't used race as a factor in admissions anyway. But the two largest—the University of Texas at Austin and Texas A&M University—did. The drop-off in minority enrollment was particularly troubling at the UT law school the first year after the *Hopwood* restrictions went into effect. The first-year law class of almost 500 students in the fall of 1997 included only four African Americans and twenty-five Hispanics. There had been thirty-one African Americans and forty-two Hispanics in the previous year's entering class. And the more flexible admissions standards set by the legislature applied only to entering undergraduate students, not to those seeking admission to law school and other professional schools.[41]

Finally, in 2003, the U.S. Supreme Court, ruling in a case from Michigan, effectively repealed *Hopwood* by holding that universities can use affirmative action programs to give minority students help in admissions, provided that racial quotas are not used. The University of Texas, among other institutions, then began steps to develop new, race-based admissions criteria. Some legislators, meanwhile, wanted to put limits on the number of students who could be admitted to a university under the 10 percent law because it was restricting admissions options at the University of Texas at Austin, consuming a large percentage of each year's freshman class. After refusing for several years to change the law, the legislature in 2009 imposed some restrictions.[42]

Does the state's future depend on increased expansion of higher education opportunities? There is general agreement that the state's future is directly tied to increased investment in institutions of higher education, such as the University of Texas at San Antonio pictured here.

Photo courtesy: Courtesy of UTSA

TUITION DEREGULATION: THE PRICE OF ADMISSION GOES UP With tax dollars becoming increasingly tight, University of Texas officials successfully lobbied the legislature in 2003 for a new law that, for the first time, gave individual university governing boards the freedom to set tuition rates independently of legislative action. By the fall of 2009, tuition and fees at state-supported universities had increased an average 72 percent, while state appropriations for student financial aid increased by a much lower rate.[43] The Legislative Study Group issued a report just prior to the 2009 session criticizing the legislature for shirking "its responsibility for funding colleges by shifting more of the burden onto the shoulders of parents and students in the form of tuition costs."[44] But the legislature, facing increasing budgetary problems, refused to change the law, even as universities continued to impose tuition increases.

Other Policy Challenges Facing Texas Today

⭐ **8.5** ... **Describe the policy challenges Texas faces in the areas of criminal justice, health and human services, and the environment.**

Texas public policy challenges are not limited to education. From crowded prisons to children's health insurance to an endangered water supply, Texas faces a number of public policy challenges in the areas of criminal justice, health and human services, and the environment.

Criminal Justice

Texas did away with public hangings on the courthouse square years ago but retained a frontier attitude toward crime and criminals, an attitude that produced a criminal justice system based more on revenge than rehabilitation. Politicians were elected to the legislature on tough, anti-crime promises to "lock 'em up and throw away the key." Once in office, they passed laws providing long sentences for more and more offenses and built more prisons. Eventually, the system was overwhelmed by sheer numbers, and crime became a bigger problem than ever.

Legislators and most other state policymakers ignored deteriorating prison conditions until U.S. District Judge William Wayne Justice of Tyler declared the prison system unconstitutional in a landmark lawsuit brought by inmates (***Ruiz v. Estelle [1980]***). He cited numerous problems, including overcrowded conditions, poor staffing levels, inadequate medical and psychiatric care for prisoners, and the use of so-called building tenders—inmates who were given positions of authority over other prisoners, whom they frequently abused. Justice ordered extensive reforms with which the state agreed to comply, and he appointed a monitor to help him supervise what was then known as the Texas Department of Corrections and is now the institutional division of the Texas Department of Criminal Justice.[45]

One key order by Justice limited the population of prison units to 95 percent of capacity to guard against a recurrence of overcrowding and allow for the housing of inmates according to their classifications. These classifications were designed to separate youthful, first-time offenders from more hardened criminals and those with special needs from the general prison population.

CROWDED PRISONS PROMPT REFORMS   The prison population limit and an increase in violent crimes in the 1980s helped produce a criminal justice crisis that lasted for several years. By the time the *Ruiz* lawsuit was settled in 1992 and the state was given more flexibility over its prison operations, Texas had spent hundreds of millions of dollars building new prisons but still could not accommodate all the offenders flooding the system. Hundreds of dangerous criminals were receiving early parole. (To learn more about Texas's prison population, see Figure 8.3.)

Many of the convicts overloading the system were nonviolent, repeat offenders—among them alcoholics and drug addicts who continued to get in trouble because they were unable to function outside the prison. Experts believed that alcoholism, drug addiction, or drug-related crimes were responsible for about 85 percent of the prison population.[46] At the urging of Governor Ann Richards in 1991, the legislature created a new alcoholism and drug abuse treatment program within the prison system, which planners hoped would reduce that recidivism.

In settling the *Ruiz* lawsuit in 1992, the state agreed to maintain safe prisons, and the federal court's active supervision of the prison system ended. Then, in 1993, the legislature enacted a major package of criminal justice reforms, including the first

***Ruiz v. Estelle* (1980)**

A lawsuit in which a federal judge in 1980 declared the Texas prison system unconstitutional and ordered sweeping, expensive reforms.

Figure 8.3 *How does the prison population of Texas compare to the incarcerated population of other large states?*

Sources: U.S. Department of Justice, Bureau of Statistics, "Prison Inmates at Midyear 2009—Statistical Tables," bjs.ojp.usdoj.gov/content/pub/pdf/pim09st.pdf; U.S. Census Bureau, *American FactFinder,* www.census.gov.

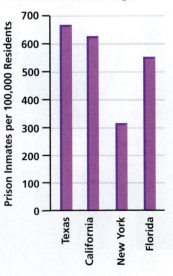

overhaul of the penal code in twenty years. The plan doubled the minimum time that violent felons would have to serve in prison—from one-fourth to one-half of their sentences—before becoming eligible for parole. To reserve more prison space for the most dangerous criminals, however, the legislature lowered the penalties for most property crimes and drug offenses. These nonviolent offenders were diverted to community corrections programs or a new system of state-run jails, to which they could be sentenced for a maximum of two years. To build 20,000 new state jail beds and additional prison units, the legislature and Texas voters also approved a $1 billion bond proposal in 1993. It was the fourth bond authorization, for a total of $3 billion, mostly for prison construction, that voters had approved in six years.

Senator John Whitmire of Houston, then-chairman of the Senate Criminal Justice Committee and an architect of the changes, said the new plan would not only be tough but also "smart" against crime. The changes were supported by some district attorneys, but other prosecutors and some law enforcement officers feared that the lighter penalties for many drug dealers and property criminals would boost the crime rate and make their jobs more difficult.

The legislature authorized doubling the size of the prison system during the 1994–1995 budget period, and a construction boom was soon underway. By the late 1990s, Texas had room for more than 150,000 inmates in its prisons, state jails, and substance abuse facilities, and the backlog of convicted felons in county jails was temporarily eliminated. But criminal justice experts warned the state would soon need even more prison space if the legislature did not enact additional sentencing and parole reforms and attack crime among juveniles. And, sure enough, within a few years the prisons were full again. By the middle of 2009, 170,000 persons were incarcerated in prisons and jails in Texas. To partially address the problem of overcrowding, the State Board of Pardons and Paroles relaxed its rules to speed up the release of convicts who had been returned to prison for minor violations of their paroles, such as not reporting to their parole officers on time.

Is there a relationship between dropouts, crime, and incarceration? Data indicate that about 80 percent of inmates are school dropouts. The students seen here are enrolled in prison schools under the jurisdiction of the Windham School District, which was created by the legislature to provide academic and vocational education to eligible prisoners in the state's correctional institutions.

Photo courtesy: AP/Wide World Photos

FIGHTING JUVENILE CRIME Although the overall crime rate in Texas decreased in the early and mid-1990s, crime committed by juveniles increased. Republican George W. Bush made juvenile justice reform a campaign issue.

The legislature responded in 1995 with a far-reaching law that cracked down on juvenile offenders and offered some prevention programs to divert troubled children from lives of crime. The law lowered from fifteen to fourteen the age at which violent offenders could be tried as adults, and it expanded the list of offenses for which delinquents could receive fixed sentences in state facilities—up to forty years for the most violent. The measure also required any child expelled from school to be referred to juvenile court, encouraged local governments to enact more curfews for teenagers, and beefed up programs for runaway youths and other disadvantaged children.

By the late 1990s, the juvenile crime rate had started to drop, and the 1995 crackdown may have been a factor. But the crackdown—

and the crowded youth detention facilities it produced— were the focus of a major state scandal several years later when in early 2007 it was alleged that some correctional officers had sexually abused young inmates in their care. In the long run, many experts believed, the success or failure of public programs in education, health care, and welfare reform would be the determining factors in Texas's war on crime, because many criminal offenders, in addition to being substance abusers, are poor and high school dropouts.

THE DEATH PENALTY   For many years, Texas has led the nation in executions. More than 470 persons, including two women, have been put to death in Texas since executions resumed in 1982, and more than 300 persons, including ten women, were on death row in the summer of 2010. Opposition is vocal, but most Texans support the death penalty. According to a Scripps Howard *Texas Poll* conducted during the 2000 presidential race, 73 percent of Texans supported the death penalty, even though 57 percent of the respondents said they believed that innocent people had been executed. Nearly nine out of ten respondents said that death row inmates should have the right to obtain free DNA testing to try to prove their innocence.[47] A *Houston Chronicle* survey conducted in 2002 had similar results. Some 69 percent of respondents supported the death penalty, even though 55 percent believed that innocent people probably had been executed.[48]

Eleven people have been released from death row after subsequent evidence, mainly the result of DNA testing, proved them innocent. As forensic and DNA testing become more sophisticated, challenges to murder convictions are becoming more commonplace. One closely watched case pending before the Texas Forensic Science Commission involves Cameron Todd Willingham, who was executed for killing his three young children in a house fire in Corsicana. New scientific evidence indicates the fire may not have been intentionally set. But, Governor Perry replaced four of the nine commissioners, delaying an official determination that the arson finding was faulty. Still, Texas "could become the first state to acknowledge officially that, since the advent of the modern judicial system, it had carried out the 'execution of a legally and factually innocent person.'"[49]

Health and Human Services

Health and human services is the area in which state government must weigh compassion against the cold realities of its budget, and Texas has been historically stingy. Texas traditionally has spent less money per capita on health and welfare than most states. Even in the 1970s, when the oil industry was still pumping a healthy amount of tax revenue into the state treasury, Texas was slapped with two federal court orders for providing inadequate care to the mentally ill and the mentally retarded in state institutions. Perhaps the tight-fisted attitude springs from the legacy of frontier colonists—perpetuated by countless politicians claiming that Texans could prevail in hard times by pulling themselves up by their bootstraps. But this perception ignores the reality that many people in modern Texas cannot pull themselves up by their bootstraps because they

THINKING NATIONALLY

Regional Patterns in Executions

Since the death penalty was reinstated in 1976, more than 1,200 executions have been carried out by the states. There is a distinct regional pattern to executions. By the summer of 2010, northeastern states had executed four individuals. Midwestern states had executed 141, and western states, 67. In sharp contrast, southern states had executed more than 1,000 people, with Texas and Virginia leading the way. Texas has executed more than 470 persons since 1982.

- What explanations can you give for the low number of executions in the northeastern region of the country?

- How do you account for the high number of executions in the South and particularly in Texas?

- Are the murder rates in the different regions of the country significantly different? If so, what explanations can you provide for these differences?

don't have any boots. According to the 2008 American Community Survey, approximately 15.8 percent of Texans—approximately one of every six—lived in poverty. Particularly hard hit are children, the elderly, and minorities.

WELFARE REFORM   By the late 1990s, welfare changes designed to break the cycle of poverty were major priorities of both state and federal governments. New laws emphasized education and job training for welfare recipients and put limits on how long they could collect benefits. In 1995, the Texas Legislature enacted a law that required recipients of public assistance to sign responsibility agreements and participate in educational or job training programs in order to receive benefits. It also imposed limits of one to three years on the time a person could collect welfare. The federal government enacted a more sweeping welfare reform law in 1996 that put a five-year lifetime limit on welfare benefits for most recipients and required able-bodied adults to go to work within two years of receiving assistance. The U.S. Congress abolished the Aid to Families with Dependent Children (AFDC) program, which had provided federal funds for every eligible welfare recipient since the 1930s. In its place, the states were given broad authority to design their own welfare programs with fixed amounts of federal money. The new federal law (TANF) also gave the states quotas to meet in finding jobs for welfare recipients and eliminated most welfare benefits for immigrants.

It will take years to fully evaluate the effectiveness of the welfare changes, but early results in Texas were mixed. State officials reported that more than 100,000 people left Texas's welfare rolls during the first half of 1997 alone. But most of them were children, and not all of the adults quickly found jobs—or at least the kind of employment that would remove them from poverty. About half of the adults who left the welfare rolls had found new jobs, while 10 percent were earning more money from existing jobs, according to an October 1997 survey by the Texas Legislative Council. The legislative researchers said that state and federal welfare reforms had helped, but they concluded that the state's strong economy was the main reason former welfare recipients were finding jobs.[50]

The state agency primarily responsible for moving people from welfare to work was the Texas Workforce Commission, which coordinated job training programs for low-income Texans. Supporters credited the agency with helping reduce the state's welfare rolls by thousands of people. But critics said the agency was training too many people for menial, minimum-wage jobs that didn't pay enough to permanently remove them from poverty. They said the commission needed to offer more training for higher paying jobs that offered a more secure future. But state officials said the economy and private employers—not the government—determined the types of jobs available.[51]

The state's welfare reform law also required poor people to attend state-run classes on how to get a job before they could receive welfare payments. "The class had no textbook and no test," wrote a newspaper reporter who attended one of the early classes conducted by state work counselors in Austin. "But the lesson was clear: Texas expects you to try to get a job before asking for welfare."[52]

More than 275,000 Texas families had left the welfare rolls by 2000. But health care coverage had become a major problem for many of them, according to a study released that year. The report by Families USA, a Washington-based advocacy group that supports universal health coverage, determined that 100,000 low-income Texas parents had lost Medicaid coverage since 1996. That was a 46 percent drop in adult Medicaid enrollees in Texas and the second-largest decline among the fifteen states that account for most of the country's uninsured people. Medicaid is a government-sponsored health insurance program for the poor. Although the study did not determine whether people who left Medicaid had other health insurance, advocates for the poor said many of the people who left Medicaid were probably former welfare recipients who had taken low-paying jobs that did not offer health insurance.

By 2006, ten years after the welfare reform law was passed, the number of families receiving welfare in Texas had decreased from 275,000 families to 150,000. But the number of Texans in poverty increased.

HEALTH INSURANCE FOR CHILDREN

Another critical health care need in Texas is insurance coverage for children. Nearly one-fourth of Texas's 5.8 million children in 1999 did not have health insurance, ranking Texas next to last among the states in that category. The legislature responded by opting into the federal program creating the Children's Health Insurance Program, or CHIP, to provide low-cost health coverage to children of the working poor, those families who earned too much to qualify for Medicaid but could not afford insurance on their own. The program was open to children younger than nineteen whose families' annual income was no more than twice the poverty level.[53]

But thousands of children lost health insurance in 2003, after the legislature reversed course and imposed stricter rules for CHIP coverage to help close a $10 billion shortfall in the state budget. Within only a few months, enrollment had dropped by about 50,000, and it dropped by thousands more within the next two years.

By 2003, Texas led the nation in the percentage of uninsured residents, with one in four people, children and adults, lacking health insurance.[54] Critics said state legislators, in cutting back on CHIP coverage, were shortsighted, because many children unable to receive preventive health care will end up in the emergency rooms of public hospitals, where treatment for serious, but preventable, illnesses will cost taxpayers even more. The legislature restored some of the CHIP cuts in 2007 but, facing opposition from Governor Rick Perry, refused additional expansion of the program in 2009. That proposal would have made health coverage available to about 80,000 additional children by raising eligibility for CHIP to 300 percent of poverty, or a maximum income of about $66,000 a year for a family of four.

REORGANIZING HEALTH AND HUMAN SERVICES

The legislature in 2003 also ordered a major reorganization of the state's health and human services agencies. The goal of the most sweeping overhaul of social services in modern Texas history was to make state government smaller and save tax dollars through administrative changes and some privatization. Republican leaders who backed the changes predicted they would benefit both the needy recipients of state services and the taxpayers footing the bill. But advocates for the poor were skeptical.

Photo courtesy: AP/Wide World Photos

What are the benefits and costs of vaccinations? There are some who object to childhood vaccination on medical and religious grounds, but immunization has been analyzed in terms of costs and benefits. The children seen here are receiving vaccinations at a center supported by the Texas Department of State Health Services.

Children and Mental Health

Among the fifty states, Texas provides fewer mental health care services for children (ages 2–17) than any other state. Of the children who experienced emotional, developmental, or behavioral problems in 2007, approximately 42 percent received care. Less than 52 percent of the children in Mississippi, Oregon, Georgia, and Florida received mental health care. States where the highest percentage of children received care (75 percent or more) were Iowa, Rhode Island, Delaware, Connecticut, and Pennsylvania.

- What explanations do you have for the low level of children's mental health care in Texas?

- Do you detect any patterns in the states that provide low levels of mental health care?

- How will the decision to provide fewer services affect Texas in the future?

It would take several years to complete the consolidation of twelve agencies into five and assess the results.

The reorganization caught the immediate attention of the business community. Several dozen companies submitted bids for consulting contracts to help the state carry out the privatization effort, but it got off to a rough start. Accenture, a Bermuda-based company, was given an $899 million state contract to operate call centers to determine applicants' eligibility for public benefits. But the company's work was soon embroiled in controversy, with many applicants complaining of delays in processing claims and lost paperwork. At one point, some applicants even faxed confidential financial and health information to a warehouse in Seattle, Washington, because a wrong phone number had been printed on an information sheet. In late 2006, state officials announced Texas was cutting the contract by $356 million and ending it two years early. Under the changes, Accenture was left primarily with the responsibility for data entry, leaving state employees to screen applicants' qualifications for food stamps, Medicaid, and other assistance.[55]

BIG TOBACCO   In a major health-related initiative, then-Texas Attorney General Dan Morales sued the tobacco industry in 1996, seeking billions of dollars in reimbursement for tax money spent to treat smoking-related illnesses. The suit also sought restrictions on tobacco companies' marketing and advertising that Morales said were targeting children.

Shortly before Texas's suit was scheduled to go to trial in early 1998, Morales and the tobacco industry negotiated a $17.3 billion settlement. Tobacco companies agreed to pay Texas and its county hospitals the huge sum over twenty-five years and end all their advertising on billboards and public transportation facilities in the state. The agreement called for Texas's first-year proceeds from the settlement, or about $1.2 billion, to be spent on anti-smoking and health care programs, mostly for children. Morales believed those expenditures were particularly important because health care had traditionally been underfunded in Texas and he considered the anti-tobacco suit a health care issue. The legislature agreed. Part of the money was used to fund the new Children's Health Insurance Program, described earlier in this section, and most of the remaining funds were used to create numerous health care–related endowments for medical schools and to establish an anti-smoking education program at the Texas Department of Health.

The way the legislature structured the anti-smoking education program, however, was controversial. Lawmakers put $200 million of the tobacco funds into an endowment, which budget writers said would ensure the most effective use of the money for years to come. Most health care providers and advocates supported that approach. But the American Cancer Society of Texas, the American Lung Association's Texas division, and the Campaign for Tobacco Free Kids objected, because the $200 million endowment initially would generate only about $10 million a year that could actually be spent. The dissenting groups said that amount was woefully inadequate for developing effective anti-smoking programs in a state as large as Texas.

Texas was not the only state to sue tobacco companies. Mississippi, Florida, and Minnesota also negotiated separate out-of-court settlements with the industry. And after Texas reached its settlement in 1998, cigarette companies negotiated a national $246 billion settlement with the remaining states.

It is ironic that Texas sued the tobacco companies on the basis of health issues but it depends on a sizeable return on the tobacco tax to fund the state's budget. In 2009, this tax generated over $1.5 billion.

Environmental Problems and Policies

Texas is blessed with an abundance of fragile natural resources that can no longer be taken for granted. But efforts to impose environmental regulations are difficult for a number of reasons. For one, Texas still has a large share of the nation's oil refining and chemical manufacturing industries, despite the 1980s oil bust. And although efforts have been made to reduce environmental risks, state policy makers are influenced by economic considerations because those same industries employ thousands of people and pump billions of dollars into the economy and the state treasury. Compounding the problem are several other apparent conflicts of interest, including the desire to attract new industries, a legacy that emphasizes individual property rights, and Texans' love for their automobiles, pickups, and sport utility vehicles.

DIRTY AIR   Air pollution has become an increasing problem in Texas since the state rushed to diversify its economy in the 1980s and attract major industries. In a national environmental survey in 1992, *City & State* magazine ranked Texas forty-eighth among the states in the quality of governmental programs protecting natural resources.[56] Texas received some additional notoriety in 1999 when Houston beat out Los Angeles for the unwanted title of the nation's "dirtiest air" city. Specifically, the Houston metropolitan area led the nation that year in the number of days—fifty-two— in which the city's air violated the national health standard for ozone, the main ingredient in smog. Los Angeles regained its first place standing in 2002, but the problems in Texas persist.[57]

Unlike large cities in many other states, Texas cities have been slow to develop local rail transportation systems. Dallas and Houston only recently built the state's first two rail transit systems, and Austin was following suit with a limited rail system of its own. But automobiles have increasingly clogged streets and freeways and spewed tons of pollutants into the air. State officials responded with anti-pollution restrictions only after being forced to do so by the federal government. To meet federal Clean Air Act standards for smog reduction, the state now requires motorists in the Houston, Dallas-Fort Worth, and certain other metropolitan areas to have special emissions inspections of their cars. And, speed limits on freeways and highways in metropolitan areas have been lowered to 55 miles per hour. In 2003, the legislature—to avoid losing millions of dollars in federal highway funding—also enacted a plan for raising state funds to pay for the emission reduction effort. The plan, among other things, increased the costs of auto title transfers and imposed surcharges on some large diesel equipment.

Many state political leaders also have preferred to encourage industries to voluntarily reduce pollution, rather than impose strict cleanup requirements. Governor George W. Bush, for example, convinced the legislature in 1999 to enact a voluntary cleanup program for many of the old industrial facilities in Texas that still had not been brought into compliance with federal clean air standards. These facilities had been built before 1971 and had initially been "grandfathered" by lawmakers that year from the higher emission-control standards placed on new industrial plants. Environmentalists complained that many of the old facilities were major polluters and urged the legislature to require them to upgrade their equipment. But state lawmakers required only "grandfathered" power plants operated by utility companies to be upgraded, while continuing voluntary compliance for the older plants in other industries. Legislators raised state emissions fees on the biggest polluters as an incentive for them to comply, but environmentalists complained that the higher fees would apply to only a handful of plants.[58]

In 2010, President Barack Obama's administration attempted to crack down on Texas's regulatory system as too lax. Efforts by the Environmental Protection Agency to

How dirty is it? According to a study published by the American Lung Association in 2010, the Houston-Baytown-Huntsville area ranked 7th in the nation in ozone pollution and 16th in year-round particle pollution.

Photo courtesy: AP/Wide World Photos

take over the permitting process for some industrial facilities from the Texas Commission on Environmental Quality sparked what was likely to be a long legal and political battle over the issue. (To learn more about the state's efforts to combat air pollution, see Politics Now: Governor Says Texas' Air Quality Improving; Critics Insist State Efforts Are Only Just a Start.)

GLOBAL WARMING   As economic development progressed in the state, Texas became a major emitter of greenhouse gases. By 2007, Texas not only led the fifty states but was responsible for more carbon dioxide emissions than the number two and three polluters, California and Pennsylvania, combined. By 2009, Ralph Nader's organization, Public Citizen, had filed suit against the Texas Commission on Environmental Quality (TCEQ). In doing so, the group hoped to block the TCEQ from issuing permits to a number of coal and petroleum coke-fired plants. In commenting on the case, TCEQ chairman Bryan Shaw stated that the verdict on the dangers of global warming was not yet in.[59]

In contradiction to Shaw's assessment, scientists at Texas A&M University issued a report in 2009 emphasizing that not only was global warming real but that, in the not-too-distant future, it would pose a potentially devastating threat to the Texas coast. These scientists predicted that global warming would cause sea levels to rise, spawn more intense hurricanes, and result in increased coastal flooding. Damage to coastal communities from hurricanes would more than triple by the 2080s.[60]

AN ENDANGERED WATER SUPPLY   Population growth and a drought in the mid-1990s increased public concern over Texas's water supply. Much of the attention of environmentalists, farmers, ranchers, and government officials initially was focused on the underground Edwards Aquifer, the sole source of water for San Antonio and its rural neighbors. A major legal battle began in 1991, when the Sierra Club sued the federal government, contending the U.S. Interior Department had violated the Endangered Species Act. The environmentalists said the department had failed to guard against excessive pumping from the underground reservoir, which could endanger salamanders that live in the aquifer or aquifer-fed springs.

The lawsuit angered many San Antonians and farmers and ranchers. But U.S. District Judge Lucius Bunton of Midland ruled in favor of the Sierra Club, warning that overpumping not only threatened endangered species but also posed a contamination threat to the aquifer itself. Bunton eventually ordered San Antonio and several smaller cities to reduce pumping from the aquifer, but his order was blocked in 1996 by the Fifth U.S. Circuit Court of Appeals in New Orleans.[61] In 1993, the Texas Legislature created the regional Edwards Aquifer Authority with the power to regulate pumping from the aquifer and to protect the reservoir from pollution. The Texas Supreme Court upheld the state law in 1996, despite the objections of landowners who contended the state was ignoring their rights.[62]

Advocates of landowners' rights argued that any pumping limitations could damage the livelihoods of farmers and ranchers and adversely affect the San Antonio economy. But environmentalists argued the future of San Antonio and the entire region was dependent on protecting water levels in the aquifer. After the drought worsened in 1996, the legislature approved a comprehensive, statewide water conservation plan in 1997.

Another water issue also has begun to attract attention. State Land Commissioner Jerry Patterson has proposed leasing state lands to private companies, which would pump groundwater for sale to cities or other entities that needed it. Patterson said such leases could raise more money for public education, but critics questioned how much water a growing state could afford to sell. (To learn more about the sale of water in Texas, see The Living Constitution: Article 16, Section 59.)

CENTRALIZED REGULATION   The legislature in 1993 centralized most of state government's environmental protection efforts into one agency, the Texas Natural Resource Conservation Commission, which consolidated separate agencies that had

Governor Says Texas' Air Quality Improving; Critics Insist State Efforts Are Only Just a Start

By R.G. Ratcliffe

May 28, 2010
Houston Chronicle
www.chron.com

AUSTIN—Gov. Rick Perry, citing improvements in Texas air quality, asked President Barack Obama on Friday to get regional Environmental Protection Agency administrators to back off efforts to take over the state's air quality permitting process for refineries and power plants.

Perry told Obama the state process has improved air quality while ensuring economic growth.

"EPA's unwarranted actions will kill good American jobs, reduce our economic output and undermine critical domestic energy and petrochemical supplies for all 50 states," Perry said in a letter to the president. "Worse still, EPA's actions are unwarranted given the tremendous air quality improvements that have been made in Texas."

Neil Carman, Clean Air Program director for the Sierra Club, said improvements in Texas' air quality stand out only because of how polluted the state was.

"The problem with the comparison of Texas to the rest of the nation is Texas has so much pollution," Carman said. "You can have a significant reduction and still be the most polluted."

Perry's letter said Texas has achieved a 22 percent reduction in ozone and a 46 percent decrease in nitrogen oxide emissions in the past decade.

"Houston is second only to Atlanta in the total percent decrease in ozone for metropolitan areas since 2000, even with a 20 percent increase in population," Perry said.

However, records from the EPA website show Houston still far exceeds Atlanta for ozone pollution.

On the American Lung Association list of most polluted cities for ozone, Houston ranked seventh and Dallas-Fort Worth ranked 13th. Atlanta was ranked 19th.

Direct federal action

The Dallas regional EPA office responded to Perry with a statement.

"EPA has been working with Texas to address deficiencies in the state's air permitting program," the statement said. "EPA in Dallas has taken another important step to address deficiencies in the state's air operating permit program by directing a Texas plant with a deficient air quality permit to seek a federally authorized permit directly from EPA."

The EPA notified state regulators this year that its studies found additional significant pollution reduction could be achieved if the state gave up its so-called flexible permitting process and replaced it with a system that required companies to start the permit process from scratch when major equipment changes were made. Texas Commission on Environmental Quality administrators disputed the EPA study. . . .

Industry likes process

The federal agency objects to the state's flexible permit process, which allows companies to fast track equipment upgrades so long as total pollution does not exceed a site's original emission's permit.

Critics say the process takes away the incentive companies have to improve plant sites, while corporations contend the financial incentive is to bring state of the art equipment online more quickly.

Critical Thinking Questions

1. Without the federal Environmental Protection Agency looking over the shoulders of state policy makers, would there have been an improvement in air quality?

2. Does the position of the governor reflect how most Texans feel about federal regulations?

3. If foot-dragging on air quality has occurred, what explanations can you offer as to why state enforcement has not been more aggressive?

The Living Constitution

The conservation and development of all of the natural resources of this State . . . are each and all hereby declared public rights and duties; and the Legislature shall pass all such laws as may be appropriate thereto. . . . There may be created within the State of Texas, or the State may be divided into, such number of conservation and reclamation districts as may be determined to be essential, which districts shall be governmental agencies and bodies politic and corporate with such powers of government and with the authority to exercise such rights, privileges and functions concerning the subject matter of this amendment as may be conferred by law.

—ARTICLE 16, SECTION 59

When Texas voters in 1917 approved a constitutional amendment giving the legislature the authority to create conservation and reclamation districts (water districts), they could hardly imagine that obscure, local districts would be at the center of twenty-first century "water wars." But that is what has occurred.

With communities throughout the Southwest facing severe water shortages, corporations and some wealthy individuals have begun to buy up land that has access to underground water. Oilman T. Boone Pickens, for example, bought land in Roberts County from which he can pump water from the Ogallala Aquifer through a pipeline to Dallas, some 300 miles away. Pickens tried to organize this water district in 2002 but was rebuffed by a group of Roberts County residents. So, during the 2006 election cycle, he gave $1.2 million to political candidates and political committees and spent another $1 million on lobbyists working the Texas Legislature in 2007. Consequently, the legislature gave Pickens virtual carte blanche to organize a special district with wide-ranging powers. The law pertaining to special districts was modified to permit people who owned property within the district but lived elsewhere to vote in the organization election. There was no doubt what the outcome of the November 2007 election on the district's creation would be. Only five voters owned land in the district, and all had business relationships with Pickens. The oilman had sold them small parcels of his huge holdings shortly after the end of the 2007 legislative session.

Using the so-called right of recapture (access to water under one's own property), Pickens anticipates pumping 200,000 acre feet of water out of the aquifer each year, which could place additional stress on the primary water source of West Texas. Using the power of eminent domain, he could potentially force landowners to sell him access to their land for a pipeline.

CRITICAL THINKING QUESTIONS

1. Should a handful of wealthy individuals have the right to "buy" natural resources to the detriment of other citizens?
2. With increased water scarcity, should a landowner have the right to capture all the water possible that is located under his or her land?
3. What laws might ensure that Texas will be able to best fulfill the state's future water needs?

specialized in protecting water, air, and other selected resources. Both industrial interests and environmentalists generally preferred the new commission, later renamed the Texas Commission on Environmental Quality, over the fragmented regulatory system that it replaced. But some environmental leaders complained that the agency, in deciding the fate of new industrial permits, all too often favored economic development over environmental protection. "I do think that overall the agency tries to be balanced, but almost inevitably they really end up leaning a little too close to industry, in part because it has the [money] to plead its case day in and day out," said Sierra Club leader Ken Kramer. But Texas Chemical Council spokesman Jon Fisher believed the agency was fair. "The bottom line in an environmental regulatory agency is one that recognizes that their job is to protect the environment and not to harass business. Likewise you don't have to hurt the environment to protect business," Fisher said.[63]

TOWARD REFORM: Prospects for Reform in the Policy-Making Process

★ **8.6** . . . **Characterize public policy reforms Texas has implemented to address contemporary challenges.**

The conservative politics of Texas, rooted in its political culture and economic interests, has produced a general legacy of incremental changes in public policies. Criminal justice, education, voting rights, and health and welfare reforms were precipitated by court cases that challenged the status quo. Yet, even with court intervention, state policy makers dragged their feet, often making the most modest changes that they hoped would satisfy the courts. On many measures of welfare and social service expenditures, Texas's per capita appropriations still rank low.

Texas is one of the most polluted states in the nation and is under increasing pressure from the federal government to strengthen its regulatory policies. But when state leaders, such as the governor, argue that federal mandates or the Environmental Protection Agency's oversight are no longer needed, serious doubt is created about the strength of new environmental initiatives coming from state government.

Energy production has dominated much of the state's economic history, and while domestic production of oil and national gas has declined, Texas leads the nation in wind power capacity. This shift to wind power reflects both private and public initiatives. In addition to research and development sponsored by state educational institutions such as the Wind Science and Engineering Research Center at Texas Tech University and the Alternative Energy Institute and Wind Energy Test Center at West Texas A&M University, the state, using federal funds, is channeling monies for renewable energy through the State Energy Conservation Office. Other state agencies such as the Lower Colorado River Authority have taken significant steps in the conversion from fossil fuels to renewable energy. (To learn more about Texas's use of wind power, see Analyzing Visuals: Texas Wind Farms.)

The transformation of the state's economy was, in part, guided by public policy, and economic development and growth are linked to actions of policy makers. Decisions to locate plants or new facilities are often shaped by governmental incentives, such as tax abatements, infrastructure development, and low-interest loans. The convergence of public and private interests played a key role in bringing high-tech incubators to Texas. Texas cities, with the support of state policy makers, made significant bids in the early 1980s to bring Microelectronics and Computer Technology Corporation (MCC), a pioneering research consortium of technology companies, to Austin.[64] As part of this bid, the University of Texas and Texas A&M University committed to upgrading their

ANALYZING VISUALS

Texas Wind Farms

The map shows the locations of current and proposed wind farms and wind conditions across the 254 counties of Texas. Examine the map, and then answer the questions.

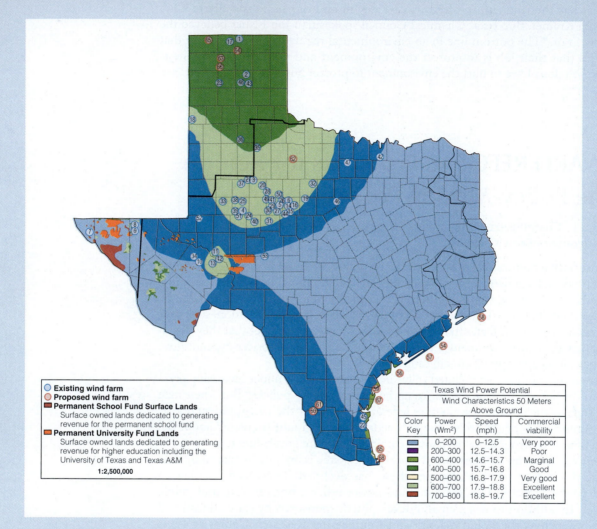

Legend:
○ **Existing wind farm**
○ **Proposed wind farm**
■ **Permanent School Fund Surface Lands**
Surface owned lands dedicated to generating revenue for the permanent school fund
■ **Permanent University Fund Lands**
Surface owned lands dedicated to generating revenue for higher education including the University of Texas and Texas A&M

1:2,500,000

Texas Wind Power Potential			
Wind Characteristics 50 Meters Above Ground			
Color Key	Power (Wm²)	Speed (mph)	Commercial viability
	0–200	0–12.5	Very poor
	200–300	12.5–14.3	Poor
	600–400	14.6–15.7	Marginal
	400–500	15.7–16.8	Good
	500–600	16.8–17.9	Very good
	600–700	17.9–18.8	Excellent
	700–800	18.8–19.7	Excellent

■ Where are most of the existing wind farms and proposed wind farms in Texas located?

■ What are some likely reasons that the wind farms have been and are being placed in these locations?

■ What sorts of issues are associated with collecting wind-generated electricity from wind farms spread over large areas? How reliable is wind energy, if it is dependent on climate conditions?

departments of computer science and electrical engineering. Now, almost thirty years later, state leaders continue to preach job creation, but the development of the strong educational system that is so crucial to the state's economic future continues to be a struggle.

Across much of the economic spectrum, employers require personnel with increased skills. Without a technologically literate workforce, these companies will not have a competitive edge in the global economy. Students and their parents are looking for high-quality education. A wide range of players, including policy makers, professionals, and advocacy groups, are pushing for reforms. But many other experts believe true reform will require increased state funding for education, and that isn't likely without a major overhaul of the state tax structure.

Major tax changes appear unlikely for now, mainly because of strong opposition to a personal income tax. But current tax sources—namely the state sales tax and local property taxes—are stretched almost to the breaking point. Texas will take steps toward enacting an income tax only when the business community decides that revenue option is essential to the state economy's future survival.

What Should I Have LEARNED?

Now that you have read this chapter, you should be able to:

⭐ **8.1 Trace the evolution of public policy in Texas, p. 236.**

Decisions by policy makers in earlier periods shaped the options available to contemporary policy makers. Previous economic downturns limited revenues available to earlier legislatures, and the laws they enacted, unless rescinded, determine available taxes. Earlier decisions to earmark specific taxes for specific purposes restrict their use today. Texans demanded local control of their schools after the end of Reconstruction, and this structure, which is still in place, requires an ongoing balancing act between the state and local school districts on funding and other educational policies. The legal concept of community property was derived from the laws of Mexico, and the principle is still found in property and family law in Texas today.

⭐ **8.2 Identify the multiple approaches to public policy analysis, p. 237.**

In addition to looking at policy as a series of stages or events in its development, numerous models can be used to help understand policy making, such as iron triangles and issue networks. In addition, policy outcomes can be understood as a product of the conflicting interests not only of private groups and individuals but also of public institutions.

⭐ **8.3 Analyze the state's budget-setting process and its central role in all public policy, p. 241.**

Texas operates with a biennial budget, which creates challenges because state agencies must anticipate their needs as much as three years in advance. Like other states, Texas prohibits deficit financing. Because Texas does not have a personal income tax, the state instead relies on regressive taxes, such as sales taxes. Budgetary problems are intensified during economic downturns.

⭐ **8.4 Evaluate current policies affecting funding, equity, and access to quality education in the areas of both public and higher education, p. 248.**

Today, Texas has more than 1,000 independent school districts governed by locally elected boards. The districts operate under educational policies primarily determined by state law and are funded by a combination of state and local property taxes. The variations in property values across the state have produced inequities in school funding, leading the courts to order the legislature to remedy the inequities. Access to higher education has also been impacted by a number of court decisions.

⭐ **8.5 Describe the policy challenges Texas faces in the areas of criminal justice, health and human services, and the environment, p. 255.**

The conservative political culture of Texas emphasizes retribution over rehabilitation for criminal behavior. Federal courts ordered the state to build new prisons to prevent overcrowding and improve conditions for inmates. But, with limited rehabilitation programs, the recidivism (return) rate of the prison population was high. Texas also has been unwilling historically to fund health and human services programs. Welfare reform has been challenging, although new federal and state laws require state officials to move thousands of people off the welfare rolls and into jobs. Texas has abundant natural resources but a lax, almost hostile attitude toward regulation. Petrochemical plants spew tons of pollutants into the air, but they also provide jobs for thousands of Texas workers and tax revenue for local and state governments. Water shortages are becoming critical in some parts of Texas, but the need to develop a comprehensive water policy is thwarted by outdated laws dealing with water and property rights.

⭐ **8.6 Characterize public policy reforms Texas has implemented to address contemporary challenges, p. 265.**

With few exceptions, policy changes have not come rapidly in Texas. Significant policy changes in education, voting rights, and criminal justice occurred with court intervention or the threat of court action. Changes in other areas tend to be incremental or piecemeal, as seen in water and environmental policies. Texas has demonstrated a long history of resistance to welfare policies, reflecting cultural values based on self-reliance. Less well understood by the general public is that conservative policy makers tend to be much more responsive to the demands and interests of the business community, which some pundits have termed welfare for the rich.

Test Yourself: Public Policy in Texas

★ **8.1 Trace the evolution of public policy in Texas, p. 236.**

Vestiges of Spanish and Mexican law can be seen in Texas
A. labor law.
B. oil and gas law.
C. intellectual property law.
D. unemployment law.
E. community property law.

★ **8.2 Identify the multiple approaches to public policy analysis, p. 237.**

Which of the following statements is least applicable to the formulation of public policy in Texas?
A. Many policies produce unintended consequences.
B. Many policies have indirect and direct benefits.
C. Most policy proposals make tradeoffs between costs and benefits.
D. Policy changes tend to be incremental and slow.
E. Most policies are under the direct control of the large urban counties.

★ **8.3 Analyze the state's budget-setting process and its central role in all public policy, p. 241.**

The Texas Legislature has the authority to borrow money for all but one of the following:
A. Highway construction.
B. Prison and jail construction.
C. Medical research conducted by research institutions.
D. Operating expenses such as salaries of state employees.
E. Construction of educational facilities.

★ **8.4 Evaluate current policies affecting funding, equity, and access to quality education in the areas of both public and higher education, p. 248.**

The biggest share of state expenditures (including federal funds appropriated by the legislature) is for
A. prisons and state jails.
B. highway construction.
C. education.
D. health and human services.
E. overall government operations.

★ **8.5 Describe the policy challenges Texas faces in the areas of criminal justice, health and human services, and the environment, p. 255.**

The landmark decision of *Ruiz* v. *Estelle* (1980) held that
A. the state's prison system violated the "cruel and unusual punishment" clause of the U.S. constitution.
B. the state's school finance system violated the state constitution.
C. the "right of recapture" of underground water on one's land was a fundamental right which could not be limited by the actions of a water district.
D. general obligation bonds were unconstitutional if they exceeded five percent of the state's annual revenue.
E. drug testing of student athletes was unconstitutional.

★ **8.6 Characterize public policy reforms Texas has implemented to address contemporary challenges, p. 265.**

Texas leads the nation in which of the following?
A. Coal production
B. Solar power
C. Electricity production
D. Wind power capacity
E. Natural gas

Essay Questions

1. Funding of public education aside, what do you perceive to be the major obstacles to improving the state's public school system?
2. What are some of the consequences of federal and state welfare policy over the past ten years?
3. Why is it so difficult to develop comprehensive statewide water policies?
4. Under what circumstances might the state of Texas adopt a personal income tax?

Key Terms

dedicated funds, p. 242
deficit financing, p. 241
Edgewood v. *Kirby*, p. 250
general obligation bonds, p. 245
House Bill 72, p. 250
income tax, p. 245

issue networks, p. 240
lottery, p. 244
"no pass, no play" rule, p. 250
Permanent University
    Fund (PUF), p. 253

property tax, p. 243
Ruiz v. *Estelle* (1980), p. 255
sales tax, p. 243
sin tax, p. 244

To Learn More on Public Policy in Texas

In the Library

Anderson, Ken. *Crime in Texas,* rev. ed. Austin: University of Texas Press, 2005.

Camarota, Steven A., and Karen Jensenius. *A Shifting Tide: Recent Trends in the Illegal Immigrant Population.* Washington, DC: Center for Immigration Studies, 2009.

Gilderbloom, John Ingram. *Invisible City: Poverty, Housing, and New Urbanism.* Austin: University of Texas Press, 2008.

Griffin, Roland C., ed. *Water Policy in Texas: Responding to the Rise in Scarcity.* Washington, DC: Resources for the Future Press, 2010.

Longo, Peter J., and David W. Yoskowitz. *Water on the Great Plains: Issues and Policies.* Lubbock: Texas Tech University Press, 2002.

Marbury, Laura Brock, and Mary E. Kelly. *Down to the Last Drop: 2009 Update—Spotlight on Groundwater Management in Texas.* New York: Environmental Defense Fund, 2009.

Marquart, James W., Sheldon Ekland-Olson, and Jonathan R. Sorensen. *The Rope, the Chair, and the Needle: Capital Punishment in Texas 1923–1990.* Austin: University of Texas Press, 1993.

North, Gerald, Jurgen North, and Judith Clarkson, eds. *The Impact of Global Warming on Texas.* Austin: University of Texas Press, 1995.

Perkinson, Robert. *Texas Tough: The Rise of America's Prison Empire.* New York: Metropolitan Books/Henry Holt, 2008.

Porter, Charles. *Spanish Water: Early Development in San Antonio.* College Station: Texas A&M Press, 2009.

Rodriquez, Louis J. and Yoshi Fukasawa, eds. *The Texas Economy: 21st Century Economic Challenges.* Lanham, MD: University Press of America, 1996.

San Miguel, Guadalupe, Jr. *"Let All of Them Take Heed": Mexican Americans and the Campaign for Educational Equality in Texas, 1910–1981.* Austin: University of Texas Press, 1987.

Shirley, Dennis. *Community Organizing for Urban School Reform.* Austin, TX: University of Texas Press, 1997.

Walsh, Jim, Frank Kemerer, and Laurie Maniotis. *The Educator's Guide to Texas School Law,* 7e. Austin: University of Texas Press, 2010.

Ward, Peter M. *Colonias and Public Policy in Texas and Mexico: Urbanization by Stealth.* Austin: University of Texas Press, 1999.

On the Web

To learn more about public policies affecting low- and middle-income people, go to the Center for Public Policy Priorities at **www.cppp.org.**

To learn more about a nonpartisan, nonprofit citizens organization committed to "honest and accountable government" in Texas, go to Common Cause of Texas at **www.commoncause.org.**

To learn more about an organization serving business interests in Texas, go to the Texas Association of Business at **www.txbiz.org.**

To learn more about state fiscal policy and other public policy issues in Texas, go to the Texas Taxpayers and Research Association at **www.ttara.org.**

Chapter 1

1. Social Science Data Analysis Network (SSDAN), *CensusScope* September 28, 2010, www.censusscope.org/us/s48/chart_popl.htm. Census 2000 analyzed by the Social Science Data Analysis Network (SSDAN).

2. Texas State Data Center and Office of the State Demographer, "Projections of the Population of Texas and Counties in Texas by Age, Sex and Race/Ethnicity for 2000–2040 (scenario 0.5)," February 2009, txsdc.utsa.edu/tpepp/2008projections/ 2008_txpopprj_txtotnum.php.

3. Texas State Data Center, "Projections of the Population of Texas."

4. During 1994, Texas passed New York in population, replacing it as the second largest state in population. The 2000 Census officially established Texas as the second largest state. California, with 37 million residents, remained the most populous state in 2009.

5. U.S. Census Bureau, *Annual Community Survey, 2008,* factfinder.census.gov/home/saff/main.html?_lang=en.

6. W. W. Newcomb Jr., *The Indians of Texas: From Prehistoric to Modern Times* (Austin: University of Texas Press, 1961), 22.

7. Newcomb, *The Indians of Texas,* 180–5.

8. Arnoldo De Leon, *Mexican Americans in Texas: A Brief History* (Arlington Heights, IL: Harlan Davidson, 1993), 7–19.

9. De Leon, *Mexican Americans in Texas,* 20.

10. Donald E. Chipman, *Spanish Texas, 1519–1821* (Austin: University of Texas Press, 1992), 242–60.

11. Terry G. Jordan, "A Century and a Half of Ethnic Change in Texas, 1836–1986," *Southwestern Historical Quarterly* 89 (April 1986): 392–4.

12. National Association of Latino Elected and Appointed Officials, *2009 National Directory of Latino Elected Officials* (Los Angeles: NALEO Education Fund, 2009). Courtesy of Salvador Sepulveda.

13. "Hispanics Key in '98 Vote, Both Parties Say," *Corpus Christi Caller-Times Interactive* September 22, 1998, corpuschristionline. com/texas98/texas20612.html; Lomi Kriel, "Dems, GOP Vie for Sought-After Hispanic Vote," *Daily Texan Online* October 16, 2003, www.dailytexanonline.com/news/2004/06/03/TopStories/ Gop-Convention.To.Rejuvenate.Support-684288.shtml; and Will Krueger, "Hispanic Leaders Looking Ahead," *Daily Texan Online* October 17, 2003, www.dailytexanonline.com/news/2003/10/17/ TopStories/Hispanic.Leaders.Looking.Ahead-531638.shtml.

14. Jordan, "A Century and a Half of Ethnic Change," 400–1; Terry G. Jordan, et al., *Texas: A Geography* (Boulder, CO: Westview, 1984), 77, 79.

15. Jordan, "A Century and a Half of Ethnic Change," 402, 404; and Jordan, et al., *Texas,* 79.

16. Joint Center for Political and Economic Studies, *National Roster of Black Elected Officials, 2002* (Washington, DC: Joint Center for Political and Economic Studies, 2003).

17. Comptroller of Public Accounts, "Lone Star Asians," *Fiscal Notes* (November 1997): 3–5; and *National Asian Pacific American Political Almanac, 2003–2004* (Los Angeles: UCLA Asian American Studies Center, 2003), 300–302.

18. Jordan, Bean, and Holmes, *Texas,* 71, 73.

19. U.S. Census Bureau, *2008 American Community Survey,* September, 2009, factfinder.census.gov/servlet/ADPGeoSearchByListServlet? ds_name=ACS_2008_1YR_G00_&_lang=en&_ts.= 294677749035.

20. Texas State Data Center and Office of the State Demographer, *2008 Total Population Estimates for Texas Metropolitan Statistical Areas,* January 2010, txsdc.utsa.edu/tpepp/2008_txpopest_msa.php.

21. U.S. Census Bureau, *2000 Census: Demographic Profiles* (September 28, 2010), censtats.census.gov/data/TX/04048.pdf.

22. The exit polls showed Bush increasing his share of the Hispanic vote in Texas in the 2004 presidential election from 43 percent to 59 percent (corrected to 49 percent). However, the 59 percent for Bush did not stand up when analyses of actual votes in heavily Hispanic counties in South Texas and heavily Hispanic precincts in Dallas were presented. See David L. Leal, et al., "The Latino Vote in the 2004 Election," *PS: Political Science and Politics* 38 (January 2005): 41–49.

23. See Pew Hispanic Center, "Latinos in California, Texas, New York, Florida, and New Jersey," Survey Brief, March 2004, www.pewhispanic.org/site/docs/pdf/LATINOS%20IN%20CA-TX - NY-FL-NJ-031904.pdf.

24. Pew Hispanic Center, "The Hispanic Vote in the 2008 Election," Nov. 7, 2008, pewresearch.org/pubs/1024/exit-poll-analysis- hispanics.

25. Pew Hispanic Center, "Hispanics and the New Administration," Jan. 15, 2009, pewhispanic.org/reports/report.php?ReportID=101.

26. Louis DeSipio, "Latino Civil and Political Participation," in Marta Tienda and Faith Mitchell, eds., *Hispanics and the Future of America* (Washington, DC: National Academies Press, 2006), 454.

27. Harold Meyerson, "The Rising Latino Tide," *American Prospect, Online Edition* (November 18, 2002), www.prospect.org/web/page .ww?section=root&name=ViewPrint&articleId=6611.

28. Louis DeSipio, *Counting on the Latino Vote: Latinos as a New Electorate* (Charlottesville: University Press of Virginia, 1996), 48–56; and *Public Broadcasting Latino Poll 2000,* State Tabulations, July 27, 2000, www.latinopoll2000.com.

29. Pew Hispanic Center, "2007 National Survey of Latinos: As Illegal Immigration Issue Heats Up, Hispanics Feel a Chill," Dec. 13, 2007, pewhispanic.org/reports/report.php?ReportID=84.

30. Carl Davis, et al., *Who Pays? A Distributional Analysis of the Tax Systems of All 50 States,* 3rd ed. (Washington, DC: Citizens for Tax Justice and the Institute on Taxation and Economic Policy, 2009), 102, www.itepnet.org/whopays3.pdf.

31. Elizabeth Mendes, "Uninsured: Highest Percentage in Texas, Lowest in Mass.," August 19, 2009, Gallup Poll, www.gallup.com/poll/ 122387/uninsured-highest-percentage-texas-lowest-mass.aspx.

32. T. R. Fehrenbach, *Seven Keys to Texas,* rev. ed. (El Paso: Texas Western, 1986), 3–4.

33. T. R. Fehrenbach, "Seven Keys to Understanding Texas," *Atlantic Monthly* (March 1975): 123–4.

34. Fehrenbach, *Seven Keys to Texas,* 22.

35. T. R. Fehrenbach, *Lone Star: A History of Texas and the Texans* (New York: Macmillan, 1968), 472–6.

36. Fehrenbach, *Seven Keys to Texas,* 29.

37. Fehrenbach, *Seven Keys to Texas,* 24–25.

38. Fehrenbach, *Seven Keys to Texas,* 76.

39. Alwyn Barr, *Texans in Revolt: The Battle for San Antonio, 1835* (Austin: University of Texas Press, 1990), 1–4.

40. William C. Brinkley, *The Texas Revolution* (Austin: Texas State Historical Association, 1952).

41. Quoted in Mark E. Nackman, *A Nation Within a Nation* (Port Washington, NY: Kennikat, 1975), 27.

42. Joe B. Frantz, *Texas: A Bicentennial History* (New York: Norton, 1976), 69.

43. Walter Lord, *A Time to Stand: The Epic of the Alamo* (Lincoln: University of Nebraska Press, 1961), 54.

44. Lord, *A Time to Stand,* 82.

45. Paul Andrew Hutton, "The Alamo: An American Epic," *American History Illustrated* (March 1986): 24.

46. Lord, *A Time to Stand*, 142.

47. Lon Tinkle, *The Alamo* (New York: McGraw-Hill, 1958), 118.

48. Gilbert M. Cuthbertson, "Individual Freedom: The Evolution of a Political Ideal," in Robert F. O'Connor, ed., *Texas Myths* (College Station: Texas A&M University Press, 1986), 179.

49. David Montejano, *Anglos and Mexicans in the Making of Texas, 1836–1986* (Austin: University of Texas Press, 1987), 305.

50. Fehrenbach, *Seven Keys to Texas*, 95.

51. Fehrenbach, *Seven Keys to Texas*, 128.

52. Samuel P. Huntington, *American Politics: The Promise of Disharmony* (Cambridge, MA: Harvard University Press, 1981), 13–60.

53. William S. Maddox and Stuart A. Lilie, *Beyond Liberal and Conservative: Reassessing the Political Spectrum* (Washington, DC: Cato Institute, 1984), 7–21.

54. Maddox and Lilie, *Beyond Liberal and Conservative*, 14–15.

55. Roscoe Martin, *The People's Party in Texas* (Austin: University of Texas Press, 1970), 31–52.

56. Martin, *The People's Party in Texas*, 82–112.

57. The Gallup Polls conducted in Texas during 2009 indicated that 43.5 percent of the respondents identified themselves as conservative, 36.0 percent identified themselves as moderates, 16.7 percent identified themselves as liberal, and 3.8 percent would not identify themselves ideologically. (Feburary 3, 2010) www.gallup.com/poll/125480/Ideology-Three-DeepSouth-States-Conservative.aspx.

58. V. O. Key Jr., *Southern Politics* (New York: Vintage Books, 1949), 261.

59. National Agriculture Statistics Service (NASS), Agricultural Statistics Board, U.S. Department of Agriculture, "Crop Production: Cotton," 12-9-2009, usda.mannlib.cornell.edu/usda/nass/CropProd//2000s/2009/CropProd-12-1-2009.txt.

60. Fehrenbach, *Seven Keys to Texas*, 52–54; and *Texas Almanac, 1986–1987* (Dallas: Dallas Morning News, 1985), 212.

61. National Agriculture Statistics Service (NASS), Agricultural Statistics Board, U.S. Department of Agriculture, "Cattle," January 29, 2010, mannlib.cornell.edu/USDA/current/CATT/CATT-01-29-2010.pdf.

62. Fehrenbach, *Seven Keys to Texas*, 58–60; Donald A. Hicks, "Advanced Industrial Development," in Anthony Champagne and Edward J. Harpham, eds., *Texas at the Crossroads: People, Politics, and Policy* (College Station: Texas A&M University Press, 1987), 49–50; *Texas Almanac, 1994–1995*, 608; Comptroller of Public Accounts, *Fiscal Notes* January 1994: 1, 14; and "The Texas Economy Online," Texas Department of Economic Development Web site, October 26, 1999, www.bidc.state.tx.us/overview/2-2te.html.

63. Bruce Wright, "Weathering the Storm," *Fiscal Notes* (March 2009).

64. Comptroller of Public Accounts, "The Texas Economies: What Makes Them Tick," *Fiscal Notes* (December 1993): 7–10.

65. Central Intelligence Agency, *The World Factbook—2009*, www.cia.gov/library/publications/the-world-factbook/

66. Ali Anari and Mark G. Dotzour, "Monthly Review of the Texas Economy—May 2009," Real Estate Center at Texas A&M University, Technical Report, 1862.

67. U.S. Census Bureau, *Small Area Income and Poverty Estimates, 2008* (November 18, 2009).

68. *Forbes*, "The Four Hundred Richest Americans," Special Report, September 30, 2009, forbes.com/lists/2009/54/rich-list-09_The-400-Richest-Americans_Rank.html.

69. U.S. Census Bureau, *2008 American Community Survey* (September 2009).

70. Daniel Elazar, *American Federalism: A View from the States*, 3rd ed. (New York: Harper and Row, 1984).

71. U.S. Census Bureau, *American Community Surveys;* U.S. Census Bureau, *Statistical Abstract*, 2009; U.S. Department of Agriculture, *Food and Nutrition Program;* The Centers for Disease Control and Prevention, *National Vital Statistics Report;* Kaiser Family Foundation, 3-7-2010 www.statehealthfacts.org; and Commonwealth Fund, "Aiming Higher: Results from a State Scorecard on Health System Performance," 2009.

72. Lawrence M. Mead, "State Political Culture and Welfare Reform," *Policy Studies Journal* 32 (May 2004): 271–296.

Chapter 2

1. Juan B. Elizondo Jr., "Ratliff: Time to Rewrite Constitution," *Austin American-Statesman* (October 28, 1999): B6; Bill Ratliff and Rob Junell, "A New Constitution for the New Millennium," *Austin American-Statesman* (December 9, 1998): A15; and Osler McCarthy, "Poll Shows Support for New Constitution," *Austin American-Statesman* (February 13, 1999): B3.

2. Ralph W. Steen, "Convention of 1836," *Handbook of Texas Online*, www.tsha.utexas.edu.

3. Joe C. Ericson, "Constitution of the Republic of Texas," *Handbook of Texas Online*, www.tsha.utexas.edu.

4. Walter L. Buenger, "Constitution of 1861," *Handbook of Texas Online*, www.tsha.utexas.edu.

5. S. S. McKay, "Constitution of 1866," *Handbook of Texas Online*, www.tsha.utexas.edu.

6. Claude Elliott, "Constitutional Convention of 1869," *Handbook of Texas Online*, www.tsha.utexas.edu.

7. Seth S. McKay, "Constitution of 1869," *Handbook of Texas Online*, www.tsha.utexas.edu.

8. John Walker Mauer, "State Constitutions in a Time of Crisis: The Case of the Texas Constitution of 1876," *Texas Law Review* 68 (June 1990): 1638–9.

9. Joe E. Ericson, "The Delegates to the Convention of 1875: A Reappraisal," *Southwestern Historical Quarterly* 67 (1963/1964): 22–27. Ericson's reappraisal of the delegates is based on Nat Q. Henderson's *Directory of the Officers and Members of the Constitutional Convention of the State of Texas, A.D. 1875* (Austin: n.p., 1875).

10. Mauer, "State Constitutions in a Time of Crisis," 1646–7.

11. Patrick G. Williams, "Of Rutabagas and Redeemers: Rethinking the Texas Constitution of 1876," *Southwestern Historical Quarterly* 106 (October 2002): 250.

12. Williams, "Of Rutabagas and Redeemers," 250–3.

13. Although the content of the section was deleted, the title remains to prevent confusion with the numbering of the remaining articles.

14. *Texas Constitution*, Article 1, sections 12 and 29, respectively.

15. Donald S. Lutz, "The Texas Constitution," in Kent L. Tedin, Donald S. Lutz, and Edward P. Fuchs, eds., *Perspectives on American and Texas Politics*, 5th ed. (Dubuque, IA: Kendall/Hunt, 1998), 45.

16. Lutz, "The Texas Constitution."

17. Janice C. May, "Constitutional Revision in Texas," in Richard H. Kraemer and Philip W. Barnes, eds., *Texas: Readings in Politics, Government, and Public Policy* (San Francisco: Chandler, 1971), 318.

18. See *Texas Constitution*, Article 16, section 44.

19. Dick Smith, "Constitutional Revision, 1876–1961," in Fred Gantt Jr., Irving O. Dawson, and Luther G. Hagard Jr., eds., *Governing Texas: Documents and Readings* (New York: Crowell, 1966), 53.

20. The amendment accounts for sections and articles of the current constitution that have only the title or section number appearing in the text. For example, Article 3, section 3a (repealed August 5, 1969).

21. Legislative Council, Analysis of Proposed Constitutional Amendments, November 2, 1999, Election (Austin, TX: Legislative Council, 1999).

22. Smith, "Constitutional Revision," 55.

23. Informational Booklet on the Proposed 1975 Revision of the Texas Constitution, 64th Legislature, 1975, 3–7; Janice C. May, *The Texas Constitutional Revision Experience in the 1970s* (Austin, TX: Sterling Swift, 1975), 25–30; and Smith, "Constitutional Revision," 51–55.

24. See Texas Advisory Commission on Intergovernmental Relations, *The Texas Constitutional Revision Commission of 1973* (Austin: Texas Advisory Commission on Intergovernmental Relations, 1972), on the importance of the commission to the convention's success.

25. May, *The Texas Constitutional Revision Experience*, 160–200.

26. "Amendment Fatigue," *Austin-American Statesman* (November 6, 1997): A14.

Chapter 3

1. V.O. Key Jr., *Politics, Parties, and Pressure Groups*, 4th ed. (New York, NY: Thomas Y. Crowell, 1958), 181–83.

2. The fifteen counties are Bexar, Brazoria, Collin, Dallas, Denton, El Paso, Fort Bend, Galveston, Harris, Hidalgo, Jefferson, Montgomery, Smith, Tarrant, and Travis.

3. Samuel J. Eldersveld and Hanes Walton Jr., *Political Parties in American Society*, 2nd ed. (New York: Bedford/St. Martin's, 2000), 106.

4. Frank B. Feigert, et al., "Texas: Incipient Polarization?" *American Review of Politics* 24 (Summer 2003): 192–3.

5. Feigert, et al., "Texas: Incipient Polarization?" 192–3.

6. Paul Lenchner, "The Party System in Texas," in Anthony Champagne and Edward J. Harpham, eds., *Texas Politics: A Reader*, 2nd ed. (New York: Norton, 1998), 165–7.

7. Louis Dubose, "Kay Bailey Finds Religion," *Texas Observer* (July 12, 1996): 4–8.

8. A. Phillips Brooks, "GOP Lieutenant Gets Close Look," *Austin American-Statesman* (August 9, 1997): B1, B7.

9. Nate Blakeslee, "Farewell to Barry G.," *Texas Observer* (July 3, 1998): 13–15; and Sam Dealey, "Bush-Whipped: The Texas GOP Undergoes a Little Soul-Searching," *American Spectator* (August 1998): 58–59.

10. Jake Bernstein, "Elephant Wars: The Christian Right Flexes Its Muscle at the Republican Convention," *Texas Observer* (July 5, 2002): 8–9, 19, 29.

11. "2006 State Republican Party Platform," Republican Party of Texas, www.texasgop.org.

12. Barbara Norrander, "Determinants of Local Party Campaign Activity," *Social Sciences Quarterly* 67 (September 1986): 567.

13. The Scripps-Howard Texas Poll question is: "Generally speaking, do you usually think of yourself as a Democrat, a Republican, an independent, or something else?" According to state law in Texas, a party member is anyone who participates in the party's primary election.

14. James A. Dryer, et al., "New Voters, Switchers, and Political Party Realignment in Texas," *Western Political Quarterly* 41 (March 1988): 155–67; Kent L. Tedin, "The Transition of Electoral Politics in Texas: 1978–1990," in Kent L. Tedin and Donald S. Lutz, eds., *Perspectives on American and Texas Politics: A Collection of Essays*, 3rd ed. (Dubuque, IA: Kendall/Hunt, 1992), 129–51; and James A. Dyer, et al., "Party Identification and Public Opinion in Texas, 1984–1994: Establishing a Competitive Party System," in Anthony Champagne and Edward J. Harpham, eds., *Texas Politics: A Reader*, 2nd ed. (New York: Norton, 1998), 108–22.

15. "Republican Party of Texas Growth Chart," Republican Party of Texas, www.texasgop.org (percentages calculated by the authors).

16. Gregory S. Thielemann and Euel Elliott, "Texas: Same As It Ever Was?" *American Review of Politics* 26 (Summer 2005): 236.

17. Thomas L. Whatley, ed., *Texas Government Newsletter* (January 24, 1983): 2.

18. Keith E. Hamm and Robert Harmel, "Legislative Party Development and the Speaker System: The Case of Texas," *Journal of Politics* 55 (November 1993): 1145–6.

19. Hamm and Harmel, "Legislative Party Development," 1145–6.

20. See R. Bruce Anderson, "Party Caucus Development and the Insurgent Minority Party in Formerly One-Party State Legislatures," *American Review of Politics* 19 (Fall 1998): 191–216.

21. *Texas Lawyer* (May 1994): 1, 28.

22. Paul Allen Beck and Frank J. Sorauf, *Party Politics in America*, 7th ed. (New York: HarperCollins, 1992), 420; Walt Borges, "The Court's Big Chill," *Texas Lawyer* (September 4, 1995): 1; Walt Borges, "The Texas Supreme Court in 1998–1999: Moderating the Counter-Revolution," A Report of Court Watch, Project of Texas Watch, www.texaswatch.org; and "Decade of Watching and Waiting: Texas Supreme Court Year-in-Review 2005–2006," Court Watch Annual Review, March 29, 2007, www.texaswatch.org.

23. Texans for Public Justice, *Austin's Oldest Profession: Texas' Top Lobby Clients & Those Who Service Them*, May 2010, info.tpj.org/reports/austinsoldest09/index.html. The exact amount of lobbying contracts cannot be established because state reporting requirements only require disclosure within a dollar range.

24. Texas Administrative Code, title 1, part 2, chapter 34, specifies the requirements for registration.

25. Kevin Bogardus, "Statehouse Revolvers," Center for Public Integrity, October 12, 2006, www.publicintegrity.org/hiredguns/report.aspx?aid=747.

26. Osler McCarthy, "Minority Lobbyists Increase Their Presence at Legislature," *Austin American-Statesman* (April 12, 1999): A1, A12.

27. Quoted in Robert Bryce, "Access Through the Lobby," *Texas Observer* (February 24, 1995): 16.

28. Bryce, "Access Through the Lobby," 16.

29. Alan Rosenthal, *The Third House: Lobbyists and Lobbying in the States* (Washington, DC: CQ Press, 1993), 190–9.

30. Texans for Public Justice, "Austin's Oldest Profession," May 2010, www.info.tpj.org/reports/austinsoldest09/index.html.

31. Rosenthal, *The Third House*, 182–90.

32. Bryce, "Access Through the Lobby," 16.

33. Texas Ethics Commission, "Political Committees Sorted by Start Date," June 15, 2010, www.ethics.state.tx.us/tedd/PACs_By_Start_Date.pdf.

34. Texans for Public Justice, "Texas PACs: 2008 Election Cycle Spending," April 2009, www.tpj.org/reports/txpac08/pacs2008.pdf.

35. Jeffrey M. Berry, *The Interest Group Society*, 2nd ed. (New York: HarperCollins, 1989), 154–7.

36. Fred Gantt Jr., *The Chief Executive in Texas: A Study in Gubernatorial Leadership* (Austin: University of Texas Press, 1964), 269–71.

37. Dave McNeely, "GOP Voters Switch to Fight Richards," *Austin American-Statesman* (April 5, 1994): A11.

38. Richard Murray, "The 1982 Texas Election in Perspective," *Texas Journal of Political Studies* 5 (Spring/Summer 1983): 49–50; and Paul Burka, "Primary Lesson," *Texas Monthly* (July 1986): 104–5.

39. W. Lance Bennett, *The Governing Crisis: Media, Money, and Marketing in American Elections* (New York: St. Martin's, 1992), 84–111.

40. Texans for Public Justice, "Money in Politex: A Guide to Money in the 2006 Texas Elections," September 2007, www.info.tpj.org/reports/politex2006/index06.html.

41. Texans for Public Justice, "Money in Politex: A Guide to Money in the 2008 Texas Elections," September 2009, www.info.tpj.org/reports/politex08/index.html.

42. Kaye Northcott, "Getting Elected," *Mother Jones* (November 1982): 18.

43. Northcott, "Getting Elected," 19.

44. Texans for Public Justice, Press Release, September 29, 2009, info
.tpj.org/reports/politex08/pressrelease08.html.

45. Texans for Public Justice, Press Release.

46. See Jon Ford, "Texas: Big Money," in Herbert E. Alexander, ed.,
Campaign Money: Reform and Reality in the States (New York: Free
Press, 1976), 78–109.

47. Quoted in David Elliot, "Image Is Everything: How TV Has
Reshaped Campaigning," *Austin American-Statesman* (October 16,
1994): A1, A8.

48. For an excellent article on Texas campaign consultants, see Juan
B. Elizondo Jr., "Political Consultants: How They Do It," *Austin
American-Statesman* (October 18, 1998): H1, H5.

49. Peggy Fikac, "Texas Governor: The Democratic 'Dream Team' Bites
the Dust," in Larry Sabato, ed., *Midterm Madness: The Elections of
2002* (Lanham, MD: Rowman and Littlefield, 2003), 259.

50. Delbert A. Taebel, et al., "The Politics of Early Voting in Texas:
Perspectives of County Party Chairs," *Texas Journal of Political Studies*
16 (Spring/Summer 1994): 43–44.

51. Robert M. Stein, "Early Voting," *Public Opinion Quarterly* 62 (Spring
1998): 57–69; and Paul Gronke, et al., "Early Voting and Turnout,"
PS: Political Science & Politics 40 (October 2007): 639–45.

52. Ruy A. Teixeira, *The Disappearing American Voter* (Washington, DC:
Brookings Institution, 1992), 12–13.

53. Morris P. Fiorina, "The Electorate at the Polls in the 1990s," in
Sandy Maisel, ed., *The Parties Respond: Changes in American Parties
and Campaigns*, 2nd ed. (Boulder, CO: Westview, 1994), 124–5.
Angus Campbell, et al., *The American Voter* (Chicago: University of
Chicago Press, 1960), 523–31, provides the classic statement of the
influence of these factors.

54. *Texas Poll Report* (Fall 1986): 4; and Kent L. Tedin, "The 1982
Election for Governor of Texas," *Texas Journal of Political Studies* 5
(Spring/ Summer 1983): 29.

55. John C. Henry, "Poll Shows Anti-White Sentiment," *Austin
American-Statesman* (December 5, 1986): B2.

56. Arthur H. Miller, et al., "Schematic Assessments of Presidential
Candidates," *American Political Science Review* 80 (June 1986): 521–40.

57. Thomas L. Whatley, ed., *Texas Government Newsletter* (November
17, 1986): 2.

58. Fox News Election Day Poll: Texas (Governor), November 8, 2002,
www.foxnews.com.

59. Gardner Selby, "Texas Voters Might Be Spectators As Parties
Choose Presidential Nominees," *Austin American-Statesman*
December 30, 2007 www.statesman.com/news/content/region/
legislature/stories/12/30/1230texpres.html.

60. State of Texas, Office of the Governor, Message, "Veto of H.B. 770,"
May 25, 2007, www.lrl.state.tx.us/scanned/vetoes/80/HB770m.pdf.

Chapter 4

1. Texas State Historical Association, "Mexican Government of Texas,"
Handbook of Texas Online, www.tsha.utexas.edu.

2. Texas State Historical Association, "Convention of 1833" and
"Republic of Texas," *Handbook of Texas Online*, www.tsha.utexas.edu.

3. Texas State Historical Association, "Congress of the Republic of
Texas," *Handbook of Texas Online*, www.tsha.utexas.edu.

4. Texas State Historical Association, "Lorenzo de Zavala," *Handbook of
Texas Online*, www.tsha.utexas.edu.

5. David Montejano, *Anglos and Mexicans in the Making of Texas,
1836–1986* (Austin: University of Texas Press, 1987), 38.

6. See J. Mason Brewer, *Negro Legislators of Texas*, 2nd ed. (Austin:
Jenkins, 1970).

7. New Hampshire, Pennsylvania, Georgia, Missouri, Massachusetts,
Connecticut, and Maine have larger lower houses. National
Conference of State Legislatures, "Population and Legislative
Size," www.ncsl.org.

8. Impeachment is just one of the constitutional means by which state
officials may be removed from office. See Article 15 of the Texas
Constitution.

9. See House Research Organization, "Constitutional Order-of-
Business Provision," *Daily Floor Report* (January 30, 2007): 2; and
Enrique Rangel, "House Members Block Rules for Bills," *Amarillo
Globe-News* (January 31, 2007).

10. National Conference of State Legislatures, "2010 Legislator
Compensation," November 2010, www.ncsl.org; and Council of
State Governments, *Book of the States 2007*, vol. 39, February 2009,
(Lexington, KY: Council of State Governments, 2007), 93–94.

11. National Conference of State Legislatures, "2008 State Legislative
Session Calendar," February 2009, www.ncsl.org.

12. See National Conference of State Legislatures, "Full and Part Time
Legislatures," June 2009, www.ncsl.org.

13. James R. Jensen, "Legislative Apportionment in Texas," *Social Studies*
2, University of Houston Public Affairs Research Center, 1964; and
David Richards, "So Long, Oscar," *Texas Observer* (November 17,
2000): 11.

14. Projections are based on a number of variables, including past
population growth, deaths, births, and immigration. It is impossible
to know before the 2010 U.S. Census is completed the exact
population count, but projections provide some indication of what
the size of legislative districts will be after the redistricting of 2011.
Texas State Data Center, "Population 2000 and Projected Population
2005–2040 by Race/Ethnicity and Migration Scenario for State of
Texas," February 2009, txsdc.utsa.edu.

15. See National Conference of State Legislatures, *Redistricting Law
2000* (Denver, CO: National Conference of State Legislatures, 1999).

16. House Research Organization, "New Districts in Place for 2002
Elections," *Interim News*, no. 77-4 (January 14, 2002).

17. Ralph A. Wooster, "Membership in Early Texas Legislatures,
1850–1860," *Southwestern Historical Quarterly* 69 (October 1965):
163–73.

18. Gary Moncrief, Richard Niemi, and Lynda Powell, "Turnover
in State Legislatures: An Update," Western Political Science
Association Annual Meeting. San Diego, CA. March 22–25, 2008.

19. Tenure calculated by authors from individual member data
(2007–2008 legislature) provided by Office of the Chief Clerk
(House) and Office of the Secretary of the Senate.

20. Thomas H. Little, et al., "Term Limits: Legislatures' Adaptation,"
Book of the States 2007, vol. 39 , 70–74. For more information on
initiative and referendum, see Shaun Bowler, Todd Donovan, and
Caroline Tolbert, eds., *Citizens as Legislators: Direct Democracy in the
United States* (Columbus: Ohio State University Press, 1998).

21. Categorization is difficult, as legislators use different terms to report
their occupations. Business, for instance, includes business, insurance,
finance, real estate, construction, etc. Members can also list more
than one occupation. Calculated by authors based on House
biographical profiles provided by Office of the Chief Clerk (House)
and Senate Media Services, "Texas Senators 80th Legislature," 2007.

22. National Conference of State Legislatures, "Women in State
Legislatures: 2009 Legislative Session," July 30, 2009, www.ncsl.org.

23. National Conference of State Legislatures, "Number of African
American Legislators 2009" and "Number of Latino Legislators
2009," January 23, 2009, www.ncsl.org.

24. Texas State Senate, "Facts About the Senate of the 81st Legislature,"
January 13, 2009, www.senate.state.tx.us:

25. See, for instance, "Sierra Club Environmental Voting Record,"
2007, www.texas.sierraclub.org; and Young Conservatives of Texas,
December 2009, "Legislative Ratings for the 81st Legislature,"
yct.org.

26. Any such ranking is partly an artifact of the votes chosen. Different record votes could have produced different results, and absences can influence one's ranking. For a description of the earlier votes, see Stefan Haag, et al., *Texas Politics and Government: Ideas, Institutions, and Policies* (New York: Addison Wesley Longman, 1997), 272; Stefan Haag, et al., *Texas Politics and Government: Ideas, Institutions, and Policies*, 2nd ed. (New York: Addison Wesley Longman, 2001), 239, and 3rd ed. (2003), 249; and Gary Keith and Stefan Haag, *Texas Politics and Government: Continuity and Change* (New York: Pearson, 2006), 107, and 2nd ed. (2008), 111.

27. Michael King, "Endangered Species?" *Austin Chronicle* July 18, 2003, www.austinchronicle.com.

28. Malcolm E. Jewell and Marcia Lynn Whicker, *Legislative Leadership in the American States* (Ann Arbor: University of Michigan Press, 1994), 194.

29. For a description of this nonparty speaker system and the current birthing of parties that threatens to undo that system, see Keith Hamm and Robert Harmel, "Legislative Party Development and the Speaker System: The Case of the Texas House," *Journal of Politics* 55 (November 1993): 1140–51.

30. *Dallas News* (December 30, 1971).

31. Gary Moncrief, "Committee Stacking and Reform in the Texas House of Representatives," *Texas Journal of Political Studies* 2:1 (1979): 47.

32. *Dallas Times-Herald* (December 1, 1980); *San Angelo Standard Times* (February 13, 1983); and *Austin American-Statesman* (January 11, 1981).

33. Jewell and Whicker, *Legislative Leadership in the American States*, 79.

34. The three were James Wilson Henderson, Hardin Richard Runnels, and Coke Stevenson. Texas Legislative Council, *Presiding Officers of the Texas Legislature, 1846–1995*, revised ed. (Austin: Texas Legislative Council, 1995), 21, 25, and 77.

35. Council of State Governments, *Book of the States 2007*, vol. 39 (Lexington, KY: Council of State Governments, 2007), 199.

36. For more detailed information, see House Research Organization, "How a Bill Becomes Law: 80th Legislature," *Focus Report* (February 1, 2007); Rules and Housekeeping Resolutions, *Daily Floor Report* (January 12 and 13, 2005); and Hugh L. Brady, *Texas House Practice*, 2nd ed. (Austin: Capitol Hill Books, 2007).

37. The Local and Consent Calendar is supposed to be reserved for noncontroversial bills (though sometimes a controversial matter will be sneaked through on it). Bills on this calendar are not usually debated; if they are contested, they will be pulled from this calendar.

38. This daily calendar actually includes several calendars. Bills are considered on Major State, General State, Emergency, Resolutions, Constitutional Amendments, Local and Consent, or Senate Calendars.

39. For an account of the incident, see Robert Heard, *The Miracle of the Killer Bees* (Austin: Honey Hill, 1981).

40. Technically, the rules only require that a majority of members of the conference committee from each chamber sign the report. This loophole allows "phantom" meetings—some conference committees never meet. The chairs simply negotiate the language behind closed doors, then present it to the others for their signatures.

41. Council of State Governments, *Book of the States 2005*, vol. 37 (Lexington, KY: Council of State Governments, 2005).

42. See the General Laws of Texas, 42nd Legislature, Regular Session, chap. 206; and Stuart A. MacCorkle and Dick Smith, *Texas Government*, 2nd ed. (New York: McGraw-Hill, 1952), 99, 160.

43. Fred Gantt Jr., *The Chief Executive in Texas: A Study in Gubernatorial Leadership* (Austin: University of Texas Press, 1964), 99.

44. MacCorkle and Smith first commented on this occurrence in the 1951 session. See MacCorkle and Smith, *Texas Government*, 99.

45. Governor Rick Perry, "Proposed 2008–09 State Budget," January 2007; and Legislative Budget Board, "Legislative Budget Estimates for the 2008–2009 Biennium."

46. Council of State Governments, *Book of the States 2004*, vol. 36 (Lexington, KY: Council of State Governments, 2004), 362.

47. Alan Rosenthal, "The Legislature: Unraveling of Institutional Fabric," in Carl E. Van Horn, ed., *The State of the States*, 3rd ed. (Washington, DC: CQ Press, 1996), 111, 124.

48. Rosenthal, "The Legislature"; and Thad Beyle, *State Government: Congressional Quarterly's Guide to Current Issues and Activities, 1998–99* (Washington, DC: CQ Press, 1998), 71.

49. 2007 List of Registered Lobbyists, Texas Ethics Commission, as of December 31, 2007, www.ethics.state.tx.us.

50. *Fort Worth Star-Telegram* (January 13, 1983).

51. See, for instance, Texans for Public Justice, "Austin's Oldest Profession: Texas' Top Lobby Clients and Those Who Service Them," August 2006, www.tpj.org.

52. See, for example, Texans for Public Justice, "Capitol Spending: Officeholder Expenditures in 2007," January 2008, www.tpj.org.

53. Steven Kreytak, "Pulling the Plug on 'Ghost Votes,'" *Austin American-Statesman* (June 27, 2008): 1.

Chapter 5

1. Sources for this material include Janet Elliott, et al., "Perry Orders Cancer Virus Vaccine for Young Girls," *Houston Chronicle* (February 3, 2007): A1; Janet Elliott, "Critics Rip Perry's Vaccine Mandate," *Houston Chronicle* (February 6, 2007): A1; Corrie MacLaggan, "Governor Defends HPV Decision," *Austin American-Statesman* (February 8, 2007); Corrie MacLaggan, "Furor Over HPV Vaccine Shocked Perry," *Austin American-Statesman* (February 23, 2007): A01; Corrie MacLaggan, "Panel Challenges Hawkins on HPV," *Austin American-Statesman* (March 1, 2007): B01; Clay Robison, "Committee Debates Cancer Vaccine Plan," *Houston Chronicle* (February 20, 2007): B1; and Janet Elliott, "House Votes to Block HPV Order," *Houston Chronicle* (March 15, 2007): B4.

2. Executive Order RP-65, February 2, 2007, www.governor.state.tx.us.

3. Linda Johnson, "Merck Ends Push in States to Get Girls Immunized," *Austin American-Statesman* (February 21, 2007): A06.

4. Fred Gantt Jr., *The Chief Executive in Texas: A Study in Gubernatorial Leadership* (Austin: University of Texas Press, 1964), 15–16. Charles Polzer lists thirty-one Spanish governors of Texas from 1717 to 1823. *Documentary Relations of the Southwest*, in Biographical Files—Governors of Texas (Austin: Center for American History, University of Texas, 1977).

5. Larry Sabato, *Goodbye to Good-Time Charlie: The American Governorship Transformed*, 2nd ed. (Washington, DC: CQ Press, 1983), 2–4.

6. See constitution of 1845 and amendment of 1850. Also see Gantt, *The Chief Executive in Texas*, 20–27.

7. Gantt, *The Chief Executive in Texas*, 30–31.

8. The 1827 Constitution included a four-year term, with a one-term limit. The constitution of the Texas Republic limited the president to a single three-year term (Sam Houston served two nonconsecutive terms). The 1845 and 1861 Constitutions included a two-year term, with a limit of no more than four years in a six-year period. The 1866 Constitution included a four-year term, with a limit of no more than eight years in a twelve-year period. The 1869 Constitution had the most liberal provisions—a four-year term of office, with no term limits. Gantt, *The Chief Executive in Texas*, 335.

9. Allan Shivers served part of Jester's term and three of his own terms, for a total of seven and one-half years; Clements's total of eight years was the longest, but they were not consecutive terms.

10. The president of the Texas Republic was paid $10,000 a year, as specified in the constitution. The salaries for the governors under

the constitutions from 1827 until 1876 varied from $2,000 to $5,000. The 1876 Constitution reduced the salary from $5,000 to $4,000. Gantt, *The Chief Executive in Texas*, 335.

11. Gantt, *The Chief Executive in Texas*, 38; Council of State Governments, *The Governor: The Office and Its Powers* (Lexington, KY: Council of State Governments, 1972); and December 2004 comparisons from Council of State Governments, *Book of the States 2007* (Lexington, KY: Council of State Governments, 2007), Table 4.3, 166.

12. Richard Hubbard became governor when the first governor under the new constitution, Richard Coke, resigned in 1876 to become a U.S. senator; William Hobby did so when Governor James Ferguson was removed from office in 1917; Coke Stevenson did so when Governor O'Daniel won a special election to the U.S. Senate in 1941; Allan Shivers did so when Governor Jester died in 1949; and Rick Perry did so in 2000 when George W. Bush resigned after winning the U.S. presidency.

13. Gantt, *The Chief Executive in Texas*, 151–2.

14. Joseph Schlesinger, "Politics, the Executive," in Herbert Jacob and Kenneth Vines, eds., *Politics in the American States: A Comparative Analysis* (Boston: Little, Brown, 1965), 220–9.

15. Sabato, *Goodbye to Good-Time Charlie*, 4–6.

16. Citizens Advisory Committee on Revision of the Constitution of Texas, "Interim Report to the 56th Legislature and the People of Texas," March 1, 1959, 20–21.

17. See Gantt, *The Chief Executive in Texas*, 29–33; and Seth McKay, "Making the Texas Constitution of 1876" (PhD diss., University of Pennsylvania, 1924).

18. In Maine, New Hampshire, New Jersey, and Tennessee, the governor is the only statewide elected official. Council of State Governments, *Book of the States 2007*, Table 4.6, 173, and Table 4.10, 181.

19. Schlesinger, "Politics, the Executive," 1965; and Schlesinger, "Politics, the Executive," in Herbert Jacob and Kenneth Vines, eds., *Politics in the American States: A Comparative Analysis*, 2nd ed. (Boston: Little, Brown, 1971), 225–34.

20. Virginia Gray, et al., *Politics in the American States*, 5th ed. (New York: HarperCollins, 1990), appendices 6.1–6.7; Thad L. Beyle, "Governors: The Middlemen and Women in Our Political System," in Virginia Gray and Herbert Jacob, eds., *Politics in the American States: A Comparative Analysis*, 6th ed. (Washington, DC: CQ Press, 1996); and Thad L. Beyle, "The Governors," in Virginia Gray and Russell Hanson, eds., *Politics in the American States: A Comparative Analysis*, 8th ed. (Washington, DC: CQ Press, 2004), 194–231. Beyle's forthcoming ranking is discussed in Pamela Prah, "Massachusetts Gov Rated Most Powerful," www.stateline.org.

21. Beyle, "The Governors," in Gray and Hanson, *Politics in the American States*: 194–231.

22. It is not clear exactly how many appointments a Texas governor makes. A 1982 analysis states that there are about 4,000 appointments, with about 2,000 subject to confirmation. Yet, a 1989 Senate study counted only 1,389 appointees. Governor George W. Bush made about 3,400 appointments in just over four years in office. See Senate Nominations Committee, "Analysis of Gubernatorial Appointees to Agencies, Boards and Commissions," December 8, 1989, 1; Charles Wiggins, et al., "The 1982 Gubernatorial Transition in Texas," in Thad L. Beyle, ed., *Gubernatorial Transitions: The 1982 Elections* (Durham, NC: Duke University, 1985), 396; and Wayne Slater, "Bush Steps Up Number of Hispanic Appointees," *Dallas Morning News* (October 12, 1999): A1.

23. The case is *Denison* v. *State*, 665 S.W.2d 754 (Tex. Crim. App. 1983). Texas Legislative Council, "Staff Memo to Senate Committee on State Affairs, Subcommittee on Nominations," January 26, 1981.

24. George Braden, *The Constitution of the State of Texas: An Annotated and Comparative Analysis*, vol. 1 (Austin: Texas Legislative Council, 1977), 327–31. See also Texas Legislative Council, "Staff Memo," 4 and 13.

25. Bruce Hight, "Senator Blocks Utility Official," *Austin American-Statesman* (September 28, 1999): C1, C2; and Bruce Hight, "Senator: PUC Decision Was 'Difficult,'" *Austin American-Statesman* (September 29, 1999): D2.

26. Wiggins, Hamm, and Balanoff, "The 1982 Gubernatorial Transition," 396.

27. See Chandler Davidson, *Race and Class in Texas Politics* (Princeton, NJ: Princeton University Press, 1990), 237.

28. Peggy Fikac, "Bush Appointing Many Females, Minorities," *San Antonio Express-News* (July 9, 2000): 14A; Kelley Shannon, "Minority Appointments Rise Slightly: Perry Has a Higher Rate than Bush, but Lower than Richards," *San Antonio Express-News* (November 28, 2003); and Wayne Slater, "Perry's Picks Offer Glimpse at Priorities: Donors, Minorities Among Appointees," *Dallas Morning News* (July 3, 2001). Perry appointment figures from Governor's Office (May 19, 2006) and from Texans for Public Justice, "Governor Perry's Patronage," April 1, 2006, www.tpj.org.

29. Wiggins, et al., "The 1982 Gubernatorial Transition in Texas," in Thad L. Beyle, ed., *Gubernatorial Transitions: The 1982 Elections* (Durham, NC: Duke University, 1985), 398.

30. Wayne Slater, "Bush Steps Up Number of Hispanic Appointees," *Dallas Morning News* (October 12, 1999): A1.

31. Texans for Public Justice, "Governor Bush's Well-Appointed Texas Officials," October 2000, and "Governor Perry's Patronage," April 1, 2006, www.tpj.org.

32. Gantt, *The Chief Executive* in Texas, 327.

33. Richard Murray and Gregory Weiher, "Texas: Ann Richards, Taking on the Challenge," in Thad L. Beyle, ed., *Governors and Hard Times* (Washington, DC: CQ Press, 1992), 186.

34. For descriptions and examples of governors' legislative prowess, see Gantt, *The Chief Executive in Texas*, 42, 237–8, 244–54.

35. William E. Atkinson, "James Allred: A Political Biography, 1899–1935," (PhD diss., Texas Christian University, 1978), 275.

36. See John Connally, *In History's Shadow: An American Odyssey* (New York: Hyperion, 1993), 226; Ann Fears Crawford and Jack Keever, *John Connally: Portrait in Power* (Austin, TX: Jenkins, 1973), 183–6; and Ben Barnes, *Barn Burning, Barn Building: Tales of a Political Life, from LBJ to George W. Bush and Beyond* (Albany, TX: Bright Sky, 2006), 77–79.

37. Council of State Governments, *Book of the States 2007*, vol. 39, Table 3.2, 76–78.

38. *Ferguson* v. *Maddox*, 263 S.W. 888 (Tex. 1924); and Gantt, *The Chief Executive in Texas*, 221.

39. Gantt, *The Chief Executive in Texas*, 39. Twenty-five states require a two-thirds vote of the total membership to override, twelve require a vote of two-thirds of those present, six require three-fifths of the total membership, and one requires three-fifths of those present, while six require just a majority of the total membership. Council of State Governments, *Book of the States 2005*, Table 3.16, 161–2. The Texas Constitution is confusing in its language about overrides of vetoes. It says that an override requires a vote of two-thirds of the members present in the chamber that passed the bill first, and two-thirds of the elected members of the chamber that passed the bill last—or, if it is a line-item veto, two-thirds of the members present in each chamber.

40. The president of the Republic of Texas had pocket-veto authority: if he refused to sign a bill passed in the last five days of a session, the bill died. No constitution since statehood has included pocket-veto authority. Braden, *The Constitution of the State of Texas*, 333.

41. House Research Organization, "Vetoes of Legislation," *Special Legislative Report*, no. 193 (1995); "Vetoes of Legislation—75th Legislature," *Special Legislative Report*, no. 75-16 (1997); "Vetoes of Legislation—76th Legislature," *Focus Report* (June 25, 1999); "Vetoes of Legislation—77th Legislature," *Focus Report* (June 26, 2001); "Vetoes of Legislation—78th Legislature," *Focus Report*

(August 5, 2003); "Vetoes of Legislation—79th Legislature," *Focus Report* (July 29, 2005); and Vetoes of Legislation—80th Legislature," *Focus Report* (July 9, 2007).

42. Texas Legislative Council, "Gubernatorial Veto: Powers, Procedures, and Override History," staff memorandum, May 22, 1990. See also Fred Gantt Jr., "The Governor's Veto in Texas: An Absolute Negative?" *Public Affairs Comment* 15 (March 1969), University of Texas Institute of Public Affairs; *Senate Journal*, May 23, 1990, 149; and *House Journal*, May 29, 1990, 192.

43. See Gantt, *The Chief Executive in Texas*, 39; and Council of State Governments, *Book of the States 2005*, Table 3.16, 161–2.

44. House Research Organization, "Texas Budget Highlights Fiscal 2004–05," *State Finance Report*, 78-3 (November 17, 2003): 5; and "Texas Budget Highlights Fiscal 2006–07," *State Finance Report*, 79-3 (January 30, 2006): 2.

45. Kendra A. Hovey and Harold A. Hovey, *Congressional Quarterly's State Fact Finder 2007: Rankings Across America* (Washington, DC: CQ Press, 2007), D-12, 113. (The book erroneously lists only five positions for Texas; apparently, the book lists only the constitutionally designated offices, omitting the elected agriculture commissioner and three railroad commissioners.)

46. *Frew* v. *Hawkins*, 540 U.S. 431(2004).

47. *Hopwood* v. *Texas*, 78 F. 3d932 (5th Cir. 1996).

48. *Ruiz* v. *Estelle*, 503 F. Supp. 1265 (S. D. Tex. 1980).

49. Texas Watch Foundation, "Consumers Question Attorney General Priorities," July 8, 2002, www.texaswatch.org.

50. Virginia H. Taylor Houston, "Surveying in Texas," *Southwestern Historical Quarterly* 65 (October 1961): 216.

51. How much land this represented is uncertain, since even the boundaries of the state were in dispute.

52. For a history and analysis of the Texas Railroad Commission, see David Prindle, *Petroleum Politics and the Texas Railroad Commission* (Austin: University of Texas Press, 1981).

53. Prindle, *Petroleum Politics and the Texas Railroad Commission*, 20, 112, and 117.

54. For a more detailed analysis of the SBOE, see House Research Organization, "State Board of Education: Controversy and Change," *Focus Report* (January 3, 2000).

55. These figures do not include regional agencies, such as river authorities, or local agencies created or funded by the state, such as the fifty community college districts.

56. See Terrence Stutz, "Court Overturns Farmers Insurance Settlement," *Dallas Morning News* (January 22, 2005): 5A.

57. Comptroller of Public Accounts, *Breaking the Mold: New Ways to Govern Texas* (Austin: CPA, 1991): 43.

58. William Gormley Jr., "Accountability Battles in State Administration," in Carl E. Van Horn, ed., *The State of the States*, 3rd ed. (Washington, DC: CQ Press, 1996), 162.

59. Gormley, "Accountability Battles in State Administration," 162.

60. Texas Sunset Advisory Commission, "Sunset Review in Texas: Summary of Process and Procedure," October 1993, 23; and "Report to the 80th Legislature," May 2007.

61. Texas Sunset Advisory Commission, "Report to the 81st Legislature," February 2009.

62. Texas Sunset Advisory Commission, "Summary of Sunset Legislation, 81st Legislature," 1.

63. Marver Bernstein, *Regulating Business by Independent Commission* (Princeton, NJ: Princeton University Press, 1955), 90.

64. *Texas Almanac 1972–73* (Dallas: A. H. Belo, 1971), 397.

65. *ACCORD Agriculture, Inc.* v. *TNRCC* No. 03-98-00340-CV Third Court of Appeals (1999).

Chapter 6

1. Sources for this material include Ralph Blumenthal, "Texas Judge Draws Outcry for Allowing an Execution," *New York Times* (October 25, 2007); April Castro, "Texas Judge Fosters Unsparing Reputation," *Boston Globe* (October 24, 2007); "Closing Time at the Death Chamber," *Austin American-Statesman* (October 6, 2007); "Justice in Texas? Not on Her Watch," *Austin American-Statesman* (October 13, 2007); Rick Casey, "Death Judge Broke Rules," *Houston Chronicle* (December 15, 2007); and Christy Hoppe, "Criminal Appeals Court Creates Emergency Filing System," *Dallas Morning News* (November 18, 2007).

2. *Baze* v. *Rees*, SS3 U.S. 3S (2008).

3. Paul Womack, "Judiciary," *Handbook of Texas Online*, October 6, 2010, www.tsha.utexas.edu/handbook/online/articles/view/JJ/jzj1.html.

4. Figures for all of the courts in the chapter are from the Office of Court Administration, *Annual Statistical Report for the Texas Judiciary, Fiscal Year 2009* (Austin, TX: Office of Court Administration, 2009), 57–59.

5. Texas Research League, "The Texas Judiciary: A Structural-Functional Overview," *Texas Courts: A Study by the Texas Research League*, Report 1 (Austin: Texas Research League, 1990), 41.

6. Office of Court Administration, "Annual Report for the Texas Judiciary: Fiscal 2009," December 2009, 46–53. www.courts.state.tx.us/pubs/AR2009/AR09.pdf (Austin, TX: Office of Court Administration, 2009).

7. Office of Court Administration, "Annual Report," 39–45.

8. Office of Court Administration, "Annual Report," 31–34.

9. The operation of the court is described in James A. Vaught, "Internal Procedures in the Texas Supreme Court," *Texas Tech Law Review* 26, no. 3 (1995): 935–58.

10. Office of Court Administration, "Annual Report," 25–27.

11. Office of Court Administration, "Annual Report," 28–30.

12. The following figures are from the Profile of Appellate and Trial Judges in the "Annual Report for the Texas Judiciary," Office of Court Administration, December 2009, 13. www.courts.state.tx.us/pubs/AR2009/AR09.pdf (Austin, TX: Office of Court Administration, 2009).

13. American Judicature Society, "Judicial Selection in the States: Appellate and General Jurisdiction Courts," October 6, 2010, www.judicialselection.us.

14. Walt Borges, "The Court's Bill Chill," *Texas Lawyer* (September 4, 1995): 1.

15. "Tort Reform Passes," *Texans for Lawsuit Reform*, October 6, 2010, www.tortreform.com/node/324#Pass.

16. Anthony Champagne, "Judicial Reform in Texas," in Anthony Champagne and Judith Haydel, eds., *Judicial Reform in the States* (New York: University Press of America, 1993), 107.

17. Texans for Public Justice, "Payola Justice: How Supreme Court Justices Raise Money from Court Litigants," February 1998, www.tpj.org/reports/payola/conclusions.html.

18. Texans for Public Justice, "Checks and Imbalances: How Texas Supreme Court Justices Raised $11 Million," April 2000, www.tpj.org/reports/checks/warchests.html.

19. Texas Watch Foundation, *The Texas Supreme Court by the Numbers: A Statistical Analysis of the Texas Supreme Court (2005–2006)*, October 5, 2006, www.txwfoundation.org/TWF/index.cfm?event=showPage&pg=release100506, and *Shifting Sands for Consumers: 2002–2003 Texas Supreme Court Year-in-Review*, October 30, 2003, www.txwfoundation.org/courtwatch/Review_2002_2003.pdf.

20. Thomas R. Phillips, "State of the Judiciary," March 29, 1999, www.supreme.courts.state.tx.us/soj99.html.

21. Office of Court Administration, *Public Trust and Confidence in the Courts and Legal Profession in Texas* (Austin, TX: Office of Court

Administration, 1998); and Office of Court Administration, *The Courts and the Legal Profession in Texas—An Insider's Perspective: A Survey of Judges, Court Personnel, and Attorneys* (Austin, TX: Office of Court Administration, 1998).

22. John Williams, "Name Game Cost GOP Candidate," *Houston Chronicle* (March 25, 2002), www.chron.com/cs/CDA/story.hts/metropolitan/williams/1307892.

23. Pamela Fridich, et al., *Lowering the Bar: Lawyers Keep Texas Appeals Judges on Retainer* (Austin: Texans for Public Justice, 2003), 2; updated by the authors.

24. David M. Horton and Ryan Kellus Turner, *Lone Star Justice* (Austin, TX: Eakin, 1999), 169–205; and Ken Anderson, *Crime in Texas* (Austin: University of Texas Press, 1997). In 2005, the Texas legislature made life without parole the only alternative to the death penalty for sentencing persons convicted of capital offenses.

25. Texas Chief Justice's Task Force on Judicial Reform, *Justice at the Crossroads: Court Improvement in Texas* (Austin, TX: 1972).

26. Texas Research League, *Texas Courts: A Study by the Texas Research League,* three reports (Austin: Texas Research League, 1990–1992).

27. Texas Research League, *Texas Courts: A Study by the Texas Research League*, Report 2, "The Texas Judiciary: A Proposal for Structural-Functional Reform" (Austin: Texas Research League, 1991), 25–27.

28. See House Research Organization, "Court System Reorganization and Administration, SB 1204 by Duncan," in *Focus Report: Major Issues of the 80th Legislature, Regular Session* (July 17, 2007), 136–8.

29. John J. Goodson, "Judicial Selection: Options for Choosing Judges in Texas," House Research Organization, *Session Focus* (March 10, 1997), 2.

30. Anthony Champagne, "Judicial Selection in Texas," in Anthony Champagne and Edward J. Harpham, eds., *Texas Politics: A Reader*, 2nd ed. (New York: Norton, 1998), 95–104.

31. SJR 33, 78th Legislature, regular session, October 6, 2010, www.capitol.state.tx.us.

32. For an overview of revision attempts, see American Judicature Society, *Judicial Selection in the States, Texas, History of Judicial Selection Reform*, October 6, 2010, www.ajs.org/js/TX_history.htm.

33. Supreme Court of Texas Judicial Campaign Finance Committee, "Report and Recommendations," Office of Court Administration, February 23, 1999, www.supreme.courts.state.tx.us/JCFSC/campaign1.htm.

34. See, for instance, Texans for Public Justice, "Payola Justice: How Supreme Court Justices Raise Money from Court Litigants," February 10, 1998, www.tpj.org/1998_02_01_archive.html; and "Checks and Imbalances: How Texas Supreme Court Justices Raised $11 Million," info.tpj.org/docs/2000/04/reports/checks/toc.html.

35. Morgan Smith, "Will SCOTUS Opinions Affect TX Judicial Elections?" *The Texas Tribune*, (August 27, 2010), www.texastribune.org/texas-legislature/texas-legislature/will-scotus-opinions-affect-tx-judicial-elections/.

Chapter 7

1. "Ike Wears Itself Out Beating Up on Texas," CNN.com, September 14, 2008, www.cnn.com.

2. Eric Berger, "Harris to Join 6-County Storm District," *Houston Chronicle,* December 21, 2009. www.chron.com/disp/story.mpl/metropolitan/6781866.html

3. U.S. Census Bureau, "Local Governments and Public School Systems by Type and State 2007," March 5, 2008, www.census.gov.

4. Dick Smith, "County Organization," *Handbook of Texas Online,* October 4, 2010, www.tsha.utexas.edu

5. George D. Braden, *The Constitution of the State of Texas: An Annotated and Comparative Analysis*, vol. 2 (Austin: Texas Advisory Commission on Intergovernmental Relations, 1977), 505.

6. See Dick Smith, "The Development of Local Government Units in Texas" (doctoral dissertation, Harvard University, 1938). See also Herman James and Irvin Stewart, "County Government in Texas," *University of Texas Bulletin,* no. 2525 (July 1, 1925).

7. Texas Association of Counties, "About Texas Counties: The History" and "About Texas Counties: Some Fun Facts," October 4, 2010, www.county.org.

8. Terrell Blodgett, "Texas Cities: The Bulwark of Democracy," 1999 William P. Hobby Jr. Distinguished Lecture, Southwest Texas State University, www.swt.edu.

9. Braden, *The Constitution of the State of Texas*, 505.

10. Those boundary disputes continue. In 2000, a court declared in favor of Denton County in its boundary dispute with Tarrant County over the now lucrative real estate between the Dallas–Fort Worth area and Denton. On appeal, the decision was reversed, and the Supreme Court upheld Tarrant County's claim. See "Boundary Battle Puts Two Counties at Odds," *County* (September/October 2003).

11. Terrell Blodgett, "City Government," *Handbook of Texas Online,* October 4, 2010, www.tsha.utexas.edu. See also Egbert Cockrell, "Municipal Home Rule with Special Reference to Texas," *Southwestern Social Science Quarterly* 1 (1920/1921): 147; and P. E. Merten, "Do Statewide Planning and the Consistency Concept Infringe on Home Rule Authority," *Journal of Planning Literature* 11 (May 1997): 564–74.

12. Steve Bickerstaff, "Voting Rights Challenges to School Boards in Texas: What Next?" *Baylor Law Review* 49 (Fall 1997): 1017.

13. *City of Clinton* v. *The Cedar Rapids and Missouri River Railroad Co.*, 24 Iowa 455 (1968).

14. U.S. Census Bureau, "Population Estimates Program," July 1, 2009, factfinder.census.gov/home/saff/main.html?_lang=en.

15. See Jim Lewis, "The County Advocates," *County* (January/February 2003).

16. While the correct punctuation for this term would be commissioners' court, constitutional and legal references designate it as commissioners court, with no apostrophe, so we use the official method throughout this chapter.

17. *Gray* v. *Sanders*, 372 U.S. 368 (1963); *Wesberry* v. *Sanders*, 376 U.S. 1 (1964); and *Reynolds* v. *Sims*, 377 U.S. 533 (1964).

18. *Avery* v. *Midland County, Texas, et al.*, 390 U.S. 474 (1968).

19. The office of county treasurer has been abolished for Tarrant, Bee, Bexar, Collin, Andrews, Gregg, El Paso, Fayette, and Nueces counties.

20. Judon Fambrough, "County Regulation of Rural Subdivisions," Land Development, Publication 1195, October 1997 (rev. 2000), recenter.tamu.edu; and "Counties Achieve 'Sea Change' on Development Authority," *County* July–August 1999, www.county.org.

21. Paul Sugg, "Last Year, Counties Were Granted Greater Authority to Address Unbridled Development. So What Happened?" *County* November–December 2000, www.county.org

22. Jim Lewis, "Election Reform: Will the Prayers Be Answered?" *County* July–August 2001, www.county.org.

23. 78th Texas Legislature, HB 1549, Regular Session, 2003, www.capitol.state.tx.us.

24. Jim Lewis, "Budget 2005," *County* (September/October 2005): 41–43.

25. "Are Legislators Too 'Fee Bill' Minded?" *County* (January/February 1997), www.county.org; Cheryl Smith, "If It Moves, Put a Fee on It," *County* (January/February 2004): 18–21; Maria Sprow, "It's About the Money, Honey: State Mandates Countywide Collections Offices for Court Fees, Fines," *County* (November/December 2005): 40–42.

26. Terrell Blodgett, "Municipal Home Rule Charters," *Public Affairs Comment* (University of Texas, 1996), 1–7; Blodgett, "Home Rule

Charters," *Handbook of Texas Online*, www.tsha.utexas.edu; Delbert Taebel, et al., *A Citizen's Guide to Home-Rule Charters in Texas Cities* (Arlington: University of Texas at Arlington, Institute of Urban Studies, 1985); and Terrell Blodgett, "Texas Cities: The Bulwark of Democracy," 1999 William P. Hobby Jr. Distinguished Lecture, Southwest Texas State University, www.swt.edu.

27. Almost all general-law cities have fewer than 5,000 people. However, even a few home-rule cities have fewer than 5,000 people. At one time, those cities had more than 5,000 people and achieved home-rule status. They then lost population. There is no requirement that a city give up its home-rule charter if it drops below 5,000 in population. For a list of home-rule cities, see *Texas Almanac 2006–2007* (Dallas: Dallas Morning News, 2006), 453–64.

28. Article 3, section 53, of the Texas Constitution prohibits the legislature from passing "any local or special law . . . regulating the affairs of counties, cities, towns, wards or school districts."

29. For Type A and Type B general-law cities, the Local Government Code specifies an aldermanic form of government. However, cities are allowed to change their charters and could adopt the council–manager form. In 2003, the legislature changed the Local Government Code to allow cities to assign duties to city officials, a provision that allows cities to create a city administrator, who performs the functions that a city manager performs in the council–manager form of government. Type C general-law cities are required to incorporate with the commission form of government. In practice, Texas cities do not incorporate as Type C cities.

30. Dale Krane, Platon Rigos, and Melvin Hill Jr., *Home Rule in America: A Fifty-State Handbook* (Washington, DC: CQ Press, 2000), 401; and Blodgett, "Texas Cities."

31. "Hurricane That Wrecked Galveston Was Deadliest in U.S. History," CNN, September 8, 2000, www.cnn.com.

32. Blodgett, "Texas Cities"; and Bradley R. Rice, "Commission Form of City Government," *Handbook of Texas Online*, www.tsha.utexas.edu.

33. "Where Do Texas Cities Get Their Money?" *Texas Town and City* 92 (January 2005): 20–21.

34. "Where Do Texas Cities Get Their Money?" Frank Sturzl, "The Courses of Municipal Revenue," *Texas Town and City* 93 (June 2006): 14–16.

35. "Municipal Fiscal Conditions Are Improving," *Texas Town and City* 92 (March 2005): 10–13.

36. Lawrence E. Jordan, "Municipal Bond Issuance in Texas: The New Realities," *Texas Town and City* 79 (December 1991): 12, 25.

37. For a history of the annexation statutes and policy battles, see Scott Houston, "Municipal Annexation in Texas: 'Is It Really That Complicated?'" Texas Municipal League, January 2008.

38. A city may carry over some of this allowance from one year to another but may expand no more than a total of 30 percent of its area in one year.

39. The ETJ ranges from one-half mile for those cities with fewer than 5,000 citizens, up to five miles from the corporate limits for cities with more than 100,000 citizens.

40. Local Government Code, chap. 42.

41. Local Government Code, section 43.121, Limited Purpose Annexation (planning, zoning, health, and safety). Section 43.130 states that citizens in a limited-purpose annexation area may vote in city council races but not bond elections. Section 43.122 limits strip annexation to at least 1,000 feet wide and no more than three miles, in most cases.

42. Senate Interim Committee on Annexation Interim Report, 76th Legislature, October 1998.

43. Local Government Code, chaps. 41–43.

44. See, for instance, Craig Smyser, "Houston's Power: As It Was," *Houston Chronicle* (June 27, 1977): 6.

45. U.S. Census, "Local Governments and Public School Systems by Type and State 2007," *Census of Governments, 2007*, www.census.gov.

46. "State Buffs Up County Statutes," *County* (July/August 1999), www.county.org.

47. Bill D. Dugatt III, "How to Create a Groundwater Conservation District," Bickerstaff, Heath, Smiley, Pollan, Kever, and McDaniel, April 8, 1999, www.bickerstaff.com; and Sugg, "Last Year, Counties Were Granted Greater Authority."

48. U.S. Census Bureau, "Local Governments and Public School Systems by Type and State 2007."

49. Texas Education Agency, *Snapshot 2008–2009*, www.tea.state.tx.us.

50. Texas Education Agency, *Snapshot 2008–2009*; and data from the National Center for Education Statistics, U.S. Department of Education, "State Education Data Profiles," reported some 9,000 schools in 2008. www.nces.ed.gov.

51. Texas Education Agency, *Snapshot 2008–2009*.

52. Texas Association of School Boards, Membership Services, telephone conversation, April 22, 2008; summary of documents of board electoral systems provided by the association.

53. "Communities in America Currently Using Proportional Voting: Cumulative Voting," Center for Voting and Democracy, October 4, 2010, www.fairvote.org.

54. *Edgewood* v. *Kirby*, 777 S.W.2d 391 (TX 1989).

Chapter 8

1. Joseph W. McKnight, "Homestead Law," *The Handbook of Texas Online*, www1.tshaonline.org/handbook/online/articles/HH/mlh2_print.html.

2. Ronald Kaiser, "Basics of the Capture Rule," Presented at the Texas Water Law Institute, November 4–5, 2004, 3.

3. Thomas R. Dye, *Understanding Public Policy*, 12th edition (Upper Saddle River, NJ: Prentice Hall, 2008), p. 1.

4. Hugh Heclo, "Issue Networks and the Executive Establishment," in Anthony King, ed., *The New American Political System* (Washington, DC: American Enterprise Institute, 1978), 88. Much of this section is based on this chapter.

5. Heclo, "Issue Networks," 88.

6. This section draws primarily from L. L. Wade and R. L. Curry, Jr., *A Logic of Public Policy: Aspects of Political Economy* (Belmont, Calif.: Wadsworth Publishing Company, Inc., 1970), Chap. 1.

7. Wade and Curry, Jr., *A Logic of Public Policy*. See Chapter 1 for an excellent introduction to the definitional issues and approaches to public policy analysis.

8. The following discussion is organized around the general stages presented by James E. Anderson, David W. Brady, Charles S. Bullock, III, and Joseph Stewart, Jr., *Public Policy and Politics in America*, 2nd ed. (Monterey, CA: Brooks/Cole Publishing Company, 1984) and Charles O. Jones, *An Introduction to the Study of Public Policy*, 2nd ed. (North Scituate, MA: Duxbury Press, 1977).

9. Anderson, et al., *Public Policy and Politics in America*, p. 8.

10. Jones, *An Introduction to the Study of Public Policy*, pp. 138–39.

11. Jones, *An Introduction to the Study of Public Policy*, p. 139.

12. Randall B. Ripley and Grace A. Franklin, *Congress, the Bureaucracy, and Public Policy*, 3rd ed. (Homewood, IL: Dorsey Press, 1984), 10.

13. Ripley and Franklin, *Congress*, 107.

14. Ripley and Franklin, *Congress*, 104.

15. Carl Davis, et al., *Who Pays? A Distributional Analysis of the Tax Systems in All 50 States*, 3rd ed. (Washington, DC: Citizens for Tax Justice and the Institute on Taxation and Economic Policy, 2009), 2.

16. Federation of Tax Administrators, "State Individual Income Taxes (Tax Rates for Tax Year 2010—as of January 1, 2010)," www.taxadmin.org/Fta/rate/ind_inc.pdf. New Hampshire and Tennessee tax income from dividends and interest but not salaries or wages.

17. Clay Robison, "Taxes in Crisis—Tax 'Quilt' Is Bursting at Seams—Lawmakers Facing Inequitable Tax Bite," *Houston Chronicle* (April 22, 1991): 1A.

18. Federation of Tax Administrators, "State Sales Tax Rates and Food & Drug Exemptions (as of January 1, 2010)," www.taxadmin.org/Fta/rates/sales.pdf.

19. Texas Comptroller of Public Accounts, "Revenue by Source for Fiscal 2009," *Window on State Government*, www.window.state.tx.us/taxbud/revenue.html.

20. Texas Comptroller, "Revenue by Source."

21. Texas Comptroller, "Revenue by Source."

22. Texas Comptroller, "Revenue by Source."

23. Federation of Tax Administrators, "State Excise Tax Rates on Cigarettes (as of January 1, 2010)," www.taxadmin.org/fta/rate/cigarette.pdf.

24. R.G. Ratcliffe, "Lottery Names Latest Director—$248 Million Expected Shortfall to Schools Seen," *Houston Chronicle* (December 17, 1997): 37A.

25. Texas Comptroller of Public Accounts, "Revenue by Source for Fiscal Year 2009."

26. Texas Bond Review Board, *Debt Affordability Study, February 2010*, 3, www.brb.state.tx.us/pub/bfo/DAS2010.pdf.

27. Texas Bond Review Board, *Debt Affordability Study*, 38.

28. R.G. Ratcliffe, "Texas Trend Relies on Bonds to Build Now," *Houston Chronicle*, (January 16, 1989): 1A.

29. Texas Bond Review Board, *Affordability Study*, 3.

30. *Rodriguez v. San Antonio Independent School District*, 337 Supp. 280, 285 (WD Tex. 1971). The trial was delayed for two years to permit extensive pretrial discovery and allow the legislature to assess the need for funding reforms. The case was subsequently stayed after appeals to the U.S. Supreme Court: *San Antonio Independent School District v. Rodriguez*, 411 U. S. (1973).

31. *Shirley Neeley, Texas Commissioner of Education, et al., v. West Orange-Cove Consolidated Independent School District, et al.*, 176 S.W.3d 746, 755 (Tex. 2005).

32. Associated Press, "38% of Teachers Thinking of Calling it Quits," *Houston Chronicle* (April 30, 1994): 36A.

33. National Education Association, news release, May 21, 2003.

34. Texas Education Agency, "Snapshot 2009 Summary Tables State Totals," *Snapshot 2008–2009*, ritter.tea.state.tx.us/perfreport/snapshot/2009/state.html.

35. Texas Virtual School Network, www.txvsn.org/TxVSNFAQ.aspx.

36. Wendy Benjaminson, "Home Schools Win Court Fight: Ruling Backs Right to Teach Their Own Children," *Houston Chronicle* (June 16, 1994): 1A.

37. U.S. Department of Education, National Center for Education Statistics, "1.5 Million Homeschooled Students in the United States in 2007," *Issue Brief*, December 2008.

38. Texas Home School Coalition, press release, January 2009.

39. *Ann Richards, et al. v. League of United Latin American Citizens, et al.*, 868 S.W.2d 306 (Tex. 1993).

40. *Hopwood, et al., v. State of Texas, et al.*, 78 F.3d 932 (5th Cir. 1996).

41. Lydia Lum, "The *Hopwood* Effect: Minorities Heading Out of State for Professional Schools," *Houston Chronicle* (August 25, 1997): 1A.

42. James C. McKinley, Jr., "Texas Vote Curbs a College Admission Guarantee Meant to Bolster Diversity," *New York Times* (May 30, 2009), www.nytimes.com/2009/05/31/education/31texas.html.

43. Texas Higher Education Coordinating Board, "Overview: Tuition Deregulation," www.thecb.state.tx.us/Reports/PDF/1527.PDF?CFID=4796841&CFTOKEN=5900171; and Clay Robison, "Since Deregulation, College Tuition Costs 39% More than 3 Years Ago—Appropriations for Financial Aid Have Not Kept Pace," *Houston Chronicle* (September 24, 2006): A1.

44. Legislative Study Group, "LSG Analysis and Recommendations on State of Higher Education in Texas—Part 1," www.texas/sg.org/LSG_Higher_ED.pdf.

45. *Ruiz v. Estelle*, 503 F. Supp. 1265 (S.D. Tex. 1980).

46. Clay Robison, et al., "Building of Prisons Under Gun—2 Legislators Say It's up to County," *Houston Chronicle* (September 8, 1991): 25A.

47. The Scripps Howard *Texas Poll*, The Scripps Howard Data Center, June 2000.

48. *Houston Chronicle*, December 31, 2002.

49. David Grann, "Trial by Fire: Did Texas Execute an Innocent Man?" *New Yorker* (September 7, 2009), www.newyorker.com/reporting/2009/09/07/090907fa_fact_grann.

50. Polly Ross Hughes, "Job Aid Drop in Welfare Rolls—Poll Responses Raise Concern," *Houston Chronicle* (October 19, 1997): 1A.

51. Bill Minutaglio, "State Workforce Commission Falls Under Increased Scrutiny—Critics Doubt Long-term Effects; Supporters Tout Welfare Numbers," *Dallas Morning News* (December 14, 1997): 1A.

52. Denise Gamino, "Welfare 'Students' Find Job Class Dull, but Attendance Is Required," *Austin American–Statesman* (December 6, 1997): B1.

53. Christopher Lee, "Applicants Flock to Health Plan—More than 23,000 Families Seek Low-cost Insurance for Children," *Dallas Morning News* (April 8, 2000): 33A.

54. Polly Ross Hughes, "Rule Changes Push Thousands of Children off Insurance Rolls," *Houston Chronicle* (November 12, 2003): 1A.

55. Janet Elliott, "State Social Services Contract—Accenture Deal to Be Reduced by $356 Million, End 2 Years Early over Backlog, Errors," *Houston Chronicle* (December 22, 2006): A1.

56. *City & State* (July 13, 1993): SG2, SG6.

57. Dina Cappiello, "Houston Avoids Title of Smoggiest U.S. City," *Houston Chronicle* (September 24, 2003): 23A.

58. Bill Dawson and Clay Robison, "76th Legislature—Compromise Will Urge Older Plants to Reduce Emissions Voluntarily," *Houston Chronicle* (May 31, 1999): 26A.

59. Chris Rizo, "Public Citizen Sues to Force Texas to Regulate Greenhouse Gases," *Southeast Texas Record* (November 7, 2009); and Associated Press, "Blame Coal: Texas Leads Carbon Emissions," MSNBC, June 2, 2007, www.msnbc.msn.com/id/19000614/.

60. Matthew Tresaugue, "Global Warming: Warning for Texas Coastal Damage Could Triple by 2080s," *Houston Chronicle* (June 2, 2009): 3B.

61. Ralph K.M. Haurwitz, "Court Blocks Order to Trim Use of Water," *Austin American-Statesman* (September 11, 1996): B1.

62. *Barshop v. Medina County Underground Water Conservation District*, 925 S.W.2d 618 (Tex. 1996).

63. *Austin American-Statesman* (September 9, 1996).

64. "Microelectronics and Computer Technology Corporation (MCC)," *Handbook of Texas Online*, www.tshaonline.org/handbook/online/articles/MM/dnm1.html.

A

Administrative Procedures Act: A statute containing Texas's rule-making process.

agriculture commissioner: The elected state official in charge of regulating and promoting agriculture.

Alamo: A San Antonio mission that was defended by Texans during their war for independence.

American Creed: A set of ideas that provide a national identity, limit government, and structure politics in America.

Anglos: Non-Hispanic whites.

annexation: Enlargement of a city's corporate limits by incorporating surrounding territory into the city.

application for discretionary review: Request for Texas Court of Criminal Appeals review, which is granted if four judges agree.

at-large-by-place: An election system in which all positions on the council or governing body are filled by city-wide elections, with each position designated as a seat, and candidates must choose which place to run for.

attorney general: The elected official who is the chief counsel for the state of Texas.

B

balanced budget: A budget in which the legislature balances expenditures with expected revenues, with no deficit.

bicameral Texas legislature: The legislature has two bodies, a House of Representatives and a Senate.

biennial legislature: A legislative body that meets in regular session only once in a two-year period.

bill: A proposed law.

budget execution authority: The authority to move money from one program to another program or from one agency to another agency.

C

captured agency: A government regulatory agency that consistently makes decisions favorable to the private interests that it regulates.

charter schools: Public schools that have flexibility from state regulations in order to encourage innovation in educational programs.

chief budget officer: The governor, who is charged with preparing the state budget proposal for the legislature.

chief executive officer: The governor as the top official of the executive branch of Texas state government.

chief of state: The governor in his or her role as the official head representing the state of Texas in its relationships with the national government, other states, and foreign dignitaries.

city commission: A form of city government in which elected members serve on the legislative body and also serve as head administrators of city programs.

clemency: The governor's authority to reduce the length of a person's prison sentence.

cockroach: A member of a constitutional convention who opposes any changes in the current constitution.

commander in chief: The governor in his or her role as head of the state militia.

commissioners court: The legislative body of a county in Texas.

committee: A subunit of the legislature, appointed to work on designated subjects.

comprehensive revision: Constitutional revision through the adoption of a new constitution.

comptroller of public accounts: The elected official who is the state's tax collector.

concurrent resolution: A legislative document intended to express the will of both chambers of the legislature, even though it does not possess the authority of law.

constitutional county court: Constitutionally mandated court for criminal and civil matters.

Constitutional Revision Commission: Group established to research and draft a constitution for a constitutional convention.

constitutionalism: Limits placed on government through a written document.

council–manager: A form of city government in which the city council and mayor hire a professional manager to run the city.

county attorney: Elected official serving as the legal officer for county government and also as a criminal prosecutor.

county auditor: Official appointed by a district judge to audit county finances.

county chairperson: Party leader in a county.

county clerk: Elected official who serves as the clerk for the commissioners court and for county records.

county commissioner: Elected official who serves on the county legislative body, the commissioners court.

county convention: County party meeting to select delegates and adopt resolutions.

county court at law: Statutory county court to relieve county judge of judicial duties.

county executive committee: Precinct chairpersons in a county who assist the county chairpersons.

county judge: Elected official who is the chief administrative officer of county government, serves on the commissioners court and may also have some judicial functions.

county tax assessor-collector: Elected official who collects taxes for the county (and perhaps for other local governments).

county treasurer: Elected official who serves as the money manager for county government.

court of appeals: Intermediate appellate court for criminal and civil appeals.

cumulative voting: A method of voting in which voters have a number of votes equal to the number of seats being filled, and voters may cast their votes all for one candidate or split them among candidates in various combinations.

D

debt: The total outstanding amount the government owes as a result of borrowing in the past.

dedicated funds: Constitutional or statutory requirements that restrict some state tax or fee revenues to spending on specific programs.

deficit financing: Borrowing money to meet operating expenses. It is prohibited by the Texas Constitution, which says that state government must operate on a pay-as-you-go basis.

deficit spending: Government spending in the current budget cycle that exceeds government revenue.

district attorney (DA): Elected official who prosecutes criminal cases.

district clerk: Elected official who is responsible for keeping the records for the district court.

district court: Court of general jurisdiction for serious crimes and high-dollar civil cases.

E

Edgewood v. _Kirby_: A unanimous and landmark decision by the Texas Supreme Court in 1989 that ordered the Texas Legislature to devise a more equitable school finance system.

engrossed bill: A bill that has been given final approval on third reading in one chamber of the legislature.

enrolled bill: A bill that has been given final approval in both chambers of the legislature and is sent to the governor.

equality: The belief that all individuals should be treated similarly, regardless of socioeconomic status.

executive commissioner of health and human services: The official appointed by the governor to oversee the state's multiagency health and human service programs.

extraterritorial jurisdiction (ETJ): The area outside a city's boundaries over which the city may exercise limited control.

F

filibuster: A formal way of halting Senate action on a bill by means of long speeches or unlimited debate.

first reading: The Texas Constitution requires three readings of a bill by the legislature; first reading is when the bill is introduced, its caption is read aloud, and it is referred to committee.

frontier era: The period when Texas was a border between American civilization and an area inhabited by a hostile, indigenous population.

G

general-law cities: Cities with fewer than 5,000 residents, governed by a general state law rather than by a locally adopted charter.

general obligation bonds (local): A method of borrowing money to pay for new construction projects such as roads, drainage, and physical facilities of a city. Generally requires citizen approval and repaid from general tax revenue.

general obligation bonds (state): A method of borrowing money to pay for new construction projects, such as prisons or mental hospitals. Interest on these bonds, which require voter approval in the form of constitutional amendments, is paid with tax revenue.

general ordinance-making authority: The legal right to adopt ordinances covering a wide array of subject areas—an authority that some cities have but counties do not.

germane: Related to the topic.

governor's message: Message that the governor delivers to the legislature, pronouncing policy goals, budget priorities, and authorizations for the legislature to act.

H

home rule: The right and authority of a local government to govern itself, rather than have the state govern it.

House Bill 72: A landmark school reform law enacted in 1984. Among other things, it reduced class sizes, required teachers to pass a literacy test to keep their jobs, and imposed the no pass, no play rule, which restricts failing students from participating in extracurricular activities.

I

income tax: A tax based on a corporation's or an individual's income. Texas is one of only a few states without a personal income tax.

individualism: The belief that each person should act in accordance with his or her own conscience.

insurance commissioner: The official appointed by the governor to direct the Department of Insurance and regulate the insurance industry.

intent calendar: The Senate calendar listing bills on which the author or sponsor has given notice of intent to move to suspend the regular order of business in order that the Senate may consider them.

issue networks: The loose and informal relationships that exist among a large number of actors who work in broad policy areas.

J

joint resolution: A legislative document that either proposes an amendment to the Texas Constitution or ratifies an amendment to the U.S. Constitution.

justice of the peace court: Local county court for minor crimes and civil suits.

L

land commissioner: The elected official responsible for managing and leasing the state's property, including oil, gas, and mineral interests.

legislative party caucus: An organization of legislators who are all of the same party, and which is formally allied with a political party.

liberal constitution: Constitution that incorporates the basic structure of government and allows the legislature to provide the details through statutes.

liberty: The belief that government should not infringe upon a person's individual rights.

local election: Election conducted by local governments to elect officials.

Local Government Code: The Texas statutory code containing state laws about local governments.

lottery: A form of gambling, conducted by many states, in which participants purchase tickets that offer an opportunity to cash in on a winning number or set of winning numbers. Voters legalized a state lottery in Texas in 1991.

M

municipal corporation: A city.

municipal court: City court with limited criminal jurisdiction.

N

nonparty legislative caucus: An organization of legislators that is based on some attribute other than party affiliation.

"no pass, no play" rule: A provision of Texas House Bill 72 that restricts a student failing a course from participating in extracurricular activities.

P

per diem: Legislators' per day allowance covering room and board expenses while on state business.

permanent party organization: Party organization that operates throughout the year, performing the party's functions.

Permanent University Fund (PUF): A land- and mineral-rich endowment that benefits the University of Texas and Texas A&M University systems, particularly the flagship universities in Austin and College Station.

petition for review: Request for Texas Supreme Court review, which is granted if four justices agree.

piecemeal revision: Constitutional revision through constitutional amendments that add or delete items.

plural executive : An executive branch in which power and policy implementation are divided among several executive agencies rather than centralized under one person; the governor does not get to appoint most agency heads.

populists: People who support the promotion of equality and of traditional values and behaviors.

precinct chairperson: Party leader in a voting precinct.

precinct convention: Precinct party meeting to select delegates and adopt resolutions.

president of the Texas Senate: The lieutenant governor of Texas, serving in his constitutional role as presiding officer of the Senate.

property tax: A tax on homes, businesses, and certain other forms of property that is the main source of revenue for local governments. The tax is based on the assessed value of the property.

proportional representation: A voting system that apportions legislative seats according to the percentage of the vote won by a particular political party.

pro-tempore (pro-tem): A legislator who serves temporarily as legislative leader in the absence of the Senate president or House Speaker.

public counsels: Officials appointed by the governor to represent the public before regulatory agencies.

Public Utility Commission: A full-time, three-member paid commission appointed by the governor to regulate public utilities in Texas.

Q

quasi-judicial: Partly judicial; authorized to conduct hearings and issue rulings.

quorum: The minimum number required to conduct business (as in a legislative body).

R

Railroad Commission: A full-time, three-member paid commission elected by the people to regulate oil and gas production in Texas.

regressive tax: The tax level increases as the wealth or ability of an individual or business to pay decreases.

regular session: The biennial 140-day session of the Texas Legislature, beginning in January of odd-numbered years.

revenue bonds: Bonds sold by governments that are repaid from the revenues generated from income-producing facilities.

revisionist: A member of a constitutional convention who will not accept less than a total revision of the current constitution.

revolving door: An exchange of personnel between private interests and public regulators.

***Ruiz v. Estelle* (1980):** A lawsuit in which a federal judge in 1980 declared the Texas prison system unconstitutional and ordered sweeping, expensive reforms.

S

sales tax: A tax charged as a set percentage of most retail purchases and many services. It is the main source of tax revenue for state government in Texas and an important source of revenue for many cities and metropolitan transit authorities.

second reading: The Texas Constitution requires three readings of a bill by the legislature; the second reading is when debate and consideration of amendments occur before the whole chamber.

Senate two-thirds rule: The rule in the Texas Senate requiring that every bill win a vote of two-thirds of the senators present to suspend the Senate's regular order of business, so that the bill may be considered.

senatorial courtesy: A process by which a governor, when selecting an appointee, defers to the state senator in whose district the nominee resides.

Sharpstown scandal: The legislative scandal of 1971–1972 that resulted in a bribery conviction of the House Speaker and other officials and set the stage for the 1973 reform session.

sheriff: Elected official who serves as the chief law enforcement officer in a county.

simple resolution: A legislative document proposing an action that affects only the one chamber in which it is being considered, such as a resolution to adopt House rules or to commend a citizen.

sin tax: A common nickname for a tax on tobacco or alcoholic beverages.

single-member districts: Election system in which a legislator runs from and represents one district rather than the entire geographic area encompassed by the government.

Speaker of the Texas House: The state representative who is elected by his or her fellow representatives to be the official leader of the House.

Speaker's lieutenants: House members who make up the Speaker's team, assisting the Speaker in leading the House, either informally, or in a role as a committee chair or other institutional leader.

Speaker's race: The campaign to determine who shall be the Speaker of the Texas House for a given biennium.

Speaker's team: The leadership team in the House, consisting of the Speaker and his or her most trusted allies among the members, most of whom the Speaker appoints to chair House committees.

special (called) session: A legislative session of up to thirty days, called by the governor, during an interim between regular sessions.

special election: Election held at a time other than general or primary elections.

State Board of Education: The fifteen-member elected body that sets some education policy for the state.

state convention: Party meeting held to adopt the party's platform, elect the party's executive committee and state chairperson, and, in a presidential election year, elect delegates to the national convention and choose presidential electors.

state executive committee: Sixty-two-member party committee that makes decisions for the party between state conventions.

state party chairperson: Party leader for the state.

state senatorial district convention: Party meeting held when a county is a part of more than one senatorial district.

statutory constitution: Constitution that incorporates detailed provisions in order to limit the powers of government.

strong mayor–council: A form of city government in which the mayor has strong powers to run the city by hiring, managing, and firing staff and controlling executive departments; the mayor also serves on the council.

sunset law: A law that sets a date for a program or regulation to expire unless reauthorized by the legislature.

T

Tejanos: Native Texans of Mexican descent.

temporary party organization: Party organization that exists for a limited time and includes several levels of conventions.

term limits: Restrictions that exist in some states about how long an individual may serve in state or local elected office.

Texan Creed: A set of ideas—primarily individualism and liberty—that shape Texas politics and government.

Texas Association of Counties: Professional association that provides information, training, and other services for Texas county officials. The group also lobbies the legislature on behalf of county governments.

Texas Commission on Environmental Quality: A full-time, three-member paid commission appointed by the governor to administer the state's environmental programs. (Formerly the Texas Natural Resource Conservation Commission.)

Texas Court of Criminal Appeals: Court of last resort in criminal cases.

Texas Education Agency: The state agency that oversees local school districts and disburses state funds to districts.

Texas Municipal League: Professional association and lobbying arm for city governments.

Texas Rangers: A mounted force of armed volunteers that provided order on the frontier.

Texas secretary of state: The state official appointed by the governor to be the keeper of the state's records, such as state laws, election data and filings, public notifications, and corporate charters.

Texas Supreme Court: Court of last resort in civil and juvenile cases.

third reading: The Texas Constitution requires three readings of a bill by the legislature; third reading is the final reading in a chamber, unless the bill returns from the other chamber with amendments.

trial *de novo*: New trial, necessary for an appeal from a court that is not a court of record.

V

veto: The formal, constitutional authority of the chief executive to reject bills passed by both houses of the legislative body, thus preventing their becoming law without further legislative action.

W

weak mayor–council: A form of city government in which the mayor has no more power than any other member of the council.

Chapter 1
1.1 B   1.2 D   1.3 C   1.4 B   1.5 C

Chapter 2
2.1 A   2.2 E   2.3 D   2.4 E

Chapter 3
3.1 E   3.2 D   3.3 C   3.4 C   3.5 D

Chapter 4
4.1 D   4.2 D   4.3 C   4.4 C   4.5 B   4.6 E
   4.7 E   4.8 D

Chapter 5
5.1 D   5.2 C   5.3 C   5.4 D   5.5 C   5.6 E   5.7 D

Chapter 6
6.1 D   6.2 E   6.3 C   6.4 D   6.5 E

Chapter 7
7.1 C   7.2 D   7.3 C   7.4 C   7.5 C

Chapter 8
8.1 E   8.2 E   8.3 D   8.4 C   8.5 B   8.6 D

TIMELINE: Selected Events in Texas Government and Politics

1965 **Reapportionment of the Texas Legislature**—As a result of a federal district court order, the Texas Legislature is compelled to redistrict its seats to conform to the "one person, one vote" rule.

1944 *Smith* v. *Allwright*—The U.S. Supreme Court rules that Texas's white primary is a violation of the Fifteenth Amendment to the U.S. Constitution.

1975 **Voting Rights Act Extended to Texas**—The 1975 amendment to the U.S. Voting Rights Act extends to Texas the prohibitions against "vote dilution" in political districts. It also requires pre-clearance by the U.S. Department of Justice of changes in redistricting plans and other election procedures.

1949 **Gilmer-Aikin Law**—Texas enacts legislation to create the first systematic statewide funding of public schools.

1945 **Texas Supreme Court Expands**—In an effort to relieve the workload of the appellate courts, a constitutional amendment increases membership on the Texas Supreme Court to nine: a chief justice and eight associate justices.

1961 **Sales Tax**—Texas adopts a state sales tax.

1974 **Constitutional Convention Unsuccessful**—The constitutional convention, composed of state legislators, fails to obtain the required votes of the delegates for submission of a new constitution to the voters.

1978 **First Republican Governor of Modern Times**—Bill Clements is elected as Texas's first Republican governor of modern times.

1980 *Ruiz v. Estelle*—A federal judge declares the Texas prison system to be unconstitutional and orders sweeping, expensive reforms.

2002 **Republican Dominance**—Republicans are elected to all statewide offices and control both houses of the Texas Legislature.

1993 **NAFTA**—The United States, Canada, and Mexico enter into the North American Free Trade Agreement, transforming Texas into a center of international trade.

2009 **Revenue Shortfall**—The Texas Legislature faces a large revenue shortfall, which threatens many state programs.

1984 **Major School Reforms**—The Texas Legislature passes a law that includes new taxes, limits on class size in the lower grades, and the "no pass, no play" rule for extracurricular activities.

2011 **Redistricting after the U.S. Census**—The Texas Legislature draws new districts based on the population data from the 2010 U.S. Census; the new districts reflect the state's diverse population of 25-plus million residents.

2000 **Longest Serving Governor**—Rick Perry becomes governor after George W. Bush resigns to become the U.S. president. Perry is the longest serving governor in the state's history.

2003 **Tuition Deregulation**—Tuition is deregulated at Texas state universities, resulting in a significant increase in student costs at public institutions.